WHO AM I
IN THE LIVES OF CHILDREN?

Fourth Edition

WHO AM I
IN THE LIVES OF CHILDREN?
An Introduction
to Teaching Young Children

STEPHANIE FEENEY
University of Hawaii

DORIS CHRISTENSEN
Early Childhood Consultant

EVA MORAVCIK
University of Hawaii

Photographs by
HELLA HAMMID

Merrill, an imprint of
Macmillan Publishing Company
New York

Collier Macmillan Canada, Inc.
Toronto

Maxwell Macmillan International Publishing Group
New York   Oxford   Singapore   Sydney

Cover photo: Hella Hammid
Editor: Linda Sullivan
Developmental Editor: Linda Kauffman Peterson
Production Editor: Mary M. Irvin
Art Coordinator: Mark D. Garrett
Text Designer: Debra A. Fargo
Cover Designer: Russ Maselli
Production Buyer: Pamela D. Bennett
This book was set in Garamond.

Copyright © 1991 by Macmillan Publishing Company.
Merrill is an imprint of Macmillan Publishing Company

Previous editions copyrighted 1987, 1983, 1979 by
Merrill Publishing Company

Printed in the United States of America

Macmillan Publishing Company
866 Third Avenue, New York, NY 10022

Collier Macmillan Canada, Inc.

Library of Congress Cataloging-in-Publication Data
Feeney, Stephanie.
    Who am I in the lives of children?: an introduc-
tion to teaching young children/Stephanie Feeney,
Doris Christensen, Eva Moravcik.—4th ed.
        p. cm.
    Includes bibliographical references and index.
    ISBN 0-675-21320-7
    1. Education, Preschool—United States.   2. Pre-
school teaching—United States.   3. Child development—United States.   4. Early childhood education—United States.   I. Christensen, Doris.   II.
Moravcik, Eva.   III. Title.
LB1140.23.F44   1990
372.11'02—dc20   90-20260
                                                                    CIP

Printing: 1 2 3 4 5 6 7 8 9   Year: 1 2 3 4

FOREWORD

Studying from a book like *Who Am I in the Lives of Children?* is not the easy way to become a teacher, but it *is* the way to become a good teacher. And the premise that, as a teacher, you need to constantly reassess your role in the lives of children is no doubt the reason this text continues to be a core in the field of early childhood education. Young children need teachers who are not machines, not simply memories. They need people with searching hearts and seeking minds, people who are always trying to better understand themselves, their job, their young charges, and the world around them. This book will surely help you become this sort of teacher.

We have all probably heard it said that good teachers are born, not made. This expression has been around for a long time, which is unfortunate because there's only a grain of truth in it and a lot of error. While it certainly helps teachers of young children to have been born with strong bodies, good eyes, keen hearing, quick reflexes, a generous share of brains,

strong backs, and healthy arches, the expression is completely inaccurate in its denial that good teachers are *made*. As teachers function in the classroom—dealing with behavior, providing instruction, coping with problems, and, most of all, preventing problems—they continually call upon skills and techniques that have become second nature to them. There is no end to their tricks of the trade. The notion that there is nothing "made" in a good teacher is an absurdity. No one is born with a skilled teacher's know-how. You have to learn it—both in your training and on the job.

One important strength of all of the editions of *Who Am I in the Lives of Children?* is the multiplicity of these practical, down-to-earth approaches in early childhood education. Interspersed throughout the text are pages of guidelines, strategies, and suggestions for coping with the many troublesome parts of teaching. Over and over the reader comes upon the statement "We have found in our experience . . . ," and then realistic, sound ideas follow.

Much as I admire this flow of valuable, concrete specifics, I admire even more the underlying concepts behind the practical approach. The authors see that teachers are made, but they also see that a teacher is more than a bundle of tricks. While a teacher is made through good professional training, a teacher is also a whole human, a product of inheritance (that grain of truth mentioned earlier), a product of professional training, *and* a product of all kinds of day-by-day experiences: as a child, as an adolescent, and as an adult. The authors respect the fact that the whole life we lead helps make us good teachers, just as the whole of life is integral to the children we teach. We teach out of all that we are: everything that has happened and happens to us—all the joys and all the sorrows. This book respects the human in you, the reader, and, as important, the humanness of children.

As the authors present their myriad ideas, you will become a part of the process and, because of this, the ideas stand a better chance of ending up as part of your perceptions, rather than remaining the authors'. This is particularly remarkable because the authors do not hide their own points of view. Time and again they use words like: "We are convinced . . ." or "We find we are no longer able to support educational approaches that . . ."

But the authors know that if teachers are to respect children, they themselves must be respected. Convinced of this, they are primarily concerned with the development of thoughtful teachers. They want people in the classroom who go through a never-ending process of questioning about themselves, about children, about the world children live in. Over and over they ask such questions as: "What are your values?" "What are you after?" "What are the ethical implications of this practice?" In its whole design, the books says to the reader: "Think, don't memorize; question, don't simply accept." The book presents a chart and says: "This is designed to help you choose . . ." It makes statements like "both self-contained and open-design classrooms can be effective, and both have drawbacks" and invites the reader to be the judge.

Many changes affecting young children have taken place since I wrote the first Foreword for the second edition. The pressures on family life continue to mount: continuing increases in divorce and separation; growing numbers of single parents; steady rises in the number of mothers in the labor force; the persistence of poverty for too many; the endangerment of our ecological systems. . . These have gone hand-in-hand with, and are reflected in, new demands placed on schools. The need for top-quality child care, especially in infant and toddler programs, becomes increasingly critical. Advocacy for children, the needs of families, and professional issues that impact the quality of early childhood education have moved to the forefront. These have not been times that build stability into children's lives.

This new edition makes a worthy contribution in this situation. The earlier strengths are all here: the clarity of the authors' stands; their down-to-earth specificity meshed with wide-ranging concerns for values and ethics; the richness of their own experiences; their honesty; their concern for the reader as a human. New content even further strengthens the book: increased coverage of professional ethics; a new chapter on play; greater emphasis on the needs of the family; an exploration of the movement toward professionalization of the field.

The adage warns, "If it ain't broke, don't fix it." The earlier edition wasn't "broke," but this edition is even better. It is very welcome at a time when more and more children, more vulnerable, are apt to be in groups at younger and younger ages for longer and longer hours. The need for sensitive, skilled teachers is especially keen. Those who read this book, puzzling and thinking as they do it, are sure to join that number.

James L. Hymes, Jr.
Carmel, California

PREFACE

Who Am I in the Lives of Children? is about becoming a teacher of young children. It provides an overview of the field of early childhood education and of programs for children between birth and age eight with a primary focus on practice in programs for preschool and kindergarten children (three through five years of age). It can be used in two and four year college programs, in courses in early childhood foundations and curriculum, and for short courses and workshops for practicing teachers. It is also suitable for helping students to acquire the competencies required for the Child Development Associate Credential.

Since the first edition of *Who Am I in the Lives of Children?* was published in 1979 we have used it in a variety of settings and geographical locations. The fourth edition reflects a process of rethinking of old ideas and acquiring and integrating new information and experiences; it also reflects numerous recent developments in the field.

When we wrote the previous editions we lived near each other and often worked in the same settings. For the last several years we have lived in different parts of the country and have not been able to write together on a regular basis. This new edition has the benefit of two periods of uninterrupted writing time, one in a quiet cabin on the slopes of Haleakala in Maui and the other in an old house on a windswept beach on Oahu. For the first time in several years we have had the opportunity to share our experiences, to discuss how these have been influenced by new developments in the field and to reflect on changes in our ways of thinking about and working with children and teachers.

We have reorganized the chapters into five broad topics and broadened the focus to include the entire early childhood age range from infancy through eight years. Part III, Living and Learning with Children, and Part IV, The Curriculum, focus on practice with children three through five years of age. At the end of each chapter in these parts, we include a section on adapting programs for infants and toddlers and primary school children.

A new chapter on children's play has been added, as has a section on health and safety curriculum. Content on teacher values, history, and the field has been reorganized. We have added more information in a number of areas of current concern including ethics, environmental issues, war play, anti-bias curriculum, appropriate software for young children, child abuse, testing and evaluation, and new approaches to literacy development. Growing national awareness of the needs of families and the resulting legislative initiatives are discussed, as are the critical issues of affordability, staff salaries, and the retention of teachers in programs for children under five. We also explore the current movement toward professionalization of the field of early childhood education.

Our basic values and philosophy remain the same. Yet revisions need to be made to reflect rapidly occurring changes. Today it is common to see articles in national and local publications concerning issues that were once exclusively discussed by people in our field. In the last presidential election child care was a major campaign issue. The societal changes that make early childhood education and the needs of families so prevalent are reflected in this new edition. Tomorrow's early childhood educators must have, in addition to a commitment to high quality education, knowledge of broader societal issues and the ability to advocate for the rights and needs of young children.

Our ideas have been profoundly shaped by the field of early childhood education, which has a unique history and philosophy. We draw upon theoretical work in psychology, human development, and education of John Dewey, Erik Erikson, Margaret Mahler, Maria Montessori, Abraham Maslow, Jean Piaget, Carl Rogers, Lev Vygotsky, and others. We have been influenced by writers who have vividly portrayed the educational process. Among them: Sylvia Ashton-Warner, Bruno Bettelheim, George Dennison, John Holt, Herb Kohl, A. S. Neill, and Vivian Paley. We have also learned a great deal from our association with many fine early childhood educators, including Barbara Biber, Barbara Bowman, Elizabeth Brady, Harriet Cuffaro, Richard Feldman, Marjorie Fields, Elizabeth Gilkeson, Randy Hitz, James L. Hymes, Elizabeth Jones, Daniel Jordan, Lilian Katz, and Docia Zavitkovsky.

We wish to recognize some of the very special people who have contributed to our growth and understanding of children and programs and who have provided invaluable assistance in structuring the material in this book. First and most important we thank the children and families we have worked with and who have taught us so much. We have learned and grown from our association with The University of Hawaii at Manoa Children's Center. We especially appreciate the staff's attention to relationships, the quality of the experiences they provide for children and families, and their tolerance of a director whose attention has been diverted by writing a book.

We continue to be deeply indebted to students in the early childhood education programs in which we have taught. We have learned a great deal from our interactions with them. Graduate students in early childhood education at the University of Hawaii, both past and present, have been a tremendous source of intellectual stimulation, feedback, and assistance in our thinking and writing. Our special thanks to Robyn Chun, Diana Ginsburg, Mary Goya, Lisa Foster, Christine Jackson, Evon Kawamoto, Mary Ann Lester, Carol Phelps, Kathleen Reinhardt, and Laverna Westfall.

We are especially grateful to students and former students who helped with research and writing of this book. Christine Jackson and Linda Buck worked with us on the chapter on children with special needs in the second and third editions (originally funded by a grant from the

Bureau of Education for the Handicapped of the U.S. Office of Education). Kathleen Reinhardt worked on research and writing on the section on literacy development for the third edition and Robyn Chun allowed us to draw from her research for Chapter 4, Child Development. A very, very special thank you to Diana Ginsburg for diligent research and thoughtful assistance in drafting revisions for chapters on the field, history, and children with special needs. Given the busy schedules of the authors it is unlikely that we could have met our publication deadline without Diana's help.

Work on professional ethics in early childhood education described in Chapter 1 was developed by Stephanie Feeney and Kenneth Kipnis, Professor of Philosophy at the University of Hawaii, under grants from the Wallace Alexander Gerbode Foundation and the National Association for the Education of Young Children. Special thanks to Lynda Stone, Assistant Professor of Educational Foundations at University of Hawaii, for her very helpful comments and to Kenneth Kipnis for his help in writing the material on professional ethics.

Special thanks to Linda McCormick, University of Hawaii Professor of Special Education, for sharing her knowledge and reviewing the chapter on special needs children; to Rebecca Severeide for sharing materials and for helpful comments; and to Anita Trubitt for contributions to sections on music curriculum and temperament. Discussions and correspondence with Robert Peters, Headmaster of Hanahauoli School in Honolulu, with Elizabeth Jones of Pacific Oaks College, and Marjorie Fields of the University of Alaska at Juneau have contributed greatly to our thinking about the topic of curriculum planning as reflected in Chapter 10.

Hella Hammid is an extraordinary photographer of children and we are delighted to be able to continue to feature her work in this book. We are also pleased that she was able to come to Hawaii to take a series of wonderful new photographs especially for this edition. Hella's photographs communicate the experience of childhood with power and sensitivity that we are sure will add to your enjoyment of this text.

New photographs for this edition were taken at the University of Hawaii at Manoa Children's Center, Hanahauoli School, Pearl Harbor Sub Base Child Development Center, and Castle Medical Center Child Development Center. We appreciate cooperation from the children, staff and parents of these schools. Photos taken for previous editions that are used here were taken at Pacific Oaks Children's School, The Harold E. Jones Child Study Center, Maggie Haves School, John Adams Child Development Center, Beverly Hills Montessori School, the Clay Street Center, St. Thomas Parish Preschool, and Hill 'n Dale Family Learning Center in California, and St. Timothy's Children's Center and the Early School in Hawaii.

This edition comes forth with an attention to detail and design that far surpasses previous editions of the text. We gratefully acknowledge the contributions of the many people at Merrill/Macmillan who helped shape this new edition: Mary Irvin, our efficient production editor; Deb Fargo, text designer; Mark Garrett, coordinator of the art and photo programs; Linda Sullivan, Editor; and Linda Peterson, our Developmental Editor, who prodded us every inch of the way.

And as always, we acknowledge the reviewers of our manuscript: Kathleen Amershek, University of Maryland–College Park; Berta Harris, San Diego City College; Wayne Reinhardt, Edmonds Community College, Seattle, Washington; and Judy Scurlock, Aiken Technical College, Augusta, Georgia.

We also acknowledge the contribution to our thinking and to our lives made by our dear friend Jean Fargo. Jean models a splendid inquiring mind and the combination of caring and rigorous thought. Thanks to Don Mickey for editing, computer consultation, coffee and much, much more. No book is written without affecting the lives of those closest to the authors. We thank, appreciate, and offer appologies to Dylan Stanfield, Denny Dobbin, Jeffrey Reese, and Don Mickey, who supported our work with patience and good humor.

S. F., D. C. and *E. M.*
Honolulu, Hawaii

CONTENTS

WHO AM I
IN THE LIVES OF CHILDREN?

INTRODUCTION

When we read a book, we like to know who wrote it and why; we also want to learn about the authors' feelings and experiences. This book grows out of our experiences as children, as adults, as learners, and as teachers. Our early school experiences included child-oriented nursery schools much like those we describe here: large, dreary, anonymous public schools; a small multinational school in Europe; and a one-room country school.

While our childhood experiences were quite different, our values are similar. We have many of the same feelings and ideas about education and we share a strong commitment to programs that are nurturing and humane and that support all aspects of children's development. This commitment has led us to many different endeavors. Among us we have been preschool teacher, social worker, kindergarten teacher, center director, consultant, parent educator, trainer of Child Development Associates, Head Start regional training officer, and college teacher. We have worked in parent cooperatives,

child care centers, preschools, infant-toddler programs, Head Start programs, public schools, resource and referral agencies, government agencies, and college settings. We have been child advocates and active members of local and national early childhood organizations.

We first wrote *Who Am I in the Lives of Children?* because we needed an introductory text that reflected our viewpoint that the personal development and professional development of teachers are inextricably linked. In addition, we wanted to emphasize the importance of reflection on values and on educational choices. We also wanted to speak to teachers and prospective teachers in as direct a way as possible, so we wrote in an informal and personal voice.

The cornerstone of this book and our work with children is what we will refer to as the *developmental* approach to early childhood education. Programs based on this approach have their roots in a long tradition of humanistic education and have been profoundly shaped by

1

the work of Friedrich Froebel, Maria Montessori, John Dewey, Arnold Gessell, Erik Erikson, Lev Vygotsky, and Jean Piaget. Programs that evolve from the developmental tradition are dedicated to the development of the whole child—physical, social, emotional, and intellectual—and are characterized by a deep respect for the individual and the recognition that individual differences must be responded to in educational settings. Such programs recognize that children learn best from direct experience and from spontaneous play. Teachers in these programs begin with children as they are and try to understand and help them grow in ways that are right for the individual rather than according to a predetermined plan. They look at children in terms of potential to be actualized and in the context of their culture and family unit.

Because we see the two as interconnected, we address the personal and professional development of the teacher. Each person who works with children develops differently because each has a distinct personality, as well as different experiences, abilities, and values. We don't want everyone to reach the same conclusions or to teach in the same way. It is important that you develop your own teaching style and philosophy and learn to reflect on your values and actions so that you continue to grow as a person and as a professional.

There are many approaches to helping others learn to teach, and each college instructor has his or her own ideas regarding the best methods for preparing people to work in early childhood programs. Sometimes prospective teachers are not given the guidance they need to discover what they value and what they want for children. Teaching teachers by focusing on content and skills is comparable to making clay figures by forming the pieces—head, arms, legs—and sticking them onto a central core. Like these clay figures which fall apart when fired, the students may not know how to respond when faced with the pressures of a classroom of lively youngsters. Our approach to teacher education is more like creating a clay figure in which each part is drawn out of the central piece of clay. Such an approach produces teachers whose work with children is an integral part of who they are.

Each chapter in this book is constructed to help you to gain awareness, acquire essential knowledge, and develop needed skills in an area of early childhood education. At the end of each chapter, you will find questions to stimulate reflection and projects designed to encourage application of the content. The bibliography at the end of each chapter includes the books that we have used for our research and have referred to in the chapter. Appendix 3, Recommended Books: Our Favorites, lists books that have been personally and professionally meaningful to us in our careers as educators of young children. These books are of special significance in the field, and we urge you to delve into them.

Who Am I in the Lives of Children? is organized into five parts. Each part and the chapters within it lay the foundation for those that follow. The first four parts provide the basic information and skills needed for working effectively with groups of young children. The final part deals with additional skills needed by early childhood educators for working with children with special needs and with families.

Part I, Foundations of Early Childhood Education, introduces some of the distinctive traditions and features of the field of early childhood education. Chapter 1, The Teacher and Values, explores the nature of the teacher of young children as a person and a professional. Chapter 2, History, describes the origins of early childhood education, and Chapter 3, The Field, presents an overview of the programs and practices that you may encounter as you begin your career. Together, these three chapters provide the context for working with young children in group settings.

Part II, Understanding Children, includes chapters designed to help teachers understand children's development and the significance of their play. Because understanding children is of central importance in early childhood education, these chapters form an essential foundation of practice. Chapter 4, Child Development, provides a basis for understanding young children. Chapter 5, Play, introduces a critical medium for children's development and discusses how teachers can support productive play. Chapter 6, Observation and Evaluation, acquaints you with the basic skills teachers use to appraise individuals and groups of children and to evaluate ways to support their growth and development.

Part III, Living and Learning with Children, focuses on the knowledge and expertise that a teacher must have in order to create a nurturing and stimulating daily program for young children. Chapter 7, A Good Place for Children, explores the importance of meeting children's basic physical and psychological needs. Chapter 8, The Learning Environment, looks at how you can structure the use of space and provide the equipment and material necessary to support children's development. Chapter 9, Relationships and Guidance, deals with how teachers can develop positive relationships with children and help them learn to work and play in a group setting. These three chapters address essential aspects of the program for children. They are based on the foundation laid down in the previous chapters and are necessary preconditions for curriculum as it is described in the chapters that follow.

Part IV, The Curriculum, addresses aspects of the curriculum in early childhood programs. Chapter 10, Planning Curriculum, presents a framework for thinking about and designing meaningful and appropriate learning experiences for young children. Chapters 11 through 14 deal with four broad areas of the early childhood curriculum: physical development, the arts, language and literacy, and cognitive development. In each chapter, we provide you with a lens through which to view development and we introduce teaching practices.

Part V, Special Relationships, presents additional skills, beyond those of regular classroom practice, needed by teachers of young children. Chapter 15, Working with Children with Special Needs, will help you to identify and work with children who require special knowledge and attention. Chapter 16, Working with Families, provides an overview of the teacher's responsibilities to families and the importance of developing good relationships with them.

The relationship of the parts and chapters of the book is graphically represented as a triangle in Figure 1. A firm foundation is essential for strength and durability. Chapters in Parts I and II lay the foundation: The Teacher and Values, History, The Field, Child Development, and Play form a base of awareness and knowledge that underlie all of our work with children. Chapter 6, Observation and Evaluation, introduces a basic and extremely valuable tool for your work in early childhood programs. You will use observation skills to look not only at children, but also at relationships, the learning environment, curriculum choices, and yourself. Observation intersects all the levels of the triangle. Chapter 7, A Good Place for Children, Chapter 8, The Learning Environment, and Chapter 9, Relationships and Guidance, rest on the foundation because they provide the structural support for a viable program. These basics for living and learning with children need to be established

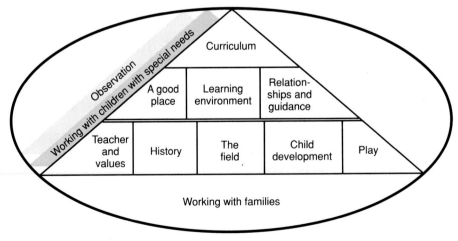

FIGURE 1
Graphic representation of parts of this book

before teachers can turn their attention to curriculum. Chapters on curriculum are placed at the apex of the triangle because they are founded upon all the rest. Chapter 15, Working with Children with Special Needs, describes the awareness, knowledge, and skill needed to work effectively with these children. Like observation, it cuts across all the areas of the triangle. Finally, Chapter 16, Working with Families, is portrayed graphically to suggest that the family provides the context for all that we do in early childhood programs.

It would be impossible to include in this book everything that you might need to know about each topic. Rather, we try to provide you with a lens through which to view the many choices *you* must make in designing meaningful and appropriate learning experiences for young children. You will play an important part in the lives of the children you will teach and their families. We hope that this book will help you to develop as a competent and nurturing teacher of young children.

PART I

FOUNDATIONS OF EARLY CHILDHOOD EDUCATION

This section introduces some of the distinctive traditions and features of the field of early childhood education. Chapter 1, The Teacher and Values, explores the nature of the teacher of young children as a person and as a professional. Chapter 2, History, describes the origins of early childhood education, and Chapter 3, The Field, presents an overview of the programs and practices that you may encounter as you begin your career. Together, these three chapters provide the context for working with young children in group settings.

CHAPTER ONE

The Teacher and Values

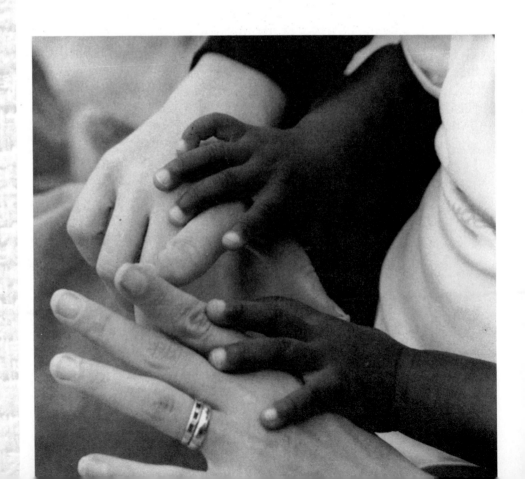

A teacher affects eternity: he can never tell where his influence stops.
—*Henry Brooks Adams*

In this chapter we explore the nature of the teacher of young children as a person and as a professional. We discuss the effect of teacher personality on young children, characteristics of effective teachers, and ways that personal values affect professional behavior. We examine the role and authority of the teacher, the core values of early childhood education, and the ethical responsibilities of teachers of young children. We also look at issues of professionalism and career opportunities in the early childhood field.

Who you are as an early childhood teacher, how you interact with people, and the kind of environment and program that you provide make a lasting impact on children, families, and society. This implies a tremendous responsibility. You may be the first adult that a child encounters for any length of time outside of the home. Most children enter early childhood programs with lively and inquisitive minds. Not all of them come to feel good about themselves, to love learning, and to regard school as a rewarding experience. Those who do are very likely to have had experiences with teachers who were caring, who enjoyed children and teaching, who respected children's lively intelligence, and who supported children in becoming thinking and feeling human beings. When teachers base what they do on genuine liking and respect for children and sound knowledge of development and early education, the children they teach are likely to come to respect themselves and others and maintain the eagerness and curiosity that mark the early years.

The purpose of this book is to help you become a teacher who nourishes the growth of children by helping them to develop their natural potential rather than by teaching separate facts, drilling on skills, or regimenting behavior. Your personality, attitudes, values, skills, and sense of professional identity all play an important role in the kind of person you will be in children's lives.

THE TEACHER AS A PERSON

Who you are forms the foundation for the professional you will become and the kinds of professional decisions you will make. Personal dimensions have an important impact on how individuals evolve into early childhood professionals.

Personal Style

Personal characteristics give people their distinctiveness. Although it is not necessary to have a particular kind of personality to be a good teacher of young children, it is important to be aware of the possible effects of your personality on your daily work with children. The individual ways you think, act, and feel are derived from a complex interaction of your inherited characteristics (temperament) and your life experience. Awareness of your characteristic reactions and individual style—tendencies to be exuberant or calm, to prefer vigorous activity or more sedentary pursuits, to prefer novelty and change or predictability and order, to prefer large groups of people or intimate gatherings, to prefer quiet solitude or the excitement of a crowd, to choose puzzling challenges or tasks that are more easily mastered—can help you understand yourself. Personality, in this sense, is neither good nor bad; it is simply a part of you. Although many kinds of people can successfully teach young children, we have observed that characteristics such as energy, enthusiasm, flexibility, resourcefulness, and the ability to tolerate disorder make it easier. As a prospective teacher, it is important that you become aware of your characteristics and how they affect others and how they fit or do not fit with the styles of the adults and children with whom you work. Awareness can help you enhance or restrain aspects of your personality when it is appropriate to do so, can help you make choices about your career, and can help you be a more sensitive teacher.

In our attempts to help our students understand themselves, we have used two of a number of available techniques for examining personality type. These are Thomas and Chess's Nine Dimensions of Temperament (Thomas and Chess 1977) and the Myers-Briggs Type Indicator (MBTI) (Myers 1980).

Pediatricians Alexander Thomas and Stella Chess refer to temperament as the observable manifestations: the "how" of behavior that explains a great deal about individual differences in style. They studied the temperament of infants (see Chapter 4) and found that newborns show definite differences in certain traits that persist over time. The nine dimensions of temperament, which are described on page 73, are a valuable starting point for understanding the personalities of adults as well. They are helpful in explaining personality differences and can be used as a tool for personal reflection (Burks and Rubenstein 1979; Trubitt 1981). For example, a college student of ours with a very low activity level reviewed the nine dimensions and realized that a highly active child in her class was not misbehaving or deviant but was simply different.

The MBTI, based on Carl Jung's views of personality types, also helps people learn about the way that they characteristically look at the world and make decisions (Keirsey and Bates 1978; McCaulley and Natter 1980). The MBTI considers four dimensions that deal with individual preferences for interacting with the world and others, ways of working, making judgments, and preference for spontaneity versus order. The MBTI also provides a basis for self-examination that can increase your awareness and give you insights about your relationships with children and adults. Most college counseling centers will administer the MBTI to students.

As you develop greater self-awareness, you can begin to observe your preferences regarding the kinds of individuals (adults and children) that you prefer to interact with and the kinds of activities and work settings that suit you best.

Awareness of your preferences will help you choose a setting that allows you to function most effectively as a teacher. If you are highly distractible and have a need for order, you might want to avoid settings with lots of noise and confusion in favor of smaller, quieter learning spaces. If you enjoy change and are not easily distracted, you might find a freer, more spontaneous environment more to your liking.

Capacity to Nurture Others

Even though the style and temperament of teachers may vary greatly, there are some personal qualities that are essential for working with young children. In order to support children's development, teachers must have the capacity for self-knowledge and the capacity for caring, compassion, and nurture. To become a person who possesses these qualities, you must know and accept yourself. Self-knowledge depends to a great extent on developing the ability to observe oneself in the same honest and non-judgmental way that one learns to observe children and to realistically appraise areas in which change may be needed. The capacity for self-knowledge and acceptance is the cornerstone for the quality of compassion that is so important in a teacher. Arthur Jersild describes it like this:

> To be compassionate, one must be able to accept the impact of any emotion, love or hate, joy, fear, or grief—tolerate it and harbor it long enough and with sufficient absorption to accept its meaning and to enter into a fellowship of feeling with the one who is moved by the emotion. This is the heroic feature of compassion in its fullest development: to be able to face the ravage of rage, the shattering impact of terror, the tenderest prompting of love, and then to embrace these in a larger context, which involves an acceptance of these feelings and an appreciation of what they mean to the one who experiences them.
>
> *(Jersild 1955, pp. 125–26)*

It is important to be open to new experiences, to acknowledge and deal with feelings, and to experience relationships in ever-increasing depth and breadth. It is also important to understand that although everyone experiences strong emotions like anger and fear at times, you can learn to choose how to respond to these feelings instead of acting on them in ways that may be damaging.

Skills in gaining trust and developing relationships are acquired as you come to know yourself better, accept yourself, and then learn more about children and how to work with them. Part of this process of development (and the major theme of this book) is to ask yourself frequently: Who am I in the lives of children? What kind of person do I want to be? What kind of teacher do I want to be? What are my strengths and what are the areas in which I need to try harder? No one of us is completely self-aware, mature, wise, compassionate, and insightful all of the time. All of us have tendencies to be defensive. It is important, however, to develop the capacity for self-awareness and some vision of the kind of behavior and relationships toward which we aspire, to be committed to a lifelong process of growth and change, and to learn to accept feedback from others as a valuable source of growth instead of something to defend against or to use to berate or belittle oneself.

Your own early experiences were very important in the formation of the way that you feel about yourself and others and your ways of responding to situations. The ability to respond in positive and healthy ways appears to be related to learning to trust others in the early years and to see the world as a basically good and nurturing place. Adults who have had their basic needs met in childhood and who have developed trust in themselves and in the world will more easily develop the ability to support the growth and development of others.

People who lack this basic trust may not have had their needs met in consistent ways in

their early lives and may find it difficult to become caring, compassionate, and nurturing. This is not to say that individuals who have had unhappy childhoods cannot be good teachers of young children. Some of the best teachers we know have made conscious decisions to overcome the painful aspects of their childhoods and to dedicate themselves to providing for children some of what they missed in their own early years.

Personal Values

Values are those things we believe to be intrinsically worthwhile; that is, they are prized and desirable in themselves. Truth, love, beauty, honesty, friendship, family, and loyalty are val-

ues. In addition to caring for children, teaching involves acting on what one believes to be right and good for them. Educational choices are made based on your commitment to help others to grow and learn and, to a great extent, on your personal values.

The development of values is a complex process that grows out of an individual's family background, religion, ethnic background, class, sex, and life experiences. Your personal history and the resulting values affect the ways that you will interact with children and adults. Values underlie most of our important life decisions. We assimilate personal values early in life without realizing it. Later, when we reflect, we are able to identify our values. Professional values are acquired much later and combine the commitments and responsibilities of a specific profession with individual values.

Your personal values have led you to the beginning steps in becoming a teacher of young children. You may have great empathy for those who are helpless and have made a personal commitment to making the world a better and more caring place. You may be committed to making the world more peaceful and have chosen early childhood education because you recognize that to do so we must begin with children. You may cherish and hold dear education and have come into this field to help young children realize their incredible potential. You may value freedom, independence, and individuality and have pursued teaching because as a teacher you can give children the opportunity to express their individuality. You may value the family as the mainstay of society and have entered this field to support families and children's connection to their families. You may value discovery, learning, aesthetics, diversity, human rights, or a respect for nature and may want to share these commitments with children. You may have religious values that you want to actualize by teaching and caring for others.

Bias and Prejudice

Everyone has personal preferences. You may prefer jazz to classical music and chocolate to pistachio ice cream. This is a matter of taste. People also have expectations based on what they have experienced in the past, what they have heard from others, and what they hope for or fear. Based on experience, you have come to expect that you will enjoy yourself if you go to a jazz concert or order chocolate ice cream.

Just as we all have preferences and expectations for things like music and food, we all have preferences and biases regarding individuals or groups of people. These preferences, unlike the ones just mentioned, have the potential for negative impact on others. Your personality,

values, and past experiences contribute to the development of inclinations to favor or reject certain individuals or groups of people *(biases)*. These inclinations may be based simply on the human tendency to feel comfortable with people who are most like ourselves. Sometimes they are so strong that they become prejudgments based on preconceptions rather than on direct experience of the individual *(prejudices)*. Prejudice creates distance. In educational settings it can result in teachers who have negative feelings about a child or family based on unfounded assumptions and then behave as if these were true.

Teachers are often unaware of their biases and prejudices and of the devastating effect that these can have. As a teacher or prospective teacher, your awareness of your own biases will be important in monitoring your behavior so that it will not have negative effects on children or their families. To learn something about your biases, begin by asking yourself the following questions and answering as honestly as you can:

- How do I respond to children who are dirty, ragged, smelly, or unattractive?
- How do I feel when children do not conform to my expectations about good or acceptable behavior?
- Are there children I immediately like or dislike or with whom I feel comfortable or uncomfortable? What are the characteristics of these children?
- Do I have strong feelings about children who are loud, verbal, and aggressive? What about children who are quiet, passive, shy, clingy, or whiny?
- Do I generally tend to prefer children of one sex?
- Do I have strong reactions to children from certain economic backgrounds, races, or cultures?
- Do I have negative feelings about working with children who are precocious, developmentally

delayed, or who have handicapping conditions?

- What are my reactions to families who have lifestyles that are very different from my own, and do these influence my feelings about their children?

The word *prejudice* means prejudgment, which can be either favorable or unfavorable. It can be harmful to be prejudiced in favor of one group of children because your feelings may affect a whole group. When less favored children observe your preferences, they may perceive themselves as less worthy.

Self-observation and resulting awareness may help you to know when you may be hurting children by rejecting them for things they cannot control. If you discover that you do have some biases (and we all do), simple awareness may be enough to help you remember the special needs of a shy child or not to overreact to an aggressive, bossy, or whiny child. Indeed, many fine teachers actively work to dispel these feelings when they occur by deliberately finding the things that they like about the child who triggers a negative reaction. The child who thus begins as one you dislike may become one for whom you feel a special affection.

If you become aware that you have strong prejudices that you cannot overcome, you should ask yourself whether there are particular children or groups of children with whom you should not work. You may even need to consider seriously whether you should become a teacher.

THE TEACHER AS A PROFESSIONAL

You are on the threshold of entering a profession with a group of individuals who share a mission, a set of values, similar training, and standards for practice and behavior. Although people have cared for and educated young children for centuries, early childhood educa-

tion is a relatively new field. As early childhood teachers strive to achieve greater recognition as professionals, they are becoming better at articulating philosophy, at basing work with children on well-understood theories, and at making choices based on their knowledge. They are taking greater pride in their work because they know that they serve children at a critical period in the life cycle. They are also becoming more aware of the moral dimension of their work and the critical need to responsibly address the recurring ethical dilemmas that arise when working in early childhood settings.

The Teacher's Role

The term *role* refers to expectations that are made of people because they hold a particular position in society. The role of the early childhood teacher has expanded as people have become more aware of the significance of early education and child care in our changing society. The career of a teacher of young children is no small undertaking, in part because the expectations accompanying the role are many, varied, and sometimes contradictory. Teachers of young children also need to interact with a number of different groups of people—most notably children, other staff members, and parents. There is wide agreement that the responsibility of the early childhood teacher, in the broadest sense, is to help children learn and grow. The way this should be translated into practice, however, is subject to debate based on differing views of what the primary focus of the early childhood program should be—to what extent facts, skills, thinking and problem solving, creativity, cooperation, and self-expression are emphasized.

Teachers of young children deal with more areas of children's lives than most other teachers. They are involved in all aspects of the child's development (social, emotional, intellectual, and physical). The focus on the whole child is critical in early childhood programs because young children are vulnerable and dependent on adults for nurture as well as education. Even though programs may differ in values, in the organization of classrooms, and in curriculum, they are similar in the breadth of the teacher's responsibilities to children.

You will play many roles as a teacher of young children, both in the classroom and outside of it. In the classroom you will be called upon to provide children with a sense of psychological comfort and security. The younger the children with whom you work, the more vulnerable they will be and the more you will need to assume some of the nurturing role of the parent. You will also organize and maintain an environment in which children live and learn;

you will collect resources, design curriculum, plan the daily program and evaluate its effectiveness, mediate relationships between children, and interact with other adults. In a single day you may function in the roles of friend, parent, colleague, interior designer, nurse, janitor, counselor, instructor, entertainer, diplomat, and sometimes even funeral director for small animals.

Another important role of the teacher is that of behavior model. The ways that you communicate, solve problems, and relate to others form a powerful model for how children and others in your classroom will behave. Children tend to do what adults *do* regardless of what adults say.

Research in schools has shown that children often learn to be aggressive or cooperative by observing adults, that children who observe adults in problem-solving tasks are able to solve problems more readily than those who have not had that experience, and that the level of thinking demonstrated by teachers sets the level for student thinking (Good and Brophy 1973; Saiwin 1969). Children's behavior will be influenced substantially by the teacher's behavior in the classroom.

Another challenge in the role of teacher of young children is working collaboratively with the other adults in the school. This may involve teaching with a co-teacher, with an assistant, or with volunteers in the classroom, as well as interacting with a director, principal, and other school personnel. It is important to learn to keep lines of communication open, to be able to share your goals and expectations, and to deal constructively with differing ideas about what is best for children or how to implement the daily program. As a new teacher, you are likely to work with people who have been teaching longer than you have and who have set ideas. You may have to learn to work in harmony while not losing your own values and ideals.

In addition to your responsibilities in the classroom, you will interact with parents on a regular basis. Because early childhood programs generally provide the first transition from home to the larger world outside of the home, the teacher plays an important role in helping parents and children learn to be apart from each other for a period of time each day. In fact, the early childhood educator may be the second adult outside the home (the first is the pediatrician) who has a relationship with the parents and the child. The role of the teacher of young children therefore involves working with parents as well as their offspring. It involves helping parents learn more about child development and positive parenting skills.

You will also interact with other agencies concerned with children, be involved in your own continuing professional development, and, on occasion, be involved in training teachers and advocating for children. You will have many roles and will be called on to perform many and varied tasks. These will, of course, vary with the age of the children you work with and their developmental needs. Work with infants and toddlers calls for nurturing behaviors as the context of learning; there is little emphasis on formal teaching. Older preschool, kindergarten, and elementary children are more able to care for themselves and need teachers to provide meaningful curriculum as well as nurture.

Differences between the Roles of Teachers and Parents

Teachers of young children are in many ways like parents, more so than teachers who work with any other age group. Yet they are not the parents of the children that they teach, and sometimes it is difficult to negotiate the fine line between these two roles. There are important similarities between parents and teachers, but there also are important differences. Lilian Katz (1980) makes a number of interesting distinctions between "mother" (defined in terms of the primary nurturing role rather than on biological relationship) and teacher that we and our students have found valuable in understanding the roles and responsibilities of each.

Katz points out that mothers and teachers need to be quite different in their level of attachment to a child. The teacher needs to appreciate every child but more realistically and less passionately than a mother does. Teachers need to keep enough distance to observe children objectively. This allows them to assess children in terms of developmental norms and to balance the needs of the individual with the welfare of the entire group. Teachers also need to be more purposeful and somewhat less spontaneous than mothers. Teachers need to have clear goals and plan activities in systematic ways to enhance specific areas of children's development.

Obviously, these are not absolute distinctions, but the relative emphasis should be different if parents and teachers are to provide what the child needs from each of them. Neither should feel guilty because they are not doing the other's job. Yet we know teachers who feel badly because they cannot love and provide for every child as if the child were their own, and we know parents who worry that they are not spending enough time teaching their children. Each group needs to know that it can complement the other in helping children grow and learn.

Many teachers in early childhood settings genuinely love and respect children. It is unrealistic, however, to expect yourself to be able to love every child all of the time. Parents love their children (a finite, relatively small number) for an infinite amount of time for no better reason than that they are intimately connected forever. Teachers love children (an ever-increasing number of them) for the limited time that they share a learning journey, because they participate in the children's daily lives and help them to learn and grow. In the same way that gardeners love flowers as they water them and pull weeds and then move on to another season and another garden, so teachers watch and nurture children with love and care and then move on to another season and another group of children.

The Teacher's Authority

The role of teacher is granted a certain authority by society: the right to give commands, expect obedience, make decisions, and take action. The most obvious source of the teacher's authority is adulthood. Because teachers are larger, stronger, and older, children acknowledge their right to give direction. Although the teacher's authority is conferred by society as a part of the role itself, it is reinforced by experience in teaching,

by skill and knowledge, and by dedication and commitment.

Learning to deal with authority is one of the first important issues that faces a prospective teacher. We have watched our college students struggle (and, as beginning teachers, struggled ourselves) with their notions of authority as they have sought to define their relationships with children in ways that felt natural and comfortable to them. Some of them try to deny the authority that comes with the role of teacher. They behave as if they are one of the "kids" and treat the children as "pals." They become confused and frustrated when the children do not respect them and treat them exactly the same way that they treat their peers. Others expect children to respect them simply because they are the teacher. They feel that children have to learn that the teacher is "boss" and to accept authority just because it is there. They try to exercise authority without earning it and are often surprised at the rebellion and resistance they encounter.

We have found the concept of natural authority described by George Dennison in his book *The Lives of Children* helpful in looking at teacher authority:

> Natural authority is a far cry from authority that is merely arbitrary. Its attributes are obvious; adults are larger, more experienced, possess more words, have entered into prior agreements among themselves. When all this takes on a positive instead of merely negative character, the children see adults as protectors and as sources of certitude, approval, novelty, skills.
>
> *(Dennison 1969, p. 124)*

There are a number of issues in teaching that relate to the proper use of authority. Most of us have encountered teachers who were harsh, punitive, or unfair and who in other ways could be described as abusing their authority. We have also experienced teachers who were not clear and consistent and who did not give us enough direction. These teachers had abdicated their

authority and left children without necessary structure and a sense of what was acceptable behavior. Authority that is authentic and lasting is based on mutual respect and not on coercion or abandonment of responsibility. It is used wisely and with compassion.

Professional Values

Each profession within a society has a set of core values that represent deeply held commitments that are consciously held because practitioners believe that they contribute to society's well-being. Through the core values of the field, early childhood educators can make a professional commitment to the kind of society they wish to live in, the kinds of educational programs they wish to work in, and the kinds of people they want to help to nurture.

The accompanying box lists the core values that have been recognized by the National Association for the Education of Young Children (NAEYC) as a part of its Code of Ethical Conduct. The list represents current consensus regarding the commitments that characterize the "good early childhood educator." The field of early childhood has a long history of emphasizing those practices that recognize and respect the humanness and dignity of people. The core values listed enable early childhood educators to formally recognize their commitments to children, to families, and to themselves. They pro-

vide the philosophic underpinnings for teaching strategies that are humane and respectful, that provide for individual choice, and that help children to develop individuality in combination with social responsibility.

In the first part of this chapter, we discussed the impact of your personal values on the kind of professional you will become. A person who chooses early childhood education as a career often does so because of a strong desire to nurture children and to contribute to their growth and development. Such people often find themselves in agreement with the spirit of the values of early childhood education. Knowledge of these values and the historical tradition from which they come helps prospective teachers to identify with the field and to make a professional commitment to working with children and families. There is a merging of personal values with professional values that can be endorsed and shared.

Value Conflicts

A number of value conflicts can arise in early childhood settings. In fact, clarifying your values and trying to understand and reconcile value differences within yourself and with others is likely to be a frequently recurring endeavor.

Value conflicts may occur within yourself. You may find that in practice you have to make some hard choices: for example, you may value creativity but find that children's spontaneous expression (a loud and enthusiastic rhythm band during morning activity time) competes with your values of tranquility and order. You may face value conflicts regarding the needs and demands of the important people in your life—between the children you teach and your own family. Or you may face value conflicts within yourself such as choosing between the work you love and other work that pays a better salary.

You are also likely to find yourself facing value conflicts with others. Teaching would be easier if the teachers you worked with, program

CORE VALUES IN EARLY CHILDHOOD EDUCATION

Standards of ethical behavior in early childhood education are based on commitment to core values that are deeply rooted in the history of our field. We have committed ourselves to:

- Appreciating childhood as a unique and valuable stage of the human life cycle;
- Basing our work with children on knowledge of child development;
- Appreciating and supporting the close ties between the child and family;
- Recognizing that children are best understood in the context of family, culture and society;
- Respecting the dignity, worth and uniqueness of each individual (child, family member and colleague);
- Helping children and adults achieve their full potential in the context of relationships that are based on trust, respect and positive regard.

Source: National Association for the Education of Young Children, Code of Ethical Conduct.

administrators, and the parents of the children you teach were in agreement with you on all educational issues and practices. This doesn't often happen in a society that is characterized by diversity. As people from different backgrounds and with different values attempt to work together, different viewpoints will surely arise. Whenever possible, differences with others need to be acknowledged and discussed if viable solutions are to be found.

Some educational disagreements are a matter of differences in goals; consider these examples: the extent to which specific academic skills versus child-chosen activities should be emphasized in programs; whether the curriculum should be preplanned or deal with concerns and issues raised by the children; the relative emphasis that should be placed on the arts, moral development, academics, scientific experimentation, peace education, computer skills, and many other educational demands. If competing views are based on strongly held value differences, and if one or another position cannot be demonstrated to be better for children, then there is no easy solution. Differences can be discussed

using the core values for guidance; compromise may be reached, or the parties to the disagreement may need to agree to disagree. Other troubling conflicts encountered in early childhood programs deal with moral responsibilities (these are discussed in the section on professional ethics that follows).

Some Thoughts about Values

In the daily life of the teacher of young children, values help determine the goals that are set and the actions that grow from these goals. Values evolve and change slowly as people gain new information and experience. Willingness to examine values is an important characteristic of a teacher who is learning and growing. Teachers who don't reflect on values are in danger of jumping from one teaching practice to another without knowing whether their actions are consistent or if they represent what they believe to be best for children. When teachers examine values, they can weigh their decisions thoughtfully and choose alternatives with more clarity and wisdom.

It is important for teachers to make every effort to behave in ways that are consistent with their values and those of the field. Sometimes teachers are not aware of their values or when their behavior may contradict what they believe their values to be. For example, we worked with teachers in a school where the values of independence and child-directed learning were clearly articulated, but the teachers did not allow children to choose their own materials from the open shelves. To avoid discrepancies between belief and action, examine your choices and how they relate to your goals for children. Not only do children emulate a teacher's behavior, but they also observe and internalize values based on the teacher's example. Only when your behavior is consistent with your values, however, do your actions have a positive impact.

Thoughtful reflection combined with knowledge of child development can help teachers to make decisions that are based on the best interests of children. We have found that teaching conflicts can be handled best when teaching teams take time together to reflect on and clarify their educational goals and values and to seek compromise in areas where there is no consensus. It is also helpful to communicate clearly values choices to parents. When problems occur, it helps to recognize that differences in values are a natural and healthy part of life in a diverse society. Though it is important to confront value conflicts thoughtfully, you can rarely resolve them neatly. As with other aspects of early childhood education, the process is important.

Occasionally, value differences between you and co-teachers, administrators, or parents may be so severe that you will find that you cannot, in good faith, continue to work in a program. Coming to this conclusion can be difficult and painful, but it may be your only alternative if differences cannot be resolved. You may find that you are more comfortable and happier teaching in a setting that more closely reflects your values; for example, a former student of ours decided to leave a program because it did not adequately address her belief in the importance of creative development. Or you may choose to leave a program when you have serious concerns that the well-being of young children is compromised.

Professional Ethics

The ethics of a profession reflect its obligations to its clients and to society. Ethics involve the members of the profession's shared process of critical, systematic reflection upon their moral obligations. The following statement by Strike, Haller, and Soltis (1988) describes the nature of professional ethics:

> First, it concerns what is the *right* thing to do, not just the most expedient or least trouble making, the *fair* or *just* thing. Moral issues are usually characterized by certain kinds of language. Words such as *right, ought, just,* and *fair* are common. Moral issues concern our duties and obligations to one another, what constitutes just or fair treatment of one another and what rights we each have. (p. 3)

Professional ethics in early childhood education reflect the field's responsibilities to the child, family, and society. The core values of the field guide teachers and other practitioners as they deliberate on ethical dilemmas by asking themselves, What should responsible early childhood educators do and what should they refuse to do?

Professional ethics help us to resolve moral dilemmas that cannot be settled by facts. Moral dilemmas require a special kind of reasoning that is characterized by exploring a case and applying moral principles (ideas about how the world ought to be). Moral principles include justice, fairness, and respect for the dignity and worth of individuals. Moral dilemmas often involve conflicting sentiments; there may be no right answer or easy solution, and choices must often be made under complex and ambiguous circumstances. For example, in a situation in which parents request that you do not allow their child to nap in school, you are caught in a conflict between obligations to the parents and to the child.

A teacher's primary responsibility is to the well-being of children; therefore, the first thing to be considered when facing a dilemma is the extent to which each alternative might cause harm or benefit. Teachers and staffs can ask themselves the following questions to help guide them in decision making:

- Might this decision cause children any harm now or in the future?
- Which choice is most worth embracing in terms of the core values of early childhood education?

A code of ethics provides guidance to practitioners who face moral decisions. Lilian

Katz and Evangeline Ward's book, *Ethical Behavior in Early Childhood Education* (1978) describes the value of ethical codes in defining and unifying a profession by moving decision making from an individual enterprise to a process based on consensus. A code of ethics provides the basis for an argument or an action. It makes it easier to behave ethically because a practitioner is acting not as an individual but as a professional governed by the principles and requirements of the field. They explain that a code of ethics assures the public that practice in a profession is based on sound and agreed upon standards that are in the best interests of society.

The guidelines contained in codes of ethics help practitioners do what they believe is right and good, not what is easiest, what is most personally beneficial, or even what makes others like them the most. Ethics are of particular concern in early childhood education because young children are so vulnerable and have little control over their lives or power to defend themselves. It is therefore extremely important that those who work in early childhood programs behave fairly and responsibly in children's behalf.

Working out standards for responsible behavior and the establishment of a code of ethics are part of the process of the development of an occupation into a profession, a process that has been going on in early childhood education for a number of years. The National Association for the Education of Young Children has recently approved a Code of Ethical Conduct (Feeney and Kipnis 1989) to guide its members in responsible professional practice. The code provides direction for thinking through and acting on some of the recurring ethical dilemmas that early childhood educators encounter in their daily work with children and families.

NAEYC's code is organized into four sections describing responsibilities to children, families, colleagues, and to community and society. The items in the code offer guidelines and principles designed to help practitioners

make responsible, ethical decisions. Items in the code are organized into ideals that describe exemplary practice and principles of required behavior. The code includes items that pertain to all professions—the importance of keeping personal information confidential—and some that are unique to early childhood education—how to balance the needs of the individual child with the needs of the group (a copy of the code is contained in Appendix 1).

FINDING YOUR PLACE IN EARLY CHILDHOOD EDUCATION

People concerned with the education and welfare of young children and trained in early childhood education can choose among a number of different jobs. Each person has to find the career that best reflects his or her interests, talents, and style. In early childhood education today, you can work directly with children from birth through age eight in a variety of programs including preschools, child care centers, parent-child programs, and elementary schools.

The job of the teacher of young children is varied and challenging; it demands knowledge, skill, sensitivity, and creativity. The job is not always easy and the roles are not always distinct. Early childhood education is especially appropriate for those who want to devote themselves to caring for children and who enjoy the spontaneous interactions that abound in daily life with young children. It can be frustrating for people who think that teaching is a matter of dispensing information or who like everything tidy and predictable. Sometimes college students who begin their careers with glorious visions of teaching young minds become discouraged when they discover how much of their time is spent mixing paint, changing pants, mopping floors, and wiping noses. Working with young children is demanding, difficult, and tiring. It can also be challenging and gratifying.

Training in early childhood education provides a valuable perspective on child development and experience that can serve in a variety of careers. Some of our students discover that working directly with young children in classrooms is just right for them. Others who want to work in the field, but who enjoy administration and contact with adults as well as children, become program directors. Still others who want to work with children individually and in more depth may choose the field of social work or counseling. In addition to these choices, careers in early childhood education can include teacher training, research, teaching child development and early childhood education in high schools, and parent education. Newer professional roles include advocates for children and families and specialists in child care resource and referral agencies. Career decisions are not set in concrete and don't have to last forever. As we grow and change, so do our needs for professional fulfillment. The more experience you have working with children of different ages in a variety of early childhood settings, the sooner it will become clear whether teaching is the right choice for you. There are many kinds of work in which you can act upon your commitment to children. What is most important is that you learn about yourself and make the best decision you can based on where you are at a particular time in your life.

DISCUSSION QUESTIONS

1. Choose a teacher you remember clearly from your own childhood. Discuss the personal qualities of that teacher. How did he or she exercise power and authority? How do you think that teacher affected children's feelings about themselves and school?
2. In a group, make a list of the characteristics of the teachers you have liked best and least in your school experiences. Discuss which of these are personal qualities and which are professional characteristics. What seems to be essential in a good teacher? Which characteristics do you think have potential to harm children and are not acceptable in teachers of young children?
3. Share your thoughts about the kind of world you would like to live in, the kinds of people who would be needed to make such a world possible, and what schools would have to be like to develop those people.
4. Reflect on the important personal values in your life and how they may have influenced your decision to go into the field of early childhood education. How might they influence the way you will teach young children and work with their families?
5. Choose an ethical issue that you have encountered or one described in this chapter and see how it might be resolved using the NAEYC Code of Ethical Conduct in Appendix 1.

PROJECTS

1. Observe a teacher in an early childhood program for at least one hour. Attempt to experience the classroom and children from the teacher's perspective. Describe as thoughtfully as you can what happened during your period of observation. What do you think the teacher was trying to accomplish? What values does the teacher appear to hold? What successes and problems were encountered? How might the teacher have been feeling about what happened? What were your feelings and reactions?

2. Choose a child and for at least one hour attempt to experience the classroom (and the child's relationship with the teacher) from the child's perspective. Describe as thoughtfully as you can what happened during your period of observation and how the child might have felt. Describe your feelings and reactions and what you learned about children and about teachers.

3. Read a book about a teacher (preferably one who teaches in a program for young children) or one of the other books listed in Appendix 3. Prepare a short review article as if you were writing for a professional newsletter. Very briefly tell something about the book and your thoughts and feelings and about the book's implications for you as a teacher of young children. Would you recommend this book to other teachers and prospective teachers? (Please do not summarize the whole book.)

4. Review briefly the events of your childhood and adolescence at home and at school. How did you feel about your early experiences and relationships as you were living through them? As you look back now, which experiences and relationships seem to have had a meaningful effect on your development as a person, and what led to your decision to become a teacher? What do you see as your potential strengths and weaknesses as a teacher or prospective teacher?

5. Observe two early childhood programs. What seemed to be the primary values of each program? What specific things about the program led to your conclusions? Which program was most consistent with your values for education and why?

6. List at least five of the most important values in your life. For each, discuss the influences and experiences that you think contributed to its development. In what ways have these values influenced your decision to enter the field of early childhood education? In what ways do they influence your values for the education of young children?

BIBLIOGRAPHY

Ade, W. 1982. Professionalism and Its Implications for the Field of Early Childhood Education. *Young Children* 37(3):25–32.

Almy, M. 1975. *The Early Childhood Educator at Work.* New York: McGraw-Hill.

Ashton-Warner, S. 1980. *Teacher.* London: Virago.

Ayers, W. 1989. *The Good Preschool Teacher.* New York: Teachers College Press.

Biber, B. 1969. *Challenges Ahead for Early Childhood Education.* Washington, D.C.: National Association for the Education of Young Children.

Burks, J., and M. Rubenstein. 1979. *Temperament Styles in Adult Interaction.* New York: Brunner/Mazel.

Callahan, J. C. 1988. *Ethical Issues in Professional Life.* New York: Oxford University Press.

Dennison, G. 1969. *The Lives of Children.* New York: Vintage Books.

Feeney, S., and K. Kipnis. 1985. Professional Ethics in Early Childhood Education. *Young Children* 40(3):54–56.

Feeney, S., and K. Kipnis. 1989. Code of Ethical Conduct and Statement of Commitment. *Young Children* 45(1):24–29.

Feeney, S., C. Phelps, and D. Stanfield. 1976. Values Examination: A Crucial Issue in Early Childhood Education. In *Early Childhood Education: It's an Art? It's a Science?,* ed. J. D. Andrews. Washington, D.C.: National Association for the Education of Young Children.

Good, T., and J. Brophy. 1973. *Looking at Classrooms.* New York: Harper & Row.

Hendrick, J. 1987. *Why Teach?* Washington, D.C.: National Association for the Education of Young Children.

Jersild, A. 1955. *When Teachers Face Themselves.* New York: Teachers College, Columbia University.

Katz, L. G. 1980. Mothering and Teaching—Some Significant Distinctions. In *Current Topics in Early Childhood Education.* Vol. 3. Norwood, Mass.: Ablex Publishing.

Katz, L. G., and E. Ward. 1978. *Ethical Behavior in Early Childhood Education.* Washington, D.C.: National Association for the Education of Young Children.

Keirsey, D., and M. Bates. 1978. *Please Understand Me: Character and Temperament Types.* Del Mar, Calif.: Prometheus Memesis Books.

Kipnis, K. 1987. How to Discuss Professional Ethics. *Young Children* 42(4):26–33.

Kohl, H. 1984. *Growing Minds: On Becoming a Teacher.* New York: Harper & Row.

Maslow, A. 1968. *Toward a Psychology of Being.* 2d ed. New York: Van Nostrand Reinhold.

McCaulley, M. H., and F. L. Natter. 1980. *Psychological Type Differences in Education.* Gainesville, Fla: Center for Application of Psychological Type.

Moustakas, C. 1982. *The Authentic Teacher.* New York: Irvington Publishers.

Myers, I. B. 1980. *Gifts Differing.* Palo Alto, Calif.: Consulting Psychologists Press.

Noddings, N. 1984. *Caring: A Feminine Approach to Ethics and Moral Education.* Berkeley, Calif.: University of California Press.

Riley, S. S. 1984. *How to Generate Values in Young Children.* Washington, D.C.: National Association for the Education of Young Children.

Rogers, C. 1969. *Freedom to Learn.* Columbus, Ohio: Merrill.

Rokeach, M. 1967. *Beliefs, Attitudes and Values.* San Francisco: Jossey-Bass.

Rosen, J. L. 1968. Personality and First Year Teachers' Relationships with Children. *The School Review* 76(3):294–311.

Saiwin, E. 1969. *Evaluation and the Work of the Teacher.* Belmont, Calif.: Wadsworth.

Seaver, J. W., C. A. Cartwright, C. B. Ward, and C. A. Heasley. 1979. *Careers with Young Children; Making Your Decision.* Washington, D.C.: National Association for the Education of Young Children.

Souper, P. 1976. *About to Teach.* London and Boston: Routedge & Kegan Paul.

Spodek, B., O. Saracho, and D. L. Peters. 1988. *Professionalism and the Early Childhood Practitioner.* New York: Teachers College Press.

Strike, K. A., E. Haller, and J. F. Soltis. 1988. *The Ethics of School Administration.* New York: Teachers College Press.

Thomas, A., and S. Chess. 1977. *Temperament and Development.* New York: Brunner/Mazel.

Trubitt, A. 1981. A Study of the Relationship of Temperament of Preschool Children and Their Teachers. Master's thesis, University of Hawaii School of Social Work, Honolulu.

Yonemura, M. V. 1986. *A Teacher at Work: Professional Development and the Early Childhood Educator.* New York: Teachers College Press.

CHAPTER TWO

History

The past is prologue
—*National Archives*

This chapter describes the historical roots of early childhood education and how persons and events in the past have influenced current programs and practices. It is written to provide you with a perspective on the origins of present philosophies and practices.

Knowledge of the history of early childhood education gives us a context for understanding where we are and where we are going as a field. A historical perspective gives the teacher a sense of early childhood education's roots in the past and an idea of the sources of current practice. Knowing about history can lead to the realization that much of what is called "innovation" in current practice has been written about and experimented with before.

Knowledge of the origins of influential programs lets you know why we do many of the things we do today. And awareness of the history of early childhood education in the United States will give you an understanding of how current developments and educational options have grown out of past ideas and practices.

Early childhood education is a fairly new field, although it has old roots and emerges from a long historical tradition. In this chapter we will discuss some notable people who applied themselves to understanding children and to making the world a better place for them to grow and learn.

Early childhood education as a special field dates from early nineteenth century Europe. However, many values and practices found in today's programs are derived from philosophers, writers, and teachers of earlier centuries. Many of today's programs have their roots in what is referred to as the *humanistic tradition* in education. The theorists who contributed to this stream of thought were concerned with issues such as the education of the whole person, interrelationships between mind and body, the quality of relationships between individuals, and the role of play in learning. They supported education that fostered individual freedom. Some believed in universal education rather than educational opportunities only for the elite. Educators in this tradition tended to see childhood as a valuable time in its own right, not just a preparation for adulthood. The humanistic tradition was slow to be accepted, particularly during the lifetimes of its innovators. Although the ideas of the educators we discuss here were sometimes influential, at other times they were regarded as radical and treated with suspicion and hostility.

In order to put our historical discussion into perspective, it helps to realize that today's concept of childhood is relatively new. Until recently, children had little status and virtually no rights. In ancient Greece, infanticide was common. Child selling was a common practice throughout the Roman empire. The Christian church condemned infanticide on the basis that every child possesses a soul, but its concept of original sin led to the interpretation of normal childish mischievousness as the work of the devil. During the Middle Ages, high mortality rates contributed to an indifferent attitude toward young children. Once children were past infancy and no longer needed constant care, they were expected to work and behave like adults. This is evident in the portrayal of children as miniature adults in the art of this period (Aries 1962). The actual years of childhood were brief, hardly longer than our current broad definition of *early* childhood as the years from birth to age eight. Most children became apprenticed to learn a trade as early as possible, and by puberty, many children were married.

A specialized field of early childhood education could not arise until the concept of childhood as a unique developmental period emerged in the sixteenth and seventeenth centuries. Aries (1962) describes two views of childhood that date from this period. The first is that the very young child, under seven, was a source of amusement, to be fussed over and coddled. The second view, that children are vulnerable and in need of protection and education, is the link with early childhood education today. By the eighteenth century, the idea was advanced that the obligations between children and parents did not rest solely on the children. Lip service, at least, was given to the notion that parents had important duties to their children, but child labor and parental cruelty were still acceptable practices.

BEGINNINGS OF EARLY CHILDHOOD EDUCATION

Some notable people in history have significantly shaped the ideas behind today's early childhood education programs. The philosophers, religious leaders, and writers we discuss in this section had an influence on the field, even though they addressed themselves to a total philosophy of education rather than to the education of young children in particular.

In ancient Greece, education was extolled as the means by which an "ideal state" could be realized. The education of young children was considered important. Later in Rome, the state subsidized an educational system, establishing grammar schools throughout the empire. What formal education there was in the early Middle Ages was under the control of the Catholic church and generally restricted to boys and young men who aspired to the religious life. Most other children were educated informally through the apprenticeship system. During the Renaissance, which began in the fourteenth century, there was a revival of interest in classical learning, but the Reformation in the sixteenth century disrupted the educational systems in many countries. After the Reformation, schooling was gradually substituted for apprenticeship as the primary vehicle for educating the young. Schools established under civil or church auspices enabled primary-aged children to learn to read and write in Latin. Charity schools for five-through eleven-year-old children were founded by churches to teach reading, writing, and arithmetic in native languages.

Many educational historians trace the humanistic tradition in education back to ancient Greece and the ideas of Plato (428–348 B.C.) and Aristotle (384–322 B.C.). Plato was concerned with developing an ethical and reasonable ruling class. Both Plato and Aristotle recognized the importance of beginning education with young children, both saw human beings as essentially good, both emphasized the development of mind and body, and both sought to create a society in which good people followed good laws.

Martin Luther (1483–1546), the religious reformer of the Renaissance whose work led to the Reformation, was a strong advocate of universal education. He believed that in order for people to take responsibility for their own salvation, they needed to read and understand the Bible for themselves. Luther believed that schools should develop the intellectual, religious, physical, emotional, and social qualities of children. An extensive school system was developed in Germany in response to Luther's views, but his goal of universal education did not become reality until nineteenth century America.

Czechoslovakian bishop John Amos Comenius (1592–1670) was a teacher and educational theorist. Like Luther, he believed in universal education. He saw all people as being equal before God and believed, therefore, that all individuals, rich or poor, common or noble, male or female, were entitled to the same education. Comenius stressed the importance of educating children while they are young and can easily be bent and formed. Schooling for the youngest began in the maternal school, the "school of the mother's knee." The mother attended to her child's physical needs and encouraged play. She might show the child

pictures of common objects contained in an illustrated book, created by Comenius and believed to be the first picture book for young children. Comenius believed that after the age of six children should attend vernacular schools to prepare them for life and for further education. Teaching in the vernacular schools was in the native language, not in Latin.

In England, the physician-philosopher John Locke (1632–1704) advocated changes in parental care and education of their children. Infants' free movements should not be restricted by the practice of swaddling them in tight strips of cloth; neither should young children be restricted from physical exploration. Rather than physical punishment, parents should use gentler forms of discipline, but they should begin to employ these when the child is quite young. The phrase *tabula rasa* (blank slate) and the idea that a young child is open to the influence of early training and education are often associated with Locke. Locke felt that learning should never become a task imposed on the child. A respectful, loving relationship is the best way for parents and teachers to inspire the child to imitate their examples and to learn.

Later, in France, the work of Jean-Jacques Rousseau (1712–1778) became influential. Rousseau, a philosopher, writer, and social theorist, was acquainted with the ideas of Locke and is now regarded as an early proponent of a child-development-based view of learning. Rousseau's ideas about proper child rearing and education were a reaction to a what he saw as corruption in government and society. He did not believe that people were born with original sin, but rather that their inherent goodness was spoiled by civilization. In the novel *Emile,* Rousseau presents his view that innate goodness will flower when people are raised out of contact with corrupt society. Rousseau felt that parents and educators should express their confidence in the natural growth process by giving children the freedom to explore and do things for themselves.

HISTORICAL CONCEPTS OF PLAY

Along with an understanding of how views of childhood and education have changed, it is useful to briefly examine the related transformation of ideas about play. In today's early childhood education programs, play is considered an important element intrinsic to children's learning. A basic knowledge of the origins and historical theories of play will help you understand those varied conceptions of play reflected in the philosophies of past and present programs for young children.

In ancient Greece and Rome, children's play appears to have been a valued activity. Structured physical play in the form of games and gymnastics began in childhood and continued to be important as recreation for adult men. The free play of young children was viewed as necessary and a way of learning. Plato recom-

mended that adults observe children's play and games to gain better understanding of them. He suggested gathering together all the village children (ages three to six) for group play under adult supervision (Caplan and Caplan 1974). A Roman, Quintilian, believed that teachers could use play to help children develop intellectually (ibid.).

After the fall of the Roman empire, play seems to have been regarded as somehow sinful. Not until after the Renaissance did play once more appear to be valued. Comenius is regarded as the first advocate of children's play during that historical period. He encouraged the classroom use of puzzles and other concrete objects as learning tools, and he contended that every school should have a playground! Locke (1632–1704) probably reflected a more common view that children indulge in play because they have nothing better to engage their minds. Within the Protestant churches, there was a faction that viewed play as the work of the devil, an activity to be severely restricted. This outlook is in diametrical opposition to Rousseau's romantic vision of the child teaching himself through his own natural, undirected play, free of adult interference and guidance. Friedrich Froebel pioneered in formulating an educational approach based on play, which he called the "highest phase of child development" (Weber 1971, p. 38). Subsequently, Maria Montessori, Margaret McMillan, and others in the United States and Europe carried the idea of learning through play beyond Froebel's conception to include free choice.

During the nineteenth and early twentieth centuries, a number of writers formulated explanations for the role of play in human development (Levy 1978). Johan Huizanga, a Dutch historian and educator, believed that among the essential components of civilization are certain forms of play—ritual, poetry, music, and dancing. Herbert Spencer, British philosopher and psychologist, introduced what has been called the *surplus energy theory,* which suggested that the purpose of play was to help man use energy that he no longer needed because of his "higher" animal status. The *recapitulation theory* of play is credited to G. S. Hall, who believed that during childhood the history of evolution is progressively relived. He saw play as an opportunity to rid the human race of primitive and unnecessary instinctual traits carried over by heredity from past generations. *Instinct theory* was developed by German philosopher and writer Karl Groos, who believed that play was a natural instinct and was necessary for children's growth and development. The *relaxation theory* posited by G. T. W. Patrick holds that play is an essential recuperative mechanism to relieve the stresses of work.

More recent theories of play strongly reflect the influence of Sigmund Freud and Jean Piaget. Freud and his followers felt that play helped children to feel more grown-up and powerful, to exert some control over their environments, and to relieve anxiety created by real-life conflicts. Play therapy, based on this theoretical framework, uses play as a therapeutic mode for working through children's conflicts and problems. Piaget believed that play contributed to and was a manifestation of cognitive development (Athey 1984). He offered a set of stages for looking at the development of children's play. (See Chapter 5 for further discussion of the purposes and benefits of play.)

EMERGENCE OF THE FIELD OF EARLY CHILDHOOD EDUCATION

Educational theorists and reformers became directly involved in the education of young children during the eighteenth and nineteenth centuries. Their work formed the basis for many modern educational practices. They were idealists, they were deeply humanitarian in their viewpoints, and they were often concerned with social reform as it affected the children of the poor.

Early childhood education as a distinct discipline had its beginning with Johann Pestalozzi (1746–1827), a Swiss who was influenced by the romantic philosophers including Rousseau. Like Luther and Comenius before him, Pestalozzi believed in universal education. He devoted his life to education, particularly for the orphaned and poor. He wrote that the first year of life was the most important in the child's development. Believing that every child was capable of learning, he suggested that instruction be adapted to each child's needs and be based on the child's natural development. He rejected the practice of memorization and advocated sensory exploration and observation as the basis of learning. He believed that children learned through self-discovery and could pace their own learning. Pestalozzi was also concerned with teaching human relationships. "My one aim was to . . . awaken a feeling of brotherhood . . . make them affectionate, just and considerate." (Braun and Edwards 1972, p. 52).

English industrialist, social philosopher, and controversial reformer Robert Owen (1771–1858), was a disciple of Pestalozzi. Owen became concerned with the poor conditions of families who worked in the cotton mills during the Industrial Revolution. He worked for reforms in their communities and established schools to improve the lives of their children, who from the age of six worked long hours in the mills alongside their parents.

Owen believed that through education, combined with an environment that allowed people to live by the principle of mutual consideration, it was possible to transform the nature of people and society. His infant school, the first in England for children three to ten years of age, had a warm, friendly atmosphere. Owen did not believe either in pressuring children to learn or in punishing them; he felt that the natural consequences of their actions would teach children right from wrong. Sensory learning, outdoor play, stories, and visitors from the community were included in the school program in an attempt to make school relevant and interesting.

Owen's ideas were considered radical in his time, and his schools did not have lasting success in England. However, many of the practices originating in Owen's schools can still be found in today's early childhood programs. These include periods of time during which children choose their activities, emphasis on a warm, nurturing, and nonpunitive teacher, and the use of spontaneous play as a vehicle for learning.

MAJOR INFLUENCES ON TODAY'S PROGRAMS

Some innovative approaches to early childhood education, developed around the turn of the century, have had a great impact on the nature of early childhood education in the United States today. As we shall see, these approaches originated in different places in response to different societal and educational concerns. They share, however, the caring and respectful attitude toward children so characteristic of the reformers just described. These approaches include the kindergarten created in Germany by Friedrich Froebel, the Montessori method developed by physician Maria Montessori in Italy, and the nursery school founded by the McMillan sisters in England. Another major influence was the progressive education movement that originated in the United States. Best known through the work of educator-philosopher John Dewey, the ideas of progressive education were applied in early childhood settings by Patty Smith Hill, Caroline Pratt, Lucy Sprague Mitchell, and Harriet Johnson.

Froebel's Kindergarten

Friedrich Wilhelm Froebel (1782–1852), the father of the modern kindergarten, established the first kindergarten program in Germany in

1837. He had studied with Pestalozzi and had been a teacher in one of his schools. The ideas of Comenius and Rousseau influenced him as well. Froebel was particularly concerned with the education of children aged three through six and also with the mother's relationship to the infant and the very young child. His innovative kindergarten program lasted three to four hours each session. Froebel believed that children were social beings, that activity was the basis for knowing, and that play was an essential part of the educational process. Froebel wanted children to have the opportunity to develop those positive impulses that came from within. The children's play was channeled by the teacher who carefully presented to them special materials and activities designed by Froebel to enhance the children's sensory and spiritual development. The materials, called *gifts,* consisted of such objects as yarn balls, blocks, wooden tablets, natural objects, and geometric shapes. These objects were intended to encourage discovery and manipulation and to lead children to an appreciation for humanity's unity with God. *Occupations* included activities like molding, cutting, folding, bead stringing, and embroidery, all aimed at fostering inventiveness and developing skills. Songs, stories, and games were selected to encourage learning the spiritual values underlying the program. Froebel held that education must begin with concrete objects from which abstract spiritual meanings could be derived. Having conceived of the kindergarten as a nurturing place for the cultivation of children's natural goodness and an extension of the home, Froebel proposed training young women as kindergarten teachers. Some graduates of his kindergarten teacher training institute immigrated to the United States, bringing with them the ideals and practices of the Froebelian kindergarten.

These early American kindergartens (the first founded in 1855) were private ventures, often established in homes and taught in German by teachers who had studied with Froebel.

Elizabeth Peabody founded the first English-speaking kindergarten in Boston in 1860. Later, after studying with Froebel's disciples in Germany, she founded the first American kindergarten teacher training school. She was very influential in winning public support for kindergartens in the United States. The first publicly supported kindergarten was opened in St. Louis in 1873. A rapid expansion of the kindergarten movement took place between 1880 and 1900, when churches, factories, labor unions, and settlement houses established kindergartens.

Two aspects of the society of that time appear to have contributed to the growth of the kindergarten. The first was the belief that because children were inherently good, they required a nurturing, benevolent environment in their early years. The second, concern for the

social problems created by the large influx of poor immigrants, gave rise to the field of philanthropic social work. Mission kindergartens for underprivileged children were established by social workers. They hoped that if young immigrant children were taught values such as responsibility, achievement, and cooperation, the children and their families would assimilate more easily into the American culture.

Early kindergartens emphasized the importance of cleanliness and courtesy, the development of manual skills, and preparation for later schooling. Froebel's gifts and occupations were used as a base for the curriculum. Physical activity was encouraged. Kindergarten children were not made to sit still, memorize, and recite, as older children were. The teacher's role was not that of taskmaster, but of affectionate leader.

Froebel believed that education for young children should differ in content and teaching methods from that for older children. The kindergarten he created represented a radical departure from the schools of his day. However, it was far more formally structured than the individualized, free play kindergarten environment espoused later by the progressives, and it little resembled what we consider to be developmentally appropriate early childhood education today.

Progressive Education

Progressive education was a reaction against the traditional forms of public schooling prevalent during the late nineteenth and early twentieth centuries. Children in the public schools passively learned skills and a predetermined curriculum by drill, rote memorization, and repetitive practice under the teacher's strict discipline.

John Dewey (1859–1952), one of the leaders of this movement for educational reform, stands as a giant among modern educational philosophers and theorists. Dewey believed that education was an integral part of life and that

practical experiences should be interwoven into the curriculum. He stressed the importance of cooperation and problem solving. The school community offered children an opportunity to practice democratic principles in group living. This "child-centered" approach to education emphasized the teacher's respect for the individual child by considering each child's needs, interests, and abilities in planning the curriculum. The child learns through doing—through experiencing and experimenting in self-directed activities, often of a practical nature. Subject areas were integrated and the role of the teacher was to watch and guide rather than to control children.

These tenets of progressive education combined with vigorous research interest in child development to trigger educational experimentation. In New York in 1916, Harriet Johnson, Caroline Pratt, and Lucy Sprague Mitchell organized the Bureau of Educational Experiments (now known as the Bank Street College of Education) as an agency for research on child development. The need for a laboratory setting for experimental education and child study led them to open a nursery school, later named the Harriet Johnson Nursery School, after its first director.

Eventually progressive education theories came under fire from educators who charged that students were not learning fundamental subjects well enough. Many educational historians now feel that Dewey was misinterpreted by many of his followers. Progressive education became associated with permissiveness, rather than with Dewey's idea that the curriculum must challenge youngsters intellectually and help them develop self-direction and responsibility. Dewey's influence in the United States waned after 1950, and progressive education as a guiding philosophy was phased out of most American schools, with the exception of a very few such as the Bank Street College of Education in New York City. It is primarily in early childhood education programs that Dewey's ideas have continued to make a contribution to American education.

Many of the ideas of the progressive movement had a rebirth and reincarnation in England in the mid-1960s in state-supported schools for five- to eight-year-olds called infant schools. These were widely discussed and written about in the United States during the 1970s (Clegg 1971; Featherstone 1971; Weber 1971). This innovative form of education for young children was inspired by teachers' experiences with children sent to the safety of the countryside during World War II. Living and working informally with groups of children, without the benefit of a school setting, teachers found that valuable relationships and learning resulted. These experiences, combined with the philosophy of Dewey and the theoretical contributions of Piaget, contributed to the new approach. It was referred to by a number of terms, including *informal education, the integrated day,* and *the open school.*

The British infant schools are part of the regular public school system and share the public school goals for teaching basic educational skills. However, the informal educational method differs a great deal from traditional, formal approaches. Its initiators believed that children had to make sense of the world around them in their own way and through their own explorations and that play formed an important part of their learning. They suggested that children developed concepts and thinking skills through direct experiences in environments prepared for learning. This approach has also been described as the *open school,* because the use of space is "open," allowing children to move freely between interest areas, and because the content is "open," derived from children's interests rather than from a prescribed curriculum. The program has also been described as having an *integrated day* because discrete subjects are not taught at specified times each day;

rather, learning is organized around tasks or projects. Curriculum content is integrated into the pursuit of these projects.

American educators began to visit the British infant schools in the late 1960s and early 1970s. In response to the enthusiasm engendered by their reports, some American schools introduced a more informal and integrated curriculum at the primary level. For a short time, Dewey's ideas returned full circle to their point of origin. But a new wave of preoccupation with reading, writing, and arithmetic basics in the 1970s and early 1980s diminished interest in such child-centered approaches to education. In the late 1980s, there was again renewed attention to the context within which the young child learns best. Now the early childhood community is issuing a fresh call for developmentally appro-

37

priate practice in programs for children from birth to age eight—another incarnation of the progressive tradition is underway.

Evolution of the Kindergarten

A period of ferment caused by conflicting philosophies began in the kindergarten movement in the 1890s and lasted for twenty years. The conservative group in the debate held to Froebelian principles and practices. The challenging group, known as the progressives, was influenced by new work in child development and by the philosophy of progressive education. The progressives wanted changes in the traditional program. By 1920, the conservative camp had yielded. The reformed kindergarten curriculum which developed incorporated many of Froebel's ideas but added a new emphasis on dramatic play, social interaction, free expression in art and music, nature study, and excursions. New unstructured materials, such as large blocks and doll houses, encouraged children's inventive play. Books and songs reflected children's interests, rather than teaching a message, and activities were inspired by the important here-and-now events, people, and objects in their daily lives.

The first professional association concerned with the education of young children in the United States was the American Froebel Union established by Peabody in 1878. In 1884, the National Education Association (NEA) established a separate department of kindergarten education. A year later the NEA recommended that kindergartens become part of the public schools. In 1892, the International Kindergarten Union (IKU) was formed to promote kindergarten education.

As kindergartens gradually moved into public schools, they met with grudging acceptance. The rigid atmosphere of the traditional primary schools, with their emphasis on drill and skill development, was sharply contrasted to the atmosphere of kindergartens which valued the development of the whole child. However, the gap gradually narrowed. Kindergarten activities like blocks, painting, and craft projects found their way into the primary grades even as primary activities filtered down into the kindergarten.

Beginning in the 1920s, kindergarten teachers in public schools were urged to prepare children for reading. The emphasis on readiness has been found in kindergartens since that time. This has often been translated into five-year-olds being prepared for upper grades through the use of workbooks and teaching techniques normally employed with older children.

To this day, the kindergarten curriculum remains an arena of educational ferment and conflict, caught between the demands of public school administrators for accountability and of early childhood educators for a child-centered approach. The debate about appropriate school learning for five-year-olds focuses on whether the purpose of the kindergarten should be to meet the developmental needs of the children or to prepare them for the academic expectations of later grades.

The Nursery School

Margaret McMillan (1860–1931) and her sister Rachel established the first open-air, play-oriented nursery school in England in 1911. The school's creation was the McMillans' response to the health problems they witnessed in school-age children of poor communities. They designed the nursery school to identify and prevent these health problems and to enhance children's physical and mental development before they entered formal schooling. Eighty years later, programs like Head Start exemplify this same purpose.

In providing for children's physical needs, the McMillans strongly emphasized the value of active outdoor work and play. Health and nutrition, perceptual-motor skills, and the development of imagination were stressed. The teacher's role was both to nurture and to informally teach children using a well-planned environment. Materials in the nursery school included those for sensory development, creative expression, gardening, nature study, and sandbox play.

American nursery schools were not only directly influenced by the English nursery school, but also by Freudian theory and Dewey's ideas on education. One of the first nursery schools in the United States was the City and Country School, established in New York City in 1913 by Caroline Pratt. In 1916, the Bureau of Educational Experiments opened its laboratory nursery school, under the direction of Harriet Johnson. In the 1920s, a number of other laboratory nursery schools were established in America, including the Laboratory Nursery School at Columbia University Teachers College organized by Patty Smith Hill. The Ruggles Street Nursery School (1922) and Training Center (1924) were directed by Abigail Eliot who had studied with Margaret McMillan in England. Unlike most laboratory nursery schools, it was similar to the McMillans' school in that it was a full-day program serving children and parents in a low-income neighborhood. Cooperative nursery schools, formed by educated middle-class parents, first began in 1915 and spread rapidly. Also founded during this period were prominent child study institutions with laboratory schools: Yale University's Clinic of Child Development in 1911, the Iowa Child Welfare Research Station in 1917, and the Merrill-Palmer Institute in Detroit in 1922. During the 1920s and 1930s, nursery schools were established in many college home economics departments to train future homemakers and to serve as centers for child development research.

Patty Smith Hill, at Columbia University's Teachers College, formed the National Committee for the Nursery School. Later, the organization's name was changed to the National Association for Nursery Education (NANE), and finally to its current name, the National Association for the Education of Young Children (NAEYC).

Nursery schools became multidisciplinary in orientation, because the early pioneers came from a number of fields, including nursing, social work, medicine, psychology, and education—hence the whole-child orientation described in this book. The earliest nursery schools were often all-day programs that emphasized the child's social, emotional, and physical growth. Cognitive development received less attention, because of the common belief that children were not ready for academic work until they entered school at the age of six. Children played freely indoors and outdoors in a rich physical environment.

In the nursery school, the child learns through interactions with people and with the environment. Children are seen as always in

transition: growing, changing, experiencing. The role of the school is to keep the paths of exploration open so that children can develop in their own ways. The daily schedule is characterized by large time blocks in which children are free to choose activities and engage in them for long periods of time. The classroom is divided into activity areas, typically those for block construction, dramatic play, art, water play, sand play, science, math, and reading.

The teacher's role in the nursery school is to create an environment that facilitates learning. Teachers also support social and emotional development by encouraging children to verbalize their feelings. Child management is carried out whenever possible by problem solving and by modifying the environment rather than by imposing adult power.

In response to new information about human intellectual development and the needs of low-income children, the traditional nursery school has continued to evolve, especially in terms of interest in children's cognitive development. What remains constant is the insistence that the child is a person whose development can benefit by play and learning activities in a carefully designed environment, which includes the presence of a sensitive teacher. Today, the term *preschool* or *child development center* is generally used to describe programs that grew out of the legacy of the nursery school.

The Montessori Method

Maria Montessori (1870–1952) was the first woman in Italy to receive a medical degree, though she is best known for her contributions to education. Early in her medical career, she devised successful approaches for working with retarded children previously regarded as incapable of learning. In 1907, she founded the *Casa Dei Bambini* (Children's House), in Rome, to explore the applicability of her educational methods to normal children. The program she designed was based on her observation of young children. She reached the conclusion that intelligence was not fixed and could be stimulated or stifled by the child's experiences. Further, she believed that children learn best through their own direct sensory experience of the world.

Montessori was undoubtedly influenced by the work of Pestalozzi, Froebel, and Freud. But the foundation for her own interest in education was her study of the French physicians Seguin's and Itard's writings on their humane methods for educating retarded children.

She was interested in the first years of life and believed that children went through *sensitive periods* during which they had interest and capacity for the development of particular knowledge and/or skills. Montessori believed that children had an inherent desire to explore and understand the world in which they lived. She saw these young explorers as self-motivated and able to seek out the kinds of experiences and knowledge most appropriate for their stage of development. Concerned with preserving the dignity of the child, she valued the development of independence and productivity.

The physical environment in a Montessori classroom was designed to be attractive and equipped with child-sized, movable furniture. Montessori stressed the importance of an orderly environment that helps children to focus on their learning and develop the ability to concentrate. The classroom is equipped with didactic materials created by Maria Montessori to help children develop their senses and learn concepts. These beautifully crafted materials are the basis for much learning in a Montessori setting. They are treated with care and respect and are displayed on open shelves so children can use them independently. The materials are graded in difficulty, and sequenced from known to unknown and from concrete to abstract. Each concept to be taught is isolated from other concepts that might be confusing or distracting. For example, if the child is learning the concept of shape, the materials will be of uniform size and color so that the attribute of shape will be isolated. Materials are also designed to have immediate, self-correcting feedback, so children know if they have completed a task successfully.

The basis for learning in a Montessori classroom is firsthand experience. The children learn by observing and by doing. Practical life experiences such as buttoning, zipping, cutting, polishing, and gardening enable children to care for themselves and the environment while building skills useful throughout life. The didactic materials help children develop the ability to concentrate. Their sense perceptions are enhanced while they learn to differentiate concepts of size, shape, color, texture, sound, and temperature. Materials for conceptual learning include those designed to teach writing, reading, and mathematics.

All learning in a Montessori classroom is cumulative. Each activity paves the way to future, more complex activities. Activities are organized primarily for individual work rather than group interaction. Children move freely about the classroom and choose their own activities. Though social-emotional development was not emphasized by Montessori, educators trained in her method believe that children develop a sense of self-esteem as they increase their competence.

Montessori schools are similar to nursery schools in that children are viewed as inquisi-

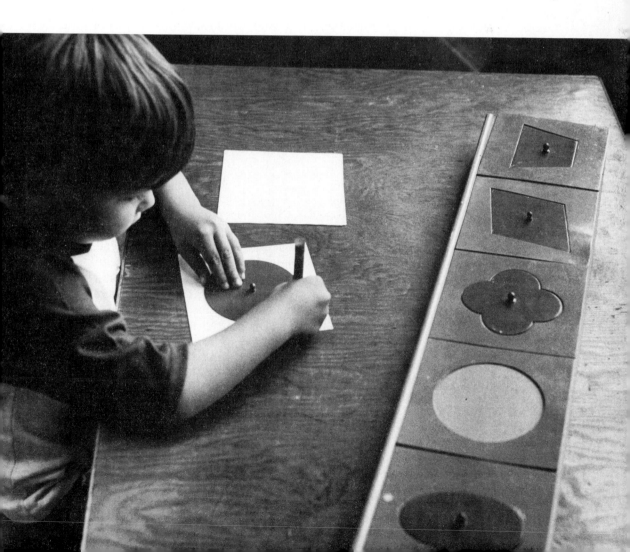

tive, self-motivated learners who are capable of selecting activities appropriate for their current needs and developmental stage. Nursery schools differ from Montessori schools in their greater emphasis on social interaction, self-expression and creativity, and multiple uses for materials.

Montessori schools were successful in Italy and eventually spread throughout the world. Early childhood programs in the United States adopted Montessori's ideas of creating a child-sized environment and using sensory materials. Although there have been private Montessori schools in the United States since 1915, the Montessori approach did not become popular here until after 1960. This renewed attention was largely due to interest in the application of Montessori's theories to the education of low-income children.

There are many Montessori schools in the United States today. Some use Montessori materials in combination with other approaches, whereas others rely exclusively on the methods and materials developed by Montessori. Even among teachers trained in her methods, there is some debate about how strictly her prescriptions should be followed and how much variation is acceptable. Two major professional associations are concerned with implementing Montessori programs, training teachers, and accrediting schools and teachers. One is the original organization, Association Montessori Internationale (AMI), with headquarters in the Netherlands; the other is the American Montessori Society (AMS) founded in 1956 in order to adapt Montessori methods to an American style of working with children.

PUBLIC POLICY AND PROGRAMS AND SERVICES FOR CHILDREN

Who is responsible for meeting the needs of America's children? This question has been, and continues to be, the subject of great debate. During the childhood years, the needs of chil-

dren are addressed by their families as well as by many other groups, including churches, voluntary associations, foundations, and local, state, and federal governments. There is no clear-cut policy guiding which needs should be met by public resources and which by private means, nor is there an overall policy regarding programs and services for children. Historically, it has been assumed that, barring disaster, families will care for their own children. Government involvement has generally been limited to the very neediest: care for orphans, protection for abused children, and food for the children of the poor.

In the United States, federal involvement in promoting the health, education, and welfare of children began with the creation of the Children's Bureau in 1912. Its charge was to investigate child health and labor, and its role was mainly to make investigations and report the findings. Since that time, the federal government established a department of Health, Education, and Welfare in 1959 and an Office of Child Development in 1969 (later called the Administration for Children, Youth, and Families). These agencies have been involved in provision of welfare to families unable to care for their own children, in health and nutrition programs, in child abuse prevention, in educational programs for low-income children, and at some times in care for children whose parents must work outside the home.

The debate regarding government's role in services to children is centered around the questions of whether intervention should occur only when the family is unable to meet children's basic needs or whether there is a greater responsibility to see that the developmental needs of all children in society are met.

In order to understand trends in child care, early education, and the policies affecting young children and their families, it is helpful to remember the larger world context. Societal changes and major political events have a powerful influence on our views of the family and our attitudes toward children. There is a tendency for social and political trends to create pendulum swings of reaction and counterreaction in educational policies.

Child Care

Provision of child care services for employed parents is a major policy issue in early childhood education today. The day nursery movement of the nineteenth century served the most desperately needy of the great waves of immigrants. By providing care for immigrant children, these privately run programs enabled parents employed in urban factories to keep their families together. Personnel in the day nurseries were largely untrained, worked long hours with very high child-adult ratios, and provided minimal care for children. In the eyes of society, the great virtue of the day nursery was that the children served were given a reprieve from even more harmful environments. These programs were primarily concerned with the health of children, the daily bath being a major event, and not with more lofty educational goals. Many day nurseries provided quite comprehensive services with long hours of operation, infant care, family education and training programs, and even counseling.

The social climate of the early twentieth century was not supportive of publicly funded child care services. These services were permissible only as a temporary response to families in need of aid during times of national political or economic crisis. They were never viewed as a basic social welfare service that government should help provide.

During the depression in the 1930s, federal child care centers, called emergency nursery schools, were established to provide relief work for teachers, custodians, cooks, nurses, and others who needed employment. These programs were phased out as the depression ended. Again, during World War II, the U.S. government became reinvolved in the business of sponsor-ing child care. This time, the purpose was to meet the needs of the large numbers of women employed in defense plants. Under the Lanham Act (1942–1946) federally funded day care centers served approximately 600,000 children in forty-one states. Private industry also sponsored child care for its workers during the war. Most notable were the two centers run by Kaiser shipyards in Portland, Oregon. The Kaiser Centers were outstanding for their comprehensive, high-quality services made available to employees with children aged eighteen months to six years.

Wartime child care services under government and industry sponsorship were contingent on that state of emergency and soon faded away. The provision of child care services during those years was merely an expedient, temporary measure intended to help win the war. Peacetime heralded a return to the image of the traditional family, with mothers in the home tending to their children. Of course, many mothers did not dutifully return home but continued their employment. As child care facilities either closed or were reduced to prewar levels, these employed mothers had limited options for child care. A patchwork of private arrangements was the common solution. The California Children's Centers were among the few survivors of the Lanham Act programs. With state funding, they continue today to serve the children of low-income full-time students and employed parents.

The postwar attitude toward women's appropriate role as homemaker, combined with the belief that children of employed mothers suffered from a lack of maternal care, gave strength to the contention that child care was at best unnecessary and at worst harmful to children. Between 1950 and 1965, the need for child care received little attention or support. Meanwhile, family life in America started to undergo major changes. The extended family system broke down as family mobility increased and the divorce rate soared. Single parents, if employed, could no longer assume complete responsibility for their young children; they had to share this responsibility with other caregivers who usually were not relatives.

The 1960s and early 1970s were a period of national concern with social reform. During this period there was a resurgence of interest in early education as a public policy issue. New research in child development, combined with a desire to counteract the effects of poverty on young children, led to the creation of a federally funded program called Project Head Start. Other compensatory programs for low-income children were started by states and private foundations. These programs were now focused on the development of the child rather than on providing a service for employed parents.

The next step was the introduction into Congress of legislation to provide child care for all working families who wanted it. A comprehensive child care services bill, passed by the U.S. House and Senate in 1971, was vetoed by President Nixon, who justified his action by stating that this measure threatened the stability of the American family. During the rest of the 1970s, attempts to pass federal child care legislation failed repeatedly. Direct federal support for early childhood programs was limited to Head Start.

In the 1980s, federal funding of early childhood programs actually declined in terms of real dollars. Federal government assistance mostly took the form of tax credits, an approach that was most beneficial to middle-class families. In the second half of the 1980s, the clamor for federal support of child care programs resulted in numerous early childhood education and child care bills being introduced into Congress. The best known of these, the Act for Better Child Care, received a great deal of support and came close to passage in the 1989 congressional session. The need for government assistance in meeting the child care needs of working families has gathered support from diverse groups in our society and it appears, as we enter the 1990s, that federal child care legislation is likely in the near future.

Programs for Low-Income Children

In the early twentieth century, educational programs for children in low socioeconomic groups existed in many American cities. These philanthropic kindergartens were intended to help children overcome the handicaps of growing up in the slums by teaching them skills and middle-class values. When kindergartens became integrated into the free public school system, special attention to the educational needs of disadvantaged children was postponed until the 1960s.

The 1957 launch of the Russian space satellite, Sputnik, generated a sense of national uneasiness and the fear that American children were being inadequately educated to compete in a scientific age. This concern led to greater emphasis on the quality of education and to curricular innovations in elementary and secondary schools, especially in the study of science and math.

At about the same time, research by Piaget, J. McVicker Hunt, and others began to dispel old ideas about intelligence being fixed and static and pointed to the impact of early experiences on later intellectual development. Researchers and educators suggested that planned intervention in the early years might enhance children's development, help them succeed in later schooling, and perhaps enable them to be more successful in their adult lives. Hence, the idea developed that early childhood programs should provide more than play opportunities for young children.

The surge of concern about the quality of American education in the 1950s and 1960s and the publicity given to this new child development research meshed with the political climate in paving the way for a whole new era in early childhood education. President Johnson's concern with the plight of the underprivileged in

America extended to a renewed interest in the lost potential of those children disadvantaged by living in poverty. The Office of Economic Opportunity was formed, and the War on Poverty was launched.

Head Start

Under the auspices of the Office of Economic Opportunity, an interdisciplinary panel representing the fields of pediatrics, education, child development, and social services was formed and directed to develop a program that might counter the effects of poverty on children. It was hoped that such a program would be effective in increasing achievement and opportunities and that it would give poor children a "head start." The resulting program, called Project Head Start, was unique in its focus on the total development of the child, in its emphasis on strengthening the family, involvement of the community, and in its provision of comprehensive services.

Head Start was begun in the summer of 1965 as a six-week demonstration project. By the fall of that year, however, it was clear that six weeks was not enough time to achieve its goals, and it was converted into a full-year program. In 1969, under the Nixon administration, responsibility for Head Start's administration was transferred from the Office of Economic Opportunity to the Office of Child Development.

As we have discussed, prior to Head Start, federal support for children's programs had been accomplished only when tied to a national emergency. The Head Start program represented a new view of child development as a valuable end in itself and an unprecedented mobilization of resources on behalf of children.

Follow Through

In 1968, the Office of Child Development authorized an experimental program called Planned Variation designed to investigate the effects of a variety of curricular approaches (models) in Head Start programs. Another new program, called Follow Through, was introduced the following year by the U.S. Office of Education in order to continue special programs for Head Start children when they entered elementary school. Follow Through was designed to explore the effects of continuity in programming from preschool through third grade. In addition, it was to explore the effects of well-defined program models on children's development and to investigate the long-range effects of various program approaches.

The study included a number of educational models that varied greatly in theory and practice. The models represented a spectrum of approaches to early childhood education based on clearly defined learning theories. Each of the models was developed under a program sponsor, usually in a university or educational research center. Models differed greatly in their values, in their assumptions about motivation, in preparation of the learning environment, in presentation of learning experiences, in teacher role, and in management strategies.

Follow Through programs can be organized into three categories that point to major program differences. Preacademic programs (for example, those developed by Siegfried Englemann and Wesley Becker at the University of Oregon and Don Bushell at the University of Kansas) advocate high teacher direction and use behavior modification techniques. Discovery models (like those developed at Bank Street College of Education in New York and the Open Education Model at Education Development Center in Massachusetts) focus on child development. They require that the teacher create a rich and stimulating classroom environment and guide children in their interactions with people and materials. Cognitive discovery models (for example, the Tucson Early Education Model, the Cognitively-Oriented Curriculum developed by Dave Weikart in Michigan, and the Responsive Environment Model from the Far West Educa-

Although research has not definitively proven the superiority of one model or group of models, the program has taught educators a great deal about program development and implementation as well as teacher training. It has also demonstrated the difficulty of doing large-scale educational research with a mobile population.

FINAL THOUGHTS

Early childhood education has a long history and a tradition of concern for the needs of children and their families. The pioneers in the field were often in advance of their time in their recognition that education had to address the whole child, not just the intellect, and in their treatment of children in ways that were respectful and appropriate for their stage of development. There has been a slow progress over the years toward more humane and egalitarian treatment of children and concern for their needs and those of their families. Much still needs to be done to educate the public and policymakers about the importance of the early years and the value to society of continuing and expanding programs and services to young children and their families.

tional Development Laboratory in California) fall somewhere in between the other two (Klein 1979).

Models were chosen by selected communities, and an effort was made to coordinate the programs so that children attended classes employing the same curricular model from preschool through third grade. The Head Start portion of the study was phased out in 1973, but the Office of Education continues to sponsor Follow Through in public schools in many of the original communities.

DISCUSSION QUESTIONS

1. Why might a teacher of young children want or need to know about the history of early childhood education and policies affecting children and families?
2. How have the programs that you have observed or worked in seemed to reflect the historical influences described in this chapter? To what extent do they appear to be similar to or different from what is described here?
3. Discuss your views about who is responsible for child care. Is it a family responsibility? A societal responsibility? What seem to be the views of your community?

PROJECTS

1. Write a research paper on one of the educators mentioned in the chapter who has had an impact on the field of early childhood education.
2. Write a book review of a biography or autobiography of one of the educators mentioned in the chapter who has had an impact on the field of early childhood education.
3. Visit an early childhood program and discuss the specific classroom practices that might be traced back to the thought and writing of the educators described in this chapter.

BIBLIOGRAPHY

Antler, J. 1987. *Lucy Sprague Mitchell: The Making of a Modern Woman*. New Haven: Yale University Press.

Aries, P. 1962. *Centuries of Childhood*. New York: Vintage Books.

Athey, I. 1984. Contributions of Play to Development. In *Child's Play: Development and Applied*, ed. T. Yawkey and A. Pellegrini. Hillside, N.J.: Lawrence Erlbaum.

Auleta, M. S. 1969. *Foundations of Early Childhood Education*. New York: Random House.

Braun, S. J., and E. P. Edwards. 1972. *History and Theory of Early Childhood Education*. Belmont, Calif.: Wadsworth.

Caplan, F., and T. Caplan. 1974. *The Power of Play*. New York: Anchor Press.

Clarke-Stewart, A. 1977. *Childcare in the Family: A Review of Research and Some Propositions for Policy*. New York: Academic Press.

Clegg, A. 1971. *Revolution in the British Primary Schools*. Washington, D.C.: National Education Association.

Dewey, J. 1972. *Experience and Education*. New York: Collier Books.

Dittman, L. L. 1980. Project Head Start Becomes a Long-Distance Runner. *Young Children* 35(6):2–9.

Featherstone, J. 1971. *Schools Where Children Learn*. New York: Liveright.

Frost, J. L., and J. B. Kissinger. 1976. *The Young Child and the Educative Process*. New York: Holt, Rinehart & Winston.

Klein, J. W. 1973. Making or Breaking It: The Teacher's Role in Model (Curriculum) Implementation. *Young Children* 28(6):359–366.

Levy, J. 1978. *Play Behavior*. New York: Wiley.

Maccoby, E. E., and M. Zellner. 1970. *Experiments in Primary Education: Aspects of Project Follow-Through*. New York: Harcourt Brace Jovanovich.

MacDonald, J. B. 1972. Introduction. In *A New Look at Progressive Education*, ed. J. R. Squire. Washington, D.C.: Association for Supervision and Curriculum Development.

Montessori, M. 1965. *Dr. Montessori's Own Handbook*. New York: Schocken Books.
——————. 1967. *The Absorbent Mind*. New York: Holt, Rinehart & Winston.
Osborn, D. K. 1980. *Early Childhood Education in Historical Perspective*. Athens, Ga.: Education Associates.
Shapiro, M. S. 1983. *Child's Garden: The Kindergarten Movement from Froebel to Dewey*. University Park, Pa.: Pennsylvania State University Press.
Schweinhart, L. J., and D. P. Weikart. 1980. *Young Children Grow Up: The Effects of the Perry Preschool Program on Youths through Age 15*. Monograph no. 7. Ypsilanti, Mich.: High/Scope Foundation.
Silberman, C. E. 1970. *Crisis in the Classroom*. New York: Random House.
Standing, E. M. 1959. *Maria Montessori: Her Life and Work*. Fresno, Calif.: Academy Library Guild.
Steiner, G. Y. 1976. *The Children's Cause*. Washington, D.C.: Brookings Institution.
Steinfels, M. O. 1973. *Who's Minding the Children?* New York: Simon & Schuster.
Weber, E. 1969. *The Kindergarten: Its Encounter with Educational Thought in America*. New York: Teachers College Press.
——————. 1984. *Ideas Influencing Early Childhood Education: A Theoretical Analysis*. New York: Teachers College Press.
Weber, L. 1971. *The English Infant School and Informal Education*. Englewood Cliffs, N.J.: Prentice-Hall.
Zigler, E., and J. Valentine. 1979. *Project Head Start: A Legacy of the War On Poverty*. New York: Free Press.

CHAPTER THREE

The Field of Early Childhood Education

The best preparation for being a happy and useful man or woman is to live fully as a child.

—The Plowden Report

This chapter is written to provide you with a perspective on the field of early childhood education, including major program approaches and policies. In it we give an overview of the field today, some major issues and trends, and possible future directions.

What do we mean by early childhood education? To what kinds of programs and services and to what age group are we referring? These questions are not as simple and clear-cut as they may first appear to be. At different times and for different purposes, the field has been defined in a number of ways. The term *early childhood education* can be used broadly to refer to efforts to educate and care for young children in schools, centers, and homes. Early childhood is variously thought of

as the period from birth to the time that children enter kindergarten, or as the years that children attend preschool—typically from ages three to five. Child development theorists define early childhood more broadly as encompassing the span from birth through age eight. In this book we give an overview, introducing you to programs for this entire age range. We focus primarily on practice in preschools and kindergarten and suggest briefly some ways in which this practice must be modified to make it appropriate for infants, toddlers, and primary-school children.

Who are the people who work with young children? The terms *early childhood educator* and *practitioner* are currently being used to encompass all of those who are involved in the care and education of young children. *Teacher* is generally used to refer to people who have completed a course of specialized training in child development and early childhood education. *Caregiver,* or *provider,* is often used to denote those who work with infants and toddlers or care for children in their homes.

What is it like to work in the field of early childhood education? Who are the people involved in it and what do they do? What are the joys, the sorrows, the potentials for growth? Learning about programs, and whenever possible experiencing them firsthand, will enable you to see a range of options and help you to identify the kinds of programs, curriculum, teaching strategies, and teacher roles you feel are compatible with your personality, educational philosophy, and career goals. Knowledge of the field also lets you see your role in it in a broader context.

In the first half of this century, most people believed that nothing important happened during the early years and that young children were not ready to learn until the age of six, when they entered formal schooling. It was generally accepted that all that children needed prior to their sixth year was a home in which their physical needs were met. Even after Freud revealed that important emotional development occurs in the early childhood years, most people held the idea that anyone who worked with children under six was "only babysitting," a phrase we sometimes still hear today.

American attitudes toward teachers of young children have been heavily influenced by the late nineteenth and early twentieth century origins of early childhood education in day nurseries, nursery schools, and kindergartens. This mixed heritage of the educationally oriented nursery school and kindergarten and the care-oriented day nursery has lent early childhood education and early childhood educators a correspondingly mixed status, character, and reputation. This is reflected in the perception that preschool and kindergarten are just preparation for the serious learning of first grade— they are not "real school." This same attitude influences pay scales: generally, the younger the children, the lower the status and salary of their teacher.

Since the early 1960s, research on the first years of life has shown that early experiences have a great impact on all aspects of a child's development. This suggests that first teachers are extremely important people in children's lives. Yet, there is a gap between research and practice. In the United States today, programs for children under five are still inadequately funded. Most are privately supported, in contrast to fully state-supported programs for children aged five years and older, although there has been an increase in the number of state-sponsored preschool programs. Federal support for early childhood education is largely limited to programs for low-income families, which serve less than a quarter of all eligible families. At the present time, however, there is a growing awareness of the critical need for new policies and programs to support American families. Quality education and care for young children are among the most important items on this agenda.

PROGRAMS FOR YOUNG CHILDREN TODAY

A number of different kinds of programs for young children are available today. These may be classified according to their purposes, which may be to enhance the development of young children by providing educational experiences, to provide child care for employed parents, or to provide education for parents. Many programs combine two or even all three of these functions. Programs may also be classified according to sponsorship and funding source, which may be public (federal, state, or local) or private. Private programs may be nonprofit, basically intended to provide a service to children and their families, or for profit, designed as a service-oriented business.

There are two basic arenas in which early childhood education occurs. The first is in settings that are designed to provide care for groups of young children, that is, center-based programs. These include preschools, child care centers, and public schools. The second major arena for child care is the home—the child's own or a caregiver's.

Center-based Programs

Preschools

Preschools are an outgrowth of the traditional nursery school, which focused on social-emotional development and provided learning through play for children three through five years of age. Beginning in the late 1960s, nursery schools began to be called preschools as their programs were modified to recognize that important cognitive development occurs in the early years. Preschool programs were structured in different ways. Some promoted play in a planned environment with learning through direct experiences. Others emphasized academic preparation for later schooling. Even though some programs concentrated on intellectual development, those in the mainstream stressed all aspects of child development—social, emotional, physical, creative, and intellectual.

Sponsorship of preschools can be public or private. Public sponsors include education and child development departments in college settings and some high school home economics departments. Their preschools are laboratory settings for training students in education and child development, while simultaneously providing a service to the school and community. Among privately sponsored programs are parent cooperatives (called co-ops). In these programs, parents hire an early childhood educator to

serve as teacher, director, and educational leader, and they commit themselves to regular, active participation in teaching and administering the school.

Traditionally, nursery schools were half-day programs that followed a public school calendar. They were common when most families did not need full-day care and mothers were available to pick up their children at midday. Many private preschools today meet the needs of employed parents by offering child care in combination with an education program. Part-day programs are still common in public schools, lab schools, and parent cooperatives. At present, there is increasing pressure to lengthen these services to eliminate the patchwork of child care arrangements needed to meet the needs of employed parents.

In most states, a growing minority of four-year-old children are in preschool programs based in the public schools. Among these are early intervention programs for children considered "at risk" for school failure, federally funded prekindergarten programs for economically disadvantaged children, special education classes for four-year-olds, some Head Start classes, and some locally funded programs for prekindergarten children and children of teen parents. As more four-year-olds enter public school programs, there is concern that these programs not become downward extensions of the elementary school. Many educators see public school programs for four-year-olds as an innovation that could bring significant social, academic, and economic benefits. Others are more cautious, worried that it will be difficult to give precedence to what is best for young children within the traditional public school structure.

Head Start is a federally funded, comprehensive preschool program. It offers low-income children developmentally appropriate educational experiences, as well as health screening and treatment, access to social services, and good nutrition. An important component of the program is parent education and involvement of parents in policy decisions. Before Head Start began in 1964, federal support for children's programs had occurred only in times of national emergency such as depression or war.

The Head Start Program has been popular with the families it serves. It has also been regarded positively by educators, policy makers, and the public. Whenever the program has been threatened by cuts in the federal budget, a groundswell of support has enabled it to survive. Moreover, the comprehensive design of the Head Start Program has had an important influence on subsequent child care policy and legislative proposals.

A recent summary of longitudinal studies of low-income children who participated in Head Start and other preschool intervention programs has shown that these programs have had a significant and lasting impact (Lazar and Darlington 1983). Studies of program participants in late adolescence and early adulthood have shown that in comparison to their peers who did not attend a quality preschool program, they are more likely to meet school standards, are less likely to be classified as underachievers, score higher on academic measures, are less likely to be placed in special education classes, engage in less delinquent behavior, and are more likely to hold jobs. The early school experiences also had a positive effect on the health and social behavior of participants and benefited their families. The vision of changing children's achievement and attitudes has been realized for those who have been able to attend, but the greater goal of ameliorating the effects of poverty has yet to be achieved. In spite of its successes, the impact of Head Start has been limited. It has, over the years, remained a demonstration program serving only a small percentage of those eligible. At last in 1990, after a decade of no real growth in federal Head Start appropriations, national support was expressed for expansion of the program.

In 1988 new bills were passed authorizing additional federal funding for programs for low-income children. Even Start, a new joint parent-child education program aimed at improving adult literacy while offering early childhood education to children between one and seven, was initiated as part of Chapter 1 legislation. This legislation also included the migrant education program for preschool children. Another bill passed was the 1988 welfare reform act that provided funding for child care services needed by welfare recipients now required to work or participate in a job training program.

Child Care Centers

Child care centers provide group care for the children of working parents and are usually open from early morning until early evening. Some centers are open later hours or provide drop-in care according to parental needs. Most centers serve children aged two through five. Some offer after-school care for school-aged children as well. Changes in state licensing regulations have enabled an increasing number of centers to add infant and toddler care services, although many early childhood educators question the wisdom of all-day center care for children under age two. The demand for these programs far exceeds the supply. Programs for infants require many adult caregivers in order to meet their basic care needs. A ratio of one caregiver to every three infants is essential to provide adequate attention to the routines of sleep, feeding, and diapering, to maintain a safe play environment, and to promote frequent, responsive adult-infant interaction.

Most centers in the United States today are privately sponsored. Some programs receive federal support through Social Services Block Grant Child Care, administered through the states. These programs provide care for children who have substantial developmental delays, children who are abused or neglected or at risk for abuse and neglect, and children whose parents are enrolled in job-training programs or whose salaries are below current poverty guidelines.

Over the past decade, the number of child care centers has grown considerably. Some relatively recent trends in child care are a movement toward more employer involvement in care arrangements for employees' children and the proliferation of franchised centers that are operated as large-scale businesses. Many new centers belong to major nationwide franchise chains. They make affordable child care available by using standardized building plans, buying equipment and supplies in large quantities, and, in some cases, by relying on a uniform curriculum and staff training materials. Many of these centers remain profitable by offering relatively low staff salaries and benefits.

Employer-sponsored Child Care Centers

Employer-sponsored child care is not a new phenomenon. It is common in Europe and has existed in the United States since the Civil War. Wartime demand for women as workers served as a stimulus for the creation of child care centers by industries. A prominent example of high-quality employer-sponsored child care with comprehensive family services is found in the Kaiser shipyard centers of World War II.

The operation of on-site or near-site employer-sponsored child care centers is one approach to enhancing employee recruitment, retention, morale, and productivity. It has been favored primarily by the military, hospitals, government agencies, and large corporations. But changing demographics of the work force, the high costs of building and operating a center, and the lack of a safe work-site location have caused employers to consider a variety of other solutions. Flextime, giving employees flexibility in arranging their work hours, may enable parents of young children to coordinate their schedules in such a way that they are less dependent on outside child care. Similarly, modern technological advances like personal computers and fax machines may permit some employees to accomplish their work in a home

Licensing and Quality Standards

Most child care programs today combine aspects of the social-welfare-oriented day nursery program and the child-development-oriented nursery school. In an era when well over half of all women with children under five are in the work force, care and education are beginning to be seen as inseparable—the child care center has become the primary delivery system for early childhood education. The age span of the children in programs now ranges from birth through elementary school age, as services are extended to include infant and toddler care and before and after school care. Unfortunately, there is still a wide range in quality—from those programs that offer excellent care and education to those that offer unsafe and inappropriate care. In 1990 there were still no federal child care standards, even for federally funded child care programs. State standards for licensing centers and for enforcing these standards vary so greatly that licensure in itself is no real guarantee of quality.

In 1984 the National Association for the Education of Young Children issued a position statement on child care licensing, urging that licensing standards adopted by states cover all forms of supplementary care for children from birth through school age, with no exemptions for any program because of its sponsorship or funding. It called for vigorous enforcement of standards that are clear, well-publicized, and congruent with current knowledge about quality care. The NAEYC has also implemented an accreditation program which identifies quality centers that surpass the minimum standards required by licensing regulations. In addition, it has issued a position statement, Developmentally Appropriate Practice in Early Childhood Programs Serving Children from Birth through Age 8, that defines appropriate practice for each age group and gives clear examples of what practices are appropriate and what ones are inappropriate.

office where they are more available to their young children. For employees whose work is tied to the workplace, family assistance options such as child care resource and referral services and partial subsidies of child care at existing child care facilities are increasingly popular. Still, perhaps only 10 percent of the larger companies have made these options available to employees. Today, with the prospect of a dwindling work force for some years to come, even small and medium-sized businesses are considering the implementation of work-family policies in their effort to recruit and retain skilled workers. Another approach is for several smaller businesses to form a consortium and jointly sponsor a child care program. As many parents seem to prefer flexibility and choice in child care arrangements, the likelihood is that most employers will subsidize diversity rather than build costly child care centers.

In the 1980s the demand for center-based child care increased more than the demand for other forms of care. Many early childhood professionals believe that there is a need for uniform national licensing standards. As child care comes to be seen as a necessary service for the majority of young families, there are many quality-related problems to be resolved: the gap between the supply and demand for child care; the shortage of child care workers; high staff turnover because of the low salaries and poor benefits; and the need for adequate funding for facilities, equipment, and educational materials.

Kindergarten

The most widely available group program for young children in our society is kindergarten. Traditionally, kindergarten attendance has been optional for five-year-olds, but recently it has become mandatory in a growing number of states. Kindergartens range from informal programs stressing socialization and the foundations for later school learning to highly structured programs that emphasize reading and utilize direct, large-group instruction to the extent of being almost indistinguishable from first- or second-grade classrooms. For many years, nearly all kindergarten programs were half-day, but the percentage of full school-day kindergartens is growing.

Kindergarten used to be viewed as the year in which young children became ready for the more formal schooling experiences of the primary years. Now five-year-olds are frequently expected to enter kindergarten ready for school. The trend to earlier academics has led school districts to adopt some or all of the following policies as a reaction to the "lack of fit" between children and the curriculum: requiring children to be older upon entry to kindergarten, mandating screening and readiness testing of children prior to entry, and creating special transitional classes for children who are not ready to meet academic expectations.

Of particular concern to early childhood educators is the growing abuse and misuse of tests given to kindergarteners. About half of the states now mandate use of developmental screening tests for three- to six-year-olds. Such tests are admirable when they are used to pinpoint those children in need of special education, health, or social services and thereby facilitate early intervention efforts. Unfortunately, test results are often used for other purposes including postponing entry into public school or assigning an extra year of kindergarten or first grade to children who do poorly on the tests. (See Chapter 6, Observation and Evaluation, for more about testing.)

Home Care

Family Day Care Homes

Child care in private homes, family day care, provides an alternative to center-based care. It is the least visible, yet most prevalent, form of privately sponsored child care in the United States today. Family day care providers care for

small numbers of children, most often infants and toddlers, in their homes. Parents choose family day care for many reasons: convenience of location, reasonable cost, flexible hours, a home atmosphere, a smaller group of children, and personalized care by a single individual, which may be better for infants and toddlers.

The care provided in these homes, like care in centers, can vary greatly. Nearly all states have some form of a regulatory system that requires registration or licensing of day care homes. There are significant state-to-state variations in setting, monitoring, and enforcing the regulations for protecting children, programming, caregiver qualifications, and the physical environment. It is estimated that fewer than 10 percent nationally of operating homes are regulated. The 1984 NAEYC Position Statement on Family Day Care Regulation called on the public to accept the responsibility for ensuring the protection and welfare of young children by acting to promote regulation of all day care homes.

Why are so few day care homes regulated? It may be that the caregiver sees this as a temporary occupation. Or it may be that the low pay and lack of status or recognition for caregivers discourage them from making a public commitment to operate a day care home. Not only does a public commitment involve abiding by regulations, it also means incurring the additional expenses of taxes, licensing fees, and insurance. A growing number of organizations provide training and support services that encourage providers to become licensed or registered to improve the quality of services. And as parents become more informed consumers of child care services, they will demand proof of licensing and adherence to standards before entrusting their children to someone else's care. But first, there needs to be a greater supply of available, quality, and affordable child care.

An important trend in family day care is the growth of resource and referral services. These services function as brokers by listing licensed homes in an area. Another trend is the formation of provider networks and professional organizations that offer education and training and sponsor lobbying efforts. Recognizing the valuable service family day care providers offer to families, people in the early childhood and human resource fields have been advocating for upgrading the quality of family day care. Ways to accomplish this include increasing standards and qualifications, providing training and supervision, subsidizing parents using this form of child care, and subsidizing insurance for licensed homes.

Nannies: In-Home Professional Child Care

The emerging nanny movement in the United States today is a response to the desire of many two-career families to have a well-trained child-care professional provide care for their children in their own home. To meet this need, a few colleges and many private agencies have opened nanny training programs. The British Nursery Nurse training program is the model on which many American programs are based. The British program is much more rigorous than most of the American programs: it involves two years of coursework and practicum followed by a national examination for certification. American programs, like their British counterparts, teach their students child development, health and nutrition, and basic principles of early childhood education. Some certificate programs are as short as six weeks, whereas others are one year in length. Colleges are beginning to offer two or four-year nanny training programs. The International Nanny Association is developing training standards for schools, standards for the increasing number of nanny placement agencies that recruit and help match employers with a nanny, and standards for the nannies themselves. Well-trained and experienced nannies can command good salaries in addition to room and board, health care benefits, sick leave, transportation, and a paid vacation.

Other Programs

Parent Education

Many kinds of programs are available for parents of young children. Such programs can take the form of parent classes and meetings dealing with topics such as child development, educational techniques, and child management; they can involve parents in working with children in early childhood classrooms; or they can provide trained visitors to work with parents and children in their homes. Programs for infants and toddlers which combine parent education with activities for children are becoming increasingly popular. Parent education, especially in combination with a good program for children, has proved to be very successful in producing positive developmental gains for young children. Parent education acknowledges that parents are their children's primary educators in the early years and that parents need to be learners as well.

Parenting education programs for adolescents are being advocated as a necessary addition to the curriculum of intermediate and high schools. The dramatic increase in births to teenage parents has major social and economic consequences for the teenagers themselves and for their children. Concern over this trend has led to the creation of new programs in schools and private social service agencies. Some programs provide services for teen parents and their babies; others focus on just the parent or the child. Head Start is among the programs responding with new approaches to young parents and children.

Sick-Child Care

An expanding service related to the growth of dual-earner families and single-parent families is sick-child care. Again, this is not a new idea: the trendsetting Kaiser shipyard centers offered this service in World War II, when it was vital that employees concentrate on the war effort. Today, programs for sick children are seen as one solution to the higher rates of absenteeism among employees with young children. In some instances, sick bays are attached to child care centers. In others, a sick child care ward in a hospital is created for the use of employees and the community. These programs usually offer care for children with mild, noncontagious illnesses. Another approach is in-home sick-child care services. Besides, or in addition to, these alternatives, many employers today are modifying their personnel policies. Some now allow parents to use their own sick leave to stay home and care for a sick child. Others are instituting family leave policies, enabling employees to take unpaid leave for such purposes as staying home with a newborn or caring for a terminally ill family member.

TRAINING AND CERTIFICATION

A number of routes can be taken to enter the field of early childhood education, and a variety of opportunities exist for training and professional development. Some people who wish to work with young children get their initial experience through volunteering or working as a substitute teacher or classroom aide. Others try out the field by enrolling in a high school or college course in child development or early childhood education. Still others go directly into a teacher education program in a two- or four-year college. Many early childhood educators were introduced to the field by directly experiencing the benefits of a good preschool for their child and family.

Professional qualifications for work in early childhood programs vary from state to state. They are based on the provisions of center licensing requirements (usually administered by social service departments), or certification for teachers (most often handled by state departments of education), or both. The minimum requirements to work with young children are good health and a high school diploma. Most states require that early childhood teachers be qualified for their jobs either by having a college degree (in some places it must be in education, early childhood education, or child development) or a CDA credential. The nationally awarded Child Development Associate (CDA) credential is based on demonstrated competency in working with young children. To teach kindergarten children, four-year-olds, or handicapped children in the public schools, a bachelor's degree is required. Child care centers generally hire teachers with an associate of arts (A.A.) or CDA. Although it is preferable for home day care providers to have an A.A. or a CDA, this is not a requirement. Persons interested in becoming a nanny should take a course offering special training. A bachelor's or master's degree in early childhood education or child development may be required for some positions involving supervision of staff or curriculum development.

States also differ in the ways in which they certify teachers; college programs are often designed to meet certification requirements. Some states give a preschool–primary teaching credential, which covers preschool through the third grade; some give a kindergarten–sixth grade certificate, with no provision for preschool teaching; and still others offer an early childhood or kindergarten endorsement in addition to standard elementary certification.

Early childhood teacher education programs can be found in many two- and four-year colleges and universities. These programs award

associate of arts or science, bachelor's, master's, and doctoral degrees in early childhood education, elementary education, or child development. The NAEYC has developed guidelines for two- and four-year college programs in early childhood education.

When early childhood programs were first introduced in colleges, they tended to be housed in home economics departments, as part of the services to farm families offered through agricultural extension service. Today, they are found in home economics departments as well as in human development departments and schools of education. In some institutions, the home economics department sponsors programs for preparation of preschool teachers; the training of kindergarten through twelfth-grade teachers is the province of the school of education.

Specialized professional training in early childhood education is essential for you to become a competent teacher who can provide positive growth experiences for young children. Research has shown that specialized teacher training in early childhood education is one of the elements critical to program quality. Teaching experience alone or a degree in another field (even elementary education) cannot provide you with the necessary knowledge of young children and early childhood program practices. There are many kinds of courses and training programs available that provide valuable information and experience for people who want to work with young children. You will need to decide which would be the most appropriate match for your interests, abilities, and professional aspirations.

CURRENT ISSUES AND PROSPECTS

Most people who work in early childhood education feel strongly that the work they do is valuable, even essential, to the well-being of children and society. Yet it is difficult for dedicated professionals to hold on to this belief, when it is reflected neither in salaries nor in relative respect and prestige.

The primary issues in early childhood education today are summed up by what is referred to as the "trilemma" of child care: the interrelationship of the need for quality programs for children, affordable child care services for parents, and adequate compensation for teachers and caregivers. The issue is also referred to as Q-C-A—quality, compensation, and affordability. The findings of National Child Care Staffing Study indicate that program quality is affected by the education of teaching staff and the adequacy of their wages. It also found that funding for child care has decreased in the past decade and that during the same period staff turnover has nearly tripled (Whitebook, Howes, and Phillips 1989, p. 4).

Most programs for young children are paid for directly by parents, not subsidized by public funds. Consequently, teacher salaries in privately supported programs for young children are much lower than salaries received by public school teachers with comparable educations and job descriptions. Without public understanding and acceptance of the importance of having well-trained, competent people working with young children, there will be no remedy to the current condition of low salaries and inadequate benefits. This makes it difficult to recruit and retain good early childhood teachers and caregivers. Few men choose to enter the field, even though many would find it rewarding. They are discouraged by the low pay and by the common stereotype that caring for young children is women's work. Other consequences of inadequate compensation are lower program quality and high staff turnover. High staff turnover is especially unfortunate, because it undermines the stability of adult-child relationships and thus affects children's ability to benefit from school experiences. Unionization is viewed by some as a possible answer to the problem of low salary and lack of benefits; others advocate political action aimed at securing more state and federal support for early childhood programs.

Early childhood services have an impact on an extremely large group of children, parents, and educators. The percentage of employed mothers of children under six is growing faster than that of any other group of mothers in the work force. Expenses for child care and education are now the average family's fourth largest expenditure. Without some public subsidy of private early childhood programs, the demand for improved wages will fall on these already financially overburdened parents.

Nearly all children from more affluent families attend some type of private preschool or child care program, but, as more and more families fall beneath the poverty line, there is a growing shortage of care for children of low-income families. For poor children, income eligibility means nothing if there are no openings in subsidized programs. The alternatives are either no service or the least expensive, unlicensed, unmonitored care. Unfortunately, when child care and education costs become prohibitively high, even middle-income parents turn to nonregulated sources of child care which offer less assurance of quality. Educators are concerned about the social stratification of young children resulting from the lack of a comprehensive early childhood policy that provides care for children from all economic groups and that takes into account the best interests of children and families.

Despite these problems, there are some bright spots. One of these is the movement toward greater professionalism and recognition

of those who work with young children. There is currently a growing sense of conviction about the uniqueness and importance of our field, along with a broadening base of support. Many organizations have issued position statements supporting the need for quality early childhood programs. Among these organizations are the National Association of Elementary School Principals, the National Association of State Boards of Education, the Council of Chief State School Officers of the National School Board Association, the Association for Supervision and Curriculum Development, and the Committee for Economic Development. Membership in the NAEYC, the largest organization of early childhood educators, has grown dramatically. The NAEYC has become increasingly involved, over the last few years, in providing standards for the field: a model of professional development for teachers, caregivers, and administrators; guidelines for two-year and four-year teacher education programs, for in-service training, and for national accreditation of quality child care programs; and a Code of Ethical Conduct. These standards contribute to growing recognition of the field as a profession.

Another positive trend was the extensive media and legislative attention that early childhood education received during the last half of the 1980s. Among the demographic trends that led to this focus of attention on the needs of young children and their families are the increasing numbers of women and children living in poverty, the rising percentage in the work force of mothers of young children, the increase in single-parent households, the rising rates of teen pregnancy, the large increase in preschool children, and the decrease in young adults entering the labor force. In recent years, more children- and family-related legislation has been introduced into Congress than ever before. There appears to be a momentum building at the federal and state levels toward action on child care, which is now being defined as a family and employment issue.

The steady growth of publicly supported kindergartens and new state-developed programs for four-year-olds is another sign of increased recognition of the value of early childhood education. As more women enter the labor force, there will be even more demand for expanded and improved child care services, as well as for new services such as infant care and child care information and referral. Child advocacy, parent education, and child care information and referral are all developing fields with new employment opportunities. Many early childhood educators are committed to child advocacy. We are becoming more sophisticated about the political process and are forming alliances with others who have similar concerns in order to heighten community awareness and influence public attitudes and legislation on behalf of young children. Certainly, there is cause for hope that the needs of young children and of those who work with them will some day receive the attention they deserve.

DISCUSSION QUESTIONS

1. Compare the purpose and sponsorship of different programs for young children that you have observed or worked in. Discuss how the teachers, parents, and children might be affected by each kind of program.
2. What programs and services are provided for young children in your community? Based on your own experience and that of other people you know, what changes need to be made and what new programs need to be initiated in order

to provide a comprehensive support system for families with children from birth through eight years of age?

3. What child care issues (for example, program quality, salaries, teacher qualifications and certification, program availability) are being discussed in your community at present? What recommendations being made and what actions (if any) are being taken?

PROJECTS

1. Survey your community and report on the kinds of programs that are available for children from birth to eight years of age (preschools, child care, programs for low-income children, public school programs). Who is responsible for licensing each kind of program? How do licensing requirements differ?
2. Research and report on training programs available for teachers of young children in your community, on how teachers are certified, and on typical salaries for teachers in different kinds of programs. What thoughts and issues are raised by your findings?
3. Observe and write a description of a program for young children in your community. Find out about its history, philosophy, sponsorship, tuition, teacher-child ratios, provisions for parent involvement, teacher qualifications, salaries, and current concerns.

BIBLIOGRAPHY

Association for Supervision and Curriculum Development. 1988. *A Resource Guide to Public School Early Childhood Programs.* Alexandria, Va.: ASCD.

Bredekamp, S. 1987. *Developmentally Appropriate Practice in Early Childhood Programs Serving Children from Birth through Age 8.* Washington, D.C.: National Association for the Education of Young Children.

Caldwell, B. M. 1989. A Comprehensive Model for Integrating Child Care and Early Childhood Education. *Teachers College Record* 90(3):404–414.

Cartwright, G. P., C. A. Cartwright, and M. E. Ward. 1981. *Educating Special Learners.* Belmont, Calif.: Wadsworth.

Clarke-Stewart, A. 1977. *Childcare in the Family: A Review of Research and Some Propositions for Policy.* New York: Academic Press.

Committee for Economic Development. 1985. *Investing in Our Children.* New York: Committee for Economic Development.

——————. 1987. *Children in Need.* New York: Committee for Economic Development.

Fromberg, D. P. 1989. Kindergarten: Current Circumstances Affecting Curriculum. *Teachers College Record* 90(3):392–403.

Frost, J. L., and J. B. Kissinger. 1976. *The Young Child and the Educative Process.* New York: Holt, Rinehart & Winston.

Galinsky, E. 1989. The Staffing Crisis. *Young Children* 44(1):2–4.

Gearheart, B. R., and M. W. Weishahn. 1976. *The Handicapped Child in the Regular Classroom.* St. Louis: C. V. Mosby.

Hymes, J. L., Jr. 1977. *Early Childhood Education: An Introduction to the Profession.* Washington, D.C.: National Association for the Education of Young Children.

――――――. 1981. *Teaching the Child Under Six.* 3d ed. Columbus, Ohio: Merrill.

――――――. n.d. *Early Childhood Education: The Year in Review.* Washington, D.C.: National Association for the Education of Young Children. Published yearly.

Jorde-Bloom, P. 1988. *A Great Place to Work: Improving Conditions for Staff in Young Children's Programs.* Washington, D.C.: National Association for the Education of Young Children.

Kagan, S. L. 1988. Current Reforms in Early Childhood Education: Are We Addressing the Issues? *Young Children* 43(2):27–32.

――――――. 1989. Early Care and Education: Tackling the Tough Issues. *Phi Delta Kappan* 7(6):433–439.

Kagan, S. L., and J. W. Newton. 1989. For Profit and Nonprofit Child Care: Similarites and Differences. *Young Children* 45(1):4–10.

Karweit, N. 1988. Quality and Quantity of Learning Time in Preprimary Programs. *The Elementary School Journal* 89(2):119–133.

Kelly, J. A. 1985. Child Care and the Role of the Public Schools. *Footnotes* 23.

Lazar, I., and R. Darlington. 1983. *As the Twig is Bent: Lasting Effects of Preschool Programs.* Hillsdale, N. J.: Lawrence Erlbaum.

Meisels, S. J. 1989. High-Stakes Testing. *Educational Leadership* 46(7):16–22.

――――――. 1987. Uses and Abuses of Developmental Screening and School Readiness Testing. *Young Children* 42(2):4–6, 68–73.

Meisels, S. J., and L. S. Sternberg. 1989. Quality Sacrificed in Proprietary Child Care. *Education Week* (June 7).

Mitchell, A. 1989. Old Baggage, New Visions: Shaping Policy for Early Childhood Programs. *Phi Delta Kappan* 70(9):664–672.

Mitchell, A., M. Seligson, and F. Marx. 1989. *Early Childhood Programs and the Public Schools: Between Promise and Practice.* Dover, Mass.: Auburn House.

National Association for the Education of Young Children. 1984. *Accreditation Criteria and Procedures of the National Academy of Early Childhood Programs.* Washington, D.C.: NAEYC.

――――――. 1988. Position Statement on Licensing and Other Forms of Regulation of Early Childhood Programs in Centers and Family Day Care Homes. *Young Children* 42(5):64–68.

Pittman, R. 1988. *Nannies.* Moravia, N.Y.: Chronicle Guidance, brief 582 (January).

Read, K. 1976. *The Nursery School: A Human Relations Laboratory.* 6th ed. Philadelphia: Saunders.

Reynolds, M. C., and J. W. Birch. 1977. *Teaching Exceptional Children in All America's Schools.* Reston, Va.: Council for Exceptional Children.

Robinson, S. L. 1987a. Kindergarten in America: 5 Major Trends. *Phi Delta Kappan* 68(7):529–530.

_____ . 1987b. Are Public Schools Ready for Four-Year-Olds?" *Principal* 66(5):26–28.

Schultz, T., and J. Lombardi. 1989. Right From the Start: A Report on the NASBE Task Force on Early Childhood Education. *Young Children* 44(2):6–10.

Seaver, J. W., C. A. Cartwright, C. B. Ward, and C. A. Heasley. 1979. *Careers with Young Children: Making Your Decision.* Washington, D.C.: National Association for the Education of Young Children.

Seefeldt, C. 1990. *Continuing Issues in Early Childhood Education.* Columbus, Ohio: Merrill.

Smith, M. M. 1989. NAEYC: Confronting Tough Issues. *Young Children* 45(1):32–37.

Spodek, B. 1973. *Early Childhood Education.* Englewood Cliffs, N.J.: Prentice-Hall.

Steinfels, M. O. 1973. *Who's Minding the Children?* New York: Simon & Schuster.

Whitebook, M., C. Howes, and D. Phillips. 1989. *Who Cares? Child Care Teachers and the Quality of Care in America: Executive Summary.* Oakland, Calif.: Child Care Employee Project.

Willer, B. A., and L. D. Johnson. 1989. *The Crisis is Real: Demographics on the Problems of Recruiting and Retaining Early Childhood Staff.* Washington, D.C.: National Association for the Education of Young Children.

Zigler, E., and S. Hunsinger. 1977. Bringing Up Daycare. *American Psychological Monitor* 7 (March).

PART II

UNDERSTANDING CHILDREN

This section includes chapters designed to help teachers understand children's development and the significance of their play. Because understanding children is of central importance in early childhood education, these chapters form an essential foundation for practice. Chapter 4, Child Development, provides a basis for understanding young children. Chapter 5, Play, introduces a critical medium for children's development and discusses how teachers can support productive play. Chapter 6, Observation and Evaluation, acquaints you with basic skills that teachers use to appraise individuals and groups of children and to evaluate how to support their growth and development.

CHAPTER FOUR

Child Development

In all the world there is no other child exactly like you. In the
millions of years that have passed, there has never been a child like
you.

—Pablo Casals

In this chapter we focus on how knowledge of child development can contribute to your understanding of children and your ability to support their growth and learning. We present some basic principles of development and explore the role and the interrelationship of biology and environment in development. We also describe physical, social-emotional, and cognitive characteristics of children from birth through the primary-grade years, discuss some major theorists who have contributed to our understanding of these, and review the implications of their theories for work with children.

The study of child development is the cornerstone of early childhood education, because an understanding of how children grow, learn, and interact is essential to nearly all the decisions we make as teachers. In early childhood education we often refer to the development of the whole child. By this we mean that children develop in the following ways: (1) they use their *physical* bodies to move competently and to explore with their senses; (2) they establish and maintain a relatively stable, positive *emotional* state and relate to others in appropriate, responsible ways in the *social* environments of home, school, and community; and (3) they have full access to *cognitive* powers to understand and find meaning in relationship to people, objects, and ideas. Early childhood educators see the importance and interconnectedness of these aspects of development and realize that each must be of equal concern to those who wish to nurture young children. Of course, not all the children you work with will be balanced, integrated, and on schedule in all areas of development, so we study child development to gain the knowledge necessary to assess the developmental status of individual children and groups of children and to plan strategies to support development.

Much of what we currently know about how children grow and develop has been learned from the researchers in developmental psychology, learning theory, and child study. In most colleges the information gathered by these researchers is brought together and taught in departments of human development, child study, or education. As you train to become a teacher of young children, you will probably be expected to take courses in child development. We have found that students are not always sure about how this coursework relates to work with young children. In this chapter we review some basic information, concepts, and theories that we find most useful to teachers and point to the implications of these ideas for their work in the classroom. As you progress through this book, you will find many references back to the ideas presented in this chapter. For example, you will see that the areas of child development study—physical, social-emotional, and cognitive—parallel the curriculum area covered in Part IV—Chapter 11: Sensing, Moving, and Growing; Chapter 12: Creating and Appreciating; Chapter 13: Communicating, and Chapter 14: Discovering and Thinking. Similarly, when we write about how to adapt teaching practices and curriculum to different age groups such as infants or school-age children we are making use of child development information that is available to us because of the careful studies of the stage-related characteristics of children that have been conducted during the past fifty years. Knowledge of development in combination with direct experience in early childhood programs will give you a basis for understanding children and making informed choices in your teaching.

PRINCIPLES OF DEVELOPMENT

Development results from changes in the child that are based on the interplay of growth, maturation, and experience. *Growth* is primarily an increase in size. *Maturation* is an increase in the complexity of organization, both physically and psychologically. *Experience* is all of a person's interactions with the environment. During the preschool years, the body of a child grows; that is, it greatly increases in size and mass. At the same time, maturation occurs; the child gradually develops control of the muscle system. Although it is not clear whether or not the maturation rate can be increased through special training, it can be retarded by environmental factors such as poor nutrition, serious illness, and the lack of experience in activities that make use of the sensing and moving capabilities of the child's body.

The same processes occur in psychological development. For example, infants lack the concept of object permanence: the awareness that even when an object is not in sight it still exists. As the child matures, the concept develops, but no amount of training seems to be able to significantly accelerate its acquisition. A lack of experience with objects that can be seen, handled, and then removed may, however, result in the concept failing to develop.

There are two basic characteristics common to all human development. First, it proceeds in a direction toward greater size and more complex organization. Second, it proceeds in an orderly and predictable manner. Physical development proceeds from the top downward (the *cephalocaudal principle*), seen most clearly in the development of the fetus. In the early stages of development, the head is half the length of the body, whereas at birth the head is one quarter the body length. This same top-down pattern is seen in motor development. The infant develops head control and reaching and grasping skills before sitting and walking. Growth and maturation also proceed from near to far (the *proximodistal law*). The large muscles closest to the center of the body grow and develop coordinated functions before the small muscles of the hands and fingers.

Since prior levels of size and complexity must precede later ones, development is sequential and cumulative. For example, before children can learn to write, they must have mastered the small-muscle coordination required to grasp objects; have learned to use implements like brushes, pencils, and scissors; have had experiences forming shapes and letters; and have seen and used written language.

The knowledge that development is a process that follows a definite sequential order, combined with information about the characteristics of each stage, lets teachers know what can generally be expected of children. Teachers can plan developmentally appropriate experiences for children based on this knowledge. Awareness of the cumulative nature of development helps teachers recognize that children cannot be expected to have understanding or skill for which their level of development has not prepared them.

New experiences that do not build from previous experiences can be meaningless or overwhelming to a child, and experiences that are not challenging or interesting may provoke boredom and restlessness. J. McVicker Hunt (1961) describes the concept of an *optimal match* between children's present level of understanding or skill and the acquisition of a new knowledge or skill. New experience needs to provide just the right amount of novelty or challenge to interest the child in engaging with something unfamiliar. Teachers can stimulate children's development by planning experiences that provide challenge and by avoiding experiences that children find frustrating (because they are too difficult) or boring (because they are too easy).

The child's actual age in years, chronological age, and stage of development are only approximately related. The direction and sequence of development are similar for every child, but each individual moves through stages at his or her own rate. Each infant enters the world with a unique biological endowment, and because the interplay of physical and environmental forces are different for every person, no two children (even from the same family) are exactly alike.

ROLE OF BIOLOGY AND ENVIRONMENT IN DEVELOPMENT

The history of thought about human development has been characterized by shifts in our beliefs about the relative impact of biological versus environmental forces on personality and behavior. Biological forces on development (sometimes referred to as *nature*) are genetic

IN THE CLASSROOM: BASIC PRINCIPLES OF DEVELOPMENT

Implications for Teachers

Principle: Growth, maturation, and experience are interrelated.

Implication: Knowledge of normal growth and understanding of the process of maturation will help you make decisions about the kinds of experiences you can provide to support each child's development.

Principle: Physical development proceeds from the top down and from near to far.

Implication: As children grow and mature, they become more capable of coordinating their movements. It is important to be aware of each child's physical capabilities so that you provide experiences that support the development of emerging abilities.

Principle: Development follows a definite sequential order and is cumulative in nature.

Implication: What a child can do and understand today is the basis of future development. If you are knowledgeable about the physical, social, emotional, and cognitive milestones each child must master before progressing to the next, you will be better able to plan a program that takes into account the wide variety of abilities you are likely to encounter, even with children who are very close in age.

Principle: The rate of development is different for each child and is only partly related to age.

Implication: In order to have developmentally appropriate expectations for children, it is essential that you observe and become acquainted with the competencies of each individual in your group.

traits or inherited capacities and are expressed in the process of growth and maturation. Environmental forces (referred to as *nurture*) have to do with the kinds of interactions and experiences that enhance or restrict the development of biological potential. In the past, there was a heated debate (sometimes called the *nature-nurture controversy*) between people who felt that either the biological endowment or the environment was the primary force in shaping human nature. Views on the subject shifted from the belief that all development was biologically

determined to the opposite view that children were infinitely malleable and that environment was all-important in shaping later behavior and achievement.

Those who believe that inheritance is of great significance in human development have focused on establishing the degree to which developmental mechanisms and individual traits are linked to biological influences. People have explored and argued for a predominantly biological basis for such things as adult-child attachment, temperamental characteristics (including sociability, and dominance-submission behavior), and general intelligence. The maturational theory of Arnold Gesell, discussed more fully later, is based on the belief that changes in children's physical and psychological development are a result of their genetic endowment.

Behaviorist theory presents the extreme opposite view that the environment is the primary determinant of how people learn, grow, and behave. John B. Watson, an American psychologist, founded the behaviorist movement. For behaviorists, the primary focus is on learning that involves change in behavior that can be observed and measured. The work of B. F. Skinner advanced behaviorism into a major theory. Skinner believed that all behavior is controlled by the environment and that all behavior can be modified by the application of scientific principles of operant conditioning.

Theorists today still debate the relative importance of biological and environmental influences on development, but there is general agreement that heredity and environment interact in complex ways and that each plays an important role in development.

Biological Factors

Today most child development specialists regard biological development as being much more important than they believed in the past two decades when the emphasis was on the powerful impact of the child-rearing environment. In fact, no one questions the hereditary basis of physical characteristics such as eye, hair, and skin color. Some other characteristics — height, weight, intelligence, predisposition to some diseases, and temperament — are significantly determined by biological inheritance, but they also can be influenced by environmental factors such as diet, exercise, nutrition, health, and living conditions.

Research on inherited temperamental characteristics conducted by physicians Alexander Thomas and Stella Chess (1977), and discussed in Chapter 2 with regard to teachers' characteristics, has influenced current views of the impor-

tance of biological inheritance. They have shown that newborns are not all alike at birth (something that parents have always known) and that there are distinct and observable differences in temperament among them that are fairly persistent over time. The work of Thomas and Chess has given us valuable insight into the importance of what the child brings into the world at birth and how it interacts with the child's experiences.

According to Chess and Thomas, babies in their first days and weeks of life can be seen to differ in nine personality characteristics:

1. *Activity level:* the proportion of inactive periods to active ones.
2. *Rhythmicity:* the regularity of cycles of hunger, excretion, sleep, and wakefulness.
3. *Distractibility:* the degree to which extraneous stimuli alter behavior.
4. *Approach-withdrawal:* the response to a new object or person.
5. *Adaptability:* the ease with which a child adapts to the environment.
6. *Attention span and persistence:* the amount of time devoted to an activity and the effect of distraction.
7. *Intensity of reaction:* the energy of response regardless of its quality or direction.
8. *Threshold of responsiveness:* the intensity of stimulation required to evoke a response.
9. *Quality of mood:* the amount of friendly, pleasant, joyful behavior as contrasted with unpleasant, unfriendly behavior.

Although these characteristics tend to persist over time, they can be modified by experience. For example, babies who tend to be fearful of novelty may adapt more easily if their behavior is understood and accepted by their parents and if they are given support in developing new patterns. Temperamental characteristics are partially explained by heredity and prenatal influences, but environment also plays an important role in shaping later behavior.

We have found the work of Chess and Thomas valuable in helping us to understand the wide range of personalities in the young children we have taught and in understanding the interplay between children's characteristics and those of the adults who relate to them.

Environmental Factors

The first five or six years of life are critical in laying the foundation for all areas of the child's later development. Research has demonstrated that the experiences of these early years have a critical impact though, as we have just pointed out, we tend to view them today as interactive with biological traits. Until the 1950s and 1960s, the prevalent view was that people matured in predictable ways according to a biologically predetermined plan. A more recent view, greatly influenced by Hunt's book *Intelligence and Experience* (1961), suggests that functioning later in childhood and adulthood are greatly influenced by early experience.

Studies conducted by Benjamin Bloom (1964) indicate that 50 percent of the characteristics associated with mature intelligence develop by the age of four and approximately 80 percent by the age of eight. Other research has shown that in humans, as in animals, there are *sensitive periods,* certain times during which an important developmental milestone is most likely to occur. Some kinds of development may not occur if a sensitive period is missed or they come about with much greater difficulty. Sensitive periods for development of physiological structures like vision occur prenatally. A comparable period for language development may occur during the first few years after birth.

Research on the importance of early experience led to the idea that preschool programs might be an antidote for the deprivation associated with extreme poverty in young children, and hence compensatory education programs

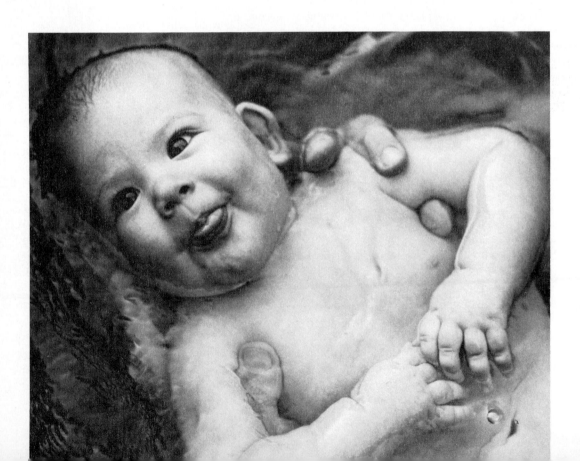

developed. Research by Lazar and others reported in Chapter 3 has presented a persuasive argument for the positive impact that quality early childhood programs can have on the lives of participating children.

A study conducted by Jerome Kagan (1973) suggests that inadequate nurture and stimulation in the early years does not necessarily cause irreversible deficiencies later in life. Kagan found that Guatemalan Indian children who were traditionally reared in ways that deprived them of daylight, adequate nutrition, and stimulation during the first two years of life, appeared to be functioning within normal ranges in all areas of development by the age of eleven. It must be pointed out, however, that the children in this study did have regular and loving contact with their mothers, and this may be what enabled later normal development. Also, they lived in a culture in which attainment of technical skills and highly abstract concepts were less likely to be required in order to be seen as fully functioning members of the community. Although repeated experiences of extreme and early deprivation may cause serious damage to the developing child, Kagan's study reminds us that human beings are remarkably resilient, and early deprivation, when countered soon enough, may be ameliorated.

Foundations of Healthy Development

Children cannot develop in an optimal manner unless their basic needs are met and they can live among nurturing adults who care for them and encourage them in their exploration of the world. Research on early childhood development and theories in the field of psychology have fundamentally changed our understanding of the minimal and the optimal conditions for healthy development.

Meeting Basic Needs

Abraham Maslow formulated a theory regarding the necessary conditions for the full development of individual human potential and described his ideas in several publications including *Toward a Psychology of Being* (1968) and *Motivation and Personality* (1970). Maslow, a major figure in *humanistic* psychology, studied people who he considered to be *self-actualized*. These individuals had an unusual zest for life, were vitally interested in the world, and got great satisfaction from their relationships and their work most of the time. As a result of his study, Maslow formulated his hierarchy of basic and growth needs. At the base of Maslow's hierarchy are the physiological needs for air, water, food, and shelter. If these needs go unmet or are only partially met, the individual may not survive or may be able to think of little else. When these basic physical needs are satisfied, the urge to feel secure becomes more pressing. This need is met when people are free from fear of hazards and threats in their environment and when they are surrounded by others who are caring and predictable. When they feel secure, people are able to focus on giving and receiving love, the pursuit of an understanding of the world, and the self-knowledge that satisfies the highest human need—that of self-actualization.

Maslow's theory does not attempt to explain either the occasional case of the individual who accomplishes great things in spite of a dismal childhood or those cases in which a person appears to have had an optimal childhood but exhibits a very low level of accomplishment. Still, Maslow's hierarchy seems to apply to some degree to most individuals. In the case of infants, toddlers, and young children, others must be available to help them meet their basic needs and to provide the conditions that free them to grow and learn.

Infants require nearly constant adult attention to their basic needs; without it, they will almost certainly suffer irreversible damage to their development. Once viewed as passive organisms engaged primarily in reflex behavior during a relatively unimportant period, infants are described today as active beings who have the ability to react to sensory stimuli, to interact with others, and to be alert to and observant of the environment. Infancy is a crucial time for laying the foundation for later development. Understanding this foundation of development will help you to meet the needs of infants and see the continuity between infancy and the preschool-age child. It is important to understand what children need to experience and achieve in the first few years of life in order to help them function productively throughout the early childhood years.

Today's specialists in child development are concerned with providing optimal conditions for development from conception through the early years. They are increasingly aware of the importance of prenatal conditions including the physical health, mental health, and nutritional status of the parents.

From within hours of birth and for a number of years after, adults must provide infants with adequate nutrition, which is, "the single most important factor affecting physical growth and development in the young child" (Horowitz 1982, p. 22). For babies' first food, most doctors and nutritionists recommend breast-feeding because mother's milk is the most nourishing food for an infant and apparently has a positive effect on the child's resistance to disease and allergy. Malnutrition in the infant and toddler has been shown to be associated with retarded mental and physical development and may be related to attentional deficits. Brain development, particularly myelination (the laying down of myelin sheaths, the nerve insulation essential in sensory integration) is impaired in malnourished children. Children with good nutrition in infancy and early childhood tend to fare better in all areas of development.

Nurturing Relationships

The second prerequisite for healthy development is a warm, intimate, continuous relationship between the infant and its primary caregiv-ers. Tender, loving care given in the context of these relationships is essential to normal physical and emotional development and helps the child to learn that the world is a safe and trustworthy place.

Research has established the significance of comforting tactile experiences such as caressing, cuddling, and rhythmic movement in the early development of all species of mammals. Harry and Margaret Harlow's well-known research showed that baby monkeys had a marked preference for contact with a terry cloth surrogate mother that provided contact comfort but no food to a wire mother that had the advantage of providing milk but that had little else to recommend in the eyes of the baby monkeys. The impetus for this research came from observations of the high mortality rates of unhandled research animals (Berger 1980; Papalia and Olds 1982).

It has also been found that a large percentage of institutionalized human infants did not survive the first year of life when there was little or no opportunity for consistent, close contact with others and where only the basic needs for nourishment and cleanliness were met. In institutions where caregivers provided frequent comforting physical contact, the mortality rate decreased sharply and infants developed normally. Other research on institutionalized and neglected children has demonstrated that those who suffer maternal deprivation in infancy often have many problems in later development. Research and clinical observation reinforce our awareness of the importance of intimate contact between the primary caregiver and the infant and how this connectedness (or failure to connect) influences all aspects of later development (Bowlby 1951). Because of the importance of these earliest relationships, there has also been a growing interest in birth procedures that are less mechanistic and more nurturing for mother and child than the traditional hospital delivery. A nontraumatic environment and contact between mother and infant in the first hours after birth appear to have a positive effect on the mother-child relationship.

Theory tells us repeatedly that children can thrive only when the proper balance of nurturance and stimulation is available. Early observation of the failure of institutionalized infants to develop normally (or even to survive) led to a concern with the social and emotional development of children who were deprived of care by their mothers and instead received substitute care in day care centers. John Bowlby did work in the middle of this century that identified attachment to the mother as an essential prerequisite for normal social and emotional development. Bowlby's work led to the conclusion that, indeed, out-of-the-home care deprived children of this vital connection to their mothers and could only result in serious psychological disorders and problems with interpersonal relationships.

Other researchers and theorists have revisited this topic in recent years and confirmed the idea that the nature of early attachments has a profound effect on development. Mary Ainsworth, who was an associate of Bowlby, conducted further research regarding the security of attachment of children to their mothers. She found that the degree of attachment between mothers and their children differed a great deal, from securely attached to those who had not attached at all. Her work confirms the belief that children must be secure in their primary relationships before they are free to fully explore the world; however, few believe that only a mother can serve this purpose. What children require is consistent, warm, and responsive nurturing by a few intimate caregivers. The caregivers can be the father, a grandmother, an uncle, the family day care provider, and a few of the regular teaching staff at the child care center of choice. This "multiple parenting" can be just as effective as a single attachment to the mother as long as there are at most a half dozen people who know and care about the child well enough to respond in a reliable and predictable

manner to the child's unique expression of needs. Although it is true that attachment is a necessary condition for optimal social and emotional development, the precise form the attachment takes is not, as long as it provides a secure base from which infants can begin to explore the world (Clarke-Stewart 1988).

Separation-Individuation

Psychoanalyst Margaret Mahler (1975) used a laboratory setting to study behavioral, social, and emotional aspects of infants and toddlers as they moved from the security of infancy to the relative independence of the preschool years. Mahler believes that children are born twice: first when they enter the world, and a second time, psychologically, at about eighteen months when they begin to be aware of an identity separate from their mother or mother figure. Mahler sees the major developmental task of infancy as the process of slowly differentiating the self from another, the acquisition of the sense of self. This process is called *separation-individuation.* The period around eighteen months is very important developmentally; even though children begin to move away from their principal caregivers and gain a feeling of pleasure in mastery, they have a continued need to maintain connectedness and to have the caregiver appreciate their developing skills and to provide continuing reassurance. Some child development specialists urge parents not to place children in care situations out of the home before they reach this important developmental landmark. Mahler's work, like that of Bowlby, has been recognized as essentially correct but subject to refinement by new research that recognizes that the consistent nurturance of children can be distributed between several adults without interrupting the operation of the developmental principles they have identified—attachment and then separation-individuation.

A Stimulating Environment

The final important condition required for infants to develop normally is an environment that provides them with novelty and stimulation and includes opportunities for sensory exploration—to hear, see, smell, taste, and touch. Interaction with people and objects in a stimulating environment in the course of play—the important work of infancy and childhood—has positive effects on subsequent intellectual development. This correlates to experimentation with animals as well. Researchers have found that rats exposed to enriched environments perform better on mazes and other measures of intelligence.

Care that satisfies the child's basic needs, nurturing relationships, and stimulating environments continue to be important throughout the early childhood years and the rest of childhood. They lay the essential foundation for later positive development.

THEORY INTO PRACTICE

Through careful observation, people have learned many facts about how children learn and grow and have developed theories to organize these facts in ways that attempt to make sense of them. A *theory* is an explanation of how the facts fit together into a form that can be used to understand the past and predict the future. Although theories aid us in understanding the world, they do not represent a truth that is static

and unchanging. As we gain new knowledge, a theory may be replaced by another theory that is simpler, more accurate, more comprehensive, or more useful.

Theories of child development differ greatly in the aspects of development on which they focus, in their underlying assumptions, and in the subjects and methods used as a basis for their conclusions. No single approach explains all aspects of children's development. Each is like a lens that focuses on some unique aspect. Knowledge of developmental theory is useful in helping you to understand children and their behavior, but it is important to keep in mind that there is no single theory today that is "right" and that ties up everything we know about children into one neat package.

In the following sections we discuss some ideas about development that are both theoretical and practical. For each aspect of development—physical, social-emotional, and cognitive—we give a brief sketch of what teachers need to know, describe the work of researchers and clinicians who have contributed to understanding this aspect of development, and explore the implications of their ideas for teaching.

Physical Development

From birth to eight years of age children undergo dramatic changes in their physical capabilities. The long, lanky seven-year-old who enjoys skating with friends and attending gymnastics class displays motor abilities that one might not predict from seeing the infant version of the same person. Physical development manifests itself in changed sleeping, eating, and toileting patterns, increased height and weight, and altered body proportions. Sensory-perceptual skills develop; large muscles become strong, flexible, and coordinated; and fine-motor strength and skill develop. Teachers of young children need to be aware of this aspect of development, for the physical competence of children influences the other aspects of their

IN THE CLASSROOM: BIOLOGICAL AND ENVIRONMENTAL FACTORS INFLUENCING DEVELOPMENT

Implications for Teachers

Factor: Heredity and environment interact to influence development.
Implication: As a teacher of young children, it is important that you read professional journals and books and attend conferences and classes to learn of new developments in research and theory. You will be able to make use of important new knowledge as you make decisions about your daily work with children.

Factor: Some characteristics and conditions are basically impossible to alter (eye, hair, and skin color and conditions such as blindness and deafness that appear before birth). Environmental factors can significantly alter other characteristics that are primarily determined by inheritance (height, weight, intelligence, and temperament).
Implication: Children come to your classroom equipped with their inheritance and their experiences as members of families. It is essential that you accept and appreciate them, that you are aware of the contribution you can realistically make to their development, and that you then work ceaselessly to provide the best that the available resources will allow.

Factor: Early experience can greatly influence later development, but all may not be lost if conditions have been less than perfect. Some research indicates that deprivation can be at least partially compensated for later.
Implication: Even though some children in your care will not have had their basic needs met by their families, you can work to make a difference by providing the best possible conditions for development now.

Factor: Nutrition is the most critical factor influencing early growth and development.
Implication: You should make use of current child nutrition information and take an active role in making certain that the children you work with receive the amount and kind of foods that will support their growth and development.

Factor: Attachment to and loving contact with warm, responsive caregivers is essential to normal physical, social, and emotional development.
Implication: It is important to recognize, appreciate, and support the intimate relationships between children and their family members and to consistently extend the most nurturing and responsive care possible to the children in your classroom. Also, you can cooperate with your coworkers to minimize the frequency with which children must undergo changes in the adults who are responsible for their care.

development, especially their self-concepts. Physically competent children may advance more rapidly than others in the cognitive domain simply because they are likely to explore more aspects of the world at an earlier age and perhaps more extensively.

Stages of Physical Development

It is important to know the stages of physical development of the children with whom you work. To get you started toward that knowledge, we outline some of the obvious and significant facts about growth patterns and physical skill attainments typical of each stage from infancy through the primary years.

Infant (birth through twelve months) development progresses very rapidly. At birth children sleep and wake in unpredictable patterns, but within the year most are sleeping through the night and taking several naps. The toothless newborn eats every few hours and obtains all nourishment from milk. By age one most children have at least twelve teeth and eat three meals plus snacks from the family table.

The grasping reflex of the newborn is largely accidental in nature—if an object comes into contact with the hand the newborn grabs.

This reflex translates into the hand and eye coordination that enables the one-year-old to meticulously pick up a pea from a plate or a piece of lint from the rug.

At birth children have no control over head movement and are nearly totally dependent on their caregivers for changes in position. Within a few months infants can lift their own heads to visually explore the world, by mid-year they can roll over when they wish, by six months some can stand, and by the end of the first year many can walk.

Toddlers (twelve to thirty-six months) refine and consolidate many of the motor abilities they have gained during the first year of life. At twelve months fingers are the tools for eating and by mid-year children enjoy using a spoon at least part of the time. By the end of the toddler stage children have all twenty of their teeth and are able to control elimination when awake and use the toilet with little assistance. Most sleep twelve or thirteen hours each day and some still wet the bed.

During the second year hand preference begins and children take up scribbling with crayons or pencils and learn how to turn the pages of a book. Great amounts of time will be devoted to picking up small items (cubes, blocks, puzzle pieces, and so forth), dropping them into a container, carrying them about, and dumping them out. At eighteen months most children can stack a couple of blocks and by age two they can manage a stack of six or more.

By fifteen months the majority of children walk. By age two nearly all run, climb up and down stairs (the same foot forward one step at a time) with a firm hold on an adult or a rail, and throw a ball in a two-handed style. Between two and three years of age children consolidate many skills and become much more independent in their ability to move about in the world and meet their own physical needs.

Preschool- and kindergarten-age children (three through five years) are exuberant and quite involved in practicing physical skills. A good deal of energy is expended each day, so most preschool-age children can easily nap for an hour or two daily, but many have learned to stay awake all day by the end of the preschool years. A young three-year-old may have an occasional daytime toileting accident, but by age four this will be a rare occurrence. Most children begin to have night control of elimination by age four or five. A few children will master night control still later and this should be treated as normal by the adults in the child's life.

Zippers, snaps, and buttons are mastered during this period and children often enjoy dressing themselves. Although a pair of scissors may still be a challenge for young three-year-olds, by age four they are able to use them with ease and by age five may have developed considerable skill with paint brushes, pens, and pencils. Many children will learn to cut along a straight line and copy a drawing of a circle or square and some will attempt to copy letters and numerals as they near the end of this period. Some five-year-olds will be able to write with good control though not great precision.

At the beginning of the preschool years large-muscle skill development may still be toddlerlike in nature. For example, a three-year-old can run but may not be able to stop and change direction with total control, whereas four-year-olds can run, vary speed and direction, and stop "on a dime." During these years children progress from throwing and catching with clumsily outstretched arms to the ability to throw a ball overhand with accuracy; from hesitant, awkward attempts at climbing to the ability to climb stairs and play structures quickly and smoothly with alternating steps. By age three most children have learned to ride a tricycle and by age four they have the strength and skill to go fast, turn sharply, and back up with accuracy and considerable speed.

Primary-age children (six through seven years) are nearly totally independent in their self-care. Toileting accidents occur only under the most trying of situations, naps are nearly unheard of, and eating patterns may closely resemble those of adults.

Handedness is clearly established and children gradually learn to differentiate their left and right sides. These children take great joy in practicing fine-motor skills such as writing, drawing, and sculpting, and during the primary years they become quite good at these.

The height and weight of children vary greatly during this period, but nearly everyone has developed the agility, stamina, strength, and skill to play team sports, bicycle around their neighborhood, skate for hours, swim, and dance with considerable grace.

Theorists' Contributions to Understanding Physical Development

Arnold Gesell (1940), who pioneered the scientific study of child development, collected observational data on children. His primary goal was to chart the growth patterns and behavior changes of children as they matured. He identified and described the age- or stage-related physical, social-emotional, cognitive, and other growth and behavior characteristics of children from birth through adolescence. Gesell and his associates gathered information under ten categories on an unspecified number of children (estimated at a few dozen for each age level). The information was then used to write summary descriptions of what the "normal" child was like at a given age—these are now called developmental norms. The resulting guidelines for what can be expected of children at various ages and stages of development have been presented in publications listed in the bibliography for this chapter. These normative data still serve as the basis for many developmental charts and screening instruments in use today.

Gesell and his group believed that maturation was the crucial factor in reaching new developmental levels. Their *maturation theory* of development holds that growth is governed by heredity and proceeds in a genetically determined sequence and that individual rate is minimally influenced by the experiences of the developing person. Because each person is genetically different, the rate at which people attain the growth and maturation necessary for learning skills and concepts will vary. Also, the Gesell group noted alternating years of good and bad behavior ("terrible twos" and "tranquil threes"), which they associated with periods of equilibrium (in balance) and disequilibrium (out of balance), that later theorists also note and incorporate into their principles of development.

The work of Gesell and his team led to the concept of readiness, a period during development in which a specific skill or response is most likely to occur. Maturational theory suggests that attempts to hasten development are futile, because progress cannot be made until the prerequisite growth and maturation have occurred within the body and mind of the individual child.

Gesell's work has been criticized because of its heavy emphasis on the role of maturation, its lack of emphasis on environmental stimulation, and because his data on ages and stages were collected from a rather limited number of subjects that were self-selected from a small geographic area and of limited socioeconomic, racial, and cultural diversity.

Implications for Teaching

The work of Gesell and his associates has, when used with proper caution, contributed a good deal that can be helpful to teachers of young children. It is used extensively by teachers, parents, and medical personnel to judge whether growth patterns and the acquisition of motor skills are proceeding as they should. We use the information Gesell and his associates gathered through careful observation to guide our decisions about when children can realistically be expected to learn how to perform specific tasks. They were among the pioneers in popularizing

the use of observation as a tool for the study of children. Observational methods are now central to the work of researchers and invaluable in the daily life of the classroom teacher (see Chapter 6 on uses of observation). Gesell's descriptions of stages of development based on averages of observational data provide us with general guidelines for expectations regarding children's development. The developmental charts in the curriculum chapters of this book are derived from this kind of normative study. Many developmental screening systems have been derived from these normative data. Screening tests and charts help us judge whether or not we should be concerned with a child's overall developmental progress or any particular aspect of a child's development.

The use of normative charts has led some people to associate average, age-related behaviors or growth levels with desirable degrees of development. Maturational theorists have taken great care to point out some critical principles that should always be considered to avoid setting up unrealistic expectations when using normative data to assess children. It is important to remember that the sequence of development does not vary, but that the rate may be very different from child to child—all children crawl or creep before they walk, but one child may begin to walk at eight months while another waits until twelve months. The family of the child who walks at eight months need not be overly proud and that of the child who walks at twelve months need not be concerned, because each child is progressing within the normal range of development.

Social and Emotional Development

The helplessness of the newborn compels adults to take responsibility for children's survival. The nearly total physical dependency of infants provides the stimulus for the first emotional bond with another person (often the mother or father) that subsequently serves as the base for further social and emotional development.

People who take primary responsibility for nurturing newborns can soon tell you a lot about the social and emotional characteristics of the children. Within days parents will be able to make definitive declarations about the temperament of their infants. Some babies are fussy, easily upset, intense, and demanding of constant attention, whereas others are calm, accepting, and content. Each child develops a characteristic way of expressing needs, joys, and concerns.

Stages of Social-Emotional Development

During the early childhood years (birth through age eight), children develop into individuals who can be described in terms of their temperament, their ability to work with others, and their perceptions of themselves. Each stage along the way has a few distinctive characteristics that affect how children will react to and interact with people, things, and experiences they encounter. Knowledge of these stage-related characteristics of social-emotional development serves as the basis for discovering ways of interacting with children in order to help them achieve healthy social-emotional development.

Infants make their needs known with their cries. The distress cries of a baby are nearly impossible for most adults to ignore. This is fortunate, for the responses of caregivers ensure the survival of infants and provide the basis for their eventual perception of the world as a trustworthy place. Infants soon learn to express a wide range of emotions through body movements and facial expressions. Within a few months after birth babies will return a smile and by the middle of the first year participate in games such as this-little-piggy and peekaboo.

Sometime between six and nine months of age most infants become somewhat antisocial as they develop a highly predictable wariness of strangers. An approaching stranger evokes

cringes, head hiding, and finally cries of protest. However, from the security of a parent's arms the feared stranger is often observed carefully and may be judged as trustworthy—especially if the parent appears pleased to see the newcomer. By age one children will again be more accepting of new people and situations.

Toddlers (twelve to thirty-six months) go on an emotional roller coaster ride from the amiability of the one-year-old, to the tyrannically expressed demands of the two-year-old, and finally back to the calmer sociability of the three-year-old. One-year-olds are egocentric, insistent on having things their way but at the same time are generally friendly, adaptive, and able to give up an assertive demand at the request of a loved adult. By age two children begin to assert themselves much more strongly, can be stubbornly self-centered, and are resistant to change as they begin their quest for autonomy.

Early in the toddler stage children like to play on their own (solitary play) or to have the exclusive attention of favorite adults. As they approach their second birthday they remain very possessive of their belongings, but they also enjoy the nearby company of other children as they play (parallel play).

Preschool- and kindergarten-age children become increasingly social. Three-year-olds tend to be friendly, curious, and generally positive in disposition. Like age two, the fourth year is often a tumultuous one during which children seem to display a different personality from minute to minute—joyful humor may be replaced by an explosive burst of temper with little or no apparent cause. By ages four and five children become more aware and begin to more clearly identify with their gender. By kindergarten most children have a reliable sense of self.

Three-year-olds enjoy adult company, can play with other children (associative play stage) and are quite able to share belongings. Peers become very important to four- and five-year-olds. Large group sociodramatic play episodes

involving recruitment of players, development of a plan, assignment of roles, and actual enactment can take up over an hour of time and require a great amount of cooperative effort and negotiating skill (cooperative play stage).

Primary-age children tend to be active, outgoing, and assertive. Children at this stage become very involved in mastering new skills and learning about the world in which they live. They practice writing the way the teacher does, learning the jump rope routines the older children know, drawing better than big brother, and mastering the rules and play of games (games-with-rules play stage). At times they may show off and brag about their recent accomplishments. If their competence is in any way challenged, they may become defensive and argumentative. Young school-age children are much more independent, but new found autonomy can create feelings of insecurity. At this age children seem to feel the need to act more grown up, so they may resist expressing the needs for affection and approval that they desperately need because they do not wish to seem to be "babies." They enjoy working cooperatively with peers, teachers, and parents and probably do so, at least in part, to secure the positive human contact they need in order to feel good about themselves.

Gender identity becomes strong during the primary years and is usually expressed by same-sex play groups that engage in play behaviors that are gender-role stereotyped. Boys and girls continue to enjoy dramatic play and become very interested in sports and games.

Theorists' Contributions to Understanding Social-Emotional Development

Theorists associated with *psychodynamic theory* have directly addressed issues related to social and emotional development. The basic concepts underlying this theoretical approach were formulated by Sigmund Freud, a nineteenth century neurologist and neuroanatomist. His theory of human development focuses on inner processes and on emotional development. Freud worked with emotionally troubled patients during a period in history in which their disturbances were believed to have an organic basis. Freud put forth the revolutionary idea that unconscious psychological processes were the source of mental illness. He developed his ideas into a framework that was the first comprehensive theory of human development describing the stages of emotional development from infancy through adolescence.

Freud introduced the idea that behavior is influenced by unconscious factors, many of which are sexually motivated, that originate in early experiences. Awareness of these is often lost to conscious memory through the mechanism of repression. Although many of the researchers who later expanded the psychodynamic model deemphasized Freud's discovery of childhood sexuality (despite the exciting stir it caused in nineteenth century Vienna), the recognition that unconscious processes frequently play an important determining role in our thought and behavior has been tremendously influential and remains a hallmark of those who have used this approach to understanding human development.

Freud's work has served as the basis for a number of other contributions to our thinking about children. Primary among theorists who have more fully elaborated psychodynamic the-

ory is Erik Erikson, whose work is influential in the thought of early childhood educators today. Erikson has described a series of stages of social and emotional development that expand Freud's original psychosexual stages to include social influences. Erikson believes that basic attitudes are formed as individuals pass through the stages and that serious problems at any stage lead to difficulty in reaching the next stage. Each stage is characterized by a major task or challenge. In infancy, the major task is the development of basic trust; for the toddler, it is the development of autonomy; for the preschooler, the development of initiative; and for the school-age child, industriousness.

For each stage, Erikson describes the potential for healthy development at one end of a continuum and the potential for development of negative and self-defeating attitudes at the other. He sees development as a product of the tension between the two extremes, with more positive than negative experiences necessary for healthy progress.

Implications for Teaching

Psychodynamic theory has contributed many important insights that have implications for teachers of young children. The development of the child is seen as progressing through a series of stages that are predictable, continuous throughout life, and influenced by many forces. Because crucial aspects of the child's development occur in the first five years when there is a great dependency on adults, the relationships between children and significant adults in their lives is seen as very important. Teachers who understand that the young child is in the process of becoming a separate person can support the conflicting needs for connectedness and independence.

Psychodynamic theory has influenced educational programs through its emphasis on early emotional development and its encouragement of creative expression as an outlet for children's

ERIKSON'S STAGES OF CHILDHOOD PSYCHOSOCIAL DEVELOPMENT

- **Trust versus mistrust (infancy):** During the first stage of development infants learn, or fail to learn, that people can be depended on and that they can depend on themselves to elicit nurturing responses from others. The quality of care an infant receives, especially in the first year of life, is essential to the development of basic trust. Through the love, nurture, and acceptance received, the infant learns that the world is a good and safe place.
- **Autonomy versus shame and doubt (toddler):** During the second stage of life, which begins at twelve to fifteen months, children develop a basic sense of autonomy: self-control and independent action. During this period they are growing rapidly. They are learning to coordinate many new patterns of action and to assert themselves as human beings. Conflict during this period centers on toilet training. If parents are accepting and easygoing, and if they recognize the child's developing need to assert independence, the child will move successfully through this stage. If adults are harsh and punitive and if the child is punished for assertive behavior, then shame and doubt may become stronger forces in the child's life.
- **Initiative versus guilt (preschool years):** This is a period of interest, active exploration, and readiness for learning. Children need to express their natural curiosity and creativity during this stage through opportunities to act on the environment. If explorations are regarded as naughtiness and if parents or teachers are overly concerned with preventing children from getting dirty or destroying things, a sense of initative may not be developed and guilt may be the more prevalent attitude.
- **Industry versus inferiority (school age):** During this period, children are ready for the challenge of new and exciting ideas and of constructing things. They need opportunities for physical, intellectual, and social accomplishment. They need many and varied interactions with materials. Success and a feeling of "I can do it!" result in a sense of industry.

Source: From *Childhood and Society,* second edition. Erik Erikson. New York: Norton. 1963.

feelings. By calling attention to unconscious forces that influence behavior, educators have become aware that children cannot consciously control their thoughts, feelings, and responses, and they are therefore less harsh in their judgments. It has also made educators increasingly aware of the importance of adult-child relationships and the psychological health of the adults who work with young children. This approach also provides insights into causes of psychological disturbance in children and techniques for treatment.

Many standard classroom practices that are regularly identified with quality programs reflect insights from and are supported by Erikson's stages of psychosocial development. These practices include:

- Low ratios with infants and toddlers because contact with warm, caring, available adults is a necessary condition for the development of the sense of *trust* that is so essential for early social and emotional development.
- The provision of many opportunities for toddlers and young preschool-age children to make choices about play activities, materials, and playmates so they develop a sense of *autonomy.*
- Adequate time to explore, plan, and carry out play episodes so that the sense of *initiative* that is central to development during the preschool years can develop.
- Opportunities to create and construct new ideas and things so that they succeed and develop the sense of *industry* that is the social-emotional task confronting school-age children.

Cognitive Development

Cognitive development is the process of becoming knowledgeable about the world. Between birth and adulthood we learn about and come to understand a great deal about the relationships among the objects, people, situations, and ideas that we encounter.

At birth infants are quite well equipped to collect information about the people and objects that fall within their sensory range—that which they can see, hear, smell, taste, and touch. However, the maturation that enables children to make sense of all that they experience evolves slowly over the first decade of life.

Stages of Cognitive Development

At each stage of development children differ in their ability to perceive, recognize, and remember people and things, to explore and relate to objects, events, and relationships, and to represent what they discover. Infants reveal their understanding of the world through their actions. Eventually each person develops the capacity to organize, make meaningful, and share their thoughts and feelings through the shared symbols of spoken and written language and number systems and through creative media such as music, art, dance, and drama.

Infants explore the world by looking, mouthing, and grasping. Mother is often the first object explored and the first person whom the infant is able to tell from others. In the early months newborns gaze at some things for long periods of time while seeming to ignore things and events that might attract their attention. It's as if the world is full of meaningless sensations and those that capture their interest are just random accidents. Later, after they have had many interactions with people and things, babies begin to make sense of happenings in their immediate world and they begin to make some choices.

Infants discover that they can make things happen by their own actions. Within a short period after birth they come to some rudimentary understanding that a loud cry will bring a concerned adult. Before long the random batting at the crib mobile will be recognized as the cause of the ringing bells and be repeated for the effect. Sometime between the middle and the end of the first year, infants demonstrate that they have begun to believe in the permanency of people and things by searching for them and protesting when they disappear from sight. Action-based problem solving appears about the same time. Infants will retrieve a toy that has rolled behind something else by removing the obstacle.

Toddlers can crawl and walk so they are better able to explore and construct an understanding of the world. Like infants, they still rely on sensory information, but they are increasingly able to make use of mental images stored in memory to recall and anticipate events. At one year of age most children have a few words available to represent the objects, people, and events with which they are most familiar. By age three children have a vocabulary of over a thousand words that they use effectively for thinking and learning.

Toddlers come to recognize that actions, objects, and ideas are represented by words. They can often recognize and name a few colors, distinguish a few objects from many, and express some concepts that have to do with space and time; for example, they can explain that the garage is near but mommy's office is far away and that mommy went to work yesterday but will stay home tomorrow.

Preschool- and kindergarten-age children use listening and looking to learn. The past three years of sensory exploration, physical manipulation, and language learning now pay off in the form of many concepts about how the social and physical world works. During this period chil-

dren become able to form more complex mental symbols of events and objects and use language to represent their ideas. Through this process language becomes the tool for constructing and communicating concepts.

"What is it?" and "How does it work?" are the frequently heard questions of three- and four-year-old children. As they pursue the answers, they construct many concepts about the qualities of things and learn to group objects by shared characteristics such as color, size, shape, and function. They explore quantity and learn that numerals (one, two, and so on) refer to a specific amount, but they are still unable to relate numerals to more than about ten objects. By age five most children understand the practical use of clocks and calendars and many associate specific events to times and days (lunch is at 11 and we stay home with our families on Saturday and Sunday). As concepts expand children are increasingly able to make and follow a plan and predict the outcomes of their own actions. Some older preschool- and kindergarten-age children may begin to be interested in representing their ideas in writing. Most will represent quite sophisticated ideas through art media and elaborate sociodramatic play episodes. Play has taken on symbolic forms in which children can pretend that they are people other than themselves and in which objects can stand for something they are not (a boy becomes a daddy and uses a block to symbolize a telephone to call his wife).

Primary-age children refine many cognitive abilities that lead to the beginning of the ability to reason logically. Symbols become effective tools for many children as they begin to learn to read and write. Some six-year-olds will be reading with considerable skill. Other children will just begin to master the skill by the end of the primary years. Early in this stage of development children judge quantity by appearance. For example, if you set out two glasses of juice, one in a short, wide glass and the other in a tall, narrow glass, many children will select the tall glass as the one that has more even when someone clearly demonstrates that the amounts are the same. Later during the primary-grade years children begin to realize that quantities remain the same even though the form may change and will no longer be fooled by how things look (this is called *conservation of quantity,* see the description of Piaget's stages in the accompanying box). Also, children become able to visualize how something will appear if it is viewed from another position in space. Children enjoy their ability to construct more complex relationships between objects and as a result become interested in collecting, sorting, and classifying things in new ways. They are now able to sequence objects from short to tall and to arrange colors from light to dark, and they take great pleasure in using these new skills in the arrangement of the clothes in their closet or the books on the shelf.

The understanding of time expands to the point where they can appreciate their own past, their family history, and historical events in their communities and the world. The ability to think logically leads to the enjoyment of games that are governed by rules and a beginning understanding of societal concepts such as laws, rules, and justice.

Theorists' Contributions to Understanding Cognitive Development

The best known approach to cognitive development comes from the work of Jean Piaget, who devoted many years of his life to the study of children's thinking. He began his career as a biologist and later became a philosopher as well. In his youth he studied how organisms adapt to their environment. His fascination with the biological adaptation of animal species evolved into an interest in how human beings adapt to their environments through their ability to use reason. Piaget's theory focuses primarily on the nature and development of logical thought. The innovative methodology that he devised for the study of children's thinking was one of Piaget's most significant contributions. His systematic, in-depth approach was based on case studies of individual children and interview techniques.

Cognitive development theory stresses adaptation as a result of the interaction between the individual and the social and physical environment. Piaget is interested in mental activity, in what the individual does in his or her interactions with the world. Piaget believes that knowledge is not given to a passive observer, rather knowledge of reality must be discovered and constructed by the activity of the child, and that children have the capacity to adapt and change (Ginsburg and Opper 1979, p. 14).

Through his observations of children, Piaget identified processes of cognitive development. As a result of interaction with the environment, the child develops organizing structures or concepts that Piaget calls schemes. Early schemes become the basis for more complex future mental structures. Piaget identifies three complementary processes that children use to organize their experience into structures for thinking and problem solving.

The first process is *assimilation,* by which a person integrates new information or experience into existing schemes or patterns of behavior. Through this process the child fits new information into his or her own framework for understanding the world. For example, the child who sees a goat for the first time and calls it a dog is trying to assimilate, or use, a structure he or she already has. Assimilation does not result in a change of schemes, but it does create growth in them and therefore contributes to development. When confronted with a new stimulus, the child will try to assimilate it into an existing scheme.

If it is not possible to fit new information or experience into existing schemes, the child engages in the second process, *accommodation*—the changing of an existing scheme to fit external reality more accurately or the creation of a new scheme. Through this process cognitive structures change and develop. The child has accommodated when she or he acquires the new scheme: goat. These structures are constructed by the child and reflect his or her understanding of the world.

The third process, *equilibration,* is based on the tendency of individuals to seek a dynamic balance between assimilation and accommodation. When there is a balance between assimilation and accommodation, the child is in a state of equilibrium. Imbalance between the two creates a state of disequilibrium. Equilibration is the process of moving from disequilibrium to equilibrium. It is through the tension and conflict of imbalanced assimilation and accommodation that intellectual growth (or adaptation) occurs.

Through the processes just described, the child progresses through a series of developmental stages that build from the interaction among three elements: existing mental structures, maturation, and experience. Piaget sees these stages as very distinct from each other. Stages occur in the same predictable sequence for everyone, although the exact age at which a child enters the next stage varies with the individual and the culture. The characteristics of each stage are summarized in the accompanying box.

The children you work with in early childhood programs will be in the sensorimotor and the preoperational stage of cognitive development. As children enter the preoperational stage, they are beginning to use symbols to represent experiences (words) in their thought processes. According to Piaget they are still bound to their perceptions and see things only from their viewpoint (egocentrism). The primary way that they learn is through direct experiences that involve sensory exploration and manipulation. During this period children are likely to focus on only one characteristic of an object or experience at a time, so they are easily deceived by appearances. One of our favorite stories that illustrates this concerns a child on his first plane

- **Sensorimotor stage**: During the sensorimotor period (from birth to approximately two years of age), the child changes from a reflex organism to one capable of thought and language. Behavior is primarily motor and the child is dependent on physical manipulation to gain information about the world. The ability to form mental images for events that cannot be readily heard, felt, seen, smelled, or tasted does not occur until age two. During this period infants learn to differentiate themselves from others and to seek stimulation and begin to develop the concept of causality.

  The important developmental task of infancy that represents a shift in development and signals progress into the next stage is called *object permanence.* Children learn that objects exist in the world apart from their relationship to them—an object may still exist even after it is out of sight.

- **Preoperational stage**: The preoperational period (between the ages of two and seven) is characterized by language acquisition and by rapid conceptual development. During this time the child evolves from one who relies on actions for understanding to one who is able to internally represent events (think conceptually). Children learn labels for experience, develop the ability to substitute a symbol (word, gesture, or object) for an object or an event that is not present. Thought is based on how things appear to the child rather than on logical reasoning.

  The early phase of this period is called *preconceptual.* Between the ages of two and four, children are egocentric, that is, they are unable to take the viewpoint of others. They tend to classify by a single salient feature. For example, they might classify all adult females as mommies. During the second, *intuitive,* phase of the preoperational period (between four and seven years), children are capable of more complex thought. They are less egocentric and more capable of social relationships. Moral feelings and moral reasoning begin during this stage.

  The developmental hallmark of the early childhood period is *conservation,* the child's realization that the amount or quantity of a substance stays the same even when its shape or location changes. It is dependent on the child's growing ability to look at things from more than one point of view at a time.

- **Concrete operations period**: During this period (between ages seven and eleven), children develop the ability to apply logical thought to concrete problems. Formal thought processes become more stable and reasonable, even though children still have to think things out in advance and try them out through direct manipulation.

- **Formal operations period**: During this final stage of cognitive development (between the ages of eleven and fifteen), children's cognitive structures reach their highest level of development, and they become able to apply logic to all classes of problems. Children develop basic principles of cause and effect and of scientific experimentation. They can weigh a situation mentally to deduce the relationships without having to try it out.

ride who turned to his mother after the plane had completed its ascent and asked, "When do we start getting smaller?"

Piaget created a whole new focus and methodology for the study of children's cognitive development. Like any pioneering work it was neither complete nor fully formulated. Kagan (1984, pp. 192–93) suggests three areas of vulnerability in Piaget's work: (1) inadequate explanation for the transition from one stage of development to the next; (2) omission of important areas of cognitive functioning such as language development; and (3) recognition that children's development is more uneven and that some competencies occur earlier than Piaget's findings indicated.

Margaret Donaldson in her book *Children's Minds* (1978) demonstrates that young children may show advanced thinking in situations that are familiar. Donaldson concludes that the extent to which children's tasks are meaningful to them has an important impact on what they will be able to do in a situation. Children can, in fact, accomplish certain developmental tasks earlier than has been thought in the past.

A number of researchers today are refining and extending Piaget's work, especially in the area of children's interactions with people. They are taking a social interactionist perspective which focuses on the role played by adults in facilitating the young child's development. The ideas of L. S. Vygotsky, a Russian psychologist who wrote during the 1930s, have contributed to this new emphasis on the social origins of language and thought. Vygotsky, like Piaget, believed that children are active in their own development and that it is an ongoing process. Vygotsky's emphasis, however, is on the relationship with other people as the major process contributing to development. In his view, young children develop in a specific social and cultural context, with early communicative interactions with adults becoming internalized to form the basis for speech and thinking. Vygotsky de-scribed development as proceeding from the interpsychic (between the child and other people) to the intrapsychic (within the child) plane. Social experiences therefore form the foundation for human development. In Vygotsky's view the development of language is primary and all human meaning is mediated by language.

Because knowledge is created through interaction with other people, it is not only important to look at the child, as Piaget did, but it is also important to focus on the interaction of the adult and child. In *Thought and Language* Vygotsky writes, "What the child can do in cooperation today he can do alone tomorrow" (1962, p. 104). Current research in child development, particularly in the areas of language literacy development, has begun to reflect this social interactionist focus.

Implications for Teaching

Piaget's work has been extremely influential in early childhood education in the United States since the late 1960s. One of his most important contributions has been to help parents and teachers to become aware that children's thinking is fundamentally different from that of adults and to focus on understanding the nature of the individual child's thought. It is important for teachers to realize that the thinking processes of children are affected by their stage of cognitive development and their prior experiences at home and school. Another important lesson that educators have gained from Piaget's work is that what is important in assessing children's intellectual development is not only their answer to a question but also the line of reasoning that led to that particular response.

Piaget's insistence that young children are always trying to construct a more coherent understanding of their world through their direct experience of it has led many educators to the belief that educational practices should allow ample opportunity for children to explore, experiment, and manipulate materials. Piaget was adamant that we cannot directly instruct children in the concepts that they need to know to move on to the next developmental stage. These concepts are acquired as a result of a complex interaction between experience, maturation, and adult mediation. He was critical of what he saw as an American tendency to hurry development rather than to let it follow its own course. Piaget was interested in the role of play in development and believed that it was the adult role to provide material and challenges and to facilitate the exchange of viewpoints between the players.

From the perspective of Vygotsky and many modern cognitive development theorists, teachers play a vitally important role in young children's learning and development because they are actually helping them to construct meaning in their lives. Teachers accomplish this through conversation that is relevant to the particular child and by helping each child to find a personal meaning in the activities offered at school.

DISCUSSION QUESTIONS

1. Reflect on your own development. How might your experiences as a developing child affect the kind of teacher you will be?
2. In what ways have you seen the developmental theories discussed in this chapter in the early childhood programs that you have visited and worked in?
3. How do you think your knowledge of child development will influence you in the classroom?

PROJECTS

1. Observe a young child, interpret, and report on his or her behavior in terms of Erikson's and Piaget's stages of childhood development.
2. Write a review of a book dealing with one of the topics in this chapter you want to learn more about. Describe the implications of what you learned for you as a teacher of young children.

BIBLIOGRAPHY

Ainsworth, M. 1979. *Patterns of Attachment*. New York: Halsted Press.
Berger, K. 1980. *The Developing Person*. New York: Worth.
Bloom, B. 1964. *Stability and Change in Human Characteristics*. New York: John Wiley & Sons.

Bowlby, J. 1951. *Maternal Care and Mental Health.* Geneva: World Health Organization.

Bruner, J. 1983. *Child's Talk: Learning to Use Language.* New York: W. W. Norton.

Clarke-Stewart, A., M. Perlmutter, and S. Friedman. 1988. *Lifelong Human Development.* New York: John Wiley & Sons.

Donaldson, M. C. 1978. *Children's Minds.* New York: W. W. Norton.

Donaldson, M. C., R. Grieve, and C. Pratt, eds. 1983. *Early Childhood Development and Education: Readings in Psychology.* New York: Guilford Press.

Elkind, D. 1981. *The Hurried Child: Growing Up Too Fast Too Soon,* Reading, Mass.: Addison-Wesley.

Erikson, E. 1963. *Childhood and Society.* 2d ed. New York: W. W. Norton.

Flavell, J. H. 1985. *Cognitive Development.* 2d ed. Englewood Cliffs, N.J.: Prentice-Hall.

Gesell, A. 1940. *The First Five Years of Life.* New York: Harper & Row.

Gesell, A., and F. L. Ilg. 1949. *Child Development: An Introduction to the Study of Human Growth.* New York: Harper & Row.

Ginsburg, H., and S. A. Opper. 1979. *Piaget's Theory of Intellectual Development.* 2d ed. Englewood Cliffs, N.J.: Prentice-Hall.

Horowitz, F. D. 1982. The First Two Years of Life: Factors Related to Thriving. In *The Young Child: Reviews of Research,* Vol. 3, ed. S. G. Moore and C. Cooper. Washington, D.C.: National Association for the Education of Young Children.

Hunt, J. McV. 1961. *Intelligence and Experience.* New York: Ronald.

Kagan, J. April, 1973. Do the First Two Years Matter? A Conversation with Jerome Kagan. *Saturday Review of Education.*

————— . 1984. *The Nature of the Child.* New York: Basic Books.

Kamii, C., and R. DeVries. 1980. *Group Games in Early Education: Implications of Piaget's Theory.* Washington, D.C.: National Association for the Education of Young Children.

Languis, M., T. Sanders, and S. Tibbs. 1980. *Brain and Learning.* Washington, D.C.: National Association for the Education of Young Children.

Mahler, M. S. 1975. *The Psychological Birth of the Human Infant: Symbiosis and Individuation.* New York: Basic Books.

Maslow, A. H. 1968. *Toward A Psychology of Being.* 2d ed. New York: Van Nostrand Reinhold.

————— . 1970. *Motivation and Personality.* 2d ed. New York: Harper & Row.

Nye, R. D. 1981. *Three Psychologies: Perspectives from Freud, Skinner and Rogers.* 2d ed. Monterey, Calif.: Brooks/Cole.

Papalia, D. E., and S. W. Olds. 1982. *A Child's World.* 3d ed. New York: McGraw-Hill.

Piaget, J. 1966. *The Origins of Intelligence in Children.* 2d ed. New York: International Universities Press.

Rogers, C. R. 1969. *Freedom to Learn.* Columbus, Ohio: Merrill.

Thomas, A., and S. Chess. 1977. *Temperament and Development.* New York: Brunner/Mazel

Thomas, R. M. 1985. *Comparing Theories of Child Development.* 2d ed. Belmont, Calif.: Wadsworth.

Tough, J. 1977. *The Development of Meaning: A Study of Children's Use of Language.* Boston: George Allen and Unwin.

Vygotsky, L. S. 1962. *Thought and Language.* Cambridge, Mass.: MIT Press.

Wadsworth, B. J. 1984. *Piaget's Theory of Cognitive and Affective Development.* 3d ed. New York: Longman.

CHAPTER FIVE

Play

For the child, the time is always now; the place, here, the action, me. He has no capacity to entertain adult notions of fantasy world and real world. He knows only one world, and that is the very real one in which and with which he plays. He is not playing at life. Play *is* life.

—*Joseph Chilton Pearce*

Play is a child's life and the means by which he comes to understand the world he lives in.

—*Susan Isaacs*

Through play, children learn what no one can teach them.

—*Lawrence Frank*

In this chapter we review the role of play in the development and learning of children and present some of the ways in which teachers can enhance and enrich the play of children in classroom settings. We discuss several ongoing issues concerning children's play.

Children all over the world play. They have played since the beginning of time. What is this activity that we call play? Even when discouraged from doing so, why do children find so many ways to play? What are the benefits of this activity? Of what significance is play to growth and development of young children? What is its role in the education process? What can you do to support this most natural of activities in your classroom?

For centuries philosophers, theologians, educators, psychologists, and parents have observed children at play and speculated about its nature and purpose. A full understanding is still not available to us, but recent theorists, research-

ers, and educators have expanded our comprehension of what play is and why it is of vital importance to the development of children.

PLAY: ITS NATURE AND VALUE

The favorite childhood play activities recalled by adults can be as diverse as "my dolls," "pretending to be the daddy in the home center at my preschool," "building a fortress in the woods with the kids in my neighborhood," or "rolling in the autumn leaves in my back yard." Children play with a wide variety of materials and engage in a wide variety of situations called play. In this section we discuss the characteristics of play, how children of different ages and developmental stages play, and what children gain from play.

Play Is a Process

Theorists, researchers, and educators have not yet agreed on a single definition of play. In their

97

attempts to describe it, however, they do tend to identify many similar characteristics that distinguish play from other behaviors.

- *Play is intrinsically motivated.* The players display personal motivation by the pleasure and focus they bring to the play. The activity is satisfying and continues for this reason, not because it meets a basic need or conforms to an external demand.
- *Play is freely chosen.* The play opportunity beckons to the child. A child may be invited to play but never compelled. The moment compulsion enters in and a task has been assigned, it becomes work, not play.
- *Play is process oriented.* Children focus on spontaneous discovery and creation and are more involved in the process of experimentation than concerned with the eventual outcome. If the play appears to be goal oriented on occasion, that is because of the spontaneous goals imposed by the players as the play unfolds, not because a teacher, parent, or even a player set a task and decided play was the process for accomplishing it.
- *Play is nonliteral.* In make-believe situations the child suspends and alters reality in the service of the play. External reality is temporarily set aside for fuller exploration of internal reality. The players are often heard saying things such as: "Let's pretend . . . ," "I'll be the fireman and you be the old man who's trapped in the building," or (holding a block) "This can be the phone."
- *Play is pleasurable, enjoyable, and engaging.* Ask adults how they can distinguish children at play and they will likely tell you "when they are having fun" or "when they are enjoying themselves" or even "when I can't get their attention for anything." Pleasurable, focused pursuit of an activity is a hallmark of play in children and adults.
- *Play is active.* Play requires physical, verbal, or mental engagement with people, objects, or ideas. We clearly recognize the rough-and-

tumble actions of the young child at play, but our own daydreams can also be called play for they are freely chosen, pursued for their own sake, process oriented, pleasurable, and engage our mental capacities.

- *Play is self rather than object oriented.* When confronted with a new or unusual object, the first order of business for most children is to find the answer to the question, What is this object and what can *it* do? Play theorists and researchers call this exploration, and they distinguish it from play. In play the basic question is, What can *I* do with this object? (Bergen 1988; Johnson, Christie, and Yawkey 1987).

Children at play are powerful creators compelled by forces from within to create a world worthy of their attention. Although the materials of their creations are their experiences with the real world, the shapes of their creations are their own. Play is simultaneously an attachment to and a detachment from the world of reality—a time during which children can act autonomously and freely and experience themselves and the world with an intensity that enables them to make the most of every moment.

Play is a *process* that supports the development of the *whole child*—a person able to sense, move, think, communicate, and create—in an integrated, developmentally appropriate way. Teachers who study play come to understand it as a natural and compelling way for children to develop and learn. They can then devise a variety of ways to support development through play.

Play Has Developmental Stages

As children grow and develop, they engage in different and increasingly complex types of play. The stages of play tend to parallel those described by cognitive and social development theorists (see Chapter 4, Child Development). In the early 1930s Mildred Parten developed categories of play that described the nature of the play relationship among the players.

Parten identified six stages of social play. The first two *(unoccupied behavior* and *on-looker)* are not seen as play behavior but as indicative of a learning style that is typified by periods of observation preceding the venture into a new situation, or as a deficit in play skill development. The four stages still in use are:

- *Solitary play* (dominates in infancy): During solitary play children play alone with toys that have attracted them. Even if other children are playing nearby, they go unnoticed.
- *Parallel play* (typical of toddlers): Children play side by side but still are engaged with their own play objects. Little interpersonal interaction occurs, but each child may be aware of and pleased by the company of a nearby friend.
- *Associative play* (seen most in young pre-school-age children): Pairs and groups of children play together in the same area and share materials. Interaction may be brisk, but cooperation and negotiation rare.
- *Cooperative play* (characteristic of older pre-school and kindergarten- and primary-age children): Groups of children actively engage one another in a sustained play episode in which they plan, negotiate, and share responsibility and leadership to attain group goals. (Parten, 1932)

Piaget was interested in play in terms of how it supported cognitive development. He developed another framework for looking at the stages of play development and divided play into three stages:

1. *Practice play* (infancy to two years) in which children explore the sensory qualities of objects and practice motor skills. This stage parallels Piaget's sensorimotor stage of development.
2. *Symbolic play* (two to seven years) in which children use objects to represent objects in reality and use make-believe actions and roles to represent situations that are familiar or

imagined. Symbolic play emerges during the preoperational period as the child is able to use mental symbols or imagery.

3. *Games with rules* (seven to eleven years) in which children recognize and follow preset rules in the interest of sustaining solitary or group play that conforms to the expectations and goals of the games. During the concrete operational period children's play is typified by games with rules, though they can be introduced to and enjoyed by much younger children (Piaget 1962).

In the late 1960s Sara Smilansky categorized play into four types that are based on but differ slightly from those of Piaget:

1. *Functional play* appears in infancy and persists through the early years. It consists of

sensory and motor exploration of toys, materials, and people. The child manipulates things in order to learn about them.

2. *Constructive play* involves building something. Toddlers stacking cubes are engaged in constructive play as is the four-year-old building with blocks. The child now manipulates objects in order to create something according to a plan.

3. *Dramatic play* involves make-believe actions and interactions where the child pretends to be other than what he or she is in reality (mommy, fire fighter, and so forth) and uses actions, objects, or words to represent other things or situations (a block for an iron, an arm movement for steering a truck, or "woof, woof" for the bark of a dog).

4. *Games with rules* require that the child behave according to preestablished rules in order to sustain legitimate play. Chutes and Ladders, dominoes, kickball, jump rope, and perhaps even peekaboo are examples.

In her recent work concerning the nature and importance of sociodramatic play, Smilansky points out that dramatic play represents a different type and potentially a higher level of play behavior. "Dramatic and sociodramatic play differs from the three other types of play in that it is *person-oriented* and not material and/or object-oriented." Dramatic play is the enactment of human relationships through symbolic representation and may be carried out in a solitary or parallel play style. Sociodramatic play involves the acting out of complex interactions in cooperation with others. There is a story line, roles to be assigned, and changes to be negotiated as the play proceeds. "Sociodramatic play allows the child to be an actor, observer and interactor simultaneously, using his abilities in a common enterprise with other children" (Smilansky and Shefatya 1990, p. 3).

An understanding of the stages of play allows teachers to provide for appropriate play experiences for children and helps them to appreciate children's play behavior. An awareness of Parten's categories makes it more likely that you will be fascinated rather than irritated by the infant who repeatedly bangs a rattle on a tray and never tires of dropping objects to the floor from a high chair. You will appreciate the movement toward social intercourse represented by the toddler who carries the basket of cubes to the block rug to build beside a special friend. Likewise, you may be concerned by the four-year-old who rarely engages in the lively interchange in the block corner, prefers to play alone with puzzles, and rarely uses materials to pretend to be something other than what he or she is. You will be sensitive to the older primary-grade student who persists in engaging others in sociodramatic play, pursues fantasy play a great deal of the time, and avoids joining games; you will be aware of the fact that the preference for games with rules usually predominates by this age and that an excessive preoccupation with dramatic play at this age is generally associated with social and cognitive immaturity. You will appreciate that a two-year-old might enjoy a game such as ring-around-the-rosy, led by a teacher, but the same child would be unlikely to ask a friend to play Chutes and Ladders. Knowledge of the types of play a child is likely to engage in enables you to plan a program that will be developmentally appropriate for the children in your class. It also gives you some important clues to use in observing the developmental progress of each child.

Play Supports Development

Child development theory tells us that children learn best through direct, hands-on experience. Play is the ultimate realization of the early childhood educator's maxim of *learning by doing*. Play is a developmentally appropriate process for learning because children engage in it spontaneously. In Chapter 10, Planning Curriculum, the balance between play and teacher-directed learning is explored further.

Play researchers continue to discover how play facilitates the development of children in all areas. We've long been able to justify our reliance on the process of play to support physical, social, and emotional development. In recent decades teachers have met with ever-increasing pressure to justify play in terms of how it might facilitate cognitive, language, and creative development. It is of particular interest to teachers and teacher educators that researchers have begun to find positive relationships between the play abilities of children and their future academic achievement and school adjustment. Competence at sociodramatic play was highly correlated with cognitive, creative, and social abilities (Smilansky and Shefatya 1990).

Role of Play in Physical Development

Children function best when they have bodies that are strong, flexible, and coordinated and when all of their senses are operating. Play contributes to the physical development of the child throughout the early childhood years.

The child at play develops physical competency in the most efficient and comprehensive manner imaginable. No teacher or staff of physical education experts could devise a curriculum that would accomplish for children what their own spontaneous play does naturally.

Newborns move their limbs and heads in quite random and uncoordinated ways and are unable to change position or location without assistance. Within the year many can walk and all can grasp and move objects in a purposeful way. During the second year running becomes a favorite activity and almost all children, unless disabled, can turn the pages of a book. A developmental chart (see Chapter 11) that graphically portrays the physical milestones of development can quickly give you an appreciation of the accomplishments of the early childhood years—from nearly no mobility at birth to the physical skills of an aspiring Olympic gymnast by age eight, from an inability to intentionally grasp an object to the ability to draw interesting pictures, write an essay, and play the piano.

Infants discover their own hands and spend hours gazing at them, flexing the fingers, and thrashing them about before their own faces. Later, they load a large hollow cube with toys, dump it all out, reload, dump, and on and on they go with this behavior for which no adult can fathom a reason. The older child will spend hours each day playing a favorite ball game and practicing the skills that the game requires.

Children have an innate drive to explore, discover, and master skills. The intense play of childhood leads naturally to the physical mastery toward which we humans seem predisposed and which, indeed, is probably essential to our survival as a species. Play is of prime importance in the development of perceptual-motor coordination and in the attainment and maintenance of the good health that is essential if optimal development is to occur.

Role of Play in Emotional Development

Therapists and educators have long appreciated the rich emotional value of play. Freud and his followers identified play as a primary way for children to express and work through their fears, anxieties, and desires. Contemporary therapists still use play as the medium for helping children deal with the feelings associated with traumatic events and disturbing situations in their lives.

Children at play take initiative, act autonomously, devise challenges, confront those challenges and in the process master their worst fears, resolve internal conflicts, act out anger, hostility, frustration, and joy, and resolve personal problems for which the "real" world offers no apparent solutions. It is no wonder that children are highly motivated to play all day.

Those of us who work with young children value play for its role in normal emotional development. Children at play feel that they are in control of their world, are practicing important skills that lead them to a sense of mastery over their environment, and are building a sense of competence that heightens self-esteem and confidence.

Role of Play in Social Development

From birth children are enmeshed in a social environment. Survival depends on the availability of more mature members of the species to be on duty at the moment of birth. For full socialization to take place adults must stay on duty for a good many years. Infants' helplessness compels us to hold them near, to speak gentle, soothing words, and to respond to their coos and cries with educated guesses about what they may need—food, fluid, warmth, cleanliness, gentle rocking, or just more hugs and soothing talk. Infants soon grow to trust the primary

adults in their lives and these first infant-caregiver bonds are the beginning of further social development. Caregivers *play* with the child in a way that is unlike anything adults do in any other life situation. You will hear a grown-up person addressing questions to the infant and then taking the infant's part to answer, "Now don't you have about the most beautiful eyes in the whole world?" "Well, of course I do, I got them from my daddy." An ordinarily dignified adult will go, "ZZZZZZZZZZZZZZZZZZZ-Gotcha!" and respond with the greatest joy when the baby laughs aloud for the first time. Soon infant-adult play progresses to games of pat-a-cake and this-little-piggy.

All this *social play* leads to increased social interaction skills. Children learn how to initiate play with relatives, family friends, and peers. In these early play encounters children learn awareness of others, cooperation, turn taking, and social language. They become aware of group membership, develop a social personality, and learn a lot about the rules and values governing the family, community, and culture. The play becomes increasingly complex and is sustained for greater periods of time. By the time children reach their second birthday most are making rudimentary attempts to portray social relationships through dramatic play. By age four or five they will have learned all the things they need to know in order to enact the most complex of social relationships with their peers in highly developed sociodramatic play. Soon after they become enchanted by rule-governed games and through this play social concepts such as fairness, justice, and cooperation evolve and influence play behavior and other social relationships.

Role of Play in Cognitive Development

Play is the primary medium through which young children make sense of their experiences and construct ideas about how the physical and social world works. The functional (or practice play) that begins in infancy and persists through life is basic to the process of learning about the properties and functions of objects and learning how things work. The constructive play of the toddler becomes the mode we use throughout life for discovering and practicing how to create from raw materials. The dramatic (or symbolic play) of preschool-age children plays a critical role in the development of representational or symbolic thought and the eventual ability to think logically and abstractly. In sociodramatic play (the most highly evolved form of dramatic play) children carry their experiences of the world into the play episode, construct an understanding of those experiences through the process of enactment in a social context (that is, with playmates), alter the understandings based on the response and input of peers, and then carry the new meanings back to their experience in the "real world" to begin anew. This circular process is one in which new information is constantly being gathered, organized, and used in new ways. It is one of the primary ways in which children construct their understanding of the world.

Sociodramatic play has emerged as an area of particular interest to play researchers because of its significance as an indicator of and role in cognitive development. A high level of competence in sociodramatic play has been found to be highly associated with cognitive maturity. Smilansky and her colleagues have developed a system for collecting information about the elements of sociodramatic play that can reliably indicate play competence in preschool-age children. It can also serve as a diagnostic tool to help teachers select the best intervention strategies for building play skill and, of course, consequently enhancing cognitive development (Smilansky and Shefatya 1990).

Play Integrates Development

Throughout this book we refer to the development of the *whole child*. At play, more than at any other time, children engage all aspects of themselves and most fully express who they are, what they are able to do, and what they know and feel. The play activities found in almost every early childhood program are rich in their potential for supporting all aspects of development.

A block area on an eight-by-ten-foot low pile carpet that contains a large shelf stocked with several hundred blocks of eight to ten different shapes and sizes, a few vehicles, animal and human figures, and a large stack of hollow blocks with boards can become a child development oasis. Three or four children playing in this area for a forty-minute period have a full range of development and learning opportunities:

- *Physical development:* Coordination and strength are enhanced as the large, hollow blocks are lifted, carried, and stacked. Small muscles develop as children hook together the tracks for the train. Sensory awareness is gained as they handle the blocks, feel the texture, and note the grain of the wood.
- *Social development:* Cooperation and negotiation skills are practiced as children work out how to share materials so they can build both a parking garage and create an office building. Interpersonal sensitivity develops as they decide whether or not to include a latecomer.
- *Emotional development:* A sense of competence is gained by creating something based on a plan and accomplished in cooperation with friends.
- *Cognitive development:* Solving the problems of balance and symmetry inherent in block play aids cognitive development, as do the planning and communication necessary to execute an agreed upon structure.

These are only a few indicators of the things a group of children might be learning and developing as they play together in the block area of their classroom. Such a list could be developed for every experience in a school setting that allows for the spontaneous play interactions of children—the manipulative area, the play yard, of course the dramatic play area, and much, much more.

Spontaneous play in the learning centers also integrates traditional curriculum areas. In the block play described, the children are creating an office building with an attached parking garage. Here are a few examples of how a teacher might intervene to broaden the learning potential into other curriculum areas.

Social studies concepts could be introduced by asking the children what they know about some of the ways people get to work. The mention of a bus might lead to *music, creative drama,* and *movement* experiences as the children help you line up a row of chairs and proceed with singing and miming "The Wheels on the Bus." A child might initiate a *reading/ writing* experience by asking you to help make a sign to label the parking garage. *Art* materials may be needed to make road signs. *Math* is occurring when one child comes up with the idea of dividing the seven cars equally between the three players.

Play integrates development and curriculum. Every play activity contributes to the developing child—*socially, emotionally, physically,* and *cognitively*—and can be presented in terms of subjects usually taught in school.

FACILITATING PLAY

Teachers of young children have a significant role in children's play. By their attitudes and their actions they support or discourage play. As they do so, they influence the depth and nature of the play.

Teacher's Attitudes

There are three positions (attitudes) that we have seen teachers of young children take in regard to play in their classrooms. The first group is not well informed about the role of play in programs for young children. To them, play is devoid of educational value and appropriate only as a break from academic tasks. They see play as an escape from reality that must not be allowed to take too much time and attention away from the real work of learning.

Others are aware that play contributes to development, but their understanding is not so complete that they trust it as a primary process for learning important skills and concepts. Although they allow time daily for "free play" both indoors and out, they devote large blocks of time to teacher-directed activities and engage children in games and provide activities that have preplanned "lessons" built into them. In the use of art materials, these teachers often direct children toward the creation of an identifiable product, they rely heavily on music and recordings to teach concepts, and they lead children in games with rules. They are using playlike activities to manipulate children into learning things that they fear will otherwise go unlearned. These teachers are trying to turn academics into play.

A third group is made up of teachers who believe it is monstrous to turn play into academics, but they masterfully uncover the academics hidden in the natural and spontaneous play of children. Such teachers ensure that children have large blocks of time in which to explore, experiment, and play in a planned environment. They develop intervention skills that extend and enrich play experiences without interrupting this most natural activity of children. For these teachers, play is not an escape from reality, but rather an in-depth exploration of reality.

Teacher's Role

Children will play regardless of the circumstances. However, what you provide and how you interact with them during their play can make a vital difference in the quality and amount of play and what they learn in the process. You can serve in many capacities as you facilitate children's play. You can:

• *Create an environment* that invites children to play.

- *Observe and evaluate* the meaning of each child's play so as to be better able to understand the child and enrich and extend the play experience.
- *Guide* the play should it become destructive or unsafe for the players.
- *Play with or tutor* by joining in at the appropriate time and level to encourage the development of play skills and to capitalize on the learning potential inherent in play.

Teacher as Creator of the Play Environment

The child at play must have the raw materials of play readily available. The essentials elements of the play environment are time, space, equipment, and materials. Information about how to provide a stimulating play environment can be found in Chapter 8, The Learning Environment, and in the chapters on curriculum.

Children of all ages must be allotted the *time* to play. The functional and constructive play of infants and toddlers can take place in relatively short time spans. Large blocks of time are required to plan and carry out the extended, rich, and fulfilling constructive and dramatic play episodes from which older preschool-age children benefit most. In kindergarten and primary classrooms the structure of the school day often eliminates large enough blocks of time for organizing, engaging in, and completing games and projects. Many adults have a vivid memory of the frustration of trying to play a game of softball during a fifteen-minute recess. If play periods are too short, children eventually give up attempts at meaningful play because of the frustration of being asked to end the play before it has truly begun.

The *spaces* for play include a variety of indoor learning centers and a well-equipped outdoor area. We naturally think of the block center and the dramatic play area as the domain of play. To support preschoolers in engaging fully in play you must also attend to the play potential of other areas—the manipulative toy center, the art area, the writing center, the library, and the outside environment. All these areas should be well defined and large enough for at least three or four children to play together. Primary schools in which play is seen as an important mode for learning employ play as a regular feature of the curriculum and organize space in ways that resemble the room arrangement of an excellent preschool. Infant and toddler play can be sustained in areas that have floor and yard space that is large enough for a variety of materials to be spread about on the floor without being overcrowded, and the variety of interest centers is unnecessary.

Equipment and *materials* are the raw materials of play. They must be plentiful enough to stimulate children. However, too much equipment, presented in a disorganized jumble, may be confusing and inhibit play. For infants and toddlers it is important to have a variety of attractive, well-constructed toys in great enough number to avoid competition and to ensure the practice of a wide range of motor skills. For toddlers it is important that you have duplicates of most items, for as soon as one child becomes involved in stacking rings on a stick a "best friend" will want to do the exact activity. Dramatic play and construction area props that are realistic tend to motivate older toddlers and young preschoolers to more frequent and elaborate dramatic play episodes. Here too, duplicate items encourage more associative and cooperative play. Older preschoolers do not need realistic replicas, and researchers have actually observed toy objects such as a telephone being passed over in play in favor of a block that was close at hand. Materials and props that relate to a theme encourage elaborate dramatic play. We have often had the urge to replace the "home" furnishings in our preschool classrooms with cubes, blocks and boards so that the area can be adapted to a variety of themes—hospital, grocery, camp site, post office, service station, airport, restaurant, and so on. In such an area a few props can suggest new possibilities for play with little rearrangement of the furnishings. For example, the addition of a small pup tent, a portable cooking kit, and a few sticks of wood to the traditional dramatic play area would be incongruous, but it would make sense among less defined furnishings. In fact, children with

some experience with camping might use the cubes, boards, and blocks to set up a picnic table, the sticks to build the fire, and proceed from there with elaborations. Consider how you can make use of the other learning centers to elaborate the play related to the theme. In the case of camping you might find books and pictures for the library area, a record of camp songs for the listening center, and a number of art and construction projects that draw on the theme.

Kindergarten- and primary-age children engage in all the types of play encountered in the earlier stages of development, but they have a greatly increased interest in games with rules. For them, cards and board games should be added to the choices available in the classroom. This is the stage during which the sports equipment required for more sophisticated games such as softball, basketball, volleyball, tetherball, and badminton can be introduced. The earlier fascination with sociodramatic play may be transformed into an interest in projects like constructing a harbor, planning a meal to share based on a theme, or performance. Sports, organized games, and performance skills learned during these years can be enjoyed in adulthood and may become the play of the adult stage of life.

Teacher as Observer

Careful observation reveals to you what is needed to support play. When you observe carefully and evaluate what you see based on child development information and the things we know about the nature and value of play, you are better able to know when to set limits, to see what you can provide to extend the play, and to realize when it would be appropriate and useful for you to become involved in a play episode.

Careful and frequent observation of play can provide you with information about changes you must make to avoid restraining and retarding the development of play skills. As mentioned, a common constraint on play is the scant time allowed for it. If children groan in unison and say, "But we just got started," you'll know you need to change something. Full and gratifying dramatic play episodes evolve through several stages—from gathering materials and planning, through the enactment of the drama, and finally to a point at which the play can only be revived by a creative invention of one of the players or a suggestion by you. The functional play and constructive play with sensory and manipulative materials common to infants, toddlers, and young preschoolers require an abundance of materials. A scarcity of materials or storage that keeps them out of reach of the children can impede play development by limiting the kinds of skills children are able to practice.

Systematic observation of play can yield important insights about the play process, about a child's stage of play development, and about the level of play that is taking place in your classroom. Several checklists and scales have been developed for looking at play behavior. These play observation scales can be used to increase your understanding of play in general and the play of the children in your classroom.

The checklists and scales often combine the social participation categories developed by Parten with more recent cognitive development play stages, including those of Piaget and Smilansky. Each researcher who develops a play scale for the purpose of investigating the nature of play behaviors provides clear definitions for each item included in the scale and gives instructions for coding the behaviors on a recording sheet. Johnson, Christie, and Yawkey (1987), in their book *Play and Early Childhood Development,* describe several scales in detail and give instructions for using them to gain valuable information about the play of children. Each scale codes for slightly different information about the play that is being observed. For example, the Parten/Piaget scale shown in Figure 5.1 uses an axis-grid arrangement to code play on its social and cognitive dimensions and

Parten/Piaget Scale			

Child's Name _____ Date _____

	Solitary	Parallel	Group
Functional			
Constructive			
Dramatic			
Games			

FIGURE 5.1

Parten/Piaget Scale

Source: Adapted from J. E. Johnson, J. F. Christie, and T. D. Yawkey, *Play and Early Childhood Development* (Glenview, Ill.: Scott, Foresman, 1987).

enables you to get a quick look at the level of play development of a child.

To develop a profile on the play behavior of each child in your class, use a sampling system over a period of several days. To begin, make a gridded sheet like the one in Figure 5.1 for each child in the class, shuffle the sheets so they will be in random order, start your sample with the top sheet, observe the child, and then place the sheet on the bottom of the pile to be used for subsequent samples on the same day. Observe the child for approximately fifteen seconds, mark the play behavior on the sheet, then move on to the next child. You can sample three children each minute, so if you had a group of fifteen you could take six samples of each child in a half hour. After four or five days you would have enough material to see typical patterns of play behavior for each child. In a classroom of infants you would probably find more play occurrences marked in the solitary-functional grid. If you were to shadow an eight-year-old for a day, many of the play behaviors would likely fall in the lower-right corner indicating games played with groups of age-mates. Four- and five-year-old children are going to be engaged in a good deal of group-oriented, dramatic play (Johnson, Christie, and Yawkey 1987).

Johnson, Christie, and Yawkey give other scales and inventories that, while more complicated, give more and different kinds of information about the play behaviors of the children you may wish to study. They also give complete information on how to use the Parten/Piaget scale and additional ways to use it for more detailed observation. Even without the more detailed instruction, this exercise gives objective information about a child's behavior and definitely sensitizes you to the amount and kind of play occurring in a classroom.

The information these scales provide can help you make appropriate decisions about when and how to intervene in the play of children. They are quite simple to use in an informal way, and with slightly more effort you can learn to use them with the precision necessary for use in research. They will lead you to an understanding of the importance of focused, directed observation of the play behaviors of children at various ages and stages of development; at the same time they will give you valuable information about the individuals you select for observation.

Teacher as Guide

A teacher who has taken the time and energy to create a well-supplied environment for children's play must plan strategies for dealing with the disorder and disruption that can occur in a group of children who are anxious to play in individualistic and creative ways. There is a delicate balance between rules that support and sustain rich play episodes and overcontrol that interferes with and constrains play. The guideline is to protect the play but not to let it get wild and uncontrolled. The basic principle is to gently and firmly insist that people and materials not be damaged. Children, like other people, are most productive when they feel safe from harm and relatively free from interference.

Dramatic play episodes that are prolonged and engrossing often attract latecomers who wish to join in. Your special role in this situation is to observe carefully to assist shy or anxious children by helping them to enter the play. Delicacy is the order of the day. It is best if you can unobtrusively help the child find a role. For example, in the camp scene you might say, "Would you like to become one of the wood gatherers? I think I know where we can find more wood." If the entering child is disruptive, you may have to ease the child into the ongoing scene by setting a task that makes use of the high energy (for example, chopping the wood). Sometimes it may be more appropriate to suggest an alternative play activity.

The hallmark of highly developed dramatic play is that the children use objects to represent things that they don't necessarily resemble. If you are overly rigid about the proper use of furnishings, equipment, and materials, you may curtail important play learning and development. We often hear teachers tell children things like "The blocks must stay in the block area" as a child moves several of them to the dramatic play area to make a second picnic table to accommodate the late arrivals. Our guideline is to reserve judgment until we see the use to which children are putting materials. If they are being used to extend a play episode, we don't discourage the activity even if it violates our adult sense of order.

Teacher as Player and Tutor

Until the 1960s the conventional wisdom was that teachers should not become directly involved in the play episodes of children. During the preceding decades play was seen as the arena in which children were to be left free to work out their inner conflicts and exercise power over their environment that was denied them in their interactions with the adult world. Your duty as an adult was to keep yourself out of the child's play world so as not to interfere with important psychological development. The only valid role allocated to the teacher was that of observer. Research in recent decades has pointed the way toward reasons for joining in children's play and ways to do so without intruding.

Research findings indicate that when teachers play with or alongside children, they lend support to the amount and quality of the play. Adult participation gives children a strong message that play is a valuable activity in its own right, so they play longer and learn new play behaviors from observing the adult. It also builds rapport with the children: as you learn more about their interests, needs, and characteristics, you are better able to interact with them around mutual interests. When teachers participate, the play episodes last much longer and become more elaborate. Of course, the teachers' participation must harmonize with the play of the children or else it will disrupt or end the play (Johnson, Christie, and Yawkey 1987).

It is essential that children maintain control of the play and that the teachers limit their role to actions and comments that extend and enrich the play. When teachers join in, it is important that they do so in a way that supports ongoing play. Sometimes children offer a role to a teacher: "Would you like a cup of coffee?" said to a teacher who is sitting near an area where a restaurant scene is being enacted is an invitation to join. If not invited, the teacher might, after a few minutes of observation, approach the player who seems to be taking leadership in assigning roles and ask to be seated as a customer, thereby gaining entry into the play. As a customer the teacher might inquire about the price of a cup of coffee, ask for cream to put in it, and praise the chef for the delicious pancakes she prepared. By asking questions, requesting service, and responding to things children have done, the teacher introduces new elements into the play without taking over.

A study conducted by Smilansky (1968) in Israel found that children from low-income families in which parents lacked a high school education engaged in less dramatic and sociodramatic play than did children from more affluent and well-educated families. Since then other researchers have found the same pattern in other countries. Smilansky identified the important elements of dramatic and sociodramatic play to be used as the basis for evaluating play skill:

- *Imitative role-play:* The child undertakes a make-believe role and expresses it in imitative action or verbalization or both.
- *Make-believe with regard to objects:* Toys, nonstructured materials, movements, or verbal declarations are substituted for real objects.

- *Make-believe with regard to actions and situations:* Verbal descriptions are substituted for actions and situations.
- *Persistence:* The child continues playing in a specific episode for at least ten minutes.
- *Interaction:* There are at least two players interacting in the context of a play episode.
- *Verbal communication:* There is some verbal interaction relating to the play episode (Smilansky and Shefatya 1990, p. 24).

Observation scales were designed to evaluate a child's play to determine whether all the elements were present and to what degree. Intervention strategies were designed to teach only the play skills that a child lacked. In this *play tutoring* a teacher demonstrates or models a missing skill until the child begins to use the skill in spontaneous play situations. For example, if a child is dependent on realistic props, the teacher might repeatedly offer substitution ideas, "Let's pretend that these jar lids are our plates" or "Let's pretend that the sand is salt," until the child begins to do so independently. It is important to note that the goal of play tutoring is to teach play skills in the context of the spontaneous play episode. The teacher does not change the content of the play by introducing new themes or taking a directing role. Play tutoring has proven effective in improving the dramatic and sociodramatic play skills of children. Improved play skills have been shown to be effective in bringing about gains in cognitive and social development.

ISSUES IN PLAY: MEDIA VIOLENCE AND TOYS, GENDER AND PLAY, AND SEX PLAY

Whenever early childhood educators and child development specialists gather, a number of issues related to play are discussed and argued heatedly. These include media-depicted violence, war toy promotions on television, and the pursuit of war play among young children. Those concerned with the welfare of young children are confronting these issues because of the prevalence today of programs with violent themes that are directed at young children. Gender-related play behaviors and stereotyping and the appropriate response to sex play also come in for their share of discussion among early childhood educators and parents. All of these issues will come up in your school, and opinions will differ among staff members and parents. Even within a family, these issues can create relationship problems when parents reject the position held by grandparents or one parent's beliefs differ radically from those of the other parent. As early childhood educators, we have a clearer mandate on how to deal with these issues—we are guided by our developmental goals for children and to some degree by a professional consensus that has emerged in recent decades.

Media Violence and War Toys

Media programming with violent themes has increased greatly during the past decade. Much of this programming is aimed at a child audience and is accompanied by the advertising of toys depicting program characters, scenes, and story lines.

Many of the children's toys advertised on television promote materialism, aggression, violence, and racial and gender stereotypes that limit children's creative play. If toys are the tools of children's learning—the nutrients of their cognitive and social growth—we have a responsibility not to provide "junk" toys just as we have a responsibility not to provide "junk" foods. In our own classrooms for preschoolers, kindergarten, and primary children we place limits on children's use of such toys and restrict the use of toys for weapons play. We do so with some misgiving because we value children's natural play impulses. However, weapons play, play with military toys, "fashion dolls," and other highly commercial materials tend to dominate children's thinking. Such materials make it difficult for children to use other materials with creativity and they limit valuable learning. They promote values that limit people and assign roles based on race, gender, age, and power. Women, people of color, and older people often are presented as incompetent and dependent.

Violent program content and the accompanying toys limit the creative play that contributes so greatly to overall development. Children tend to use the program-based toys to imitate the stereotypic behavior of the characters and the violent story action of the programs, and do not create new play episodes with different behaviors and situations. Imitation and repetition replace imagination and creativity (Carlsson-Paige and Levin 1987).

Why are children so attracted to these toys? Young children are fascinated by images of power—large creatures, monsters, superheroes, weapons, and machines. In a world where they are virtually powerless it is not surprising that young children are drawn to power. Instead of allowing inappropriate materials in school, help young children to feel more empowered by giving them real choices. Peer approval also has a role in the attraction to war toys. When one child has a highly prized toy, others want one with an intensity that is frightening. Eliminating the toys from the environment limits this kind of peer pressure. Commercial children's TV is essentially advertisements for products. Agonized parents talk about the intense desire evoked by sophisticated marketing aimed at children through TV. A highly marketed toy attracts children out of proportion to its play value.

Instead of allowing these toys into the classroom, teachers can provide positive toys for children. However reasonable these limits on war toys appear, they are difficult to explain to children, and sometimes to their parents. We explain our specific concerns with militaristic, moralistic, and stereotypic toys to parents. We discuss restrictions with children in more general and simple ways. Here are some examples:

- **Rule**: Toys from home may be shown but not played with at school. **Reason**: When someone has home toys, other people want them and they forget about playing with school toys. School is a place for special school toys.[1]
- **Rule**: Toys may be used for constructing things that don't hurt. **Reason**: Even pretend shooting and fighting hurt people's ears and feelings and they keep other people from playing more peacefully.

The National Association for the Education of Young Children adopted and published its Position Statement on Media Violence in Children's Lives (1990) in which the negative effect of violent programming on children's development was summarized and recommendations were made for steps to be taken to minimize children's exposure to violence through the media. The NAEYC supports legislative action to reinstate guidelines for the content of programs, the elimination of programs linked to toys, and advertising standards for toys to ensure psychological as well as physical safety.

Gender and Play Behavior

Every child establishes a gender identity—a clear understanding of whether she or he is a girl or a boy. Between ages two and three most children are able to state their gender and that of others, but it is an opinion that is subject to a change because it is often based on external features such as clothing and hair length. During the preschool years children attain a stable gender identity in which they realize that a change in appearance will not result in a change of gender. Instead, it is related to the genitalia with which you are born. Gender identity and sex role identity are different but interrelated concepts that seem to be necessary preconditions for the development of gender stereotyping concepts.

Sex role identity consists of the concepts built into our culture about the activities, personality characteristics, occupations, and abilities that are appropriate for each gender. Differences exist in the behavior and characteristics of boys and girls, but it is difficult to determine the degree to which these are influenced by biology and environment. Strong evidence exists for a biological basis for two commonly identified differences—better spatial ability and more aggressiveness in males—but the social environment can influence the expression of these characteristics. Some of the differences found in the ways girls and boys play can be attributed in part to these biological influences (Schickedanz, Schickedanz, and Forsyth 1982). Many gender-related play characteristics may be influenced by both environment and inheritance, but it is difficult at this time to assign primary influence to one or the other.

The causes may remain a mystery but differences do exist between the ways girls and boys play at different ages. Boys at all ages engage in active play of a rough-and-tumble

---

[1]Note: Very young children and children just beginning school often need a home toy as a "bridge" between home and school. We do not restrict these transitional objects which are usually a stuffed toy or a blanket from infancy.

nature, get into fights, use the outdoors, and play in groups more than girls do. Girls begin to prefer same-sex playmates earlier than boys but both do so between two and five years of age. By age five girls begin to be interested in cross-sex play but boys tend to persist in their same-sex preference throughout the elementary years. The approach to materials and toys differs in both choice and uses. Girls prefer art materials, dolls, and small constructive toys and play with them in quieter ways. Boys prefer blocks and wheeled vehicles and play with them more noisily and repetitiously. Girls play with toys regardless of the gender category people ordinarily assign to the item, whereas boys avoid "girl's toys." Boys appear to prefer larger groups of playmates from preschool age through the primary years; girls show a marked preference for a small group.

Boys and girls engage in different styles of play and some of the differences may be attributed to gender stereotyping. Many people base their responses to children on strong, rigid ideas of what is appropriate treatment, activities, behavior, and objects for the gender of the child. As newborns, girls are described as little, soft,

and pretty and boys as big, strong, and active, even when identical in size and activity level. The books families and teachers read to children and give to children to read depict boys in a larger range of occupations and as more active, competent, and adventurous, whereas girls play supporting roles and need help to overcome incompetence and fearfulness.

Some teachers and parents, either purposefully or unintentionally, reinforce the gender-based play preferences and biases of children and do little to counter them. Others give so much attention to combating gender stereotypes that it becomes the curriculum of the school and the home at the exclusion of other important content. We believe it is reasonable for teachers to take assertive steps to overcome and avoid gender stereotyping in the books and materials offered to girls and boys—to make certain that both males and females are depicted in a variety of family and occupational roles. The environment can be altered to encourage children to play with other than sex-typed materials. Boys are more attracted to dramatic play areas when the areas are expanded beyond the traditional home-kitchen scene. Girls may be encouraged into the block play area by integrating it with the dramatic play area. Teachers who practice ball skills with a small group of girls and get a group of boys involved in a cooking activity are taking small, important steps toward breaking down the gender stereotypes that limit the choices of males and females in our culture.

Sex Play

In a typical preschool sex and sex play often emerge as subjects of interest and concern. Children bring their interest in sexuality to your attention through their play and questions. Human beings are sensual and sexual from birth. They enjoy sensations that are pleasurable including being warm, dry, and fed and being rocked, hugged, and cuddled. It is in this context that first feelings of sexuality emerge and these are more than genital sensations.

Feelings and ideas about sexuality develop over time and begin with first experiences of being loved and held, of discovering one's own body, and by observing others. It's natural and normal for young children to be curious about their bodies and their sexuality. Children try out all their ideas about the world through play and it makes sense that they try to understand sex through play. Younger preschoolers play through sensory exploration and their sex play often involves simply looking and touching. The mode of play that is most common for four- and five-year-olds is fantasy, or "pretend," play. They try to figure out relationships in all their play. Their sex play is just a part of the exploration of social roles, but it is often more disturbing to adults than the sensory play of infants and toddlers. Children may try grown-up sexual roles. Four- and five-year-olds pretend to be fire fighters, cooks, and superheroes and similarly they try out sexual roles.

Because most adults have strong feelings about sexuality, you may find yourself, your co-workers, or children's parents reacting strongly to children's sex play. Children will not understand these strong reactions and may become confused, frightened, or feel ashamed.

Before sex play occurs there are many things you can do. You will want to use proper vocabulary to discuss body parts as you talk to children about the day-to-day life in the classroom so that you and the children have a comfortable vocabulary for talking about all aspects of their play. ("Put your hands on your ankles, on your back, on your spine, on your buttocks." "Yes, that doll has a penis, just like the boys in our class; he's a boy baby.") Communicate that bodies are beautiful and that people's feelings and bodies deserve to be cared for and respected. ("I love to see your strong arms stretching as you pump on the swing!" "Would you like me to rub your back to help you fall asleep?" "Gabriel is saying he doesn't want anyone to sit on his lap right now."

What should you do when children in your classroom are involved in sexual exploratory play? Talking openly and nonjudgmentally is best. Let children know that people have different feelings about bodies and privacy and that feelings change as people get older. "Little children wear diapers that must be changed by an adult and like to play in the water without any clothes on; older children use the bathroom alone and often want to wear a bathing suit." Similarly, schools may have different rules than homes so that everyone will feel comfortable at school. You will want to state the guideline that is appropriate to your school and community. ("At our school the children always wear clothes except during sprinkler play.") It is important to let children know what activities are not permissible in your program. Let them know that some activities are restricted because they can hurt (like putting a stick in your vagina or anus) and others are private and saved for private places and times (like taking a bath).

FINAL THOUGHTS

To develop, children need to play. The United Nations General Assembly, in November 1989, approved a convention on the rights of the child that put forth that every child in the world must have the right to play. Yet, we encounter children who are either too deprived or too affluent to have adequate play opportunities.

Over 12 million American children live in poverty and are vulnerable to stresses associated with inadequate shelter, food, health care, and child care. Many children are routinely traumatized by violence on the streets of our cities, in media presentations, and in their homes. Chil-

dren who live in deprived and threatening situations are likely to be deprived of play opportunities and to experience emotional upheaval throughout their growing years.

For the more affluent segment of our society we need to advocate for play as an inoculation against the pressures that are imposed on children. Children who are compelled to conform to adult standards of behavior, to excel academically at an early age, and to master skills associated with a developmental stage they have not yet entered are often being stressed to the limits of endurance. To them the play time they can "steal" from their busy schedule of dance lessons, soccer practice, birthday parties, and school may be all that keeps life from being intolerable. Optimal development requires challenges, but also requires relief from the burdensome responsibility we impose on some children. Play may save some children and other people from burnout at an early age (Elkind 1981).

The full realization of the learning potential of play ensures that you will value it in its own right and make fuller use of it in your teaching. In our enthusiasm to capitalize on play as a tool for promoting development we are in danger of losing sight of the exuberant, joyful, and nonsensical aspects of play. Let us value equally the risk-taking, crazy-acting, running-wild exhilaration of being able to scream at the top of your lungs, to laugh hysterically, and to run, fall, tumble, or roll in an uncontrolled way without external or internal restraint. The uninhibited quality of play behaviors distinguishes child from adult, play from nonplay. The restraint built into most adults is sometimes imposed on children and such children are a sad sight for an adult who appreciates the exuberance of play and who understands the power of play for leading us to a full realization of our human potential.

DISCUSSION QUESTIONS

1. Recall your favorite play activity from childhood. What did you enjoy about the activity? What do you remember about how your parents and teachers responded to your play? Did they encourage it? Discourage it?
2. Think about a classroom you have recently observed. Discuss the ways the children played. How did the teachers facilitate play? What seemed to be their attitudes toward play in their classroom? What seemed to be their position regarding war play, product- or media-related toys, sex play, and gender stereotyping?

PROJECTS

1. Write a letter to a group of parents who have been questioning you about why their children play so much in your classroom. Explain your rationale for making play an important part of your program.
2. Observe an early childhood classroom for a half day and report on the following:
   - The types of social play the children engage in.
   - The stages of play shown by children.
   - What the teachers attitudes toward and beliefs about play seem to be.
   - What the teachers do to facilitate play in their programs.
   - What the teachers' attitudes appear to be toward the issues of war play, toys based on media characters, sex play, and gender stereotyping in their classrooms.
3. Interview two teachers and report on their responses about the following subjects:
   - Their views of the role of play in their classroom and in the development of the children they teach.
   - What they do to facilitate play in their program.
   - How they handle the issues of war play, war toys, gender stereotyping, and sex play in their program.

BIBLIOGRAPHY

Bergen, D. ed. 1988. *Play as a Medium for Learning and Development: A Handbook of Theory and Practice.* Portsmouth, N.H.: Heinemann.

Bredekamp, S. 1987. *Developmentally Appropriate Practice in Early Childhood Programs Serving Children from Birth Through Age 8.* Expanded ed. Washington, D.C.: National Association for the Education of Young Children.

Bruner, J. S., A. Jolly, and K. Sylva. 1976. *Play: Its Role in Development and Evolution.* New York: Basic Books.

Caplan, F., and T. Caplan. 1973. *The Power of Play.* New York: Anchor Press/Doubleday.

Carlsson-Paige, N., and D. E. Levin. 1987. *The War Play Dilemma: Balancing Needs and Values in the Early Childhood Classroom.* New York: Teachers College Press.

Elkind, D. 1981. *The Hurried Child: Growing Up Too Fast Too Soon.* Menlo Park, Calif.: Addison-Wesley.

Johnson, J. E., J. F. Christie, and T. D. Yawkey. 1987. *Play and Early Childhood Development.* Glenview, Ill.: Scott, Foresman.

McKee, J. S. ed. 1986. *Play: Working Partner of Growth.* Wheaton, Md.: Association for Childhood Education International.

Monignan-Nourot, P., B. Scales, and J. Van Hoorn with M. Almy. 1987. *Looking at Children's Play: A Bridge Between Theory and Practice.* New York: Teachers College Press.

National Association for the Education of Young Children. 1990. NAEYC Position Statement on Media Violence in Children's Lives. *Young Children* 45(5): 18–21.

Parten, M. B. 1932. Social Participation Among Preschool Children. *Journal of Abnormal Psychology* 27(3): 243–69.

Piaget, J. 1962. *Play, Dreams and Imitation in Childhood.* New York: W. W. Norton.

Rogers, C. S., and J. K. Sawyers. 1988. *Play in the Lives of Children.* Washington, D.C.: National Association for the Education of Young Children.

Schickedanz, J. A., K. I. Schickedanz, and P.D. Forsyth. 1982. *Toward Understanding Children.* Boston and Toronto: Little, Brown.

Smilansky, S. 1968. *The Effects of Sociodramatic Play on Disadvantaged Pre-School Children.* New York: John Wiley & Sons.

Smilansky, S., and Shefatya, L. 1990. *Facilitating Play: A Medium for Promoting Cognitive, Socio-Emotional and Academic Development in Young Children.* Gaithersburg, Md: Psychosocial & Educational Publications.

CHAPTER SIX

Observation and Evaluation

You see, but you do not observe.
—*Arthur Conan Doyle*

Bring with you a heart that watches and receives.
—*Wordsworth*

This chapter is about observation and evaluation techniques as ways of learning about young children. Its primary focus is to help you to develop skill in observing. Guidelines are given for learning to write observations and for using observational data in your work with children. We also discuss a range of other ways that teachers can gather and analyze information to help them in making educational decisions

Children are ever-changing and endlessly intriguing. Those who are interested in learning more about children have devised many ways to study their growth and development. Methods for studying children range from informal observations conducted during the course of the school day to formal measures that are administered under controlled conditions to compare individual chil-

dren to large groups of their peers. All of these methods share the goal of helping us to provide better, more responsive, and more appropriate education.

Observation is your most basic technique for understanding children—the foundation for all the other ways that you will learn about them and improve your teaching. It is the most important way, especially because there are many things that children cannot express through spoken language but that can be inferred by watching them.

In the course of your daily work as a teacher, you will be called upon to gather information to help you in making appraisals of children's development. The information you gather will be used for a variety of purposes: to monitor the development and progress of individual children and to plan appropriate experiences for them; to learn more about problems and help to solve them; to collect data about children to share with parents at conferences; as a basis for choosing and evaluating equipment, materials, and curriculum; to aid in making decisions such as whether a child should be placed with older children or should move on to the next school experience.

The kind of evaluation techniques that you use will depend on what you need to know and for what purpose. Evaluation can be based on (1) informal observations of children, (2) formal, structured observational techniques developed to focus on aspects of the child that you want to know more about, or (3) standardized instruments for screening, assessment, and testing.

OBSERVATION

> Paul, a fragile-looking, curly haired, just turned 3-year-old, drags a laundry basket into the shade of a big tree. He sits down in the laundry basket and stretches his legs. "I fit! I'm three!" he says, holding up three fingers. Paul rocks his body and the basket back and forth, "I'm rocking the cradle. I'm rocking the cradle." He rocks and rocks until the basket tips and with a wide-eyed look of surprise he spills onto the ground. Paul stands up and smiles. He turns the basket over and hits it on the top several times listening to the hollow drumming sounds that his thumping makes. Then he lifts up the edge of the basket and crawls underneath. He crouches under the basket, peering out through the holes at the playground and announces, "I'm going to hatch the cradle." He stands up wearing the basket like a turtle's shell, "I hatched!"

The ability to observe—to "read" and understand children—is one of the most important and satisfying skills that a teacher of young children can develop. It will help you to know and understand individuals, plan more effectively, and evaluate your teaching. More importantly, observation is the magic window that enables you to see into the child. By watching Paul and his laundry basket with our hearts and minds, we learn about who he is, we know about how he is learning and growing, and we gain an empathy toward him that helps us to be his advocate and his friend.

Observation is the basis for much of the work that is done by teachers of young children, and it is used in some form in almost every chapter in this book. Teachers observe children, curriculum, and classroom environments. In a less structured, but no less important way, they also observe themselves, their values, their relationships, and their own feelings and reactions. When teachers apply what they know about observation to themselves, they gain greater self-awareness. It is difficult to be objective about yourself but as you watch your own behavior and interactions you can learn more about how you feel and respond in various situations, and realize the impact of your behavior on others.

Observation will provide you with information so you can respond effectively to the needs of a frightened or angry child, so you can intervene to resolve recurring problems between two children, so you know what equipment and materials are being used and how, and so you know what children are learning and experiencing each day. It also helps you to identify a child who needs more stimulation or a child who might be troubled, handicapped, or abused and needs help. Observation will help you to communicate about children to parents, teachers, administrators, and other professionals.

Learning to Observe

To observe is to take notice, to watch attentively, to focus on one particular part of a complex environment. It means perceiving both the whole picture and the significant detail. Learning to observe involves more than casual looking, and it is not nearly as easy as one might think. To make useful observations of children and class-

IN THE CLASSROOM: USES OF OBSERVATION

Through observation teachers develop:

- In-depth understanding of individual children—how they think, feel, and view the world; their interests, skills, characteristic responses; and areas of strength and weakness.
- Increased sensitivity to children in general—awareness of the range of development and a heightened awareness of the unique qualities of childhood and the world of children.
- Understanding of the kinds of social relationships among children and among children and adults, and how these can be facilitated in school.
- Awareness of the class environment, schedule, and program, how well these are meeting the needs of children and staff, and how they might be improved.
- Greater self-awareness.

rooms requires training and practice. You must be clear about why you are observing and be willing to gather information and impressions with a receptive eye and mind.

Observation consists of selecting a focus and watching attentively. The information you collect increases your understanding and gives you insight into the meaning of children's behavior and of the impact of classroom practice. Systematic recorded observations reveal trends and patterns in behavior. They enable you to increase your objectivity, because conclusions based on recorded observation can correct for misperceptions and biases that can occur when conclusions are based on recall and memory alone.

The consistent practice of observation in the classroom will help you develop *child sense*—a feeling for how individual children and groups of children are feeling and functioning. This deep understanding is based on a great deal of experience in observing individuals and groups of children over time. We know that observing can generate a sense of connectedness, greater understanding and hence empathy, caring, and concern.

The Observation Process

In order to observe more objectively and separate out feelings and reactions from what is actually seen, it is useful to divide the observations process into three components:

- Data gathering—what you see and hear.
- Interpreting—what you think it means.
- Acknowledging feelings and reactions—how it makes you feel.

Data Gathering

The first and most essential step in the observation process is to watch and listen carefully, to experience as completely as possible while attempting to suspend interpretation and evaluation. This involves consciously focusing while quieting the inner voice that usually adds a running commentary explaining and evaluating situations. An effective teacher of young children has the ability to wait and see what is really happening instead of drawing conclusions based on hurriedly gathered impressions. Such "intensive waiting" (Nyberg 1971, p. 168) requires that expectations be suspended and that you be receptive to what *is* really happening: behaviors, feelings, and patterns. It doesn't mean that you must become an impersonal machine, but it does require you to carefully separate what you see from what you might have wanted or feared to see.

To know what is actually taking place you must avoid value judgments and try to reduce the distortions that are the result of biases, defenses, or preconceptions. Objectivity is difficult because you are a participant in the life of the classroom that you observe, and you both influence the people in it and are influenced by them. If you are aware of your impact on the situation and its impact on you, you can work toward becoming a more objective observer.

It is also helpful to be aware of your characteristics as an observer. When you realize what you tend to focus on, you can also get an idea of what you characteristically ignore. As you increase the range of things that you attend to, you are also likely to improve your ability to write more detailed and comprehensive observations. We have our college students observe a bowl of goldfish. Each student chooses one fish to write about. Some students describe the minute detail of the fish's anatomy as a biologist might, some look at the fish in the context of its environment (bowl, sand, water, and other fish), and some describe the interactions among the fishes. Not only do students learn something about the features they tend to observe from this exercise, but they are surprised to find how different the observations of the same fish are and how much they attribute human feelings and motivations to them.

Millie Almy and Celia Genishi say of keen observers of children:

> They study facial expression, note the steady and the shifting look, the tightly or loosely held jaw and lips, the grimaces and the smiles. They hear not only words but tones, pitch, strain, hesitation, and pauses. They note body posture, slumping shoulders and puppet-on-a-string gestures, as contrasted with flowing, graceful

> movements and accurate, efficient coordination. They see all the details in relation to the settings where the behavior takes place. The clenched hands and intent frown seen in the reading period are different from the freedom and joie de vivre of the playground. These finer details, this attention to its quality, provide clues to the meaning of behavior. (Almy and Genishi 1979, pp. 39–40)

As Almy and Genishi suggest, a good observer goes far beyond the obvious. The more teachers know about children the more differentiated and refined their observations become. They focus on features of a child's body, build, posture, tone of voice, appearance, grooming, ways of moving and manipulating objects, mood, interactions with others, and many other attributes. Keen observers know that children communicate a great deal through their bodies—facial expression; body tension; the language of hands, fingers, and eyebrows; the tilt of a head or shoulder—as much as through their spoken words and obvious actions.

Interpreting

The second basic step in the classroom observation process is to make interpretations based on what you have seen and heard. Although behavior is observable and can be described more or less accurately, the sources of behavior are not visible and may only be inferred. You need to observe closely and then seek the relationship between the observed behavior and its unobservable cause. You can never truly know why a child behaves as he or she does, but you will make decisions based on your assumptions about children's behavior every day. It is important that you develop skill in making interpretations based on *what you actually observed.*

Interpreting a child's behavior is difficult because so many factors—stage of development, health, culture, and individual experience—combine in complex ways to determine how an individual acts in a given situation. The

same behavior can mean very different things in different children. A piercing scream from Lisa Marie means that she's seriously hurt; the same type of scream from Kerri means anger or frustration.

Individual observers may interpret the same behavior or incident in dissimilar ways. For example, several of our college students noticed a little girl who was lying in a large cement pipe in the yard of a preschool they were visiting. One thought that she was withdrawn and antisocial; another was convinced that she was lonely, unhappy, and in need of comforting; and the third felt that she was just taking a few moments for quiet contemplation. Obviously they needed more information about the child and the events that preceded their observation to make accurate and meaningful interpretations.

When you need to communicate information you have gathered about a child to another person, you will add your interpretations to descriptive data to give a more complete picture of the child or situation. Watching a little longer after you have come to a conclusion is never amiss—the extra information may change your mind. Since two people viewing the same child or incident will often have different perceptions, it is useful to be tentative in your interpretations. It is also helpful to discuss your interpretations with someone else. Becoming aware of different perspectives can help you to realize how difficult it is to interpret accurately.

Acknowledging Feelings and Reactions

The third step in the observation process is to notice and acknowledge your feelings and reactions separately from more objective data and interpretation. You then have the opportunity to reflect on your personal reactions without distorting the observation. These feelings and reactions don't belong in a file on the child or in the written information that you share with the child's family or other professionals. They are a useful part of your training in learning to observe. In the beginning, deliberately take time to note your feelings and reactions. Later, in many cases, it will be enough to take note of them and correct for any biases they might create.

Writing Observations

Just watching carefully will often be enough to give you helpful information about a child or a situation. At other times you will need to write

your observations to have a permanent record for yourself or to share with co-teachers, parents, or other professionals. Learning to write clear, concise, meaningful observations takes time, commitment, and practice.

As a classroom teacher you will usually have to observe while you are in action in the classroom, or you may try to find a few brief moments to get a more detached look at a child or situation. As a college student you should have many opportunities to really focus on a child or a group in order to develop your observation skills. You will need to learn to observe unobtrusively. Enter the group quietly and sit at children's eye level, close enough to see and hear but not so close that you distract the children with your presence. Don't get involved while you are observing unless it is necessary to protect a child. Briefly answer children's questions about who you are and what you are doing ("I am learning about what children do in your classroom.") and try not to get involved in extended conversations. Take time just to watch; you will have other opportunities to get involved.

Description

When you write an observation, it is important to clearly separate objective data (description) and interpretation. Good description uses clear language and communicates enough information to convey the uniqueness of the subject of the observation. To retain the clarity of your impressions, you may find it useful to take notes inconspicuously while you are in the classroom observing or to write soon after the observation is made. Some teachers carry a small notebook and pencil in a big pocket of an apron or leave a box with file cards in a convenient corner of the classroom so that they can easily jot down some notes in the course of their work.

Following are guidelines for writing observations of children. At first your writing may be awkward and you may have difficulty deciding how much to record. The following suggestions have helped our college students develop skill in writing child observations. To capture the vitality of the situation your descriptions should report what you see as you see it happening in the present tense.

If you are writing for someone unfamiliar with your setting, begin with the context for the observation: where you are (the school, location, indoors or outdoors, area of the classroom) and who and what you are observing (an individual child, a group of children, or a specific interaction). If the reader is not familiar with the child, you will want to give a brief description next. If your reader is familiar with the child and the setting, you will simply note who you are observing, where, the date, and the time of your observation.

The first thing to do in writing an observation is to note basic physical attributes that will help the reader to visualize the child: age, sex, size, build, facial features, coloring, distinguishing markings. A plain physical description sets the stage but gives little sense of the distinctiveness of a child. For example: "She is an Oriental girl, approximately four years of age, shorter than her peers. She has a slight build, oval face, and brown hair and eyes." Your observation will communicate more if you elaborate on the basic physical description with some of the child's unique personal qualities: body stance, way of moving, facial expression, gestures, tone of voice. This conveys a better picture of the child as a unique individual. It will take practice to find a balance of vivid imagery and objectivity. The following version conveys a much more vivid sense of the child whose physical attributes were described above: "She has black eyebrows and lashes, brown hair, almond-shaped eyes, a fair, smooth complexion, pouting lips, and a small up-turned nose. She is slim and almost fragile looking and strolls from activity to activity with small, light steps, her eyes alert and her head turning occasionally from side to side. Her arms hang slightly away from her body and swing with the rhythm of her stroll."

The next step is to describe what happens—the child's activities and interactions. The addition of expressive detail, including body language, and interactions with people and with materials communicates more than a bare bones description. To capture a full picture be sure to look at a child in a variety of situations—characteristic choice of activities, things that he or she seems to enjoy or avoid, arrival, behavior at meals, transitions, and nap times.

The language used in recording should capture the subtleties and complexities of children's behavior. Carefully chosen words convey the essence of the person and situation and are an important part of writing vivid descriptions. Adverbs and adjectives enhance our ability to visualize the subject of the observation: "He rushes eagerly from the block area to the easels" instead of "He walks very fast." In choosing modifiers avoid words that have a strong emotional impact or bias built into them. Describe what a child *does* instead of giving your views on what he or she *is*. Opinions of children such as pretty, cute, bright, attractive, good, messy, slow, or naughty are best avoided in description and interpretation as these are value judgments. Describing a child in these terms tells more about the values of the observer than the nature of the child. Since the observations you write may be shared with others, you have the responsibility to convey useful information that is as free as possible from personal bias or unsubstantiated evaluations.

A good description is specific, but it does not give so much detail that the point is lost. Broad general statements do not convey much information and are not very effective in capturing important qualities of the child or interaction. For example, the statement that "John is stringing beads" does not tell the reader very much. We have a better picture of the child and situation when the observer tells us, "John has an intent look on his face, his tongue protrudes slightly from between his teeth, and it appears that all of his concentration is focused on the beads." Additional details such as when John worked with the beads, how long he worked, how he worked, who he worked with, and the feelings he projected as he worked might also increase the reader's ability to understand the child and the situation.

Writing Interpretations Based on Description

Interpretations based on written descriptions make it possible for others to read what you have written and decide whether or not they agree with your conclusions. For this reason, it is vital that your interpretations be based on descriptive data. Others can then offer their insight and you benefit from the collective experience of all who review your observation. Descriptions of the same child or incident written by different observers can be helpful because each of us tends to notice different

things. It is also eye opening to have several individuals interpret the same written description of a situation. We encourage our students to make liberal use of the words *might* and *seems to* in their written interpretations to underscore the tentative nature of conclusions about children's needs, feelings, and motivation.

We use the format shown in Table 6.1 to help our students learn to write interpretation based on data. We recommend no less than a half hour for each observation of a child. During the actual observation, students use the left column to record what they see. As soon after observing as possible, they write some tentative interpretations and note any feelings or other impressions in the right column.

With this format shown in Table 6.1, you are able to review your description, add other possible interpretations, and decide if you have enough data to substantiate your conclusions. If not, you

TABLE 6.1
Format for Writing Interpretation Based on Data

Description	Interpretation/Feelings
Joshua enters the classroom well ahead of his father and makes a beeline for the block corner where John and Thomas have a large unit block structure well in progress. J. drops his lunch box in the middle of the rug and begins issuing directions—"Make it go this way"—as he takes a block from Thomas and begins a second wall at a right angle to the first. "Get more of the big kind," J. says to John.	Excitement at being in school with his friends Enters activity quickly A little bossy? Impulsive?
The two quickly join in and proceed with J.'s plan as J.'s father approaches, observes a few moments, and then interrupts to tell J. to take his lunch box to his cubby.	Accepted as a leader among his peers?
J. acknowledges the request with an impatient glance and says, "Just a minute Dad," and continues to direct the building with even more vigor and hurriedness.	Expects to have a say in what happens to him
Father says, "You can come back to the blocks after you've. . ." J. grimaces and scrambles over the wall, grabs the lunch box, runs to his cubby, and deposits it inside. It falls to the floor as he turns to rush back to the blocks.	Follows through on request—retains focus on self-identified task
Father intercepts him halfway and points him back to his cubby and pushes him gently from behind. J. stops, looks up at Father, and laughs as if sharing a joke.	Sense of humor, trust in father

can observe the child in other settings to see if the behaviors are repeated and characteristic or simply the outcome of a particular situation.

Your written summary should be based on several observations, state your conclusions concisely, and cite the descriptive data on which they are based. A teacher who has made several more observations of Joshua might write the following: "Joshua appears to be a leader and to be well respected by the other boys. Although his behavior can appear 'bossy,' John and Thomas accept his directives and do not seem upset by, or resistant to, his stepping into their work. Joshua is enthusiastic about learning, will stay with a task for a long time, and dislikes being diverted from it. He will cooperate with adults if he has warning and a little encouragement and if they respect his purposes."

Observational Methods of Child Study

To develop more awareness of a child or of a situation it may be sufficient to simply take time to stop and observe and then mentally note what is going on. If your goal is to learn about a child for a particular purpose, such as referral to a program or service, then some form of systematic data gathering is called for. Anecdotal records, time samples, event samples, checklists, and case studies are *informal* observational methods that involve teacher observations of children in the course of their daily classroom activities. They differ in the degree to which they are systematized.

The particular method you choose depends on what you want to know about and how you think you might best find it out. If you understand what information each can give you and think carefully about the purpose of the observation, you will be able to select an approach that will contribute to your teaching.

A structured observational technique can help to confirm a hypothesis or gather more information about something you have noticed. For example, you may use a time sample to determine what percentage of the time a seemingly withdrawn child is actually spending in passive activity and how much time the child is more actively involved.

Observational techniques have some common characteristics. They begin with a focus (a particular child, behavior, interaction, classroom practice, material) and a specific attribute that is being observed (how often a behavior occurs, what precipitates it). Many are conducted within a set time frame, which may be very short (every minute for fifteen-minute periods) or which may be longer (any time a behavior occurs during a week).

Anecdotal Records

The most frequently used form of observation is the anecdotal record, a written, narrative description of a child's behavior and interactions in the course of the school day. Anecdotal records are essential tools of teachers of young children. It is important to learn to write them well. You will find that they help you meet the needs of the children you teach.

In writing an anecdotal record, you will first think about some of the things that are important to learn about the child and then write them, or anything else that occurs, whenever the time permits. For example:

- Behavior or interactions that seem typical for the child.

- Behavior or interactions that seem atypical for the child.
- Achievement of a developmental milestone, the first time the child masters a new skill or engages in a new activity.
- Incidents and interactions that convey the nature of the child's social relationships and emotional reactions in the school setting.
- Behavior or interactions relating to an area of special concern you or the child's parents have.

We have used a *sharing notebook* to keep anecdotal records. Each child in our class had a notebook and the teacher and the child's parents were invited to share observations and experiences in it.

It is valuable to write anecdotal notes for all of the children in your classroom on a regular basis. Anecdotal records can also be made with special emphasis on children about whom you have questions or concerns and those children who are "invisible"—so inconspicuous that they tend to be forgotten. If it is possible, take some notes each day. They may be just key words or fragments of information with details that you fill in later. These records become part of your collection of information about each child and need to be filed with all other confidential records.

Time Samples

A time sample tracks a child's behavior at regular intervals. It is not a record of everything that happens. A teacher who uses this technique attempts to ascertain systematically how often a particular behavior (hitting, fantasy play, thumb sucking) is actually occuring. A time sample will be conducted enough times to obtain a good idea of the frequency of the behavior—a minimum of three are needed as the basis for any interpretation. You may want to sample weeks or months later if you think that there has been a change.

To collect a time sample divide the total observation time into smaller segments. A sim-

ple checklist or code may be devised to help you quickly record what type of behavior is occurring. For example, *R* may stand for rejects interaction and *I* may stand for initiates interaction (see Figure 6.1). During a time sample, you will note what behavior is occurring at precise intervals. The behavior is recorded and the results are analyzed. The information can be used as a basis for drawing conclusions about the frequency and relative importance of particular behaviors.

We once designed a time sample to test our belief that a child named Danny was initiating an excessive number of conflicts with others. Several staff members felt that they spent a great deal of time each day intervening in the conflicts that he provoked. Another teacher had difficulty understanding this because she perceived Danny as a positive and cooperative person. The time sample was very simple. We agreed to track how frequently Danny and the two friends with whom he was often in conflict actually initiated interaction and whether it was positive or negative. The outcome of three fifteen-minute time samples on each child uncovered that Danny had many more positive than negative interactions and that this was also true of his friends. We discovered, however, that Danny initiated interactions three times more frequently than his two playmates. This helped explain our different perceptions of Danny and helped us to understand why we felt taxed by our frequent interventions. Our increased understanding helped us to become more trusting and to allow him more opportunity to handle interpersonal problems on his own.

Event Samples

An event sample is used when teachers want to understand more about a particular behavior. It is closely related to time sampling but is employed when a behavior tends to occur in a particular setting rather than during a predictable time period. In an event sample, the observer watches for a particular behavior or

Time Sample 1

A fifteen-minute record sampled once every minute during choice time indoors.

Child: Mary Ann

Time: _____   Date: _____

Activity	solitary observation	solitary play	cooperative play	fighting/arguing
	√√√√√	√√√√√√	√√	√√

Time Sample 2

Code: I = initiates, S = solitary, R = rejects, A = accepts, C = child, T = Teacher, x = continues

Child: Michael

Time: _____   Date: _____

9:30 S	9:35 x	9:40 x
9:31 x	9:36 S	9:41 AT
9:32 x	9:37 IC	9:42 AC
9:33 RC	9:38 RC	9:43 x
9:34 S	9:39 S	9:44 x

FIGURE 6.1
Two examples of time samples

interaction and then records exactly what preceded the event, what happened during the event, and what the consequences of the event were. The goal is to assist in solving the child's problem (Wortham 1990) Like an anecdotal record, this type of observation relies on the skill of the observer in making detailed descriptions. For example, if you think a child has been engaging in a lot of aggressive behavior, you may want to write a description of what precedes every aggressive act, exactly what happens, and what follows the behavior. You may discover that the behavior is only happening before lunch or nap or at the end of the day, or is triggered by interaction with one child or group of children. This type of observation can help you to better understand the nature of a child's behavior.

Teacher-Developed Checklists

Teachers can create checklists to help them to gather information: which children have acquired a particular skill or concept, how often a child engages in a particular behavior, children's play preferences, or how materials and equipment in the classroom are being used. These are a useful, relatively simple way to find out what children are doing or not doing and what is working in the classroom. A checklist can also provide an informal development profile of each child in the class. Figure 6.2 is a checklist of skills in different developmental areas that we devel-

IN THE CLASSROOM: DEVELOPMENTAL CHECKLIST

Child's Name _____

Dates of Attendance _____

Teacher's Name _____

Code: N = never   R = rarely   S = sometimes   O = often   A = always

Classroom activities preferred

_____ Unit blocks
_____ Hollow blocks
_____ Toys and games
_____ Dramatic play
_____ Sensory activities
_____ Library area
_____ Math/Science area
_____ Writing center
_____ Art media

Comments

Outside activities preferred

_____ Climbing
_____ Swinging
_____ Trikes/wagons
_____ Social play
_____ Investigation
_____ Sand/water

Comments

Characteristics during group activities

Circle Time:
_____ Interested/attentive
_____ Stays focused
_____ Participates
_____ Waits turn

Discussions:
_____ Understands
_____ Interested/attentive
_____ Stays focused
_____ Waits turn
_____ Participates

Group activities enjoyed:
_____ Music/movement
_____ Listening to stories
_____ Story playing
_____ Trips

Comments

Health and routines

_____ Separates easily
_____ Self-sufficient in toileting
_____ Manages hygiene routines (hand washing, nose blowing, etc.)

Snack and lunch:
_____ Eats and enjoys
_____ Self-sufficient
_____ Uses social skills
_____ Cleans up

Nap:
_____ Rests quietly
_____ Sleeps
_____ Handles own mat, etc.

Comments

FIGURE 6.2
Checklist for developmental skills

Social and emotional development

_____ Interested in new things

_____ Involved in play with others

_____ Initiates constructive choice

_____ Can work independently

_____ Has positive self-concept

_____ Works in a group

_____ Realistically evaluates own abilities

_____ Initiates play with others

_____ Shows self-control

_____ Shares and takes turns

_____ Expresses feelings

_____ Takes leader role

_____ Accepts limits

_____ Takes follower role

_____ Can problem-solve

_____ Defends own rights

_____ Is persistent

_____ Accepts rights and needs of others

_____ Shows satisfaction in play

_____ Accepted by group

_____ Is generally happy

_____ Has special friends

Comments

Physical development

Large motor:

_____ Interested/active

_____ Shows confidence

_____ Shows reasonable caution

_____ Shows endurance/stamina

_____ Demonstrates flexibility, coordination and strength

Demonstrates these skills:

_____ Runs   _____ Swings

_____ Climbs   _____ Hops

_____ Balances   _____ Gallops

_____ Jumps   _____ Skips

Comments

Small motor:

_____ Interested/participates

_____ Has strength

_____ Shows coordination

Demonstrates these skills:

_____ Builds with manipulative toys

_____ Uses dough and clay with ease

_____ Cuts with scissors

_____ Can cut out forms

_____ Uses pens, pencils with pincer grip

_____ Can make representational forms and letters

Comments

IN THE CLASSROOM: SELECTING AN INFORMAL OBSERVATIONAL METHOD

In order to	Use
Record a behavior or interaction or the achievement of a milestone	Anecdotal record
Ascertain how often a type of behavior occurs	Time sample
Understand why or when a particular behavior occurs	Event sample
Gather information about children's play preferences, individual progress, how materials and equipment are being used	Teacher-developed checklists

oped for a group of four-year-olds to help in assessing the developmental progress of individual children and for individualizing the program.

Case Studies

Periodically you will need to conduct a case study—an intensive analysis of a child in order to explore a problem in some depth with members of your staff, to share with a specialist, to make a referral for special services, or to use as a guide for discussion in a parent conference. As a college student, you are likely to be required to write a case study to help you learn to pull together all of your observations into a comprehensive picture of a child.

A case study can include anecdotal and structured observations collected over a period of time in a variety of settings by you or other staff members, a review of health and other records, data from conversations with parents, assessment data from standardized instruments (described in the next section), samples of the child's work, and reports of discussions with other adults who have worked with the child.

The case study weaves a rich tapestry of a child's life. From the data collected you will seek deeper understanding of feelings and behavior,

the appropriate next steps in the classroom, and other needed actions such as consultation with parents and referral for services.

STANDARDIZED EVALUATION PROCEDURES

In the past, most evaluation of children in early childhood programs was based on teachers' observations. Today more emphasis is being placed on *formal* evaluation methods, even though many early childhood educators are concerned that this may not be appropriate for young children.

A standardized instrument has a clearly defined purpose. Each item has been carefully studied. Two kinds of data are used to establish the dependability of these instruments: *validity,* or accuracy, the degree to which it measures what it claims to measure; and *reliability,* or consistency, how often identical results can be obtained with the same instrument. Standardized evaluation procedures are either *norm referenced,* comparing an individual child's performance on the instrument with that of an external norm established by administering the instrument to a large sample of children; or *criterion referenced,* relating the child's performance to a standard of achievement but not comparing the child to a reference group.

Evaluation instruments are standardized on selected groups of children. They may not be as useful a measure for other groups of children with different cultures and different experiences. Traits that are related to culture or experience may seem to indicate a developmental problem where none exists. For example, a test used in Hawaii asked children to respond to questions relating to snowsuits, mittens, and snow shovels; their "incorrect" responses were not due to developmental delay but to lack of experience with the items. This test was subsequently revised to be valid in a tropical setting.

An instrument also reflects the values of the people who created it—what they believe is worthwhile for a child of a particular age to know, to do, or to have experienced. If you are ever called upon to evaluate a standardized instrument, you will want to determine if it is a good fit for your school and your group of children.

In recent years there has been a dramatic increase in the use of standardized evaluation procedures in programs for young children. Standardized evaluation procedures that are commonly used in early childhood programs include:

- *Screening:* a brief evaluation designed to identify children who may need further evaluation and educational intervention.
- *Assessment:* in-depth evaluation of what a child actually can do.
- *Readiness* and *achievement tests:* measures that determine readiness to benefit from a specific program or curriculum or determine level of school achievement.

Screening

Screening is a relatively fast and efficient way to initially evaluate children for a variety of kinds of problems. Every child is screened, in some way,

beginning at birth. The newborn is observed for obvious defects. Simple screening such as observation and testing of heart rate, muscle tone, and respiration occurs in the first few minutes after birth. As children grow and develop, they encounter other forms of screening in the course of regular medical care.

Another important kind of screening occurs in school settings for the purpose of identifying children who might have developmental delays or disabling conditions. The goal is to identify children who may need further evaluation so that specialized services can be provided as early as possible.

Appropriate screening can bring about remarkable improvements in children's lives. Generations of children entering the Head Start program have been screened: those with hearing losses have discovered a new world of sound, those with visual impairments have been given the gift of good sight, and those with other medical conditions have had them treated. Some children have been identified by the screening as at risk for learning problems, have been evaluated, and have received special services to help them overcome problems and enter school able to keep up with their peers.

Screening instruments are relatively short, have few items, look at a number of developmental areas, and can be administered and interpreted by trained professionals or volunteers. Screening identifies children who need to be looked at more carefully. A child should *never* be labeled on the basis of screening, because screening *cannot* predict future success or failure, prescribe specific treatment or curriculum, or diagnose handicapping conditions. Even if no children with problems or delays are identified, information from screening can help you to understand the range of development of the children in your care.

Commonly used screening instruments include *Early Screening Inventory* (Meisels and Wiske), the *McCarthy Screening Test* (McCarthy), *Developmental Indicators for the Assessment of*

Learning—DIAL (Childcraft Educational Corporation), the *Minneapolis Preschool Screening Test* (Lichtenstein), and the *Denver Developmental Screening Test* (LADOCA Project Publishing Foundation, Inc.).

Screening services vary from community to community and from state to state. Many have *Childfind* programs to make parents and other adults aware of the importance of early identification. Some communities provide screening when children first enter kindergarten or first grade. As an early childhood educator you may participate in choosing or administering a screening instrument and be involved in follow-up. If formal screening is not available in your school or community, informal screening through sensitive observation can also identify children who need further evaluation.

Children who are identified through screening as being at risk may be referred to an interdisciplinary diagnostic team that includes a physician, psychologist, speech, hearing, or physical therapists, and classroom teacher. The team will evaluate whether or not a serious problem exists, what it seems to be (diagnosis), and the kind of placement and services that would be most appropriate (treatment). Chapter 15, Working with Children with Special Needs, provides more information on the referral process. Sometimes screening will indicate problems that are not severe enough to warrant special services through the schools but that do need to be acted upon by the child's family. In these cases, teachers should inform parents that the child needs to be evaluated and follow up with the family to assure that the child receives the needed service.

Choosing a Screening Instrument

No method of screening is foolproof. Some children with developmental delays will remain undetected, whereas others who have no serious delays will be identified as needing further evaluation. One criterion for choosing a screening instrument is how often children are missed or falsely identified. Be very careful in reporting screening results because false identification may label children and worry families unnecessarily.

Good screening instruments are valid and reliable and focus on performance in a wide range of developmental areas (speech, understanding of language, affect, perception, large- and fine-motor skills). They are more likely to appropriately identify children if they use the language or dialect of the community: children not tested in their first language will not reflect their true abilities. Similarly, they should be adaptable to the experience and cultural background of the children. Good screening instruments also involve information from parents who know the child and have important information to contribute.

Assessment

Assessment is a multifaceted procedure for appraising children's skills. It helps you learn about children's actual functioning in the classroom by identifying patterns of strengths and weaknesses. Assessment instruments give a profile of a child's abilities in a variety of tasks and settings. They are criterion referenced; that is, they reflect a child's degree of mastery over a skill or sequence of skills. Assessments are not meant to label children, but rather to give teachers information so that they can design appropriate experiences for individual children and groups.

Commonly used assessments include the *Brigance Diagnostic Inventory of Early Development* (Curriculum Associates), *Learning Accomplishment Profile—LAP* (Kaplan School Supply), *Portage Guide to Early Education* (Portage Project, Portage, Wisc.), *Illinois Test of Psycholinguistic Ability—ITPA* (University of Illinois Press), *Peabody Picture Vocabulary Test—PPVT* (American Guidance Service), and the *Cognitive Skills Assessment Battery* (Teachers College Press).

An assessment instrument is usually administered, interpreted, and used by teachers and other school personnel such as speech-language specialists. It may take weeks or even months to completely administer an assessment in a number of skill areas. In some settings assessment may be a process that continues throughout the school year. Teachers may administer it early in the year to identify skills the child already has and then design experiences and activities to help the child to move to the next step. The child may be assessed again later in the year and the process repeated. Results may help you discuss program goals and content. They are a part of the information you will share with parents.

Classroom assessments often include guidelines for lessons and materials that are designed to develop specific skills. Although these may provide good ideas, they should be used in the context of activities that are meaningful to children. Teachers should never teach assessment items in isolation or use them as the basis for curriculum.

Classroom assessment may also serve a screening purpose, especially if no other screening has been done. Results can give an indication that a child may have a problem. A very general guideline is that if there is a six-month lag in language or a one-year delay in any other area, the child should be watched carefully and receive special attention in the area of the deficit. If the delay is greater, the child may need a diagnostic evaluation.

Choosing an Assessment Instrument

Like screening instruments, assessments only measure what can be observed and what their authors believe to be important. They may not assess what you or your colleagues value. There is debate among early childhood educators concerning whether or not it is possible to test children for the complex range of skills that we attempt to develop in early childhood programs. If you feel that the use of an assessment instrument is appropriate for your program, be aware of the limitations of the instrument and continue to use your own informal observations to create a more comprehensive picture of a child.

When you choose a classroom assessment, it is important to consider the use you wish to make of the results. With your purpose in mind, you can select an instrument that will suit your needs and the needs of the children in your classroom. If you use information from classroom assessments in the design of your program, then the day-to-day reality of life in your classroom will be tied to that assessment. Used well, this can help you to create a program that is developmentally appropriate and responsive to the needs of individuals. Used incorrectly, children may be required to learn items from the assessment in isolation and school may turn into drudgery for them.

Assessment can give you information that will be helpful in planning for children. Good assessment instruments have goals for children that are similar to or compatible with the goals of your program. They provide guidelines for use and can be easily administered and interpreted by school personnel—criteria for success are clearly spelled out. They can be used with the language or dialect of the school's population and can be adapted to reflect the culture and typical experience of its children. Good assessments involve age-appropriate responses and timing (manipulative and verbal rather than written responses and short testing periods followed by rest intervals).

Readiness and Achievement Tests

In some early childhood programs standardized tests are used to evaluate children. Readiness and achievement tests involve examining children (individually or in groups) to assess their capability and achievement and to make judgments regarding their performance based on the performance of others.

Readiness tests focus on existing levels of skills, performance, and knowledge. They are used to assess the child's ability to profit from a particular program of instruction and their proper purpose is to facilitate program planning. *Achievement tests* measure what a child has actually learned—the extent to which he or she has acquired information or mastered identified skills that have been taught. Achievement tests should be used to determine the effectiveness of instruction.

Readiness tests that are commonly used in early childhood programs include the *Metropolitan Readiness Test* (Harcourt Brace Jovanovich) and the *Gesell School Readiness Test* (Programs for Education Publishers). Achievement tests include the *Peabody Individual Achievement Test* (American Guidance Service), the *Wide Range Achievement Test* (Jastak Associates) and

the *Boehm Test of Basic Concepts* (Psychological Corp.).

Clarity of purpose, a clear manual with adequate information about standardization procedures, reliability and validity, clear directions, and appropriateness to the group of children to be tested should all be considered in selecting a standardized test.

Issues in Standardized Testing

At present, standardized testing in early childhood programs is being heatedly debated. Those who advocate the use of these tests maintain that they allow for the comparison of children's test scores with those of a representative group who have taken the same test. They believe that

having comparative data and a national frame of reference is helpful in assessing the effectiveness of instruction and in making decisions about admissions and placements. They also claim that data from standardized tests are helpful in justifying programs and proving accountability to funding sources.

Critics of standardized testing, including a growing number of early childhood and other educators (Cryan 1986; Kamii 1990; Wortham 1990), raise many issues and concerns. Some of the most frequently cited are listed here:

- Test results may not be valid and reliable because it is so difficult to administer tests to young children—they may be beyond children's developmental capabilities or the children's behavior may be unduly influenced by mood or by the test situation.
- Tests measure a narrow range of objectives, mostly cognitive and language abilities, and miss important objectives of early childhood education like creativity, problem solving, and social competence.
- Tests do not reflect current theory and research on how children learn.
- Tests are culturally and economically biased.
- Tests are often inappropriately administered and interpreted.
- Teachers who want children to do well on tests may introduce skills too early or alter their curriculum and "teach to the test," resulting in teaching methods and content that are inappropriate for young children.
- Tests are often used for purposes for which they were not intended. For example, readiness tests are being used to identify children who need special services.
- Test results are used more often to pass judgment (sometimes resulting in labeling of children) than for improving classroom practice.
- Test results are being misapplied and used to keep children out of school, retain them in the same grade for a second year, place them in remedial classes, or make unwarranted placements in special education classrooms.

The NAEYC has developed a position statement to address these issues and to help ensure that testing is used appropriately:

> NAEYC believes that the most important consideration in evaluating and using standardized tests is the *utility criterion:* The purpose of testing must be to improve services for children and to ensure that children benefit from their educational experiences. Decisions about testing and assessment instruments must be based on the usefulness of the assessment procedure for improving services to children and improving outcomes for children. (NAEYC 1988, p. 44)

The NAEYC offers the following guidelines for decisions regarding testing in early childhood settings:

- All standardized tests used in early childhood programs must be reliable and valid according to technical standards of test development.
- Decisions that have a major impact on children such as enrollment, retention, or assignment to remedial or special classes should be based on multiple sources of information and should never be based on a single test score.
- It is the professional responsibility of administrators and teachers to critically evaluate, carefully select, and use standardized tests only for the purposes for which they are intended and for which data exist demonstrating the test's validity.
- It is the professional responsibility of administrators and teachers to be knowledgeable about testing and to interpret test results accurately and cautiously to parents, school personnel, and the media (NAEYC 1988, pp. 44–45).

Administering Tests to Young Children

Testing young children has a number of inherent difficulties. Children are unfamiliar with test taking, they cannot read and write or are just developing these skills, and they may have a problem paying attention for the length of time required to take the test. Moreover, the performance of a young child on any one occasion is subject to extreme variability and can be greatly influenced by the events of the day, immediate surroundings, health, feelings, and relationship with the person giving the test. Tests should be given only by people who are knowledgeable about child development, who are qualified to administer the test, and who are skilled at establishing rapport with children.

The way a test is administered can also have an influence on the validity of its results. We observed a situation in which entering kindergarteners were given a screening test as they began school in the fall. The test was conducted in the school cafeteria—a forbidding place even for a child who is familiar with it. Each part of the test was given at a different station and by a different person. The testing conditions led us to wonder if the results obtained in this situation were truly indicative of the children's abilities.

If you find yourself administering a standardized test (it is most likely to be an assessment that will be administered to individual children), the following suggestions may be helpful in making it a happier experience for everyone involved. The first thing that you will want to do is to take enough time to build rapport. This will be much easier if you have some prior relationship with the child or children. If you do not know a child well or he or she is fearful, it may be helpful to invite a parent into the test setting. If a child is uncomfortable or unfamiliar with the procedures, you can give him or her some time to explore the materials before testing begins.

Begin as soon as you feel the child is comfortable in the testing situation. Make sure that you know the procedures and that all of the materials are ready and easily accessible. Keep transitions short and verbal directions short, simple, and clear. Let a nonverbal child be actively involved in a task. Break up the sitting

and attending time by alternating active and sit-down tasks. If possible, change physical space (move from table to floor). If the child does not get comfortable or refuses to participate in spite of your best efforts, reschedule the test for another time (adapted from Bailie et al. 1980, pp. 48–57).

FINAL THOUGHTS

There are advantages and disadvantages and appropriate uses and potential abuses of each of the approaches described in this chapter. Observational methods are invaluable in helping teachers to increase their sensitivity and to make sound educational decisions based on in-depth knowledge of children. They are useful because they are simple, flexible, and adaptable to a wide range of situations. Also, when teachers devise their own observational methods, they can evaluate what they are interested in and concerned about. Observation may need to be supplemented by other forms of data, but it is always the best beginning point for learning about children.

When the primary purpose of evaluation is to identify developmental problems, to assess achievement, to compare the individual to a large group of peers, or to gather information about children's progress in a systematic way, then standardized evaluation measures may be called for. Properly chosen and administered, screening instruments can point to children whose problems might not otherwise be discovered until they were having serious problems in school. We believe that all children should be screened appropriately for health and learning problems.

Unfortunately, standardized testing is too often used at present to determine which children fit existing programs and to exclude those who do not "make the grade," rather than to study children and make educational programs responsive to their needs and developmental stage.

No one instrument or occasion will disclose everything you need to know about a child. Early childhood educators need to be aware of the many different ways of gathering information, to know the advantages and disadvantages of each type, and to remain sensitive and flexible in their approach to evaluation.

DISCUSSION QUESTIONS

1. Why is it important for teachers of young children to know about screening, classroom assessments, and readiness and achievement tests? What experiences did you have as a child or teacher with these forms of assessment? Do you think that these instruments were used for the benefit of children? What are your feelings about them?
2. Think about the programs you have observed or worked in. How were observations of children made and used? What other kinds of evaluations were used? What reactions do you have to what you observed?

PROJECTS

1. Observe a child for a period of at least half an hour and describe:
   • The physical attributes of the child.
   • Some of the child's unique qualities.
   • The activities and interactions the child engaged in during the period of the observation.
   • Your inferences regarding what the child might have been thinking, feeling, and doing.
   • Any strong feelings and reactions elicited in you by the observation.
2. Collect three half-hour anecdotal records on a child of your choice using the format in Table 6.1. Write a summary of your impressions based on your observations.
3. Using a commercially prepared assessment instrument, assess a child in one developmental area. Describe the experience and answer the following questions: What does the assessment tell you about the child? What doesn't it tell you that you might want or need to know? To what extent were the assessment results consistent or not consistent with your observations of the child? What does this experience suggest to you about the possible advantages or disadvantages of using commercial instruments?
4. Write a "portrait of a child" based on extensive anecdotal observations over time of one child. Include:
   • A profile of the child's physical, social-emotional, and intellectual development.

- The child's development in terms of norms for his or her age group and in comparison to his or her peers in the classroom.
- How you see the child progressing developmentally (strengths and weaknesses).
- Your impression of how well the school setting is meeting the child's needs and what the school could be doing to better meet them.

BIBLIOGRAPHY

Almy, M., and C. Genishi. 1979. *Ways of Studying Children.* rev. ed. New York: Teachers College Press.

Bagnato, S. J., J. T. Neisworth, and S. M. Munson. 1989. *Linking: Developmental Assessment and Early Intervention.* Rockville, Md: Aspen Publishers.

Bailie, L., S. Bender, C. Jackson, C. Watada, and J. Zane. 1980. *A Manual to Identify and Serve Children with Specific Learning Disabilities: Ages 3–5.* Honolulu: Department of Education.

Beaty, J. J. 1990. *Observing Development of the Young Child.* 2d ed. Columbus, Ohio: Merrill.

Bentzen, W. R. 1985. *Seeing Young Children: A Guide to Observing and Recording.* Albany, N.Y.: Delmar.

Boehm, A. E., and R. Weinberg. 1987. *The Classroom Observer: A Guide for Developing Observation Skills.* New York: Teachers College Press.

Cartwright, C., and P. Cartwright. 1984. *Developing Observation Skills.* 2d ed. New York: McGraw-Hill.

Cohen, D. H., and V. Stern. 1983. *Observing and Recording the Behavior of Young Children.* 4th ed. New York: Teachers College Press.

Cryan, J. R. 1986. Evaluation: Plague or Promise? *Childhood Education* 62(5): 344–50.

Genishi, C. 1983. Observational Research Methods for Childhood Education. In *Handbook of Research in Early Childhood Education,* ed. B. Spodek. New York: Free Press.

Gunnoe, L. W. 1979. Informal Assessment and Individualized Educational Planning. In *Special Education and Development,* ed. S. Meisels. Baltimore: University Park Press.

Kamii, C., ed. 1990. *Achievement Testing in the Early Grades.* Washington. D. C.: National Association for the Education of Young Children.

Meisels, S. J. 1989. *Developmental Screening in Early Childhood Education.* 3d ed. Washington, D. C.: National Association for the Education of Young Children.

_____ . 1987. Uses and Abuses of Developmental Screening and School Readiness Testing. *Young Children* 42(2):4–6, 68–73.

National Association for the Education of Young Children. 1988. Position Statement on Standardized Testing of Young Children, Three Through Eight Years of Age. *Young Children* 43(3):42–47.

Nyberg, D. 1971. *Tough and Tender Learning.* Palo Alto, Calif.: National Press Books.

Read, K., P. Gardner, and B. C. Mahler. 1987. *Early Childhood Programs: Human Relationships and Learning.* 8th ed. New York: Holt, Rinehart & Winston.

Seefeldt, C. 1990. Assessing Young Children. In *Continuing Issues in Early Childhood Education,* ed. C. Seefeldt. Columbus, Ohio: Merrill.

Szasz, Susanne. 1978. *The Unspoken Language of Children.* New York: W. W. Norton.

Wortham, S. C. 1990. *Tests and Measurements in Early Childhood Education.* Columbus, Ohio: Merrill.

PART III

LIVING AND LEARNING WITH CHILDREN

This cluster of chapters focuses on the knowledge and expertise that a teacher must have in order to create a nurturing and stimulating daily program for young children. Chapter 7, A Good Place for Children, explores the importance of meeting children's basic physical and psychological needs. Chapter 8, The Learning Environment, looks at how you can structure the use of space and provide the equipment and material necessary to support children's development. Chapter 9, Relationships and Guidance, deals with how teachers can develop positive relationships with children and help them learn to work and play in a group setting. These chapters address essential aspects of the program for children. They are based on the foundation laid down in the previous chapters and are necessary preconditions for curriculum as it is described in the chapters that follow.

CHAPTER SEVEN

A Good Place for Children

We must have . . . a place where children can have a whole group of adults they can trust.

—Margaret Mead

This chapter explores factors to be considered in meeting the physical and emotional needs of children in early childhood programs. First we look at the ways in which a program for young children ensures their safety and health. Then we look at ways you can help children with the first separation from their parents— when they enter your program. Guidelines are provided for how you can design and handle routines and transitions each day and throughout the year. We also look at endings and what you can do to help children adjust to a new class or program, to the transition to their next school, or to the departure of their teacher.

Early childhood programs are children's second home, and teachers and other children are their extended family. Although this is particularly true for children in full-day centers and for very young children, it is true for all young children, even those in partial-day programs, kindergartens, and primary grades. What do we want for children in their second homes? What do they need to thrive?

A good place for children is flexible enough to be responsive to their needs while stable enough to provide security over many hours. The quality of relationships, the design of the environment, and the program schedule will make, or fail to make, the program a place where children can grow and learn.

A SAFE AND HEALTHY PLACE

It seems obvious that although there are many important aspects of a teacher's role, maintaining safety and health comes first in the eyes of the world and the families served. Safe and healthy environments protect children from

IN THE CLASSROOM: SAFETY CHECKLIST

_____ Building and furnishings are free of rust and splinters.
_____ Furniture is stable.
_____ Equipment is unbroken and in good working order.
_____ Rugs are secured or backed with nonskid material.
_____ The classroom and grounds are free of hazardous debris.
_____ Emergency exits are clearly marked and clear of clutter.
_____ Bolts and rough edges on equipment and furniture are recessed or covered.
_____ The environment is arranged so that the teacher can easily supervise all activity centers.
_____ Electric outlets are covered in programs for children under the age of five.
_____ Electric cords do not cross pathways.
_____ Toxic materials are locked out of children's reach.
_____ Entrances and yard are secure. Staff can monitor strangers entering the facility.
_____ Hot water taps are turned off or are turned down so that hot water does not scald.
_____ Sharp tools and glass items are out of children's reach.
_____ Places where children use water have nonskid floors or coverings.
_____ The yard is fenced and gates have childproof latches.
_____ There are no poisonous plants growing in the yard.
_____ There is a soft medium beneath climbing, swinging, and sliding apparatuses.
_____ Permanent outdoor equipment is anchored securely and movable equipment is stable.

Emergency Prevention and Preparation

_____ A telephone is available and is easily accessible. Emergency numbers are posted nearby.
_____ Records for each child include permission for emergency treatment and health records.
_____ A medical practitioner and facility are prepared to provide emergency care and advice.

hazards and ensure that children have access to the elements that assure health. As you focus on the important goals of helping young children learn and develop a positive self-concept, you need to make sure safety and health are not overlooked.

It is fundamental that a program be both psychologically and physically safe and healthy for children. Psychological health and safety involve the child's perceptions. Children can tell when and where they are welcome. They know that they are in a safe place when their needs are

_____ Teachers are trained in first aid. Certificates are current.

_____ A first aid kit is adequately stocked, easily available, and marked for visibility.

_____ A first aid handbook is available.

_____ Ratios are low enough so that emergencies can be handled without endangering children.

_____ A fire extinguisher is available and functional, and teachers know how to use it.

_____ An emergency evacuation plan is posted. The fire department has evaluated it.

_____ Emergency evacuation procedures are practiced monthly.

_____ A plan for civil defense emergencies exists and is known to staff.

_____ A sign-out procedure is followed and well known to staff.

_____ A first aid kit (which includes emergency phone numbers, parental consent for treatment forms, change for the telephone, and an emergency plan) is carried on trips.

_____ Children are appropriately, legally, and safely restrained in cars.

_____ A plan exists for safe classroom coverage in case a child must be taken to the hospital.

Special Concerns in Infant-Toddler Programs

_____ Cribs, gates, and playpens have slats less than $2\frac{3}{8}$ inches apart or mesh less than $\frac{1}{4}$ inch in diameter.

_____ Cribs, childgates, and playpens have locking devices that work.

_____ Mattresses fit snugly in cribs.

_____ Dangling strings do not hang from cribs and playpens.

_____ High chairs and walkers are stable and are used in locations away from stairs and doors.

_____ Strollers and carriages are stable and have adequate brakes.

_____ Strollers, high chairs, and walkers have restraining straps.

_____ Windows and mirrors are made of shatterproof material.

_____ Toys are at least $1\frac{1}{2}$ inches in diameter.

cared for and when adults show respect in the ways they listen to and talk with them. In psychologically safe and healthy programs children do not fear rejection or humiliation. They are comfortable and feel secure. This sense of safety depends on warm, consistent adults who are physically accessible to children. Teachers contribute to psychological health by being encouraging and by believing in children's competence. They support this belief by creating environments in which it is safe to experiment and acceptable to make mistakes. They accept children as unique people with their own pace and stage of development.

When children know that both you and the environment are trustworthy, they can direct their energy to exploring and experimenting in a setting designed to help them learn and grow. When you know that children are safe and healthy in the environment you designed, you are able to devote your energy to helping them use the environment fully.

A Safe Place

A good environment for children is safe physically as well as psychologically. It has basically sound facilities, equipment, and materials. It is arranged to minimize hazards and ensure safety. Adult-child ratios are low enough and group size small enough so that staff can always supervise children well. Additionally, safety involves making sure of the security of the program. Yards, gates, and doors ensure that children do not leave without supervision and that the threshold of the program is crossed only by those who have permission to do so. Sign-in and sign-out procedures and staff awareness preclude a child leaving with strangers or noncustodial adults.

Preparation enables you to minimize potential hazards. Problems can then be taken care of before they exist or handled effectively when they are unavoidable. Preparedness involves anticipation of such situations as fires and accidents.

Use of a safety checklist, like the one in the accompanying box, can help you to quickly evaluate the safety and preparedness of an early childhood setting. We strongly recommend that you use a resource such as *Healthy Young Children* (Kendrick, Kaufmann, and Messenger 1989) to gain awareness of the broad scope of safety and health concerns in programs for young children.

It is important to remain attentive to health and safety not only as you design the environment but also in everyday practice. Children need information in new situations such as on trips and in the introduction of new equipment, materials, or experiences. You can help them recognize hazards and activities that may be dangerous and teach them procedures for handling potential hazards. For example, this is how we have discussed using a knife with four-, five-, and six-year-olds: "This is a knife. One side is sharp and the other side isn't. When you cut with a knife it's important to have the sharp side down and to make sure that your fingers aren't under the cutting blade. Hold onto the handle with one hand and use the other hand to push down—that way you won't accidentally get cut."

When children understand routines and precautions they are usually willing to cooperate. As in other areas of guidance, it is more effective to tell children what to do and why rather than insisting that they stop something: "Please climb on the jungle gym instead of the table. The table might tip from your weight and you might fall."

Many safety measures are absolutely necessary for the well-being of all young children, but others are not as clear-cut. Some precautions change as children reach new developmental stages. For example, covering electric outlets is not necessary for premobile infants; it is essential with mobile infants, toddlers, and young preschoolers; and it is unnecessary with kindergarten and primary-school children.

We cannot protect children from all hazards. In the real and complex world of the classroom, we must often make choices between greater safety and learning. Such choices are influenced by the age, experience, temperament, and skills of the children, the size of the group, the adult-child ratio, the situation, the purpose and policies of the program, and the philosophy and beliefs of the staff. Typical concerns include the use of potentially hazardous tools (like sharp knives and scissors), exposure to challenging environments (like an inclined trikeway), and the restriction of common materials and equipment (such as electric outlets and sticks). As you consider these gray areas, you must make safety decisions consciously and not simply react to an immediate concern or embrace an easy solution to a current problem.

A Healthy Place

In the first early childhood programs an emphasis on health was common. As more was learned about children's intellectual and social growth, less attention was paid to health. Health problems and epidemics today have been traced to child care centers, and public health practitioners have pointed to the need to look at the fundamentals of health in early childhood environments. Failure to meet the health guidelines in the accreditation standards of the National Association for the Education of Young Children has been reported as one of the most frequent areas of deficiency.

Healthy environments are clean and provide children and teachers with the necessary facilities, materials, and routines for maintaining health: water, washing and toilet facilities, good light, ventilation and heat, nutritious food, and a clean environment. Teachers ensure health by attending to health routines (such as diapering and hand washing), preventing potential hazards (such as preventing child access to toxic cleaning supplies), keeping health records, and having plans and policies for health routines and emergencies.

Every teacher needs to have basic training for coping with minor health emergencies such as fevers and vomiting and for recognizing when a child needs to be referred to a physician or dentist and when a child should be isolated from others for health reasons. After receiving such training ourselves, we were struck by the fact that adults who work with young children are at high risk of contracting disease and that the most effective and important preventive measure is conscientious and thorough hand washing. In some programs a nurse or health aide will look after health situations, in others you will be responsible. In general, the younger the children, the greater the need to be health conscious in group settings.

Recently educators have become aware of pollutants that are prevalent in our program environments. These pollutants are of particular concern because young children are more vulnerable to them because of their size and stage of development. Teachers need to be particularly concerned with making sure that asbestos, lead, pesticides, and other chemical toxins are absent from the settings in which they teach.

The upsurge in infant-toddler programs provides new challenges to early childhood educators. Infants and toddlers are at once more vulnerable and at the same time present greater health hazards in group settings than do older children. Children under the age of three are smaller and have immature organs and body systems; they have less immunity and are at greater health risk because they explore the world by touching and mouthing.

Many diseases, some irritating and others life threatening, can be spread through contamination via unsanitary diapering. Diarrheal diseases, hepatitis A, hepatitis B, and pinworms are commonly associated with unsanitary diapering and improper hand washing. Concerns with very serious diseases such as hepatitis and AIDS have led to the now common recommendation that diapering be conducted with the adult wearing

IN THE CLASSROOM: HEALTH CHECKLIST

_____ Clean drinking water is available to children at all times.

_____ Tissue, soap, paper towels, and toilet paper are available where children can reach.

_____ Toilet facilities are clean and easily accessible to children at all times.

_____ Soiled clothes are stored in closed plastic bags away from children's play areas.

_____ Children and adults wash their hands after toileting and before handling food.

_____ Tables are cleaned prior to meals, snacks, and food preparation.

_____ Nutritious foods are chosen for meals, snacks, and cooking activities.

_____ Food is not withheld as punishment or used as a reward.

_____ Food is stored and prepared in a safe and sanitary fashion.

_____ Children brush their teeth after meals and toothbrushes are stored hygienically.

_____ Records on children's health include emergency phone numbers and allergy and medication information.

_____ Health records are well organized and accessible.

_____ Policy and procedures exist for isolating sick children within the setting or for removing them from the setting.

_____ A basic manual of childhood health and disease is available.

_____ Program has written health policies which are given to parents.

_____ There are clean, individual napping arrangements for each child.

_____ There are extra clean clothes for children.

_____ Floors are mopped and rugs are vacuumed daily.

_____ Garbage cans are lined and the liner is changed daily.

---

disposable gloves that are changed for each child.

It is helpful to periodically evaluate for health by using a checklist such as the one in the accompanying box.

GOOD BEGINNINGS

Beginnings are times of change, excitement, and hope. They are also times of stress, fear, and anxiety. They are a time to say farewell to the security of the familiar and to go forward to meet new challenges. Life is composed of many beginnings; some are large and stressful, others are small and easy to deal with. Teachers can guide children over the sometimes rocky paths of the transition between home and classroom and the transitions within and between the early childhood programs.

The Transition from Home

During infancy children have a limited sense of themselves as individuals; they bond with and feel they are part of their primary caregivers. Between the ages of eighteen and thirty-six months children forge their sense of themselves

_____ Garbage is emptied daily and garbage cans that contain food are covered.

_____ Animal cages are cleaned frequently and regularly as needed.

_____ There is a source of ventilation so that the air is clean and fresh.

_____ Air conditioners, air filters, humidifiers, and dehumidifiers are cleaned often to minimize pollutants.

_____ Windows and doors are opened regularly to let out pollutants.

_____ The temperature is regulated as necessary.

_____ There is adequate light for children to see easily as they work without areas of darkness or shadows falling on children's work. As much as possible light is from natural sources with incandescent or full-spectrum fluorescent light used when necessary.

Special Concerns in Infant-Toddler Programs

_____ Healthful diapering procedures are known and practiced.

_____ Changing tables are covered with paper during use and cleaned with disinfecting solution after each use.

_____ Daily records are kept on children's food intake and other health concerns; information is shared with parents.

_____ Each child has individual sleeping arrangements and bedding; linens are changed weekly or as necessary.

_____ Toys are washed regularly.

_____ Bottles are kept refrigerated.

_____ Clothes are changed as necessary.

as individuals who are separate from their parents. Achieving this sense of separateness can be an anxiety-fraught experience filled with frightening realizations ("I can exist separately from my parents, they can exist without me!"), unnamed fears ("Will I be abandoned? Am I a bad child who deserves abandonment?"), and sometimes of frighteningly intense anger ("I hate my parents who refuse to perfectly understand and meet my needs"). Although there are individual variations, generally, by the time children are three years old, their initial sense of separateness and identity is formed. They begin to understand that neither their parents, the world, nor they themselves are either all good or all bad.

All of us can recall the anxious feelings we had in relation to separating from the familiar: leaving our childhood home, moving to a new city, starting a new job, becoming a parent. With a lifetime of experience behind us, we can still remember the stomach-clutching anxiety that accompanied those changes. When young children enter your program, they face an unfamiliar world. They are assaulted by sensations: new people, noises, objects, smells, and activities. They may have had little experience with being parted from their parents, with being among many children, or with making choices. This strangeness is made less traumatic when teachers and parents work together.

Teachers help children and their parents to realize that the bonds that exist between them are strong enough to thrive despite separation. At the same time, teachers need to help children build relationships in the new setting. When children trust their teachers and feel assured of their own competence, they become comfortable enough to benefit from their school experiences. They adapt more easily when they know that their parents have confidence in the school and in the teachers.

Children can make the transition from home best when the introduction is gradual and when they have an opportunity to integrate familiar aspects of their homes into their new lives in the classroom. One way to accomplish this is a home visit by the teacher before the child's first day in the program. Such a visit gives the child the opportunity to experience their teacher from the security of his or her own environment. During visits, teachers build the base of later relationships with children and learn about their homes and families. Such visits are also opportunities for parents to get to know and to develop confidence in the teacher.

Classroom visits by parents and children are another way to provide the information needed for children to feel comfortable and competent in the new setting. It is essential that all children experience their classroom in the company of a familiar adult. A visit orients the child to the setting, the teacher, and the materials. In some programs, initial visits occur during the course of a regular day: the child and parent sit in on an hour or two of the program. In other places, a special orientation for several new children or individual parent-child visits outside of regular program hours may precede the child's first day. Whatever its form, the initial visit helps prepare both child and parent for the new experience.

First Days and First Weeks

Your goal for the first day is to begin to know children and to help them get to know you, one another, and the routines of the program. Because adjustment on the first day can be difficult, parents are often asked to spend part or all of the day with their child. In general, toddlers and young preschoolers have a more difficult time making a transition to a new setting than do infants or older children. It is not uncommon for the parents of a toddler to spend a week gradually preparing to leave a child for a full day. It is equally common for a four-year-old to pointedly ask a parent when the parent is

going home at the end of the first hour together in the program. Each child, however, responds in his or her own way. We have taught toddlers who had no difficulty saying goodbye to their parents after only minimal preparation and four-year-olds who wept and clung to their mothers each day months after the beginning of school. The temperament and experience of both parent and child will interact with the kind of preparation that you provide to make each child's entrance into school unique.

School policies on handling the initial transition into a new class or program vary. Many programs require that parents or other familiar caregivers spend time with the child during the first days. Parents often resist spending this kind of time in the program, and employers are rarely sympathetic to this need. In our experience, many parents come only if the program requires it. Also in our experience, the parents' time and energy are well worth the effort in terms of the child's experience at school. You will need administrative support and may even want to work with others to develop a letter for employers to help them understand the value of providing this kind of support to their employees who are parents.

Individual children react differently on their first day; some want to touch and try everything, some are cautious observers, and others want to

---

IN THE CLASSROOM: SUGGESTIONS FOR THE FIRST DAY

- If possible, have children begin with a short first day. Children who have had little experience with school may have absorbed all they can in an hour.
- Encourage a parent, other relative, or familiar caregiver to spend all or part of the first day at school with the child.
- Greet children and their parents by name as they arrive and say goodbye as they depart.
- Show the children the location of the toilet and the water fountain. Show them how they work and accompany them when they seem uncertain.
- Show clearly what you expect of children but do not try to teach everything they will need to know on the first day. Avoid being overly concerned if children cannot meet seemingly simple expectations.
- Encourage children to bring a special toy or comfort object to help provide a tangible bridge between home and school. Some children are comforted by a photograph or tape recording of family members.
- Allow children to borrow a book or toy from the classroom to provide the same bridge when they return to their homes.
- Provide an interesting but limited number of age-appropriate materials in the environment. These could include blocks, books, simple puzzles and manipulative toys, dolls, and crayons.
- Provide soothing open-ended materials like water, sand, and dough.
- Provide time for independent exploration of materials.
- Provide an activity like a song or story that helps children to feel that they are a part of a group.

stay close to their parents. All children carefully observe the behavior of the teacher and the arrangement of the environment so they can understand what is expected of them and find out how the teacher will react. It is especially important to be aware of what you say and do those first days. You will want to be calm and caring, letting children know that you will help and protect them in this new, and possibly scary, place. Since so much is unknown, the environment, the activities, and the schedule of the first day should be simple to allow children to focus on a few new experiences at a time. This will allow them to understand what is happening without being fearful of doing the wrong thing.

Eventually, parents must go and the child will be left in your classroom. Almost all children experience anxiety at this time. Although some children overcome this easily, others express their anxiety through tears, tantrums, or angry words, and still others become despon-

dent and quietly wait while sucking thumbs or holding comfort objects. Some, not as visibly upset, may have toilet accidents or nightmares, or they may angrily reject their parents when it's time to go home. A few will appear fine for a few days or a week and then will react very strongly as if it were the first day. Our interpretation of this delayed response is that, as the novelty of the new experience wears thin, the child realizes that going to school will henceforth be a perpetual part of life—one that involves little personal choice. If a reaction persists or is extreme, it may mean that the child needs a more gradual or a delayed entrance into the program.

Many children, especially young ones, need the reassurance of physical contact with an adult during the first days and weeks. If you teach in a program where many children begin at the same time, you may sometimes feel like a mother opossum moving about the classroom with the

---

IN THE CLASSROOM: SUGGESTIONS FOR FIRST WEEKS

- Hold children who need extra reassurance.
- Have children bring photographs of their families to school to be held onto or looked at in times of stress. Have parents make a tape recording of home voices and sounds to play to a child in distress.
- Avoid abrupt or major changes and excitement (fire drills, films, trips, room rearrangement).
- Continue to greet children and parents by name each day as they arrive and as they depart. Keep parents informed of how their child is adjusting.
- Help children to know their school by taking small excursions to important places in it: the parent room, the play yard, other classes, the library, the office, the kitchen, and so on.
- Make sure that familiar, homelike materials are available in the classroom: pillows, stuffed toys, and personal comfort objects.
- Have play materials available that encourage children to role-play familiar home situations.
- Sing name songs to help children to get to know one another and to acknowledge each child during group meetings.

small bodies of young children clinging to you. As they become comfortable, most children will find more interesting things to do. For many children a treasured blanket, stuffed animal, or piece of clothing is important in the separation process. These very personal possessions are comforting reminders of home that help some children feel secure. It is important that children be allowed to keep them near. With time, comfort objects become less evident and may only be needed when a child is under stress or having a nap.

During the first weeks, children begin to adjust and learn to trust and feel competent. They become accustomed to the daily rhythm of activities linked by transitions, learn that they can care for many of their own needs, and discover that you will be there to help when needed. The most important tasks of the first weeks are to develop trust, to build relationships, and to establish routines. It is not nearly as important to create an exciting curriculum. You will want to ensure that children's successes outnumber their failures and that your expectations of them are realistic. It is a time when you learn what children can and cannot do. These observations will help you to plan a program that is appropriate to the individual children.

As children become more comfortable, you can begin enriching the environment with materials, activities, and trips that might have been overwhelming at first. By understanding and supporting children as they go through the separation process during the first days and weeks, you help prepare them to be active and competent learners.

A GOOD DAY

A typical day in any program for young children is an artful blend of routines and learning experiences linked by smooth transitions. We think of the daily ebb and flow of teaching-learning activities and routines as being part of a

larger experience of living and learning with children.

The Daily Schedule

The program day is influenced by the needs and developmental stage of the children and your observations of individuals and by your values and the values and concerns of parents, community, and the school administration. It is also influenced by the physical setting, the length of the program day, and the time of year.

Both spontaneous and teacher-planned activities occur daily in every carefully prepared program for young children, but spontaneous activities and an emphasis on play predominate. In informal programs curriculum is often emergent: it evolves from the interests and experiences of the children. Teachers lead a few key activities each day, observe children's interests and responses, and work to support these in spontaneous play and planned activities. In more formal programs there are more teacher-directed activities. In such settings there tends to be less emphasis on "free play."

Children's Needs and Developmental Stages

Early childhood programs must include provisions for children's needs and take into account developmental differences. All children need time for rest, personal hygiene, and nourishment. It is important that there are periods of vigorous activity and quiet and daily times when choice is permitted to allow for individual interest and attention. In programs for younger children, teachers must remain flexible since younger children's needs vary greatly. At 10 A.M.

we visited a group of toddlers: Aimee was lying down and drinking a bottle, Ian was having a nap, Walden was rocking on the rocking horse, Nadine was cuddling on a teacher's lap, and Jonathan was using the toilet. A rigid schedule could not meet such diverse needs and would inevitably lead to frustration for teacher and children. Typical schedules for different age groups might have the following characteristics:

- **Infants**: Each child regulates him or herself—meals, rests, active and quiet times.
- **Toddlers**: Regular meals, snacks, and rest with active and quiet times occurring in response to children's needs and interests.
- **Preschoolers and kindergartners**: Scheduled eating and rest times and flexibly scheduled group and outdoor times.
- **Primary-school children**: Routines scheduled as above with closer adherence to plans for group and activity times.

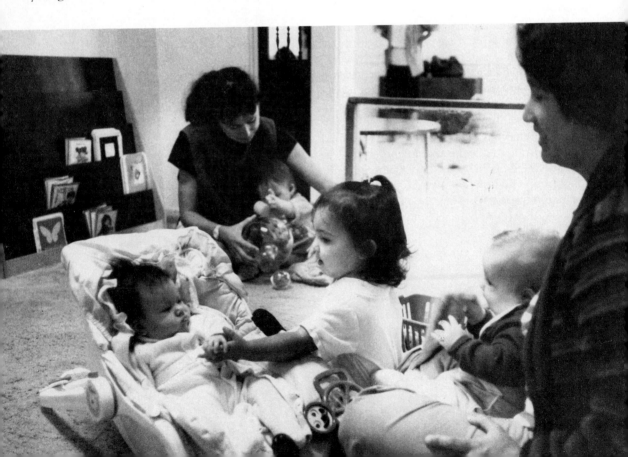

Values and Goals

Your values and goals are among your most important considerations in planning your schedule. If you value creativity and the development of responsibility, you will allow fairly large blocks of time (one to two hours) during which children choose their own activities and teachers work with individuals and small groups. If you emphasize the acquisition of knowledge and skills, larger portions of the day may be directly guided by the teacher, leaving less time for free choice. In such programs, time will be divided into smaller units to enable you to better hold and direct the attention of children. Without a consideration of your values and the implications of your scheduling decisions you may inadvertently fail to foster the very things you most care about.

Physical Setting

The building in which you teach will influence the arrangement of the learning environment and how you use time. If you teach in a building that houses only your program and has sufficient space for younger children to be separated from older ones, it is relatively easy to arrange the day so that it meets the basic needs of all age groups. Where space is limited or facilities are shared with other programs, it may be more difficult to meet the needs of various groups. You may need to work out ways to accommodate different eating and resting schedules, separation of rest and activity areas, and use of bathrooms and playgrounds. If the bathroom or playground is located at a great distance from the classroom, you will have to take this into account in your planning. Young children are not ready to use the toilet on a schedule, so you may have to plan frequent trips to make sure that children have adequate access to bathrooms. Even if children are capable of traversing the distance between classroom and yard or toilet on their own, you may need to schedule supervision to ensure their safety and security.

Length of the Program Day

If you teach in a morning-only program, some routines may be unnecessary. If children come to you in the morning after a good night's sleep and a hearty breakfast and depart in time to eat lunch and take an afternoon nap at home, scheduled rest time is unnecessary and a light snack is usually sufficient. In such a program the practice of having an enforced rest period with children on mats or seated at tables with heads on folded arms will probably meet with resistance and is a waste of your limited time together. In a short program, a good blend of outdoor activity and indoor activities with a short snack break will provide for a pleasant, productive half-day experience.

A program ending in the late afternoon must provide lunch, a mid-day rest, and snack periods to avoid overstimulated, hungry children. Children who spend eight- to eleven-hour days in an early childhood program are spending about 60 percent of their waking hours in an institutional setting. This is a significant portion of a young child's life, and the center is very much a second home. It is especially important to pay close attention to the quality of relationships, to the design of the environment, and to scheduling.

Children in full-day programs may stay eight to eleven hours, but staff members in such programs generally remain for only six to eight hours. The children are often cared for by separate morning and afternoon staffs. The coordination of the staff transition must help children to maintain their sense of trust in the setting if they are to benefit from the experiences offered in the latter part of the day.

Since "school" traditionally takes place in the morning hours, there is often a misperception that those who care for young children in the hours following the mid-day rest are somehow less important than those who perform the same tasks in the morning. Involving afternoon staff in program planning and recognizing the vital tasks they accomplish is one way to overcome this perception and maintain program quality throughout the day.

After School Programs

In kindergarten and primary-school settings the afternoon, or after school, program is separate and has a distinctly different mission from the morning program. It is designed to ensure children's well-being while parents are at work. After school programs are losing their merely custodial status as there is growing recognition that children continue to need high-quality care and education throughout the day. However, children who have been in structured, group settings all morning require a different, more relaxed afternoon. Good after school programs address children's needs with opportunities for play, socialization, and self-selected work. Although many parents see after school programs as homework mills, and some homework can be incorporated, primary-school children need the opportunity to play in the second half of their second home.

Time of Year

A program day may differ greatly from the beginning of the year to the end. During the first days, weeks, and even months, your program day must allow time to help children become accustomed to routines and new activities. As the year progresses, children will have mastered routines, become accustomed to working independently, and will be more able to cooperate in group activities. Your schedule can be adjusted accordingly. Group times can be planned for longer periods as children gain group skills. Scheduled routines, like toileting, may be omitted as children become independent and no longer require support and supervision.

Staff-Child Ratio and Group Size

The number of staff members in relation to the number of children is an important factor in how you structure the day. In a program with an adult-child ratio of one to seven, events, routines, and activities can be scheduled with a great deal more flexibility than if you work in a program with one adult for every fifteen children. With lower ratios you need not personally meet the needs of so many children and so are free to be more spontaneous and to plan for activities that have an unpredictable time frame or that require more intense teacher-child interaction.

The size of the group will also influence the day. With smaller groups you have more flexibility in planning because you can make spontaneous changes without disrupting others. You are able to give your full attention to individuals because there are fewer people to attend to. Larger groups require more advance planning for the use of facilities (playgrounds, vans, and lunchrooms), and you must stick more closely to the schedule to meet the needs of other groups. Beyond a certain group size, no matter how low your ratios, you meet inevitable problems. Large groups of young children are noisy, overstimulating, and stressful.

The NAEYC, which credentials quality early childhood programs, has set standards for adult-child ratios and group size as shown in Table 7.1.

Routines

Regardless of whether your program lasts for three hours or ten, there are some recurring events in the basic structure of a day for young children. Arrival must provide a smooth transition from home. Opportunities must be available for nourishment, rest, diapering or toileting, and learning experiences. The end of each child's day should provide a sense of closure.

Teachers of young children have long accepted the routine parts of daily living as legitimate and important aspects of the child's daily experience. They recognize that children must have their basic needs met; that they must feel safe, secure, and accepted before they can begin to learn; and that a primary task of young children is to develop competence in indepen-

TABLE 7.1

NAEYC Standards for Adult-Child Ratios and Group Size

Age of Children \ Group Size	6	8	10	12	14	16	18	20	22	24
Infants (birth–12 mo.)	1:3	1:4								
Toddlers (12–24 mo.)	1:3	1:4	1:5	1:4						
Two-year-olds (24–36 mo.)		1:4	1:5	1:6						
Two- and three-year-olds			1:5	1:6	1:7*					
Three-year-olds			1:5	1:6	1:7	1:8*				
Three- and four-year-olds					1:7	1:8	1:9	1:10*		
Four-year-olds						1:8	1:9	1:10*		
Four- and five-year-olds						1:8	1:9	1:10*		
Five-year-olds						1:8	1:9	1:10		
Six- to eight-year-olds (school age)								1:10	1:11	1:12

*Smaller group sizes and lower staff-child ratios are optimal. Larger group sizes and higher staff-child ratios are acceptable only in cases where staff are highly qualified.

Source: "Table of Standards for adult-child ratios and group sizes," in *Accreditation Criteria and Procedures,* Sue Bredekamp, Ed. pp. 24. Washington, DC: NAEYC 1984.

dently meeting their physical and social needs. As a teacher of young children, you will want to give routines—the regular and more or less unvarying parts of classroom life—attention and thoughtful planning, just as you do other aspects of the program. When daily routines are predictable, children know what to expect and have the resources they need for ordering and understanding their experiences. When you communicate your good reasons for establishing a routine and your commitment to having it work, children will usually cooperate and participate willingly.

Arrival

Arrival each day should be a friendly, predictable event. It is important to establish a routine that allows every parent and child to be greeted. An arrival period during which you are free to personally greet and talk briefly with every parent and child sets a relaxed tone. At this time you can notice if each child is in good health and appears ready to participate in the daily program. Arrival time may be one of the few regular contacts you have with parents and it can be a good time for exchanging information. In some programs, the staff member who opens the center is available to greet the family and help each child make the transition into the classroom. In programs where all the children arrive at the same time, the whole staff may gather to greet families.

Toileting, Diapering, and Toilet Learning

When you work with young children, you have no choice but to be concerned with some very basic aspects of life. These include the healthy management of diapering and children's development of toilet skills. Early childhood educators have a serious, professional need to understand the process of diapering and toileting.

Diapering is a multistep process that includes health practices such as washing hands before and after and disinfecting diapering surfaces to prevent contamination and the spread of disease. It also includes an important psychological component. Young children's emotional health, self-image, and ability to become independent are intimately tied to how they are treated during diapering and how they are helped to develop toilet skills. *Healthy Young Children* (Kendrick, Kaufmann, and Messenger 1989) presents an excellent step-by-step diapering procedure.

Children only gradually become self-reliant in using the toilet. There is no set age when all children should be independent. Between the ages of two and three young children generally are ready to learn to use the toilet independently. Children have an easier time managing toilets when the fixtures are child-sized and when clothing is manageable. They become comfortable when teachers are patient and when some attention is paid to making the bathroom pleasant. Teachers may need to accompany reluctant or inexperienced children to the toilet to reassure them. Stable step stools to enable children to comfortably reach the toilet and washbasin are essential if there are adult-sized fixtures.

Toilet mishaps are a normal aspect of a child's life and may be a regular feature of your day. A child who is genuinely upset may need to be sheltered from public awareness and given help with cleanup. Other children may need only a small amount of direction and encouragement to take care of their own change of clothes.

Mealtimes and Snacks

Some of the nicest moments of the day occur when teachers and children sit down and eat together. Snacks and meals are pleasant when they are orderly enough to focus on eating and casual enough to be a social experience.

Independence can be fostered as children participate in meal preparation and serving. For example, children can spread their own peanut butter on a cracker or pour their own juice. Children gain self-help skills when meals are served family style with bowls of food and small pitchers passed so that children can serve themselves.

Resistance and fears about eating are common. You should neither force children to eat nor deny them the opportunity to eat. Food should never be withheld from children as punishment nor used as a reward. Young children become restless and irritable when they are expected to wait until everyone is served or while others finish. They may become anxious and unable to eat if they are hurried. Many problems can be avoided if you have a set routine for children who have finished eating before the rest of the group, for example, allowing them to leave the table to read a book or to play quietly with a game or toy.

Not all families are able to feed their children a good breakfast before their early arrival. Because of this, it is important that a nutritious snack or breakfast be served in the morning and that snacks and meals are planned to meet children's daily nutritional requirements. In many states the USDA child care food program guidelines form the licensing standard for meals and snacks provided in early childhood programs. Good snacks for young children should include at least two of the basic food groups and should consist of minimally processed foods that are low in fat and added salt and sugar. Fresh fruits or vegetables, whole grain bread or cereal, milk, cheese, and peanut butter are all components of healthful snacks.

If parents provide children's food, you will need to give culturally sensitive guidance concerning appropriate meals brought from home. Some programs ask parents to send a snack if the child will be in school at the end of the day. This

helps children and parents to have more pleasant departure times without the "arsenic hour"
syndrome of tired parents and hungry, whining
children.

Cleanup

Cleanup prepares the classroom for the next
activity and is a natural and necessary part of
living with others. Children begin to understand
that they are members of a community and that
they need to share in the responsibility for
maintaining cleanliness and order. Although
cleanup is seldom a favorite activity, it need not
be hard or unpleasant. Much of the drudgery
that often surrounds cleanup comes from the
attitude that is projected by adults. When you
participate in cleanup with an attitude of expect-
ant goodwill (I feel good about doing this and I
expect that you share my feeling), children
generally are also cheerful and cooperative.
Often teachers make cleanup the punishment
that children must endure for the pleasure of
play; such an attitude discourages not only
cleanup but also play itself. Children frequently
resist cleanup when they are forced to straighten
up large messes without assistance—to a young
child such a mess may appear overwhelming
and impossible to clean. Although it is often
actually easier to do it yourself than to insist on
children's participation, your expectation and
firm but gentle follow-through will help children become able and responsible members of
their group.

Rest Time

Rest time can be a positive experience for
children and adults if children are tired, if the
environment is made restful, and if children
understand the importance of relaxing their
minds and bodies. As with other routines, it is
essential that children feel secure. If they are
fearful of the school setting, they will be unable
to relax. Most children under the age of five will
sleep if the environment is soothing and com-

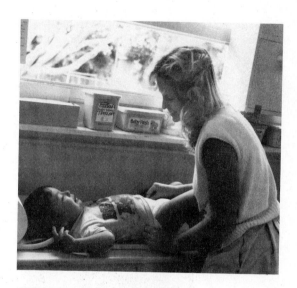

fortable. Every child needs a mat or cot for sleeping. To create an atmosphere conducive to rest and sleep, dim the lights, play quiet music, and allow children to cuddle personal comfort objects such as a favorite stuffed toy or a blanket.

When you are helping children to fall asleep, it is important to be calming. Focus on children as they begin to rest, gently rub their backs, avoid speaking to others, and whisper when you must speak. Wait until most of the children are sleeping before you begin any other tasks. Children who nap will generally do so for at least one hour. When they are finished resting, children should be free to put away their mats and play quietly.

Children who do not sleep will respond to rest time positively if, after an initial rest, they are allowed to look at books and play quietly. Children who regularly do not sleep can rest away from others so that their activity is not disturbing. Preschool children who are unable to sleep can have a rest period of at least half an hour and should not be required to lie down for more than one hour. Six- to eight-year-olds also benefit from short quiet times in their day. In many programs this is combined with an opportunity for sustained silent reading, or SSR time. The length of rest for nonsleeping children should be based on the individual's need and ability to relax.

Rest time may provide a quiet period for teachers to collect themselves and do some planning or preparation. However, the length of nap and rest periods should be based on children's need for rest and not on the desire of teachers to accomplish their tasks.

Transitions

Each time a scheduled activity or routine ends, there is a transition—a time of gathering children together or of movement into a new activity. Transition times can be smooth and relaxed if they are well planned and if children are prepared for them.

IN THE CLASSROOM: SUGGESTIONS FOR ROUTINES AND TRANSITIONS

- Offer help when children request it or show unusual frustration, even if the task is one you know they ordinarily can do independently.
- Be flexible about time while maintaining the usual sequence of events. (Activity time might be lengthened if it doesn't mean skipping another important activity.)
- Acknowledge cooperation by commenting on individual and group efforts rather than by making negative comparisons. ("Thanks for the help Vernon!" not "I wish everyone cleaned tables as well as Vernon.")
- Ignore noncooperation as much as possible or give an alternative that is neither punishing nor rewarding. ("If you are not helping, you may wait at that table." "Please come stand by the door, I'm afraid someone will be hurt when you push in the bathroom.")
- Give children several minutes warning before any transition begins.
- Maintain your communication style and tempo of movement during transitions. (It is disruptive if you suddenly start barking orders and rushing around.)
- Avoid having children wait in lines or large groups with nothing to do.
- Give clearly stated reasons for transition. ("We'll all clean up now so that we can sit down to lunch together.")
- Offer choices only when there really is a choice and avoid offering choices you are unwilling to allow. ("It's time to go inside now," not "Would you like to go in?")

Teachers and children may perceive transitions differently. As the teacher, you have responsibility for moving children from one activity or routine to the next according to a preconceived plan based on the needs of the children and your program goals. Children who do not know the reasons for the changes may respond to transitions as interruptions of things they would prefer to continue doing.

In nearly all programs, transitions take up between 20 percent and 30 percent of the total time (Berk 1976). Transitions can be times of frustration and conflict for you and children. Transitions in which many children are gathered together can often be avoided by having chil-

dren go on to the next activity independently, for example, by letting children go outside after they have finished cleaning up their area rather than waiting for the entire group to finish. Other transitions can be turned into productive time by using them as opportunities to share songs and fingerplays, for games, or for listening to relaxing music or looking at books.

When children are leaving a group to go on to the next activity, you can use techniques that avoid a chaotic stampede or excessive regimentation. You may use chants and songs that include a child's name and what to do next; for example, "This is the way JOHN washes his hands everyday at lunchtime" (for older chil-

IN THE CLASSROOM: SOME IDEAS FOR TRANSITIONS BETWEEN ACTIVITIES

- **Clues:** Give a clue about the child's family, vacation, pet, or home. A child whose mom is named Donna and whose dad is named Skip can go.
- **Riddles:** Ask a riddle about something related to the curriculum theme: What grows in the ground, gives shade to sit in, makes a good place to climb, and is a place for birds to build their nests. The guesser can go.
- **Verse:** Sing "Old MacDonald" (or a similar endless song). Ask children to think of a verse; they can go when their verse has been sung.
- **Props:** At activity time bring an item from each center for each child. As you bring out the item, ask a child to describe it, name its place, and take it there to play.
- **Friends:** Select a child to pick a friend with whom to leave the group.
- **Games:** For example, play the lost-and-found game. Choose a child. Say, "Police officer Maya, there's a lost child who's wearing blue shorts and a Batman t-shirt. Can you help me find him." When Maya finds the child she leaves and the found child becomes the police officer.
- **Name songs:** Sing a name song like "Get On Board Everybody" or "Hello" and have children leave when their name is sung.

dren the name can be spelled out), or "Everyone wearing red (or stripes) can hop like a bunny to the playground."

Experienced teachers design many creative ways for making transitions smooth, interesting learning experiences. You may wish to collect such ideas and invent your own.

Departure

The end of the program day should provide a smooth transition back to life at home with the family. Departure time can provide an opportunity to talk to parents about the child's experiences. Sharing this information helps parents know what kind of a day their child has had and understand the behavior and needs of their child at home. For example, a child who usually naps but does not on a particular day may be unusually irritable, and a parent who knows this may respond with an early bedtime. Sharing some basic information about the child's day

with parents is essential in programs for infants and toddlers. Parents need to know about feeding, elimination, rest, and variations in the normal activity and behavior of the child.

If all children leave at the same time, departure can be structured to provide closure. Teachers may read a story, go over the events of the day, and plan for the next day. If the children leave at different times throughout the afternoon, a staff member should be available to share information with parents as they say farewell to each parent and child.

GOOD ENDINGS

In every classroom for young children, there are endings. Just as beginnings require special thought and planning, so endings require special care. The relationships that children build during their first school experiences can be very close, and it can be painful when they end. For

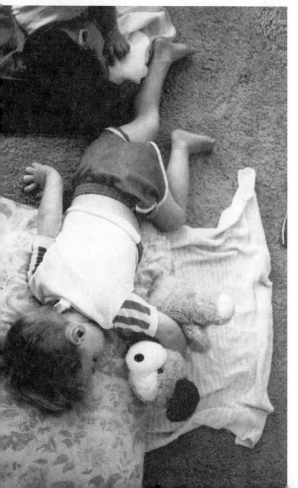

many children, this may be the first time that an important tie has ended.

Changing Classes and Teachers

When children remain in a program for more than a year, they will usually experience at least one change of class or teacher. In programs that follow a ten-month or public school calendar, this will occur in September after a long summer vacation. In full-year programs, this change may occur when the teacher feels that a child is ready for a new group or when space is needed in the group for younger children entering the program.

Although many children are ready and eager to move on to a new class, some are not. Transition to a new group requires the cooperation of both teachers and parents. The change to a new class can arouse feelings of anxiety similar to those experienced during the initial days of school, and similar techniques can help make a bridge between the old and new class. The transition is made easier when children know about their new class, when they can carry something familiar with them into the experience, and when the transition can be gradual. It also helps if children feel their parents and their first teacher have confidence in the new group and teacher.

Allow children in transition to make visits to their next class accompanied by their first teacher or a special friend. Let them visit for an activity time that they especially enjoy, perhaps circle time one day and activity time another day so that they can discover new materials and companions. On the official day of transition, have the child take responsibility for transferring personal belongings and setting up a new cubby. Going back to the old room to share lunch or nap or simply to visit for a few minutes helps the child feel secure.

When Teachers Leave

Teachers, like children, take vacations, become sick, and eventually end their association with a school. Sometimes these events take place during the course of a year. When a teacher leaves either permanently or for an extended period of time, children experience feelings of loss. They may be sad that you are gone and angry with you when you return. They may be fearful of the change and feel less secure until they build a relationship with the new teacher. Many programs for young children use team teaching as one way of minimizing the upsets of staff absences and departures. When children relate closely to two or more adults in the school, it will be less traumatic when one of them leaves.

When you know that you or a teacher you work with will leave, it is important to consider the impact on children in timing and to make adequate preparations for the transition. In one program we know, a teacher announced she would leave her job the same day that her co-teacher was going on a long-planned, much-deserved six-week leave. Although this teacher had given several weeks notice, the impact on the children was serious. The three- and four-year-old children in the class were plagued by nightmares, bed-wetting, and fears about school that the skilled substitute teacher and new teacher were unable to avert. In another program we know, a teacher learned that her husband was to be transferred out of state; as a result, she would move and leave her position, but at the same time that her coworker had planned to leave her job and move to another part of the country. This teacher talked about the change with her coworker and decided to leave the program six weeks before her move to give another teacher a chance to become familiar to the children. A teacher who understands and takes seriously her or his responsibility to children considers the impact of personal decisions on children and adjusts them to cause minimal harm.

Leave-taking is a natural part of relationships. Young children can accept this more easily if adults do. During times of transition, minimize changes in the environment and routines. Most importantly, help children understand that teachers leave schools because of changes in their own lives and not in response to the behavior or actions of children or their families.

The Next School

Children in early childhood programs go on to other schools. The "real world" of school can be a very different kind of place from a nurturing developmental program. One of your jobs is to prepare the children in your class when they make the transition to the next school.

Children may anticipate starting their new schools with both interest and concern. You can aid in the transition by helping to strengthen children's sense of themselves as competent, successful individuals by acknowledging the growth that has taken place and by mentioning how this will be useful in their new school. ("You really know how to take care of your own lunch now, Mark. You're going to be able to handle it all by yourself in kindergarten.")

Early childhood programs should not be boot camps or training grounds for the next school! The time that children spend in early childhood programs should be spent on experiences that are appropriate for the early years. It may be beneficial, however, to use the last few weeks before a transition to another school to help children learn skills they will need. The more that you know about the schools in your community, the better able you will be to prepare children for transitions. If children will be expected to know about responding to bells, changing classes in response to a bell, standing in lines, getting their lunch from the cafeteria, doing work sheets, or raising hands, you can help them to learn these skills in a short time. At the end of the program year, when children are more mature, they will be more able to learn such skills. If you are in contact with the teachers in the next school, you may be able to obtain more specific information or even take the children to see their prospective school and teacher. Tell the children that they are practicing for their next school and role play some of the routines they will be expected to follow. When children know what to expect and feel comfortable and self-confident, they start school more positively. Parents and teachers can work together during this new transition to make it a beginning filled with enthusiasm and hope.

Adaptations for Primary-School Children

All young children need a safe, healthy place where teachers attend to the quality of the routines and transitions of the program. These aspects of the program assume a much greater importance for younger children. For primary-school children these issues are handled in a slightly different way.

Beginnings

A child entering a primary grade has had at least a full year of school. These more experienced children handle the transition to a new class or school with much greater ease. The days and weeks of transition described here will be pared down to a few days. An orientation visit is still a valuable opportunity for an older child to get to know the teacher and the environment without the pressure of also beginning school work and new relationships. The first days and weeks for a new class of primary-school children will have a different rhythm than the rest of the school year. When you use this time to build a positive group concept and provide lots of success and enjoyment, you help to create a good beginning for primary-school children.

A Good Day

The daily schedule in a primary-school program is influenced by the bureaucracy in which it is housed. Large elementary schools impose a structure of weekly assemblies, special classes, scheduled lunch and recess times, and teacher lunch hours and playground duty. Larger groups and higher child-teacher ratios are common. Within this structure, teachers plan a good day for the children in their class. Children's ever-increasing maturity allows you to forgo planned toileting and naps. Arrivals and departures may need little of your attention. Your role as a teacher in a primary school is to build routines that allow for maximal independence and ritual that brings a sense of security for the children you teach. This means a focus that has less to do with physical needs and more with psychological needs. A good way to start each day, for example, is a group gathering to share news, sing a song, and map out the day's direction. A good daily relaxation is sustained silent reading stretched out on a comfortable rug. And a good way to finish each day is listening to a chapter from a great book.

Good Endings

Everyone experiences some trepidation when anticipating change. Primary-school children of-ten enjoy looking forward to new events in their lives—new teachers, new classes, new challenges. Familiarity with the changes about to take place and time to talk about their hopes and fears will allow primary-school children, like their preschool and kindergarten compatriots, to fill endings with hope and promise.

DISCUSSION QUESTIONS

1. Recall a change in your life that involved separation from friends and family or a familiar place. How did you feel? What strategies did you use to cope with the transition? What do your responses suggest to you regarding working with children who are undergoing separation?
2. Remember your first day of school or your first day in a new school or class. What stands out in your memory? What was most reassuring? What was most frightening? Why?
3. Remember an early school experience. What are your memories of daily schedule and routines, arrival and departure? How were health and safety cared for?
4. Remember leaving a school at the end of the year or leaving to go to another school. How did you feel? What did your teacher do? What made it easy or difficult?

PROJECTS

1. Observe and keep a journal on a child during the first days and weeks of his or her school experience. Report on the child's responses to the school, the teacher's techniques for supporting the child, and the parents' reactions to the experience. Describe what you learned from your observation and its possible implications for you as a teacher.
2. Observe and describe an early childhood classroom, focusing on schedule, routines, and transitions. Comment on their effectiveness. What changes would you suggest to better meet the needs of the children? Why? What are the implications of what you learned for you as a future teacher.
3. Interview two teachers about how they handle children entering the school, issues of separation, and their ways of preparing children for the next class or school. Compare and contrast their responses. What are your thoughts about what they do and the implications for you as a future teacher?

4. Interview two teachers concerning any major health or safety issues that they have faced. What were the issues and how did they come to their attention? How were they handled? What community resources were used? What did they learn? Compare the two situations and suggest the implications for you as a teacher.

BIBLIOGRAPHY

Abt Associates. 1979. *Final Report of the National Day Care Study: Children at the Center.* Cambridge, Mass.: Contract No. HEW-10507401100.

Berger, A. S. 1971. Anxiety in Young Children. *Young Children.* 27 (October): 5–11.

Berk, L. E. 1976. How Well Do Classroom Practices Reflect Teacher Goals? *Young Children.* 33 (November): 64–69.

Blakely, B., R. Blau, E.H. Brady, C. Streibert, A. Zavitkovsky, and D. Zavitkovsky. 1989. *Activities for School Age Child Care,* rev. ed. Washington, D.C.: National Association for the Education of Young Children.

Bowlby, J. 1973. *Attachment and Loss.* London: Hogarth Press and Institute of Psychoanalysis.

Child Health Alert. Newsletter concerning current issues in children's health (P.O. Box 338, Newton Highlands, MA 02161).

Galinsky, E. 1971a. *School Beginnings: The First Day* (sound filmstrip). New York: Bank Street College of Education.

―――――. 1971b. *School Beginnings: The First Weeks* (sound filmstrip). New York: Bank Street College of Education.

Harms, T., and R. Clifford. 1980. *The Day Care Environment Rating Scale.* New York: Teachers College Press.

Hirsch, E., n.d. *Transition Periods: Stumbling Blocks of Education.* New York: Early Childhood Education Council of New York.

Janis, M.G. 1965. *A Two Year Old Goes to Nursery School: A Case Study of Separation Reaction.* Washington, D.C.: National Association for the Education of Young Children.

Jervis, K., ed. 1984. *Separation: Strategies for Helping Two to Four Year Olds.* Washington, D.C.: National Association for the Education of Young Children.

Kaplan, L.J. 1978. *Oneness and Separation: From Infant to Individual.* New York: Simon & Schuster.

Katz, L.G. 1977. Education or Excitement. In *Talks with Teachers,* ed. Lilian Katz. Washington, D.C.: National Association for the Education of Young Children.

Kendrick, A.S., R. Kaufmann, and K.P. Messenger. 1989. *Healthy Young Children: A Manual for Providers.* Washington, D.C.: National Association for the Education of Young Children.

Lazar, I., and R. Darlington. 1979. *Lasting Effects After Preschool: Summary Report.* Washington: U.S. Department of Health and Human Services, Administration of Child, Youth and Families.

National Academy of Early Childhood Programs. 1984. *Accreditation Criteria & Procedures.* S. Bredekamp, Ed. Washington, D.C.: National Association for the Education of Young Children.

Pantell, R.H., J.F. Fries, and D.M. Vickery. 1984. *Taking Care of Your Child.* Reading, Mass.: Addison-Wesley.

Read, K.B., and J. Patterson. 1980. *The Nursery School: Human Relationships and Learning.* 7th ed. New York: Holt, Rinehart & Winston.

Steinfels, M.O. 1973. *Who's Minding the Children?* New York: Simon & Schuster.

Stevens, J.H., and M. Matthews. 1978. *Mother/Child Father/Child Relationships.* Washington, D.C.: National Association for the Education of Young Children.

CHAPTER EIGHT

The Learning Environment

There is no behavior apart from environment.
—*Robert Sommer*

In this chapter, we discuss the environment of the early childhood program and its influence on children's development. We explore how an environment communicates to children and we offer guidelines to help you design spaces and choose equipment and materials. We introduce a number of specific dimensions and discuss how these can help in evaluating and modifying environments so they better meet children's needs.

The environment speaks to children. When they enter the classroom they can tell if it is a place intended for them and how it is best used. A cozy corner with a rug, cushions, and books says, "Sit down here and look at books." A ladder supported by two sawhorses and connected to the ground by a plank suggests, "Climb up, go across any way you can

think of, and jump down." An airy environment with light, color, warmth, and interesting materials to be explored sends a clear message: "We care—this is a place for children." In such settings, there is enough space to move comfortably, the furnishings are child sized, and the arrangement suggests how materials can be used.

Learning environments can meet the needs of children and support teacher values and developmental goals. As you design the environment you make choices that directly influence the quality of the child's relationship to other people and to learning materials. In making these choices, you need to consider three basic questions:

- Is the environment appropriate for the developmental stage of the children?
- How does the environment affect human relationships—among children, among adults and children, and among adults?
- How does the environment facilitate children's learning and development?

ORGANIZING SPACE FOR LEARNING

The kind of facility that houses a program is the first aspect that influences the environment you create. In the design of facilities, early childhood programs have frequently been afterthoughts and have been housed in buildings created for other purposes. Although these settings may not be ideal, they can be workable and even charming. We have known and loved programs in converted homes, church sanctuaries, basements, apartment buildings, offices, coffee houses, and storefronts.

The design of a building may suggest certain types of use. The way that you and children actually use the space may be different. Buildings with self-contained classrooms are designed so that single classes of children and their teachers work within four walls where most of the materials needed for learning will be found. Each group of children is intended to spend most of the time in "their" room. Teachers often use self-contained classrooms this way, but they can also use them in teams. Each room then is given particular functions (for example, one room may be the messy activity room with space for art and sensory activities). Groups of children have access to more than one room and their teachers have larger amounts of space within which to create a learning environment.

Open-design buildings, whether created for classrooms or converted, are constructed so that many people (sometimes all of the children in the school) will be within one room most of the time. Teachers can work in teams and arrange large interest centers throughout the open room, or they can try to create self-contained "classrooms" using dividers, furniture, and taped lines to suggest walls.

Extremes of either type of classroom are not optimal. We have seen teachers and children confined in classrooms that were little larger than closets and we have seen rooms housing over a hundred children where noise and confusion precluded conversation or concentra-

tion. Research suggests that program size and group size are two of the most important indicators of quality in child care. Smaller programs and smaller group size have a positive effect on children. It is possible to gain the advantages of a small program and small group in self-contained classrooms; it is virtually impossible to do so in open classrooms that house groups of more than twenty.

Both self-contained and open-design classrooms offer advantages and both have drawbacks. Self-contained classrooms offer children and teachers a homelike atmosphere, a pride of ownership in the classroom, and a feeling of security and belonging that is especially beneficial for very young children. Some self-contained classrooms are not large enough to provide the greater variety that teachers would like and that older or more experienced children may need. Large open-design classrooms offer more space, more variety, and more diversity. They are, however, usually noisy and may be distracting and confusing to children and frustrating to teachers who prefer to have greater control over the use of space. Large rooms with many children are inappropriate for infants and toddlers who thrive in environments that are more sheltered from stimulation and that are more like homes.

Program environments vary in the degree to which they can change, but building structure is not flexible. Although your first thoughts in accepting a job may not be about the environment, remember that this is a place where you will spend many hours of your waking life. It is important to make sure that it is one in which you can work effectively and comfortably.

We call classrooms in which arrangement allows activities to occur simultaneously with maximum child direction *child centered*. These settings tend to be natural, casual, relaxed, and spontaneous. A child-centered environment is a classroom where children work either individually or in small groups. Both quiet and noisy activities happen throughout much of the day.

Content-centered early childhood programs are represented by classrooms where teacher-selected and teacher-directed learning prevail. In these environments there is greater regularity, and they lack the spontaneity and freedom characteristic of more child-centered settings.

The organization of the learning environment can be viewed on a continuum from *child centered* to *content centered*.[1] The extreme, and inappropriate, content-centered end of the con-

tinuum is represented by early childhood programs, often in kindergartens and primary schools, where children spend much of their day seated at tables or desks while the teacher lectures or provides seat work. The extreme, and also inappropriate, child-centered end of the continuum is a center where materials are provided with little organization and minimal teacher planning or interaction. Classrooms for young children fall in many places between these extremes. They are most appropriate when they are informal in structure and rich in materials *and* when teachers plan to provide many and diverse experiences for children. Teachers who understand child development design space that gives children opportunities to move, interact, explore, and manipulate. The

[1]Our use of the terms *child centered* and *content centered* came after considerable debate. We rejected *open* versus *closed* because these terms often refer to architecture or the arrangement of space, and *structured* versus *unstructured* because we feel that all programs have structure that may be more or less visible.

developmental needs of young children require that they move their bodies frequently. They learn through physical interaction, manipulation, and sensory experience and not through paper and pencil tasks. An atmosphere of warmth and informality meets the social-emotional needs of young children.

Arrangement of Indoor Space

To create an appropriate classroom environment, many early childhood programs organize space into interest or learning centers. These may include areas for art, science, blocks, books, dramatic play, sensory materials, music, woodworking, and manipulatives. Learning centers are appropriate for children throughout the early childhood years. Typically they are found in classrooms for four- and five-year-olds, but they are also effective in programs for toddlers and school-age children.

When you design a classroom with interest centers, it is a good idea to begin by defining areas for different types of activities: messy, active, quiet, large group, small group. Areas that have particular requirements can be located first. Quiet areas should be separated from noisy areas. The art area should be near water and will be easier to clean up if it has an uncarpeted

floor. The block area should be set out of pathways between centers. It needs space to encourage complex building. We prefer low-pile carpeting to reduce noise—one-by-two-foot floorboards for building on are helpful if the area is carpeted. Other areas can be arranged in the remaining space with the purpose and requirements of the areas kept in mind. The library area will require good lighting. The science area may need an electric outlet for an aquarium. The record player in the listening or music center will also need access to electricity.

Aesthetics is another aspect to consider in arranging a classroom. We believe that children's classrooms should be among the most beautiful of places. Attention to the aesthetic quality of the environment means looking for ways to make aspects of the classroom harmonious (for example, by paying attention to color and design and by grouping shelves or chairs of the same color or design in one area) and by eliminating clutter. The accompanying box gives suggestions for the aesthetic enhancement of environments for young children.

Before you finish arranging your classroom space, and whenever you are about to change the environment, observe the room from the viewpoint of a child by sitting on the floor. Observe from the entrance and from each of the interest centers. Notice what you can see in each location—what is most attractive and what is most distracting. Your view now may be quite different from what you perceive from your regular height, and it will help you to design an environment that works for children.

Arrangement of Outdoor Space

Every program for young children also needs an outdoor play area. Just as there is variety in the buildings that house the programs, there is also variety in the available outdoor space. Unfortunately, large yards carefully designed for young children are the exception rather than the rule and programs often have to make do with far less than is desirable. Educators' ideas about the purpose and importance of outdoor environments have changed: an empty asphalt parking lot is no longer considered adequate. Since we know that children are learning all the time, not just when they are in the classroom, outdoor space and equipment should support a range of developmental goals: physical, social, cognitive, and creative. They also can be used for an endless variety of learning activities. Whether your outdoor space is a rooftop or a well-kept garden, there are things you can do to enhance

IN THE CLASSROOM: SUGGESTIONS FOR AESTHETIC ENHANCEMENT OF ENVIRONMENTS

- **Color:** Bright colors will dominate a room and may detract from art and natural beauty present. If you have a choice, select soft, light, neutral colors for walls and ceilings. Try to color coordinate learning centers so that children begin to see them as wholes rather than as parts. Avoid having many different kinds of patterns in any one place—they can be distracting and overstimulating.
- **Furnishings:** Group similar furniture together. Keep colors natural and neutral so as to focus children's attention on the learning materials on the shelves. When you are choosing furnishings, select wood rather than metal or plastic. If you must paint furniture, use one neutral color for everything so that you have greater flexibility in moving it from space to space. Have a cleaning day periodically—give children brushes and warm, soapy water and let them scrub the furniture on a sunny, warm day.
- **Storage:** Rotate materials on shelves rather than crowding them together. Crowded shelves look unattractive and are hard for children to maintain. Baskets make excellent and attractive storage containers. If you use storage tubs, try to put all the same kind together on one shelf. If you use cardboard boxes for storage, cover them with plain-colored paper or paint them.
- **Decoration:** Mount and display children's artwork. Provide artwork by fine artists and avoid garish, stereotyped, faded, or tattered posters. Make sure that much artwork (both by children and adult artists) is displayed at children's eye level. Use shelf tops as places for displaying sculpture, plants, and items of natural beauty like shells, stones, and fish tanks. Avoid storing teacher's materials on the tops of shelves—if there is no other choice create a teacher cubby using a covered box or storage tub.
- **Outdoors:** Design or arrange play structures to be an extension of nature rather than an intrusion upon it. If possible use natural materials like wood and hemp rather than painted metal, plastic, or fiberglass. Provide adequate storage to help to maintain materials. Involve children, parents, and other staff in keeping outdoor areas free of litter. Add small details like a garden or a rock arrangement to show that the outdoors is also a place that deserves attention and care.

the space to meet children's needs. Animals, gardens, sandboxes, and water play areas located outdoors can be the source of science, math, language development, and creative activities. Messy art materials like clay and finger paint are especially well suited to outdoor use. Many learning experiences take on new dimensions when they go on outdoors. A story about trees, for example, read in the shade of an oak provides concrete experience and carries new meaning.

The outdoor area is typically used as a site for physical development apparatus. Playground equipment and play structures are important components of the outdoor environment and should be organized and designed thoughtfully with safety and developmental goals in mind. In play yards that are used by children of a wide range of ages and with different degrees of strength and ability, there should be equipment that provides challenge and success at a number of different levels. Toddlers and younger children require different challenges than older preschoolers or kindergartners. If you work with younger children, you will want to make sure that play structures are lower and wider (to accommodate a child who needs time to climb up or down) and less steep. You will also want to minimize irreversible choices (for example, tall slides from which you can't back down). Older children require greater variety and more challenge in ways to get up and down. Older children also need additional movable equipment for organized games. We have found softer and more natural materials preferable for playground structures. Wood, hemp, and rubber are aesthetically pleasing and safe.

If there is not enough play equipment for the numbers of children or if there is insufficient variety or challenge, additional equipment can be improvised from tires, cable spools, ropes, cargo nets, and planks. Such improvisation can be a major effort that will be greatly assisted by involvement of parents and the community. Whether the equipment is purchased or impro-

vised, this part of your environment requires thoughtful planning and evaluation on a regular basis.

EQUIPPING AN EARLY CHILDHOOD PROGRAM

Equipment and materials suggest direction and provide raw materials for children's exploration, development, and learning. Generally, *equipment* refers to furniture and other large and expensive items such as easels and climbing structures. *Materials* usually refers to smaller, less expensive items such as puzzles, books, games, and toys. Consumables like paint, paper, glue, and tape are referred to as *supplies*. Through interaction with well-designed equipment and materials, children develop large- and small-muscle coordination, concepts about the world, creativity and self-expression, social skills, and self-awareness.

Both boys and girls need experiences with the same kind and variety of learning materials. Special care is needed to provide materials and present activities without subtly suggesting that one sex will find a particular material more attractive.

Selecting Equipment and Materials

When you bring any item into a learning environment, it will influence children. Good equipment and materials are attractive. They have sensory appeal—they feel good to touch and hold. They are sturdy and not easily broken and can be kept in good repair. Since they are the tools of learning, they must work properly and fit children's size, abilities, and interests. They must be nontoxic, adequately clean, and free of hazards like broken sharp parts.

Natural materials like sand and water, and supplies like paint and paper, are important materials which we consider in a slightly different way: their durability is not an issue and they suit a wide range of developmental stages and abilities. Primary concern must be given to the safety of natural materials and supplies and to having a sufficient quantity for the number of children.

Basic Furnishings

Environments for young children require furnishings that support classroom activities and respond to the needs of children. We favor wood because of its aesthetic appeal and sturdiness and because it is easier to maintain over many years than plastic or metal. Furnishings must be stable, portable, and have rounded corners and edges. Furniture should be proportioned to the size of the children. When seated in chairs at tables, children's feet should touch the floor and their elbows should rest comfortably on tabletops. Toddlers are better able to manage squat four-legged stools than chairs which tend to tip. Children should be able to reach the top of the easel. Small tables where several children can sit provide greater flexibility than large tables. Every child needs space for the storage of clothing and personal belongings. Manufactured or improvised *cubbyholes* meet this need. Low, open shelves are essential for the storage of materials that children use independently. Children should be able to see over shelves when standing to discourage climbing. Storage of this kind allows children to make choices and encourages them to become responsible for cleanup. A shelf especially designed for books invites reading by displaying the books with their covers facing the children. Since it is relatively easy for young children to return the books to such a shelf, it helps to protect books.

Adequate storage must also be provided for the adults who work with children. Materials that must be closely supervised such as cleaning supplies, files, first aid equipment, and teachers' personal belongings need secure storage within the classroom or nearby areas.

Equipment and Materials for Learning

An environment that supports the development of young children will have many different materials that can be thought about in categories which lend themselves to planning and organization. We have found it helpful to organize these into the following groups.

- Natural materials
- Active play equipment
- Construction materials
- Manipulative materials
- Dramatic play materials
- Art materials
- Books
- Cognitive materials
- Computers
- Television and video

Natural Materials. Sand, clay, water, and other natural materials provide children with rich sensory experiences and an opportunity to learn about mathematical concepts such as volume and measurement. Simple observation of almost any child will tell you that these are satisfying play materials. They are open ended and can be used in many ways. Children learn about the properties of substances through pouring, feeling, and mixing. They may be soothed by the responsiveness of the materials and can safely vent strong emotions in their play with them. Cooperative and imaginative play is fostered as children work together with them. Sand and water play areas are often found out of doors but they can also be provided indoors with tubs and water tables.

Active Play Equipment. Equipment for active play offers opportunity for vigorous movement and exploration. Active play helps children develop and explore their physical limits, develop creativity, release energy, and learn many spatial concepts (up, down, under, over) by experiencing them with their bodies.

Simple, inexpensive equipment such as sturdy wooden boxes, planks, tires, cardboard cartons, and natural structures such as logs, trees, and boulders can present appropriate challenges and encourage active play. Swings, slides, seesaws, rocking toys, tricycles, and wagons offer opportunities to use and develop the large muscles of the arms and legs and provide experience in balance and coordination. Rubber, wood, and hemp are more responsive than concrete and metal and are less likely to cause injuries. To ensure safety and appropriate challenge, all manufactured active play equipment should be scaled to fit the children.

Construction Materials. Construction toys like blocks and Lego™ help develop fine-motor coordination and strength, enhance imagination, and provide opportunities for children to work together. The use of these materials provides learning experiences in measurement, ratio, and problem solving.

A set of hardwood unit blocks is an essential part of a learning environment for young children. As well as providing the learning experiences of other construction materials, they also demonstrate mathematical relationships. For example, children experience that several blocks of one size are equivalent to one larger block. Blocks provide a medium through which children can express their growing understanding of their world. You can enhance and extend block play by adding toy cars, trucks, human and animal figures, and other props. In order for blocks to be fully used children need adequate space and sufficient time for block play. Clearly marked block storage shelves are important in helping children to find the appropriate blocks for their constructions and to enable them to take responsibility for cleanup.

Manipulative Materials. Manipulative materials like puzzles, beads, and pegboards are designed to give children practice in hand-eye coordination and to help develop the small muscles of their fingers and hands. These experiences are important preparation for writing.

They also expose children to such concepts as color, size, and shape which help in the ability to recognize letters and words. Children have opportunities to solve problems and be creative as they work with these materials.

Dramatic Play Materials. Dramatic play materials provide learning experiences and allow children to practice the skills of daily living. Manipulation of the physical environment, such as putting on clothes with buttons and zippers, and management of relationships are both learned skills. Children imitate the actions of the important grown-ups in their lives through dramatic play and thus learn about how different roles might feel.

Dramatic play materials can be organized in an interest center that includes dress-up clothes for different kinds of work and play, from different cultures, for different ages, and for both men and women. To prevent clutter clothes can be stored in sturdy, attractive boxes with lids. They can be organized by occupation or role types and brought out as desired. Dolls representing a variety of racial backgrounds and common objects of daily life such as kitchenware, books, furnishings, and tools also form part of the equipment of the dramatic play area.

Often dramatic play centers are organized into a "home" area emphasizing domestic activity. They can be changed to present other options: a post office, hospital, store, bus, farm, camp, or restaurant. Even though the home theme relates to the most common and powerful experience in children's lives, children themselves find new ways to vary the theme. In one classroom we observed children become a lively family of spiders when they spread a crocheted shawl between chairs to become a giant web. You can respond to children's dramatic play by adding appropriate materials when you observe a new interest developing; for example, you can contribute fire hats, a rain slicker, boots, and a length of hose when the children are pretending to be fire fighters rescuing the baby.

Art Materials. Art materials provide opportunities for creative expression, problem solving, and physical and sensory development. A good selection of art materials should include paint, crayons, dough, glue, clay, and collage materials. Chapter 12 provides a more detailed explanation of art materials and their uses for different age groups.

Books. The best way to help children to feel the joy of reading and become motivated to read is to have good books available and to use them often. Children need many opportunities to look at books, to hear stories, and to see adults using and enjoying books. The use of books is encouraged when you provide a book area that is comfortable, quiet, well lit, and stocked with a selection of good-quality children's books. Well-cared-for, appropriate books displayed at children's eye level on an uncrowded bookshelf with the covers visible invite children to use them. In Chapter 13 we describe criteria for selecting good books for children across the early childhood age span.

Cognitive Materials. All the types of materials and equipment we have just described contribute to intellectual development. Activities such as woodworking, cooking, and block building are especially important in helping children develop concepts. In addition, materials such as scales, balances, lotto, and matching games are specifically designed to help children learn about the world through the processes of comparison, classification, and measurement. Teachers can make games to teach concepts about the world. Many of the materials based on the work of Maria Montessori are designed to teach young children specific concepts through the manipulation of attractive materials. Chapter 14 provides information about the use of materials in the curriculum areas of math, science, and social studies.

Computers. Computers are another type of equipment that can contribute to children's development. They are not a substitute for the traditional play materials of early childhood education but they can be useful additions. Indeed, the question today is not *if* our children will become computer literate but *when*.

Debate about the answer to the question "when" is ongoing. Some educators have embraced the concept of computers in the early childhood classroom with great enthusiasm and little contemplation. Some equate computer competence with language competence; they fear that waiting will mean passing over a critical period and thus developing competence will be more difficult. Others have reacted to the idea of presenting computers to young children with indignance ("I know it isn't good for children so we shouldn't try it.") These educators fear that children may be robbed of the critical concrete learning opportunities of early childhood if computers are introduced too early; they believe that computers are too symbolic and abstract to be appropriate for young children. Neither of these points of view reflects that children, given choice, tend to select appropriate experiences and that eager learners of all ages have embraced computer use when it meets their needs, as we can attest from personal experience.

Remember that computers are powerful tools not electronic sorcerers. The issues that they bring up—the goals of education, appropriate methods of instruction, and hothousing young children—are not unique to computers. Computers can entertain, teach, and serve. They can free beginning learners from the tyranny of rote memorization and painful drill by making available calculators, spelling checkers, word processors, and programs that teach repetitive skills in entertaining formats. They also can be abused if impressive technology is substituted for understanding and sound practice.

As you might expect, research suggests that children's response to computers varies with their developmental stage. Children who have yet to begin symbolic drawing and who do not yet understand the concept of the printed word are more interested in and need concrete play materials. Computers in their classrooms are of only momentary interest. Children who do have these basic concepts (usually ages four and above) become fascinated by computers with age-appropriate programs and seem to see them as responsive television sets, and they are delighted to be in control of them.

The ways that computers are used and the purposes to which they are put can vary enormously. Although the technology of computers is innovative, many programs are simply electronic workbooks. As workbooks they can be more appropriate than the paper and pencil kind because they give immediate feedback and can select the appropriate skill level. However, even the best computer workbooks do no more than develop rote learning. Truly innovative and appropriate programs for young children can help them develop critical thinking skills and creativity, learn about computers and programming, and perhaps most important, help them learn to be confident members of the community of computer users.

Appropriate software (programs) for young children have been developed. If your school has funds to purchase computers for educational use, it is important to remember that not all computers are equal. You will need to do research to find the system that has software that meets your needs and is consistent with your values.

Early in the microcomputer revolution software for young children began to be developed. Like selecting any other educational material, selecting software requires making thoughtful choices that reflect appropriate goals and objectives. What makes software appropriate for young children?

- Concepts taught by the software must be *developmentally appropriate*. The concepts should be those young children can understand because they are concrete.
- The software must be *open ended*. Open-ended software allows a great deal of child choice and child direction. The *child chooses* what to do and when.
- The *pace* must be set by the child and not by the program.
- Programs must motivate with an intrinsically appealing *process* (such as exploring a computer-created environment) rather than with an extrinsic reward (such as a smiling face appearing in response to giving the correct answer to a computer-generated problem).

Television and Video. Television has been with us now for forty years and it is in the homes of virtually all young children in our society. Because television is so prevalent, it is impossible to ignore it as a force in children's lives. Also because of its prevalence, it is not something that children need to come to school to experience. In fact, most children will spend far more time in their lives in front of a television set than they will in school.

Children's television programming has been with us for nearly as long as television. All children's programs are not equal. They can be thoughtfully produced like the work of Fred Rogers and the Children's Television Workshop or they can be mere marketing devices for selling breakfast cereals and promoting war toys.

Television is present in many schools. Television, and its servant video recorders, have uses and abuses in early childhood programs. Used as a "plug-in drug" to keep children entertained and quiet in lieu of teacher contact and appropriate curriculum, television is an abuse and does not belong in early childhood programs. Used occasionally as a teaching tool with appropriate content and active teacher involvement, it can contribute to your teaching goals.

If television is present in your program you will need to decide if and how you will use it. What criteria can you use to choose or reject television in your classroom? Reject television for the following reasons:

- It is used on a regular basis for segments of more than ten or fifteen minutes.
- You do not know or have no control over the programs that will be watched.
- Programs talk down to children or are designed for an older audience and are above the heads of the children in your group.
- It is used as a baby-sitter.

Choose television for these reasons:

- It is used in short segments that you have previewed and like.
- Programs contribute to curriculum goals.
- You have time to sit and watch with a small group of children and talk with them about what they have viewed.
- Programs address children respectfully and are geared to their age.

The future will, no doubt, hold many changes for television. As more and more schools have video cameras and recorders, it becomes possible for teachers to use television to serve their curriculum. New technology in the form of interactive video-computer programs may eventually hold exciting possibilities for primary-school children. We believe that the abstract nature of a television program, however well done, makes it inappropriate as a major educational tool before primary school.

Arrangement and Storage

Attention to storage can contribute to the smooth functioning of a classroom as well as to its aesthetic quality. Uncrowded materials that are stored in attractive containers make the room a pleasant place in which to live and work. A thoughtfully organized classroom helps children to understand and maintain order.

JONES'S DIMENSIONS OF TEACHING-LEARNING ENVIRONMENTS

Hard-Soft describes the character of the environment. Softness changes the character and feeling of the environment and what happens in it. Homes are responsive because they have comfortable furnishings, carpets, decorations, and lighting. Softness is conducive to greater productivity, better craftsmanship, higher motivation and morale, and lower absenteeism. Early childhood classrooms provide a bridge between home and school and need to reflect the softness of homes. Hard environments are characterized by indestructible materials such as cement, garish or unattractive colors of paint, and harsh lighting. Hard environments are created because the clients (children, prisoners, the general public) are expected to damage soft, vulnerable settings and because such settings are viewed as serious and conducive to work. Teachers soften an environment with warm, physical contact with children and by providing comfortable furniture such as couches, pillows, rugs, grass, sand, furry animals, soft toys, sling and tire swings, dough, fingerpaint, clay, mud, water, and other messy materials.

Open-Closed is the degree to which materials, storage, program, and teacher behavior restrict children. The balance between open and closed varies both with the space and with the changing needs of children over time. Materials can be viewed as a continuum with closed materials such as puzzles, which have only one right way of being used, on one end with open materials where alternatives are virtually unlimited, such as sand and water, on the other end. Open materials inspire children to be innovative and to create their own challenges. Open-closed does not mean good-bad. Materials that are closed can be rewarding for children when the task provides both sufficient challenge and opportunities to succeed. Overly difficult materials cause frustration, and damage to the material is likely to follow. Younger or less experienced children require more access to open materials. Older, more experienced children also need and enjoy open materials but they enjoy closed challenges. When children appear bored or frustrated, the cause might be in the balance of open-closed experiences.

Simple-Complex describes the ways that equipment holds children's interest. Classrooms for inexperienced or less mature children need to be simple to enable them to focus and make choices without being overwhelmed. Older children can handle additional complexity. Complexity can be added by materials

Keep in mind that your classroom's primary function is to encourage children to engage with materials, a sometimes disorderly process. Avoid being excessively concerned with maintaining constant order while children are working, because such concern can be disruptive. Instead, work on building an environment and routines that contribute to helping children return to order as a worthwhile phase of the activity.

It is important that all new materials be introduced to children. This can be accomplished in a small group where children can talk or teachers. Entering the dramatic play area and saying "I think this baby is hungry" makes the environment more complex. *Simple* materials have one obvious use; they do not allow children to manipulate or improvise. They include trikes, slides, puzzles, and concept games. *Complex* materials allow children to use two different play materials together making play less predictable and more interesting; they hold children's attention for a longer period of time. They include a sandbox with tools, blocks with props, collage with paint. *Super* materials offer a larger number of possibilities and hold children's attention much longer. They include climbing structures with the addition of hollow blocks, sand with tools and water, dramatic play area equipped with furnishings, dress-up clothes, props, and dolls.

Intrusion-Seclusion concerns who and what crosses the boundaries between rooms; people, sights, sounds, and events within the center and from outside. Intrusion adds novelty and stimulation and enriches learning. Seclusion, shelter from stimulation, provides the opportunity to concentrate, think, and be alone. When opportunities for seclusion do not exist, children often create their own seclusion by hiding or by withdrawing emotionally. Tables or easels set up against walls provide *partial seclusion; insulated spaces,* with protection on three sides, allow a small group to share privacy; *hiding spaces*—cozy closed places in crates, lofts, or under a table—allow one or two children to escape the stimulus of the classroom.

Low Mobility-High Mobility characterizes activities by physical involvement and motion. High mobility involves large-muscle activities and active motion. Low mobility involves small-muscle, sedentary activities. It is important to provide opportunities for both. Classrooms can include miniature trampolines and access to outside yards. Quiet activities like painting, books, and table games can be provided outdoors where low mobility is often neglected. Teachers provide space, materials, encouragement, and model involvement in both high and low mobility. Since girls often have large-motor deficits, it is especially important that female teachers model high-mobility activity.

Source: E. Jones, *Dimensions of Teaching-Learning Environments: Handbook for Teachers* (Pasadena, Calif.: Pacific Oaks, 1977).

with you about safe and appropriate ways to use, store, and care for equipment. Although such an approach may seem time-consuming, it saves both time and materials and gives children the information they need to be full participants in the life of the classroom.

Materials that are reserved for special use by teachers need to be stored so they are clearly out of children's reach or view. If materials are stored on low, open shelves, they tell children that they are available for their use. When children look at the environment, they should be able to tell at a glance what materials are available to them. Low, open storage encourages independence and responsibility by allowing children to choose and return materials on their own. You may wish to aid this independence by creating a system to help children understand and participate in classroom organization. Materials can be stored in containers labeled with pictures of the contents. Shelves and materials can be coded with self-adhesive colored dots. Outlines of equipment can be drawn on shelves to help children match the equipment to its proper place.

MAKING THE ENVIRONMENT WORK

When you are planning an environment, you need to consider what kinds of experiences you want children to have. Arrangement of learning environments influences what happens within them. Robert Sommer, a psychologist who has studied the effect of environment on behavior, has said that "there is no behavior apart from environment, even in utero" (Sommer 1974, p. 19).

Look at the space and the equipment that are available and consider what you wish the environment to communicate to children. Keep in mind their age and experience. Create interest centers and make the environment as safe, aesthetic, and as supportive as you can. Since adults will spend time in the classroom, address their needs too. Create a corner where they can sit and relax on an adult-sized comfortable chair or couch.

Designing a learning environment is not a one-time event; it is an ongoing process. As you live and work with children, you will wish to remain sensitive to the ways their needs change as they grow and learn. Plan on regularly reevaluating and changing the environment. Any setting can be modified and improved.

Using a checklist, like the one at the end of this chapter which we designed for our students,

or the Harms-Clifford *Early Childhood Environmental Rating Scale* (Harms and Clifford 1980), and reviewing accreditation guidelines designed by the NAEYC can help you take a structured approach to this part of your work. We have found it helpful to use specific dimensions, or attributes, described by Elizabeth Jones in *Dimensions of Teaching-Learning Environments* (1977) as another kind of lens through which to observe and evaluate our environments.

ADAPTING THE ENVIRONMENT FOR DIFFERENT AGES

The basic guidelines for designing environments for preschool- and kindergarten-age children apply to programs for younger and older children as well, with some modifications.

Infants and Toddlers

Development and needs dictate the kinds of environments that work for infants and toddlers. Large, undivided rooms with many children and adults make it difficult for infants and toddlers to form bonds with caregivers and to follow their own schedules for eating, sleeping, and playing. They thrive in environments that, like homes, have fewer people and rooms that are more sheltered from stimulation.

Because a program for infants and toddlers has a larger number of adults per child, more space per child is required. Diaper changing is a prominent feature of the daily program, so a changing area with a sink and hot water is essential for health.

Learning centers as typically found in preschool programs are effective in programs for toddlers, but a room for infants can have a simpler arrangement. Clean, carpeted surfaces for playing and crawling, different levels for mobile infants to crawl onto, and a special area set aside for sleeping are desirable. Outdoors, low, wide climbing structures without irreversible choices, shady places, and a variety of different surfaces for walking and crawling make a good environment.

Furnishings

Manufacturers are still developing appropriate furniture for infant-toddler programs. Some equipment, like high chairs and playpens, is designed for home use and does not meet group-care needs. It may take extra effort to find appropriate furniture for an infant-toddler group. Special furnishings for infants and toddlers include the following:

- A sturdy changing table at a comfortable height for the adults in the program (we prefer changing tables that have a built-in trash can and space for each child's supplies).
- A secure sleeping place for each infant in the program.
- Low shelves that toddlers can see over.
- Small dramatic play furniture without cupboard doors that pinch fingers.
- Comfortable adult chairs for holding and rocking children.
- Squat four-legged stools for toddlers and tray chairs for infants.
- Stable equipment or cruise bars so children can pull up when they are ready to take first steps.

Equipment and Materials

Natural materials are generally safe and satisfying for infants and toddlers. The younger the children, however, the more you will need to supervise. A few substitute materials prevent problems:

For	Substitute
Clay	Dough
Sand	Flour, cornmeal, oatmeal, or rice

Active play equipment needs to be low to the ground and more stable than for older children. Challenges that toddlers and infants can master

include structures with ramps and entrances and exits to be climbed into and out of. Riding vehicles, pull toys that are stable without joints that pinch, low belt swings, and swings with seat belts are possibilities. Special attention should be paid to the surfaces under and around the active play equipment.

Construction materials must be larger and simpler than those for older children. It is particularly important that they are large so they cannot be swallowed, that they can withstand frequent sanitizing, and that pieces hold together easily. Light plastic or cardboard hollow blocks are better than heavy hardwood hollow blocks. Larger props are better for use with unit blocks. Be sure to have several identical toys and many pieces that are the same so that children can engage in parallel play.

Manipulative materials, like all toys for infants and toddlers, must be large and sturdy enough to withstand frequent sanitizing. They can include homemade toys like plastic bottles with clothes pegs to drop inside and commercially made equipment like busy boxes. Infants and toddlers often interpret everyday objects as manipulative toys, so it is necessary to keep these out of their reach if they are unsafe or inappropriate.

Dramatic play materials include simple hats, pieces of cloth, and clothes with few fasteners. Tote bags, dolls, and a few lightweight aluminum pots allow a range of dramatic play. Children will incorporate manipulative toys in their first efforts at symbolic, dramatic play.

Primary-School Children

The greater adaptability of school-age children allows a number of different kinds of environments to work well. Self-contained classrooms, several rooms, or large divided rooms can be used. Primary-school children thrive in environments that they can really own, where they can feel that they participate in taking responsibility for the classroom.

Learning centers as are typically found in preschool programs are very effective in programs for primary children. Space for individuals to work alone and space for the group to come together are also important. Carpeted surfaces for reading, working, and playing, places to be alone or work with a friend, and space for ongoing projects are all important in a primary classroom.

Equipment and Materials

Natural materials are used by primary-school children in ways that are more task oriented; for example, children might compare and contrast different natural materials and record the differences. Water might be channeled with pipes and tubing or the workings of a waterwheel or an aqueduct can be explored. Clay will be used to construct objects that can be fired and principles of claywork can be learned. Sand might be closely observed and different sands can be examined.

Active play equipment needs to be especially sturdy to withstand heavier bodies and the inventive minds that create many new challenges. Children need to be able to go higher, jump further, and learn new skills such as sliding down long poles, balancing along high balance beams, and turning on parallel bars. Hard surfaces for jumping rope and bouncing balls are needed. Hoops, bats, and balls for organized games are important.

Construction toys require greater intricacy and challenge. Primary children also enjoy the challenge of duplicating the complex structures portrayed on the boxes and in the direction pamphlets with which these toys often come.

Manipulative materials can include more complex games and toys such as jigsaw puzzles and real-life tasks such as cooking, woodworking, sewing, playing an instrument, or using a keyboard or an abacus. Specific equipment for the development of fine-motor skills can be combined with cognitive tasks such as following pattern cards for geoboards, attribute blocks, and beads.

Dramatic play materials can be fancier and more elaborate. Older children will make extensive use of props and may return to the same gear over and over to complete a costume or to a set of props to perfectly match a character. Encourage children to think of what is needed and create wish lists so that they can begin to gather the props for their play. Older children often want to extend dramatic play into dramatic performance and may find guidance helpful in presenting their dramas to the other children in the class.

Art materials can be more sophisticated. You might want a studio in the classroom where children can select a mode for creative expression.

Cognitive materials can be the cornerstone of a primary-school program as children seriously take on learning challenges.

Computers can become an integral classroom tool. Older children will make extensive use of computers in the classroom for writing and for learning about the technology.

IN THE CLASSROOM: LEARNING ENVIRONMENT CHECKLIST

Overall Atmosphere and Arrangement

Room Arrangement

_____ Room is well lit.
_____ Room is relatively sheltered from noise and outside stimulus.
_____ Room is orderly and attractive.
_____ Room is appropriately ventilated and temperature controlled.
_____ Paths do not lead through work areas.
_____ Noisy areas are separate from quiet areas.
_____ Shelf tops are uncluttered.
_____ Separate storage is provided for teachers.

Aesthetics

_____ Walls are painted in neutral, coordinated colors.
_____ Patterns, colors, and storage in centers coordinate.
_____ Activity centers are decorated with art prints, children's art, interesting photographs, book covers, and educational and parent displays. They are free of materials that promote products or depict media characters.
_____ Items of beauty such as flowers, plants, or sculpture are provided.
_____ Many pictures and displays are at children's eye level.

Space for:

_____ Block center
_____ Library
_____ Dramatic play center
_____ Manipulative toy center
_____ Art center
_____ Writing center (may be in art)
_____ Science/math center
_____ Private area for children
_____ Space for large-group gathering
_____ Space for messy activities
_____ Space for active play
_____ Space for small-group gathering

Furnishings

_____ Low, open shelves for each center
_____ Clean carpets
_____ Comfortable adult-sized furniture
_____ Low tables sized to children
_____ Easel sized to children
_____ Chairs sized to children
_____ High or closed shelves
_____ Adult-sized chair or sofa
_____ Enough chairs and table space for the number of children who use the classroom at any one time

Equipment

_____ Each center has equipment.
_____ Equipment is complete and unbroken.

continued

_____ Living creatures kept as pets are in clean cages, runs, or aquariums.
_____ Plants and animals are fed, have water, and are protected.

Checklist for Classroom Areas

Block Center

Location/space
_____ Located out of traffic pattern

Furnishings
_____ Low, open shelves with adequate space for all blocks to be stored easily
_____ Low-napped carpet to build on

Materials
_____ 100+ hardwood unit blocks for every four children using the area
_____ Ten to twenty-five shapes
_____ Figures and vehicles
_____ Posters or photographs to stimulate building

Organization
_____ Blocks arranged in order on shelf
_____ Marked for cleanup

For infants and toddlers
_____ May be omitted in infant rooms
_____ May be simplified for toddlers
_____ If present, includes large-scale props

For primary-school children
_____ Center larger and more complex
_____ 200+ blocks and at least fifteen block shapes
_____ Many props
_____ Paper and pens for writing signs
_____ Structures allowed to stay up for several days

Dramatic Play Center

Furniture
_____ Child-sized table with at least two chairs
_____ Open shelves for storage
_____ Small cupboard with closing doors
_____ Full-length mirror
_____ "Bed" sturdy enough to hold a child

Materials
_____ Materials in good condition
_____ Small-sized adult men's and women's clothes typical of daily life
_____ Uniforms, costumes, and props for different cultures and occupations
_____ Props to encourage multiage pretend play
_____ Posters and photographs depicting family, fantasy, and careers
_____ Two telephones

Organization
_____ Props and costumes organized into kits for easy storage and variation
_____ Shelves and hangers marked to help children in cleanup
_____ Clutter minimized with materials rotated with children's interests and themes

For infants and toddlers
_____ Small nonbinding clothes
_____ Big aluminum or plastic pots
_____ One doll per child

For primary-school children
_____ Prop boxes on shelf
_____ Full-length and handheld mirror
_____ Costumes

Library

Location and space
_____ Located away from noisy activities and traffic pattern
_____ Well lit
_____ Decorated with art prints, book covers, and posters

Furnishings
_____ Low shelf that displays books' front covers
_____ Comfortable, clean pillows, chairs, and carpeting
_____ Big comfortable chair where an adult can sit with a child and read

Books
_____ In good condition
_____ Appropriate for developmental stage of children in program
_____ Represent a variety of styles of illustration
_____ Do not depict negative stereotypes
_____ Not based on commercial products
_____ Depict multiethnic and multiage characters in nonstereotyped roles
_____ Depict females and males involved in nurturing and adventuring with a range of skills and occupations

Organization
_____ Includes a balance of different kinds of books
_____ Fiction: realistic and fantasy
_____ Accurate informational books
_____ Mood and concept books
_____ Poetry
_____ New and classic books (Caldecott and other award winners)

For infants and toddlers
_____ Board and cloth books
_____ Big cushions

For primary-school children
_____ Larger center
_____ Child-authored books
_____ Listening center with book-record sets
_____ Books that can be borrowed

continued

Manipulative Toy Center

Furnishings
_____ Low, open shelf to store materials
_____ Comfortable carpet or low tables for work

Organization
_____ Located close to work space
_____ Materials arranged in an orderly and attractive manner

Materials
_____ A variety of materials that require different skills
_____ Several choices for every child (two to three per child)
_____ Complete toys with pieces unbroken
_____ Complete puzzles

For infants and toddlers
_____ Pieces at least 1½-inch in diameter
_____ Puzzles with two to five pieces

For primary-school children
_____ Jigsaw puzzles
_____ Larger sets of toys with wheels, gears, etc.
_____ Directions and patterns

Art Center

Furniture
_____ Easel adjusted so that the smallest child can reach the top of one side
_____ Open, low shelves
_____ High or closed shelves for restricted materials

Equipment
_____ A variety of brushes (long and short handles, wide and narrow)
_____ Trays
_____ Airtight storage containers
_____ Clay boards and clay tools
_____ Bowls, spoons, and measuring tools
_____ Plastic cups or containers
_____ Scissors that cut well in either hand
_____ Dough boards and tools

Supplies
_____ Tempera paints in primary colors, black, and white
_____ Base or paint for finger painting
_____ Unwrapped crayons
_____ Nontoxic felt pens
_____ Potter's clay
_____ Food color
_____ Special papers (construction, tissue)
_____ Wide-weave fabric
_____ Recycled materials for use in activities and storage (cardboard, styrofoam, wrapping paper, ribbons, fabric scraps, plastic jars, jar lids)

_____ Watercolors
_____ Plain typing paper
_____ Flour, salt, and oil for dough and paste
_____ White glue
_____ Yarn

For infants and toddlers
_____ May omit potter's clay
_____ Large crayons
_____ Large chalk
_____ Short, wide brushes

For primary-school children
_____ Include pencil crayons
_____ Include oil-base modeling clay

Writing Center

Furniture
_____ Proportioned table and chairs
_____ Low, open, marked shelves for storage

Supplies
_____ Storage baskets, jars, or cans for pens, crayons, and pencils
_____ Peeled crayons
_____ Nontoxic felt marking pens
_____ Hole punch
_____ Paper cut in uniform sizes
_____ Recycled envelopes
_____ Sharpened primary pencils
_____ Yarn
_____ Rulers, protractors

For infants and toddlers
_____ Omit pencils
_____ Large crayons

For primary-school children
_____ Pencil- and thin wax crayons
_____ Lined paper
_____ Dictionary or word file
_____ Staplers

Science/Math Center

Furniture
_____ Low, open shelves for storage
_____ Low table or counter
_____ Water and sand table

General materials
_____ Trays
_____ Measuring cups and spoons
_____ Plastic tubs and pitchers
_____ Accurate information books
_____ Balance and scale
_____ Sorting trays
_____ Sorting collections (buttons, rocks, etc.)
_____ Photographs and posters that illustrate concepts

continued

Science materials

_____ Aquariums, insect and animal cages
_____ Probes
_____ Machinery to investigate and disassemble
_____ Magnifying glass
_____ Airtight containers for storage

Math materials

_____ Materials that illustrate sequence and proportion (e.g., Cuisenaire rods)
_____ Attribute beads or blocks
_____ Concept games
_____ Colored cubes

For infants and toddlers

_____ Omit tools and delicate equipment

For primary-school children

_____ Tools like knives and scissors

Outside Environment

Space

_____ Space for group to run and play
_____ Hard surface for vehicles away from other play
_____ Comfortable surfaces for sitting and lying
_____ Access to water for drinking and play
_____ Sand and dirt for digging
_____ Shelter from sun, wind, rain
_____ Plants

Equipment

_____ For climbing, sliding, swinging
_____ Sand and water tubs or tables
_____ Storage for sand and water tools
_____ Tools for digging and pouring
_____ Baskets and bags for ball storage

_____ Wheeled riding vehicles
_____ Portable equipment
_____ Wading pool
_____ Hoses and buckets

Materials

_____ Water and sand table or tub
_____ Large playground balls that bounce
_____ Props to encourage active play: parachutes, rope

For infants and toddlers

_____ Push vehicles

For primary-school children

_____ Cargo nets and ropes

A Woodworking Area

_____ Low, sturdy table for woodworking
_____ Small functional hammers, saws, drills, vise
_____ Wide-headed nails
_____ Soft wood scraps

FINAL THOUGHTS

Your home changes as you change. It reflects your needs, tastes, activity, and life. It grows with you and your family. Creating an environment for children and making it work is also a process of growth. It allows you to use your knowledge of children's development, your sensitivity in observation, and your creativity. As you gain greater skill and information, and as you devote time, energy, and resources to the environment, it will better meet children's needs. Such creation is a challenging and very satisfying aspect of being a teacher of young children.

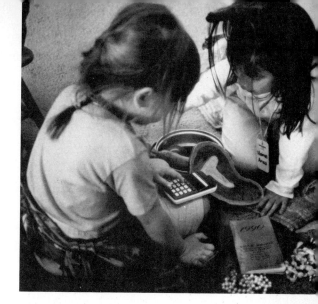

DISCUSSION QUESTIONS

1. Remember an early school experience. What stands out in your memory about the classroom, the playground, the equipment and materials, space for personal belongings, storage and distribution of materials, and the aesthetics of the setting?
2. Think about a program in which you have observed or worked. Discuss the arrangement of the classroom, the playground, the equipment and materials, space for children's belongings, storage and distribution of materials, and the aesthetics of the setting.
3. Refer to the box on Jones's dimensions of teaching-learning environments in this chapter to reflect on your college classroom. How might you change it to make it more effective for learning?

PROJECTS

1. Observe a classroom from a child's view by kneeling or sitting on a low chair. Observe from this perspective from the entrance and the interest centers. Write down all that you can see in each location. Go back to each position and observe it again from your regular height. Describe your experience. Did you experience the environment differently when you viewed it from a child's perspective? What did you learn about this classroom? What did you learn about the design of environments for children?
2. Observe a classroom focusing on the nature and arrangement of indoor space, the content and organization of outdoor space, equipment and materials, storage

and distribution of materials, the kinds of displays, and aesthetic aspects of the environment. Draw a diagram of the space. Discuss your thoughts about the environment and how you might change or modify it to better support the development of the children.

3. Plan your ideal environment for young children. Include a diagram of the indoor and outdoor spaces and a list of the equipment you would include. Describe your environment and explain your decisions in terms of your values and your goals for children.

4. Observe a classroom using the learning environment checklist on pp. 191–196. What centers are present and which are missing? What equipment and materials are not present in each of the areas? Analyze the adequacy of the environment in supporting children's physical, creative, language, and cognitive development. Discuss your thoughts about the environment and how you might change or modify it to better support the development of the children.

5. Observe a classroom and analyze it using Jones's dimensions of teaching-learning environments. Discuss your thoughts about the environment and how you might change or modify it to better support the development of the children.

BIBLIOGRAPHY

Bredekamp, S. 1987. *Developmentally Appropriate Practice in Early Childhood Programs Serving Children from Birth Through Age 8.* expanded ed. Washington, D.C.: National Association for the Education of Young Children.

CDA National Credentialing Program. 1976. *Preschool Caregivers in Center-Based Programs: Child Development Associate Assessment System and Competency Standards.* Washington, D.C.: CDA National Credentialing Program.

Child Health Alert. n.d. Newsletter concerning current issues in children's health (P.O. Box 338, Newton Highlands, MA 02161).

Feeney, S., and M. Magarick. 1984. Choosing Good Toys for Young Children. *Young Children.* 40(1)21–25.

Feeney, S., and E. Moravcik. 1987. A Thing of Beauty: Aesthetic Development and Young Children. *Young Children* 42(6):7–15.

Gandini, L. 1984. Not Just Anywhere: Making Child Care Centers into Particular Places. *Beginnings* (Summer): 3–8.

Gordon, T. 1974. *T.E.T.: Teacher Effectiveness Training.* New York: David McKay.

Gross, D. W. 1972. Equipping a Classroom for Young Children. In *Ideas that Work with Young Children,* ed. K. R. Baker. Washington, D.C.: National Association for the Education of Young Children.

Greenman, J. 1988. *Caring Spaces, Learning Places: Children's Environments that Work.* Redmond, Wash.: Exchange Press.

Harms, T. 1972. Evaluating Settings for Learning. In *Ideas that Work with Young Children.* ed. K. R. Baker. Washington, D.C.: National Association for the Education of Young Children.

Harms, T., and R. Clifford. 1980. *Early Childhood Environment Rating Scale.* New York: Teachers College Press.

Hill, D. M. 1977. *Mud, Sand and Water.* Washington, D.C.: National Association for the Education of Young Children.

Hirsch, E. 1984. *The Block Book.* Washington, D.C.: National Association for the Education of Young Children.

Howes, V. M. 1974. *Informal Teaching in the Open Classroom.* New York: Macmillan.

Jones, E. 1977. *Dimensions of Teaching-Learning Environments: Handbook for Teachers.* Pasadena, Calif.: Pacific Oaks.

Jones, E., and E. Prescott. 1978. *Dimensions of Teaching-Learning Environments II: Focus on Daycare.* Pasadena, Calif.: Pacific Oaks.

Kritchevsky, S., and E. Prescott, with L. Walling. 1969. *Physical Space: Planning Environments for Young Children.* Washington, D.C.: National Association for the Education of Young Children.

National Academy of Early Childhood Programs. 1984. *Accreditation Criteria & Procedures.* Washington, D.C.: National Association for the Education of Young Children.

Pantell, R. H., J. F. Fries, and D. M. Vickery. 1984. *Taking Care of Your Child.* Reading, Mass.: Addison-Wesley.

Phillips, D. A. 1987. *Quality in Childcare: What Does Research Tell Us?* Washington, D.C.: National Association for the Education of Young Children.

Prescott, E. 1978. Is Day Care as Good as a Good Home? *Young Children* 33(2)16–23.

Rausher, S. R., and T. Young. 1974. *Sexism: Teachers and Young Children.* New York: Early Childhood Education Council of New York City.

Ross, M. 1981. *The Aesthetic Imperative: Relevance and Responsibility in Arts Education.* Oxford: Pergamon Press.

Silberman, C. E. 1973. *The Open Classroom Reader.* New York: Random House.

Sommer, R. 1969. *Personal Space: The Behavioral Basis for Design.* Englewood Cliffs, N.J.: Prentice-Hall.

——————. 1974. *Tight Spaces.* Englewood Cliffs, N.J.: Prentice-Hall.

Sprung, B. 1975. *Non-Sexist Education for Young Children: A Practical Guide.* New York: Citation Press.

Stone, J. G. 1970. *Play and Playgrounds.* Washington, D.C.: National Association for the Education of Young Children.

CHAPTER NINE

Relationships and Guidance

Nothing I have ever learned of value was taught to me by an ogre.
Nothing do I regret more in my life than that my teachers were not
my friends. Nothing ever heightened my being or deepened my
learning more than being loved.

—*J. T. Dillon*

This chapter is about some of the most critical aspects of working in an early childhood program: developing positive teacher-child relationships, managing a classroom to support children's learning and relationships, and handling the conflicts that inevitably occur in groups of young children. We focus on approaches that enhance children's self-concepts and help them learn to live and work productively in group settings.

As a teacher of young children, you have a profound effect on every child you teach. No two children are alike and what you do, how you do it, and when you do it can be of great importance in their perceptions of you and of themselves. It is important that you strive to develop knowledge, skills, and sensitivity, so that your efforts to guide behavior are appropriate for the individual and supportive of children's positive sense of themselves.

Learning to create caring, supportive relationships with children is one of the most essential and rewarding tasks of the teacher. These relationships influence children's self-concepts, determine the quality of their educational experiences, and contribute to their deciding if school is a safe and trustworthy place to be. Only when they feel safe, cared for, and secure will they have the confidence to learn. Building positive relationships with children and creating a smoothly functioning classroom are the foundation for your teaching. Accomplishing these things involves skills in relating to and communicating with children, anticipating and preventing problems, developing rules to guide children's behavior, and utilizing effective techniques for managing the group and dealing with conflict.

SELF-CONCEPT

As children develop, they form concepts about the world and how it works; they also form concepts about themselves. Self-concept is the total picture that children have about themselves, based on their own perceptions and on what others tell them. One of the goals of early childhood education is to help children develop strong, positive, and realistic self-concepts. Self-concept influences children's ability to develop meaningful relationships with people, ideas, and the physical world. It includes perceptions of the physical self, of social and cognitive qualities, and of competence.

Children's self-concept is subject to change. They are greatly influenced by the "mirror" that significant people in their lives hold up to them and on how family members, peers, and teachers relate to them. Self-concept begins to develop in the first days and weeks of life and continues to build and change over time. Parents are usually children's first and most influential sources of information about who they are. It is from parents that children begin to establish their identities as individuals of a gender, race, and culture. They learn from parents whether this identity is desirable or undesirable. In families, children first learn whether they are acceptable or not. Their first appraisal of their intellectual potential and whether or not they are likely to succeed in the academic world also comes from their parents.

First teachers exert a similar influence on children's self-concepts. We have seen children enter early childhood programs with negative feelings about themselves and exit with a much more positive view. We recall $3\frac{1}{2}$-year-old Becky who entered a program unspeaking, thumb sucking, unwilling to engage with other children or to attempt simple classroom activities, and responding to all activities with a defeated "I can't." Becky's teachers gave her verbal and nonverbal encouragement, allowed her the time she needed to speak, and made sure she had a chance to try new activities, even if she failed to take advantage of the opportunity. They explained to other children, "Becky feels shy right now, but someday she may feel like talking and playing. We can just enjoy having her with us. We'll offer her a turn even if she doesn't want one." The teachers noted what Becky could do well and started to send other children to her as a resource. Becky did not become a social leader overnight, but gradually she began to appear more comfortable. Other children became happy to have her as a friend and Becky spent less and less time sleepily sucking her thumb. By the end of the year Becky was a somewhat quiet but enthusiastic member of the group.

As an early childhood educator, you are a significant person who has the power to influence children's sense of themselves. What you do may not be nearly as important as how you do it and what kind of person you are as you teach. Young children need teachers who accept them as they are and who encourage them to value and positively evaluate themselves. It is not necessary to love all the children you teach all the time, nor is it realistic to expect to. It is essential, however, that you communicate genuine respect and caring.

For you to be able to enhance the self-concept of children you must yourself possess a positive self-concept.

> Affirmation of self precedes affirmation of others, and an authentic adult can do much to induce and bolster a child's affirmation of himself by displaying rich and open feelings toward him, by showing unyielding confidence in him, and by providing and sharing with him genuine human encounters. *(Yamamoto 1972, p. 17)*

You need not view yourself as perfect to have a positive self-concept. We all have self-doubts and awareness of our own faults. Instead, you must appreciate your strengths, acknowledge your weaknesses, and have an inner acceptance of who you are. If you are unable to accept yourself, you may have difficulty being truly accepting of children however much you may think you like them.

Viewed broadly, this entire book is about how you can provide experiences that enhance the self-concepts of children. Many of your roles as a teacher can further this goal. Environments can be arranged to provide positive experiences, to encourage independence and responsibility, and to celebrate the individuals who make up the class. Routines can ensure that each child feels safe, secure, and capable. The curriculum can be designed to contribute to each child's positive sense of self. Perhaps most importantly, and the reason we include self-concept in this chapter, the ways that you relate to children, manage the group, and deal with interpersonal problems can have a profound effect on how the children view themselves as people and as learners.

At different ages and stages early childhood educators use different techniques to help children develop a positive self-concept. Frequent, affectionate physical and verbal contact, responsiveness to a baby's needs, and the provision of attractive, appropriate materials provide a sense of being valued. A comfortable environment with many safe yeses and few nos, with enough toys, laps, and hugs, and with a positive view of their struggles help toddlers to feel good about themselves. Preschoolers come to have a positive self-concept when they are valued for what they can do, are given many opportunities to do things for themselves, given lots of interesting things to do, and are forgiven for their lapses into asocial behavior. Lots of affectionate contact with adults who appreciate them, respect them, and provide clear limits completes the picture. Primary-school children feel good about themselves as they take on more and more real and meaningful learning and work. They need the guidance of warm, consistent adults who understand that they are capable and worthwhile people.

BUILDING RELATIONSHIPS WITH CHILDREN

An important part of your teaching role is to develop caring and supportive relationships with children. These relationships form the foundation from which children will explore, create, discover, communicate, and relate to others in early childhood programs. Children cannot be productive when they feel threatened, anxious, or uncertain.

Research on teaching and learning supports the view that good interpersonal relationships

are of primary importance in effective teaching (Gazda 1975). Good relationships between children and teachers, like all good human relationships, are characterized by the qualities of honesty, empathy, respect, trust, and warmth. They are authentic and not forced or artificial. In such relationships children must be safe from fear of physical and psychological harm that can make the teacher and the school potentially dangerous. Relationships and children's feelings about schools, teachers, and learning can be irreparably damaged by tactics such as corporal punishment and humiliation. They are damaging to children and a misuse of a teacher's power.

The most effective teachers we know have relationships with children that are characterized by appreciation and respect for the individual. These teachers feel good about their work and have clear and developmentally appropriate expectations of children based on knowledge of child development. They enjoy and often share in young children's viewpoints and are sometimes playful with them. Although they seem to gain children's willing compliance, they do not demand unquestioning obedience; in fact they welcome questions as signs of growing independence. These teachers see children as partners not adversaries. Nancy Weber-Schwartz (1987) describes them as professional and *not* patient, because patient teachers see themselves as martyrs, struggling through adversity imposed by the children. The professional teacher celebrates the children's growth with them.

Since each child is unique, your relationship with each child will also be unique. With capable and confident children, you too may be exuberant and join their play. With hesitant or awkward children, you may simply add an encouraging presence, a word of confidence, a touch, or a shared joy in success. You are also an individual so you will have your own unique style of relating with children.

COMMUNICATION

The quality of your relationships with children will be based to a great extent on your skill in communicating with them. How you communicate and what you communicate affect how children feel about themselves and the degree of safety and trust they feel in your classroom. Respectful communication conveys to children that you value their feelings and thoughts and that you trust their capacity to grow and learn.

Basic abilities that will help you be effective in communicating with children include the ability to listen and perceive their meanings accurately, the capacity to respond clearly and authentically, awareness of barriers to communication, and willingness to try to overcome these barriers. In our comments about communication, we will draw heavily on a book that we have found very helpful in developing our communication skills, *Teacher Effectiveness Training* by Thomas Gordon (1974).

Listening

The first skill that you will need to develop is the ability to listen. By this we mean that you truly understand the message that a child is giving. Listening well requires that you pay careful attention to words, gestures, body stance, movement, and tone of voice. Often we receive one message from a person's words while their body and expression convey something else. Young children's nonverbal messages are frequently your best source of information about their thoughts and feelings because their verbal skills may not be very well developed.

The more you know about a child (age; social, language, and cognitive abilities; family background and experiences), the better you will be at really understanding what that child is trying to communicate to you. The combination of this general knowledge plus attention to the immediate situation will enable you to understand the meaning behind the words and behavior at a particular time. We recently observed a three-year-old who was having a hard time at the beginning of his first school year. The morning was punctuated by bouts of crying and calling, "I want my Mommy!" As the children left circle time to play at different centers, the boy's crying started again and the cry for mommy took a new and more desperate tone accompanied by a dancelike motion. His observant teacher approached him, spoke with him quietly, and then led him off toward the bathroom. She had used her observations of this child, her awareness of his day at school, and her knowledge of three-year-olds to understand what the problem really was.

Listening also means being obviously attentive. You can demonstrate your attentiveness and "listen" better if you make eye contact with a child, crouch or sit at his or her level, and give responsive verbal and nonverbal feedback that says "I hear you, I am listening."

Roadblocks

Sometimes a teacher's response to a child's problem blocks communication. Gordon (1974) calls these responses the language of unacceptance or *roadblocks* to communication. This kind of response can tell a child that his or her ideas are unacceptable or irrelevant. Gordon describes twelve categories of roadblocks. Recognition of what they are and how they block communication will be helpful in observing yourself and learning new ways of responding to children's problems. Following are examples of Gordon's twelve roadblocks in a situation when a child will not come inside at the end of an outdoor play period. The child says, "I don't want to come inside."

1. *Ordering, commanding, directing:* "You are disobeying me. You must come in right now."

2. *Warning, threatening:* "If you don't come inside, you may not have a snack this morning."

3. *Moralizing, preaching, giving "shoulds" and "oughts":* "All of the other children are coming inside. You should come with your friends."

4. *Advising, offering solutions or suggestions:* "You need to play with your friends inside the classroom so that you won't miss activity time."

5. *Teaching, lecturing, giving logical arguments:* "If you stay outside you will miss activity time and you will be alone with no one to play with."

6. *Judging, criticizing, disagreeing, blaming:* "You always want to do something that you aren't supposed to and I am really tired of it," or "Why are you being so difficult?"

7. *Name calling, stereotyping, labeling:* "Only babies want to play outside all the time; big children come inside to activity time."

8. *Interpreting, analyzing, diagnosing:* "You must be lonely all by yourself. Do you wish you had a friend?"

9. *Praising, agreeing, giving positive evaluations:* "You're really a terrific helper. We need you inside."

10. *Reassuring, sympathizing, consoling, supporting:* "I know how you feel. You know, when I was a little girl I always wanted to play outside all the time too."

11. *Questioning, probing, interrogating:* "What's the matter with you today? Don't you feel well?"

12. *Withdrawing, distracting, humoring, diverting:* "Have you seen the new puzzles we just got? You're really going to like them."

As you read these you may be saying to yourself, "These don't all sound so bad. What can I possibly say that would not be a roadblock?" A response that is not a roadblock is one that will help you find out what the problem really is and that avoids leaping to conclusions before you have all the information. Effective responses respect and acknowledge children and allow them to tell you what is troubling them. For example:

CHILD: I don't want to come inside.

TEACHER: Really? Do you want to tell me about that?

or

I see that you'd rather stay outside right now. What is going on?

In some situations responses like questioning and interpreting are perfectly appropriate, but not when they are used before the child has a chance to express his or her problem. When you respond to children's concerns by telling them what to do or by warning them about the consequences of their actions, it can create a dependency on you to solve their problems or may make them angry and defensive. If you attempt to persuade them to your viewpoint, you may discourage exploration as well as communication. Similarly, evaluating children (positively or negatively) can effectively halt their attempts to share their feelings. Criticism or ridicule makes all of us feel foolish and unacceptable. Avoiding talking about feelings or problems by analyzing them or by distracting or humoring the child may communicate disregard for the child's true feelings. What all of the roadblocks have in common is that they keep you from focusing on what is really happening in the situation. Some of these responses (such as questioning, interpreting, or giving advice) may be used profitably once you really understand the child's needs and concerns.

Responding

The responses you make to children demonstrate that you listened and understood their communications, both meaning and feelings. What you say and your nonverbal messages communicate that you really heard. Timing, the quality and register of your voice, facial expression, gestures, and body posture often convey more to a child than the words you use. Remember that even highly verbal preschoolers were nontalkers only a year or two ago. It is easy to be misled into thinking that language is their first mode of response—it is not.

An appropriate response to a child's words can be to simply listen quietly and acknowledge what you have heard with a nod, smile, or word of encouragement. Children then know that you are paying attention to them and that you care. Such responses give more time to a child who is struggling to express ideas and feelings in words, and they may give you time to try to piece together the words and body language of a very young child.

Words of encouragement invite further communication. They say, "I'd like to hear more about that." You may want to think about what you will say to encourage children. Statements like, "I see," "Tell me more," "Yes," "Is there anything else you want to tell me?" and "Thank you for telling me" are encouraging responses.

Sometimes, despite our best efforts to understand children, we make mistakes. To avoid doing so you can restate what you think a child has communicated to you or ask a question that is an interpretation of a child's message. This allows the child to confirm your interpretation or correct any misunderstandings. For example, we recently heard a child say, "I want poopoo." Her teacher responded, "Are you looking for the purple pen?" which the child confirmed.

It is useful to look at communication as a code for a person's feelings as well as thoughts. How you interpret what the other person means may be accurate or inaccurate. *Active listening* is the term used by Gordon to describe a process in which you listen and respond appropriately to the feeling as well as the content of a message. You give the child the opportunity to clarify the message and express the feelings involved. Here are two examples of a situation where a child's words and actions had different meanings and the teacher used active listening:

Situation 1:

A two-year-old child, during the first month of school, was absentmindedly stacking blocks. His teacher walked by and the child said, "When is my Mommy coming?" The child's voice, face, and body communicated worry and sadness. The teacher responded, "Do you miss your Mommy? It sounds like you wish you could see her right now."

Situation 2:

A four-year-old child, during her fifth month of school, was intently building an elaborate block structure. The teacher walked by and the child said, "When is my Daddy coming?" The child's face, voice, and body communicated intense concentration. The teacher responded, "Are you worried you'll have to stop before you're finished?"

The teachers in both of these examples used knowledge of the children and their situations as well as observing nonverbal cues to make an educated guess regarding each child's feelings. They then helped the children to feel free to talk further about their concerns and needs and gave them the opportunity to correct the teachers' perceptions. When you use active listening, you help the child feel free to think, discuss, question, and explore. Active listening is especially valuable because it demonstrates to children that you really care about how they feel.

Communicating with Children When You Have a Problem

You demonstrate understanding of children's problems through your willingness to listen to them and hear their feelings. When you have a problem, when your needs and rights are being violated, or when a situation makes you uncomfortable or unhappy, listening does not help. Sending an *I-message,* another technique described by Gordon, is a way to communicate your problems and feelings without telling

children that they are wrong or that you don't respect or care for them.

Feelings, especially unpleasant ones, can be difficult to share, but collected negative feelings can come out harshly and may damage relationships. If you don't maintain your own rights in the classroom or if you try so hard to be nice that your needs are not met and respected, you may find yourself disliking children.

When you give an I-message, you maintain your rights, get your point across, and avoid hurting children or your relationship with them. An effective I-message has three elements:

1. A statement of the condition or behavior that is problematic.
2. A statement of the effect on you.
3. A statement of the feelings generated within you.

A teacher who is having trouble reading a story to a group of children might give the following I-message: "When you talk during the story, it's hard for others to hear and I feel frustrated." This statement does not send a negative evaluation, and it leaves the solution in the hands of the child. A more common response than the one above might be to respond with a roadblock: "Stop talking! You will have to leave the circle if you can't be quiet." Such a *you-message* focuses on the child's behavior in a blaming or evaluating manner, ignores the effect of the behavior on others, and imposes a solution on the child. It denies the child the opportunity to solve the problem.

I-messages communicate that even if you don't like a particular behavior or situation, you trust that the child is caring enough and capable of helping to solve the problem. Often the behavior will stop once the child knows that it causes a problem.

Conversing with Children

Teachers who love their work genuinely appreciate and respect young children. They show this through conversation in which both the teacher and child share their ideas and feelings.

Good conversations begin with genuine shared interest. The workings of the plumbing, the quality of the easel paint, the traits of a favorite character from a story or television show, home, family, the world, and thousands of other shared experiences make up the content of conversations between teachers and children. Too frequently teachers talk with children only to give directions, handle problems, pronounce facts, or teach skills and concepts. Even though these are parts of every teacher's day, they are not the stuff of which relationships and communication are built.

A conversation with a child requires some special techniques and an investment of time and attention. Since there is a size difference that interferes with adult-to-child conversation, get down to the child's level, make eye contact, and speak in a relaxed and natural voice using words and a style of speech that is not unlike the way you talk with your own friends. There is also a vast difference in experience between you and young children. To minimize this you need to talk about things that are within both of your experience. The emotional tone of your words need not be highly modified for children but it should express your real feelings. Obviously you cannot talk about all the adult aspects of your life, but it is possible to have worthwhile and enjoyable exchanges with children.

Praise Versus Encouragement

For many years teachers were taught that praise is an important teaching tool; they were told to use it generously with children in their class-

IN THE CLASSROOM: SOME DIFFERENCES BETWEEN PRAISE AND ENCOURAGEMENT

Content

- Praise is about externals.
  "That is the best painting I ever saw."
- Encouragement is about internals.
  "It's really satisfying when you finish a painting that you have worked on so hard, isn't it?"

Focus

- Praise focuses on the person or product.
  "Good girl!"
  "That's beautiful!"
- Encouragement focuses on the effort or feeling.
  "You worked for a long time on that."
  "You really concentrated while you were painting."

Source

- Praise originates with the one who praises.
  "I love your picture!" (I evaluate you.)
  Encouragement originates with the one who is encouraged.
- "It looks like you feel really proud of that picture." (You evaluate yourself.)

---

rooms. Praise, it was said, makes children feel good about themselves and motivates good behavior and learning. This is part of the folk wisdom of teaching, especially in the elementary school. Today, some psychologists and educators are raising questions about the effectiveness and even possible negative consequences of excessive and inappropriate use of praise (Farson 1988; Hitz and Driscoll 1988).

Praise, though it may make a child feel good for a moment, implies a judgment and can also create anxiety—inviting dependency on adult judgment and fear of negative evaluation. It is not conducive to self-reliance, self-direction, or self-control. We often see praise used in classrooms not as genuine recognition of positive behavior but as manipulation. The statement favored by many teachers, "I like how Amy is sitting!" is rarely meant to acknowledge Amy's good behavior; rather, it is a way to get another child who is not behaving into line. Although this is more humane than bawling out the disruptive child, it can generate negative feelings toward the "good" child who is always being commended and, more important, it dilutes the value of authentic praise.

Praise that is not genuine ("That's beautiful!" for every picture the teacher sees) and praise used to manipulate behavior can result in lack of faith in the teacher's judgment or even evoke defensiveness and hostility. Genuine praise, sometimes called *encouragement* to distinguish it from judgmental praise, gives children information about what the teacher appreciates and encourages internal sources of evaluation rather than reliance on external judgments.

Barriers to Communication

When you are aware of those things that get in the way of communication, you can work to avoid them. Barriers to communication include physical distractions, personal bias, inappropriate or disrespectful ways of talking, and roadblocks that stand in the way of really hearing what someone is saying.

Distractions in the environment can create barriers. If the environment is too noisy, crowded, or uncomfortably hot or cold, it is difficult to focus on what another person is saying. Communication is facilitated when you make the environment a comfortable place.

Strong feelings about an individual's appearance, race, culture, or personality may also hinder communication. As we discussed in Chapter 1, The Teacher and Values, everyone has some biases, but these need not damage relationships. You can be aware of and thoughtful about your own strong feelings with the goals of not letting them be apparent and becoming more tolerant of others. Your example will help children and other staff members learn to be accepting as well.

Communication can be hindered when you are unaware of the effect of your words on others. It is not respectful or appropriate (nor is it true communication) to talk to others about children in their presence, to talk through a child for the benefit of the adults or other children who might be listening. Similarly, sarcasm and humor at children's expense while pretending to talk with them is disrespectful.

Another barrier to communication can be the manner in which teachers speak to children. "Cute," condescending, or artificially sweet ways of talking send the message to children that they are not worthy of sincerity and respect. Teachers who have a genuine interest in children speak to them without such artificiality and never cut a conversation short because the subject matter isn't "nice."

The degree to which a teacher's talking dominates conversations also may be a barrier. Teachers often talk a great deal and leave little time for children's responses. Perhaps teachers feel that such talking is a part of their role, or maybe they are uncomfortable with silence or are uninterested in what children have to say. Continual talking gives little opportunity or encouragement for children to express ideas and feelings.

The challenge in communication is to keep alive your own awareness of the ways you talk and respond. Notice the circumstances that surround children's active and eager communication with you or another adult and contrast it with the times when the child withdraws or conversation is difficult. Be aware of the times when you feel threatened or turned off by other people and try to learn from these situations.

CLASSROOM MANAGEMENT

Another important element of your role as a teacher, and one that may be quite new and unfamiliar to you, is managing a group of children. You may have decided to enter the field of early childhood education because you enjoy children and like to watch them grow and learn. It can be surprising and discouraging to discover that in spite of love and care your classroom can sometimes be chaotic and filled with discord.

You have spent many years learning to be responsible for your own behavior, but it is quite another thing to learn to manage the behavior of others—especially a group of lively young children. The younger the children are, the less likely it is that they will be skilled in relating to others or functioning in group settings, and the more likely it will be part of your task as a teacher to help them learn these things.

IN THE CLASSROOM: ANTICIPATING AND PREVENTING PROBLEMS

Arranging the Environment

- Set up well-defined centers that are physically separate from one another.
- Make sure there is enough space for children to play without stepping on one another (at least 35 sq. ft. of space per child).
- Keep activity centers out of paths between areas, the doors, or the bathroom.
- Position library and writing centers so you can work in them and see the rest of the room.
- Arrange the furniture to avoid corridors which invite running and noise.
- Provide space for children to work with others and other space where they can be sheltered from the group.

Selecting and Arranging Materials

- Make sure there are several appropriate and appealing choices for each child in the room.
- Introduce several new or appealing activities simultaneously or make sure that there are enough materials for every child to use a new activity the day it is introduced.
- Clearly mark shelves so that children know where materials belong.
- Avoid crowded shelves.
- Remove broken or damaged materials.
- For younger children, make sure there are several identical or similar materials.

Planning the Schedule

- Plan opportunities for both energetic physical activity and restful activity in any half-day period.
- Plan time for activity that is self-selected and for group activity.
- Plan a more flexible structure for younger children.
- Maintain the same, well-organized routines and transitions every day.

Teacher Behavior

- Remember that your own behavior is the most powerful teacher—model what you want children to do.
- Make sure that the curriculum includes talking about feelings.
- Teach about cooperation and nonviolent resolution of conflict before problems occur.
- Avoid teacher tasks that are unrelated to children (for example, phone calls).
- Encourage children to take out materials, clean up, and tend to their own belongings.
- Think about new activities, materials, and events ahead of time to anticipate possible problems.

Anticipating and Preventing Problems

When children have opportunities for interesting things to do, sufficient time to complete activities, and access to caring adults, they are likely to enjoy school and to learn. Before a child steps through the door of your room on the first day of school there is important planning that you can do to ensure that problems will be kept to a minimum. An orderly environment with well-defined space, lots to do, and a schedule that is developmentally appropriate, with well-organized routines and transition times, will contribute greatly to the functioning of a classroom.

The box on p. 211 contains strategies and guidelines that can help you plan a classroom where children's self-esteem is supported and where problems are minimized.

Rules

Rules enable people to exist together in harmony. They are clearly stated expectations and guidelines for behavior that are essential for making a classroom function effectively. Children need to learn many things about life in school: what behaviors are acceptable, how to handle routines and materials, and how space is to be used. Frequently problems in the school setting occur because children lack information. You will need to communicate your expectations with clarity and simplicity. A rule is a statement of your expectations.

Rules for young children need to be simple enough so that they can be easily understood and few enough to remember. Establish only those rules that are necessary for making the setting function. A few general rules that address important principles of behavior are better than a laundry list that addresses every conceivable situation.

Rules should guide children to do something rather than deny them an activity. They must also be appropriate to the developmental level of the children. It is unreasonable, for example, to make a rule requiring young children not to move or talk. Children respect rules when they understand the reasons for them and when the behavior required is within their ability. Following are some examples of rules and their reasons:

RULE: Walk and talk quietly where people are working.

REASON: If there are lots of people working with lots of things, children can be hurt when they move quickly, and noise makes it hard for people to work.

RULE: Treat people gently.

REASON: Children cannot work and play at school if they are afraid of getting hurt.

RULE: Use toys and games carefully.

REASON: Toys and games can get lost or broken if they are not used carefully. Then we would not have them to use anymore.

RULE: Put toys and games away when you are done.

REASON: When toys and games are left out, it's difficult to find them again.

We have observed two kinds of problems with rules in early childhood programs: either there are too many rules or rules are vague or unclear. When there are too many rules, it is difficult for children to remember them. Teachers then spend much of their time enforcing rules or else they can only enforce the rules sporadically without clarity about which are most important.

When there are not enough rules or rules are ambiguous, children lack necessary direction and limits. A rule such as "blocks are for playing" fails to address the issue of using blocks as weapons or missiles and hence can be misunderstood and not followed. A clearer rule would be, "Use blocks only for building." Inadequate rules can jeopardize the safety and orderliness of the environment and children and can result in injuries, broken equipment, and chaos.

Rules are mutual guidelines for behavior that all of the members of a group must understand and support. Children abide by rules that are clearly stated and consistently enforced. In agreeing to a rule both teacher and child are making a commitment to the safety and well-being of the individuals in the group. You can help children understand the underlying principles of your shared rules by repeating the reasons for them and by reminding children that the rules are there to protect all of the children—including themselves.

Group Dynamics

Skilled teachers understand the dynamics of groups and know techniques for managing them that help children to follow the rules, stay on task, and minimize disruption from the minor problems that occur in every classroom.

Kounin (1970) has described group skills held by teachers who have well-managed and productive classrooms:

- *With-it-ness:* The ability to be aware of what is going on in the classroom and to deal with inappropriate behavior quickly and effectively.
- *Overlappingness:* The ability to deal with a number of events at the same time.
- *Flow or momentum:* The ability to keep activities moving in a smooth flow without digressions and distractions.
- *Group focus:* Awareness of the fact that they are working with a group at all times, alerting the group before changes in activity and keeping all of the children involved. Teachers are sometimes so busy focusing on individual children that they lose track of the group.

Awareness and management of the group is an essential aspect of teaching young children. The accompanying box gives some techniques that we have found helpful over the years in managing a group of young children.

Managing Large-Group Time

In working with young children, group management skills are especially important during those times of day when the teacher meets with all of the children in a large group. These times work best when they have a wide appeal, allow children to be actively involved, and are relatively short (ten to fifteen minutes for younger preschoolers). As children grow older, their interest in and ability to participate meaningfully and for longer amounts of time increases (up to half an hour). When leading a large group, you are the center of the learning experience—the leader and entertainer—and the children respond to your direction. Your sensitivity to the mood and energy of the group and your ability to respond to it will determine whether or not you keep your audience interested, involved, and cooperative. A large group will fail if it

IN THE CLASSROOM: SUGGESTIONS FOR GROUP MANAGEMENT

- As the noise level during group time rises, talk more softly. Children often will listen out of curiosity and the noise will diminish.
- Position yourself so that you can see what is happening throughout the classroom.
- To get children's attention, move close to them, crouch down to their level, and speak directly to them. Avoid shouting across the room or yard or addressing the group about a problem with an individual.
- Use children's names positively and frequently so that they don't fear something negative when you address them by name.
- Indicate what to do rather than what not to do when correcting behavior. People often feel rebellious and challenged when they are told what not to do.

For	*Substitute*
"Don't run with the scissors."	"Please walk when you carry scissors so no one will get hurt."
"Don't get paint on your clothes."	"Wear a smock so you won't get paint on your clothes."
"Don't tear the book."	"Turn the pages carefully."
"Don't poke the guinea pig."	"Use very gentle pats and quiet voices so you don't scare the guinea pig."

- When a child doesn't respond appropriately to the above examples, give the child two acceptable choices. Choices help people to feel powerful and in control.

  "Please walk when you carry scissors so no one will get hurt. I'd be happy to carry the scissors while you go outside to run."

  "Wear a smock so you won't get paint on your clothes. You may use pens or crayons if you don't want to cover up your new overalls today."

  "Turn the book's pages carefully—you can use newspaper if you'd like to tear."

- Avoid giving children choices that you are unwilling or unable to allow. "Would you give me the knife?" is not appropriate when you mean "I must have the knife right now; it is dangerous!"

requires too much waiting or if children lack interest. When you reach the limits of children's interest you need to say, "That's all for today." Beginning teachers often find managing large groups taxing. Learning to read and respond to a group takes time, experience, and self-confidence.

Dealing with Conflicts and Problems

No matter how carefully you plan, some conflicts and problems will inevitably arise in a group of young children. Conflict is a part of life both inside and outside of the classroom. Young children are just beginning to develop the knowledge, attitudes, and skills needed for living with groups of people and for dealing with their feelings. Not infrequently they come into opposition with you and with each other. Sometimes teachers are uncomfortable with conflicts and see them as barriers to their "real" job of teaching. It is more productive to see conflicts as opportunities to help young children develop self-control and self-discipline; to teach about cooperative, nonviolent conflict resolution; and to help children learn to be contributing members of a group.

When children have conflicts, teachers can offer guidance to help them learn to control and redirect disruptive behavior. In doing this you need to respect and accept the child. You can help children understand the effects of their behavior on themselves, on others, and on the total functioning of the school environment.

You can become sensitive to the struggles, feelings, and situations that bring children into confrontation with one another. Many children lash out when they are tired or frustrated. Regardless of the circumstances, children need to learn that although they must not act in ways that hurt people or property, it is all right to have strong feelings and to express them. When conflict threatens to cause serious harm, you must act immediately. With practice, children can learn to tell each other how they feel and

what they want instead of striking out when a confrontation occurs. When conflicts occur it is more effective to ask *what* can be done so that children can return to their activities than to ask *why* they came into conflict. Causality is usually complex, and if you didn't see the confrontation you are unlikely to get an accurate picture of what occurred. In the long run it is more productive to help the children to find a solution to their problem than to try to serve as judge of the situation.

You show respect for children by helping them understand the possible consequences of undesirable behavior and giving them the option of controlling behavior themselves. Such an approach indicates that you see them as mature and intelligent enough to control their own behavior. Acknowledging acceptable behavior and communicating clearly when and how a behavior is unacceptable are effective management strategies and help children to develop self-control.

The way you deal with conflict is an important model for young children. They can experience that conflict is a part of life that, while not pleasant, is an opportunity for problem solving rather than something that is violently disrupting and harshly controlled.

Discipline Versus Punishment

Dealing with problems and conflict is not always easy. As you struggle for classroom "control," you may wonder how (or if) this is possible without resorting to negative and punitive techniques. It may be helpful to understand the differences between punishment and discipline.

Discipline is a process designed to help children develop self-control—to learn, understand, and use constructive behaviors instead of misbehavior. Appropriate action resulting from discipline is the result of internal control. *Punishment* is an act designed to stop unwanted behavior by inflicting retribution that is painful or unpleasant. It does not teach alternatives or

IN THE CLASSROOM: EXAMPLES OF WAYS OF TALKING WITH CHILDREN ABOUT PROBLEMS

- "I won't let you hurt Harrison. You can tell him that it makes you mad when he takes your truck and ask him to give it back to you."
- "I can see you're angry about what happened. How can you let him know?"
- "Let's think of some other ways to handle this problem."
- "Batman is an outside game. It isn't safe for the classroom. Please choose something else to play right now."
- "There's only room for five people at the cooking table. Would you like to wait in the writing center or would you like to put your name on the list for cooking tomorrow?"
- "I know you want to keep playing but it's outside time now. Would you like to put all the blocks away by yourself or would you like me to help you?"
- "That hurt Althea's feelings and she's really sad now. Please stay with me— maybe we can help her feel better."
- "There isn't room for five children on the tire swing. Would you like to choose who goes first or shall I help?"
- "What can we do to solve this problem so that you can go back to building your tower?"

enhance understanding. "Good" behavior resulting from punishment is the outcome of fear.

Corporal punishment is never acceptable in an early childhood program because it demonstrates that it is all right to hurt someone if you are big enough. Additionally, although children who have been physically punished may behave appropriately when there is an adult threatening them, at later times they tend to show increased aggressive behavior (Honig 1985).

The central goal of discipline is to help a child learn self-control. How you achieve this goal will depend on the values you have for children, your comfort level with children's behaviors, the demands and constraints of the school setting, and your ability to communicate effectively.

Three Theoretical Approaches

A number of programs have been designed to help teachers address problems and conflicts in the classroom. Three of the best known of these are based on differing theoretical approaches. In this section we will discuss the humanistic approach based on the work of Carl Rogers, the democratic approach based on the work of Alfred Adler, and the behaviorist approach based on the work of B. F. Skinner. All can offer useful techniques for helping teachers deal with classroom problems.

The Humanistic Approach. The humanistic philosophy and therapeutic practices of Rogers have been applied to classroom management by a number of interpreters including Haim Ginott (1972) and Thomas Gordon (1974). In this approach, the values of positive self-regard and individual responsibility are emphasized. The teacher's central tasks are to develop good relationships between individuals and within groups, and to help children realize their unique potential and their capacity to see the world and themselves positively.

To accomplish these goals, teachers need the skills for achieving open, honest, and authentic communication that we described at the beginning of this chapter. They also need to be able to send nonjudgmental messages to children about the effects of behavior and engage in problem solving to find mutually acceptable solutions.

Gordon gives guidelines for handling problems by involving children in finding creative and mutually acceptable solutions to interpersonal conflicts. In this problem-solving process you begin by defining the problem and then invite the child to join you in figuring out a solution:

Define the Problem First

TEACHER: When you run and holler in the room it's dangerous and it makes it hard for people to work. What shall we do about that?

CHILD: I could run behind the block shelf—no one is playing there.

TEACHER: That's one solution, can you think of any more?

CHILD: I could run outside or I could climb on the inside climber instead.

Together Think about Whether the Solution Will Work

TEACHER: Do you think it would work to run behind the block shelf?

CHILD: No, there's not enough room.

TEACHER: There's no teacher outside right now so that won't work either. Would climbing on the inside climber work?

CHILD.: Yes.

TEACHER: I'm so glad your idea worked. The room is a much better place for all of us to work now.

We find that young children are often interested in and able to go through this simple problem-solving process. When we have consistently involved children in handling problems with us, we have found that they also start to do this quite effectively in their own problems with peers.

Our college students often ask us what to do when I-messages and problem solving don't work. Used consistently with goodwill these techniques will be effective with many children. If a child is having trouble cooperating and the teacher's patient efforts to elicit cooperation are unsuccessful, the teacher may use a more directive technique (depending on the age of the child and the frequency and seriousness of the problem). A child's repeated failure to cooperate is often indicative of a deeper problem. It may suggest stress in the home or inconsistency between the discipline used in home and school.

The Democratic Approach.   Rudolf Dreikurs (1969) has interpreted and applied to classrooms many of the ideas of Adler's individual psychology. In the democratic approach, the individual's ability to function cooperatively in social settings is valued. Children are viewed as social beings with a strong desire to be part of a group. Disruptive behavior is seen as a result of not knowing how to be part of the group in a positive and cooperative manner. When children feel unsuccessful in gaining acceptance within the group, they become discouraged and try to gain entrance in disruptive ways.

The central task in this approach is to help children discover appropriate ways of gaining approval and becoming respectful and responsible members of a group of peers. This is done by establishing a group in which the teacher functions as the leader and employs the democratic concepts of respect, cooperation, and participation in decision making. The rules for group living and the consequences for breaking the rules are first established. If a child uses a toy to hurt someone else, the *logical consequence* might be to lose the opportunity to play with that toy. In following through on the consequence the teacher would be calm and would not be angry but simply say, "You may not play with that now. You used it to hurt; you may play with it another time." Children confront the direct consequences of their behavior and thus learn the laws of living as a member of society.

The use of a *time-out* period as a consequence of unacceptable behavior comes from the democratic approach. A child whose behavior seems out of control may need time away from the group to calm down until he or she is able to return to acceptable group behavior. Providing a safe space away from others for a child to regain composure can be helpful. Time-out used as an island for calm reflection can be an effective and humane way to help children gain self-control. We have sometimes observed it incorrectly used as a punishment. The key elements in time-out are that it is not punitive and that it is self-regulated—the child determines when to return to the group.

The democratic approach to guidance relies heavily on teacher control of the consequences and on children relating the consequences to their past behavior. In order to be effective with young children, the rules must be few, the consequences very clear, and the follow-through consistent, timely, and just.

The Behaviorist Approach.   The behavior management principles and techniques developed by Skinner have been interpreted and applied to classroom discipline by many theorists and educators. These professionals see all behavior as a function of learning, so that procedures for evoking desired behaviors and changing undesired ones can be taught. They believe that children misbehave because they have been improperly rewarded.

The behaviorist approach stresses the shaping of children's actions in desired directions through the creation of purposeful and orderly learning environments. Teachers' actions can reinforce negative behavior; it is important, therefore, that teachers ignore what is undesirable and reward desired behavior. When used in classrooms, behavior management techniques help teachers to control events so that the children behave according to the prescriptions of the adult. The teacher does not engage in conflict, but rather decides which behavior is to be reinforced and which is to be extinguished. Children who have severe behavior problems may respond well to this systematic approach.

All teachers use behaviorist principles some of the time either knowingly or unknowingly. When you smile at a shy child who attempts a new activity for the first time, you are providing reinforcement. When you fail to respond to a child whose demanding behavior is disruptive, you are avoiding reinforcing it. We find it most useful to become aware of how we reinforce behavior and what is rewarding to different children. We recently observed a teacher who took a child on her lap and gently stroked his back while she explained why he should not have hit another child. Her actions were more powerful than her words and the child was rewarded for his aggression. If she had realized that this child was using negative strategies to gain her attention, she might have taken special care not to reinforce disruptive behavior and to give him attention when he was doing something positive.

An approach that is currently in vogue in many schools, Lee Canter's Assertive Discipline, is based on behaviorist principles. Teachers who use this method record children's unacceptable behavior on the chalkboard using a system of check marks. Consequences for each checkmark are predetermined. Although there are teachers who like this approach for its consistency, some early childhood educators (Gartrell 1987; Hitz 1988) have reservations about it. They question the equity of a system in which every infraction of rules (a whispered comment to a neighbor or a painful poke) is treated in exactly the same way in spite of the intention, the severity, and the consequences. Another criticism is that this and other behaviorist techniques do not actively involve children in becoming responsible for their own actions.

Applying the Theories. All of these management approaches can be used in ways that take into account individual needs and that are respectful of children. Each has value in different kinds of situations. The communication and problem-solving skills used in humanistic approaches are helpful for building relationships and dealing with everyday upsets and problems. They work well when children have few deep-seated problems and are used to dealing with

adults in verbal reciprocal relationships. They are less immediately effective with children who are not used to this kind of relationship or with very young children who have limited verbal ability. Other strategies may, at least initially, need to be employed with these children.

When conflicts arise, the democratic approach may help children understand the mistaken strategies that they have adopted and allow them to redirect their behavior more positively. And when destructive patterns have developed and become habitual, the consistency and power of reinforcement techniques may be effective in changing or eliminating the behaviors. In our opinion, behaviorist techniques are called for only after humanistic and democratic approaches have failed. We do not believe that behaviorist techniques are appropriate for normal young children who will respond to much gentler approaches, though we have found them helpful in working with children whose behavior was very disruptive. Katz's paper "Condition with Caution" (1971) reminds us that behaviorist techniques are only appropriate when negative behavior is an outcome of conditioning. Other approaches are called for when disruptive behavior is caused by emotional problems or by a lack of information about what's appropriate.

It is important to keep in mind the fit between what you do and your long-term goals for children. Without this awareness you can accumulate a grab bag of techniques that "work," that is, control immediate behavior problems. Your decisions about the success of management techniques should focus on whether the outcome is likely to have long-term positive effects rather than on whether the technique is effective at that moment.

The Troubled Child

Every teacher will encounter troubled children. Sometimes it will be a child who is having a bad day, sometimes one who is going through a hard time, and at other times a child who has serious problems beyond the scope of your training and resources (see Chapter 15, Working with Children with Special Needs, for more information about identifying and working with children with severe emotional problems). These problems can take the form of rudeness, resistance, rebellion, withdrawal, and even violent outbursts. It can be frustrating and it can make you angry when a child hurts others or refuses to comply with your classroom rules. Some troubled children are regarded as "difficult" not only because they misbehave but also because they can make teachers feel incompetent.

In dealing with a troubled child first remember that all behavior has a cause. Try to look at and understand the behavior from the child's point of view. When you do so you will almost always recognize stresses in the child's life that make the behavior understandable. Children who have frequent problems and outbursts may be telling you that they need help. Teachers, parents, administrators, and local mental health professionals need to work together to make sure that a child who is in emotional distress receives help.

For many years we have found guidelines in Bruno Bettelheim's book *Love Is Not Enough* (1950) helpful for handling destructive behavior and for reassuring violent children. Bettelheim suggests telling these children that you will not allow them to hurt themselves or other people, nor will you let anyone hurt them. As children learn that their feelings will be respected, their needs met, and that they will be protected from retaliation, they may turn less to destructive behavior.

A child who is fiercely lashing out and hurting self or others must be physically restrained. This can be done gently and firmly. Hold the child from behind so that you can contain flailing arms and legs. Although you may be upset, speak calmly and let the child know that as soon as he or she regains self-control you will let him or her go. If your environment contains safe, open space away from others, you might wish to take an out-of-control child to a space where the angry feelings can be worked out in vigorous physical activity that does not harm anyone. Violent outbursts are usually short lived, especially if you help children learn to control themselves—and if you believe that they can.

In addition to helping a child negotiate problems you can provide alternatives to disruptive behavior. This is especially important if the behaviors have been found useful in other settings or have been used to fulfill basic emotional needs. Children may need time, courage, and your persistent encouragement to change from old reliable behaviors to new untested ones, even when the old behaviors no longer work. The time children are in the process of changing can be the most frustrating time for a teacher.

The discipline techniques that work with the other children in a classroom will work with difficult children, but you will find yourself more challenged in trying to apply them. Change does not happen overnight and you may find yourself needing special strategies and support as you help a child to become a functional member of the group. In addition to being clear, consistent, and following the other strategies previously mentioned in working with a difficult child, we find these techniques helpful:

- Identify the things that you genuinely like about the child and tell him or her.
- Identify for the child what he or she is doing correctly.
- Let the child know you are committed to helping him or her make it in the classroom and that you believe that will happen.
- Have sincere, positive, physical contact with the child every day.
- Notice your own aggravation and find ways to release it away from children.
- Find a coworker to talk to during the days when the child's behavior is giving you difficulty.

Also keep in mind that there are some children who need more intensive supervision and help than you are able to provide in a regular classroom. You need to try your best to help a troubled child learn to function in school. But when the child is not improving in spite of your best efforts, it is time to call in parents for a conference, to have a mental health specialist observe the child, or even to make a referral to a setting that specializes in working with troubled children.

ADAPTING FOR DIFFERENT AGES

This chapter, like the rest of this book, addresses general techniques and strategies that are appropriate for working with children between birth and age eight. And like the rest of this book, we pay particular attention to the years from three to five. If you work with infants and toddlers or if you work with primary-school children, you will find that there are some differences in the ways you establish rapport and guide children.

Infants and Toddlers

When you relate to infants and toddlers you communicate with your whole being—voice, body, and heart all communicate. The best teachers of infants and toddlers that we know talk to even the youngest child with the tone and respect that they would use with a friend. They always explain what they are doing before they move a child and give time and attention to each interaction from play, to feeding, to diapering. For these teachers there is no such thing as routine. When a toddler behaves in an unacceptable way or an infant's action must be stopped, teachers who understand this age very gently and clearly explain what must be done and why. "I can't let you pull my hair. That hurts me. Here, you can hold your red rattle." Do the children understand? Infants and toddlers, like the rest of us, understand kindness and respect; understanding the words may come much later.

Primary-School Children

Older children also have different needs and require slightly different teaching strategies. The hallmark of the primary-school years is the development of feelings of competence. Primary-school children need teachers who speak with clear authority, who like them a lot, and who are extremely fair. Your clear excitement about learning, your confidence in their ability to live up to your high expectations, and your willingness to let them be responsible will be the relationship foundation upon which your work with primary-age children will be based. Their greater competence and experience will also enable primary-school children to engage in more creative and challenging testing behavior. A sense of humor helps. The most effective teachers of primary-age children that we know are warm and down-to-earth. They are able to combine the capacity for affection, a sense of humor and fun, and a no-nonsense approach to serious matters that serves them well and makes their children their biggest fans.

FINAL THOUGHTS

Despite the good advice and good examples that you receive in your college courses, you will likely find that your first experiences in trying to manage a group of children will be challenging. It's important to realize that children will test you to find out what they can expect from you in order to feel secure in their classroom. Any teacher, experienced or not, will be tested by children during their first days with a group. Experienced teachers are usually clearer about their expectations of children and communicate these from the very beginning in words, body language, and behavior. Children quickly become "well behaved" with them, in a way that may seem like magic to a new teacher. Less experienced teachers often hesitate and send mixed messages. Children respond with continued testing. When you become clear on your expectations and how to communicate them effectively, teaching becomes much easier. Clarity comes with time, practice, and patience.

DISCUSSION QUESTIONS

1. Recall a relationship you had with a teacher. What can you remember about the way this teacher listened to and spoke with you? What were your feelings about the teacher and the classroom? What implications might this memory have for you as a teacher?
2. Recall an experience at home or school that made you feel good about yourself. What implications might this memory have for you as a teacher?
3. Recall an incident in which you were punished or reprimanded in school. What happened? How did you feel and what were the effects on you? What do you wish had happened? What implications might this have for you as a teacher?
4. What rules and management techniques do you remember as a child in school? Were they effective? What were your feelings about them?
5. Think about a classroom you have recently observed or that you have worked in. Discuss the ways that teachers communicate with children and the kinds of relationships they have with them. How do teachers handle rules, manage the group (especially at large-group times), and deal with interpersonal conflicts?

PROJECTS

1. Observe a teacher in an early childhood classroom and describe her or his communication and relationships with children. Include ways of conversing with children; how she or he listened, responded, and communicated problems; and any barriers or roadblocks to communication. In what ways did you observe the teacher using praise or encouragement? Discuss implications for children's self-concepts, your feelings and reactions, and the possible implications of this observation for you as a teacher.
2. Observe a teacher in an early childhood classroom and describe the ways that she or he managed the classroom. Include your observations of the teacher's approach to anticipating and preventing problems, the use of rules, and skill in group management. Discuss implications for children's self-concepts, your feelings and reactions, and the possible implications of this observation for you as a teacher.
3. Observe a teacher in an early childhood classroom and describe his or her ways of handling interpersonal problems. Include your observations of the use of discipline versus punishment in handling conflicts. What evidence did you see of the use of the theoretical approaches described in this chapter? Discuss implications for children's self-concepts, your feelings and reactions, and the possible implications of this observation for you as a teacher.

BIBLIOGRAPHY

Bettelheim, B. 1950. *Love Is Not Enough.* New York: Free Press.

Bredekamp, S. 1988. *Developmentally Appropriate Practice in Early Childhood Programs Serving Children from Birth Through Age 8.* Expanded ed. Washington, D.C.: National Association for the Education of Young Children.

Canter, L. 1988. Assertive Discipline and the Search for the Perfect Classroom. *Young Children* 43(2):24.

Carkhuff, R. R. 1972. *The Art of Helping.* Amherst: Human Resources Development.

Charles, C. M. 1985. *Building Classroom Discipline.* 2d ed. New York: Longman.

Combs, A.W., A. C. Richards, and F. Richards. 1976. *Perceptual Psychology.* New York: Harper & Row.

Dillon, J. T. 1971. *Personal Teaching.* Columbus, Ohio: Merrill.

Dinkmeyer, D., G. D. McKay, and D. Dinkmeyer, Jr. 1980. *Systematic Training for Effective Parenting* (kit with leaders' manual). Circle Pines, Minn.: American Guidance Service.

Dreikurs, R. 1969. *Psychology in the Classroom.* New York: Harper & Row.

Erikson, E. H. 1963. *Childhood and Society.* New York: W.W. Norton.

Essa, E. 1990. *A Practical Guide to Solving Preschool Behavior Problems.* 2d ed. Albany, N.Y.: Delmar.

Evertson, C., E. Emmer, B. Clements, J. Sanford, and M. Worsham. 1984. *Classroom Management for Elementary Teachers.* Englewood Cliffs, N.J.: Prentice-Hall.

Faber, A., and E. Mazlish. 1980. *How to Talk So Kids Will Listen and Listen So Kids Will Talk.* New York: Avon Books.

Fargo, J.M. 1974. *Education for Parenthood in the Community College.* Ph.D. diss., University of Washington, Seattle.

Farson, R.E. 1988. Praise Reappraised in *Harvard Business Review.* Boston.

Gartrell, D. 1987. Assertive Discipline: Unhealthy for Children and Other Living Things. *Young Children* 42(2):10–11.

——————. 1987. Punishment or Guidance? *Young Children* 42(3):55–61.

Gazda, G.M. 1975. *Human Relations Development.* Boston: Allyn & Bacon.

Ginott, H. 1972. *Teacher and Child.* New York: Macmillan.

Gordon, T. 1974. *Teacher Effectiveness Training.* New York: David McKay.

Hitz, R. 1988. Assertive Discipline: A Response to Lee Canter. *Young Children* 43(2):25–26.

Hitz, R., and A. Driscoll, 1988. Praise or Encouragement: New Insights into Praise. *Young Children* 43(5):6–13.

Honig, A.S. 1985. Compliance, Control and Discipline, Part 2. *Young Children* 40(3):47–52.

Jones, E., ed. 1978. *Joys and Risks in Teaching Young Children.* Pasadena, Calif.: Pacific Oaks.

Katz, L.G. 1971. Condition with Caution: Think Thrice Before Conditioning. *Preschool Education Newsletter* (February).

Kounin, J. 1970. *Discipline and Group Management in Classrooms.* New York: Holt, Rinehart & Winston.

Marion, M. 1987. *Guidance of Young Children.* 2d ed. Columbus, Ohio: Merrill.

Maslow, A. 1968. *Toward a Psychology of Being.* New York: Van Nostrand Reinhold.

National Association for the Education of Young Children. 1987. Ideas That Work With Young Children: Good Discipline Is, in Large Part, the Result of a Fantastic Curriculum! *Young Children* 42(3):49–51.

Stone, J.G. 1979. *Discipline.* Washington, D.C.: National Association for the Education of Young Children.

Weichert, S. 1989. *Keeping the Peace.* Philadelphia: New Society Publishers.

Weber-Schwartz, N. 1987. Patience or Understanding. *Young Children* (3):52–53.

Yamamoto, K., ed. 1972. *The Child and His Image.* Boston: Houghton Mifflin.

PART IV

THE CURRICULUM

The five chapters in this section deal with aspects of the curriculum in the early childhood program. Chapter 10, Curriculum Planning, presents a framework for thinking about and designing meaningful and appropriate learning experiences for young children. Chapters 11 through 14 deal with four broad areas of early childhood curriculum: physical development, the arts, language and literacy, and cognitive development. In each chapter we provide you with a lens through which to view development and an introduction to effective teaching practices.

CHAPTER TEN

Curriculum Planning

"Would you tell me, please, which way to go from here?" asked Alice. "That depends a good deal on where you want to get to," said the cat.

—Lewis Carroll

Awareness of alternatives and the bases of choices distinguishes the competent teacher from the merely intuitive one.

—Elizabeth Brady

In this chapter we explore the nature of curriculum and the things that need to be considered in planning curriculum for young children. We discuss long-term and short-term planning, the selection of appropriate themes, unit planning, the planning of activities, and how these can be thoughtfully combined to provide a developmentally appropriate and meaningful program for children.

Alice's conversation with the Cheshire Cat suggests an important issue in working with young children. How can teachers decide what they are to do in their classrooms if they do not know where they are going? A companion to the question, "Who am I in the lives of children?" is "Why are you involved in the lives of children?" or, put another way, "What are you trying to accomplish as a teacher—for children and for society?"

Young children are learning all the time and from all of their experiences, both in and out of school. Teachers need to ask: "How, when, and in what ways do I want to intervene in this natural process?" Because children are so interested in the world, the choices about what to teach in an early childhood program are almost infinite. Nevertheless, choices must be thoughtful and appropriate for the children you teach. Planning is essential.

WHAT IS CURRICULUM?

In early childhood education definitions of curriculum cover a broad range. At one end are those that focus on everything a child experiences throughout a school day, planned and unplanned, sometimes summed up by the following phrase: Curriculum is what happens. At the other end are definitions that focus on planned learning experiences. It may help to reconcile these somewhat disparate views if we think about curriculum in terms of what teachers intend (*the planned curriculum*) and what is actually perceived and experienced by the children (*the experienced curriculum*).

We define curriculum in this book as the planned experiences designed to enhance children's social, emotional, cognitive, and physical development. In this chapter we give an overview of the curriculum planning process, and in the four chapters that follow we describe in more detail how teacher-planned experiences can support these four areas of children's development. Curriculum can be seen as consisting of three interconnected parts: the nature of the learner (*who* is taught), the content or subject matter (*what* is taught), and the process or the actual engagement of children with planned learning opportunities (*how* it is taught). Teaching is the process by which a person mediates between another person and the world to facilitate learning. But remember that what children learn does not always directly correspond to what teachers believe they have taught, so it is important to keep checking to find out what children have actually experienced.

The three components of curriculum (learner, content, and process) are inextricably linked, and each needs to be considered carefully in designing meaningful learning experiences for children. Early childhood educators are trained in child development, so they tend to place great emphasis on who and how they teach and less attention on what they teach. In contrast, in elementary and secondary schools where teachers have more background in curriculum, there has been greater emphasis on content, what is taught, and less on the learner.

The planning process for curriculum for learners of all ages includes the following seven elements, each of which must receive careful attention:

1. Reflection on educational mission or purpose. Statements of purpose may include

aims (inspirational ideals based on philosophy and values), *goals* (broad desired learning outcomes), and *objectives* (intended learning outcomes stated in specific terms).
2. Selection of content.
3. Organization of content.
5. Ways of delivering the curriculum—strategies or methods.
6. Planned activities (lessons).
7. Evaluation.

These elements interact with each other; decisions made in one area will have an impact on the others. Curriculum needs to be carefully considered if teachers are to avoid having a grab bag of unrelated activities. Thought must be given to the progression of curriculum over time, so that children have mastered simpler skills and understandings before they are introduced to more difficult ones, and so that there is a logical progression between activities and topics.

DESIGNING CURRICULUM

Curriculum is a product of its time. It changes as society changes and as knowledge of children and learning changes. It is based on a vision of the society, on a philosophy of the role of education, and on some structured way to translate this vision into learning experiences. According to Ralph Tyler, whose writing on curriculum theory has been influential for many years, curriculum can originate from three broad sources: (1) beliefs about what is true and important to know; (2) learners and their patterns of development; and (3) knowledge or subject matter (Armstrong 1989). Planning curriculum involves a series of choices which are often based on changing educational goals and values. These choices are reflected in a hypothetical pendulum that swings in cycles alternating between an emphasis on the nature and interests of the learner and emphasis on the subject matter—what is to be learned. For example, in the 1960s and early 1970s many American schools emphasized the child-directed project approach that characterized the British Infant Schools of that time; this approach was followed by a back-to-basics movement that stressed the three Rs, traditionally taught, as the most desirable approach to curriculum. Because of its historical roots, early childhood education has always placed primary emphasis on the learner. Nevertheless, over the past several decades there has been strong pressure, based on the concern that children get an early start in academics, to increase attention to the teaching of specific subject matter and to paper and pencil tasks.

There is a very wide range of curriculum in early childhood education today. Many programs nurture the natural curiosity and exuberance of childhood with a meaningful and intellectually stimulating program that combines child-chosen play and developmentally appropriate planned activities. Some programs fail to provide stimulation and rely on a few unvarying play areas; the same manipulatives, crayons and paper, outdoor equipment, well-used books, and a meager selection of blocks each day. Others provide a mishmash of unrelated activities posing as curriculum. For example, we once observed a unit on transportation that involved easel painting on truck-shaped paper, singing "The Wheels on the Bus," and making cars of celery; the teacher did nothing to help the children see the connection between these activities and activities in their daily lives. Still other programs base planning on workbooks or inappropriate prepackaged materials that appeal to adults but expect children to learn from abstract tasks that are not meaningful or appropriate.

Factors to Consider in Designing Curriculum

Teachers make many decisions as they plan programs for children. They consider what the program content should be, how it should be organized, and how it should be delivered to the children. These decisions should take into account the philosophy and goals of the program, knowledge of child development, the value of the content to the children, and the nature of the children, families, and community.

Goals, Values, and Program Philosophy

One of the most basic challenges for education and for those who work to further it is to become clear about educational goals. Schools for young children are a powerful force in influencing "not only the excellence of intellect but in shaping the feelings, the attitudes, the values, the sense of self and the dreaming of what is to be, the images of good and evil in the world about the visions of what the life . . . might be" (Biber 1969, p. 8).

What you teach and how you teach it must reflect your values for society and your long-term goals for children. It is best to begin the curriculum development process by reflecting on these things. We live in a society that is characterized by diversity in every arena of life and one of the places in which this is most apparent is in people's educational beliefs, goals, and values. There are many different and contradictory points of view regarding what is best for children and how they should be educated. These differences cannot be ignored. As Barbara Biber says,

> It is either blind or false or a little of both to think that we all have fundamentally the same goals—as teachers, as parents, as citizens—and that our differences concern only how to best accomplish these purposes. It seems of major importance to me that we discard superficial, albeit friendly neutrality and work at clarifying and stating our goals and the priorities within them.
>
> *(Biber 1969, p. 8)*

Many early childhood programs have a statement of philosophy that makes clear the program's purpose, goals, and values and its assumptions about children and learning. This philosophy and your own values and goals can provide valuable guidance in decision making regarding the content and process of the daily program for children.

Knowledge of Child Development

A hallmark of the field of early childhood education is that teachers base program practice on knowledge of child development. This knowledge enables them to plan activities for children at the appropriate level for their age and for their individual needs and interests.

According to NAEYC's *Guidelines for Developmentally Appropriate Practice,* developmental appropriateness has two dimensions: age appropriateness and individual appropriateness. *Age appropriateness* refers to the universal, predictable sequences of growth and change that occur in all children during the first eight years of life. Knowledge of typical development of children within the age span served by a program provides a framework from which teachers prepare the learning environment and plan appropriate experiences. *Individual appropriateness* refers to the fact that each child is a unique person with an individual pattern and timing of growth as well as individual personality, learning style, and family background. Both the curriculum and adults' interactions with children should be responsive to individual differences in interest, style, and ability (Bredekamp 1987).

What's Worth Knowing?

Choosing what to teach is a vital and important task. But planning curriculum will have little value if what you are teaching isn't worth knowing. What is worth knowing when you are two, three, four, five, six, seven, or eight years old? This crucial question has guided the ways in which we have thought and written about curriculum since we first heard it posed by Lilian Katz a number of years ago.

What is worth knowing? It is certainly worth knowing about yourself, how to function in your world—your family and community—and about the world you live in. We can see this as we watch a two-year-old's triumphant, "Me can!" a three-year-old's passion for pretending to be the mommy, or a five-year-old's fascination with insects. What about teaching shapes, colors, numbers, classification, seriation, conservation of volume, the alphabet, phonics, or prepositions? These are isolated skills and fragments of knowledge. It is valuable to know these things, but they can be learned as children pursue tasks and learn about things that are interesting and meaningful to them. They have little relevance to children's lives when they are taught in isolation.

Families and Community

What you teach and how you teach must also be considered in terms of the background of the children and families, their culture and community characteristics and values.

A curriculum that promotes acceptance of diversity is desirable in every classroom. The predominant cultures of the children in your program must be the point of departure for curriculum. A classroom with a predominantly Samoan, Native-American, or Mexican-American population, for example, should reflect the children's culture as well as providing experience with other cultures.

A frequently occurring issue in early childhood education today is pressure from families for schools to emphasize academic skills. Such pressure is felt in programs for disadvantaged children where parents are anxious for their children to break out of the cycle of poverty. It is felt in "exclusive" programs where parents want their young children to gain admission to private schools with highly competitive entrance requirements. This concern may influence your program as you make your academic content, while developmentally appropriate, more visible than you might in a program where families are more concerned with other issues.

Your community and geography will influence what you teach. In Hawaii, when the air is filled with volcanic haze or the TV news is filled with stories of eruptions, volcanoes are a natural and important topic of study. The study of earthquakes might well be the most relevant curriculum in the days following a major quake.

Choosing Curriculum Content

After you are clear about your program's purpose and your broad goals for children, you will begin to consider the content, or knowledge, that is to be taught. Several starting points are possible for selecting what you will teach. In some programs the curriculum grows from observation and assessment of developmental needs and tasks of young children, from play in a planned environment, and from carefully chosen themes that enhance children's understanding of the world and that integrate subject matter into meaningful learning. In these programs, children are given ample opportunity to discover and construct knowledge for themselves.

Other programs will have a preselected curriculum based on specific concepts, knowledge, or skills to be learned ("Our curriculum this month is shapes and colors, the alphabet, and numbers to 10."), on tasks intended to describe development ("We are teaching seriation, classification, and number conservation."), or on a commercial product ("We use the DISTAR or PEEK program."). These mandated sources of content are often not meaningful or developmentally appropriate for young children, and they may replace thoughtful consideration of individual and group interests and needs.

Every teacher wants to teach important things. But who decides what is important and what guides teachers as they decide what and how to teach? Curriculum decisions vary from setting to setting. In early childhood programs based on child development, they are generally

made by the teacher who works with a group of children on a daily basis and who knows them very well. Sometimes a program's administrators or education specialists will participate in planning. They may be a valuable source of assistance but in our opinion they should serve as consultants to the planning process, not dictate it. In some preschools and many elementary schools curriculum decisions are made by curriculum committees, administrators, and boards of education. This type of planning may enhance coordination and articulation between classes, but the needs of a particular group of children can easily be lost in a top-down decision-making process. Even when curriculum is chosen by others, you still have choices about the method by which you will teach and the relative importance that you place on the different aspects of the curriculum.

There is room for a wide range of differing personal commitments and alternative ways of translating them into classroom practice. Programs vary in the extent to which they place emphasis on social, emotional, intellectual, and physical goals. Some educators believe that we must begin with feelings and relationships, others believe that it is more important to begin with skills and concepts to be learned. As we visit programs we see a wide range of practices and of curriculum content.

As we suggested in Chapter 8, The Learning Environment, programs for young children can be thought of as existing on a continuum between two poles—child-centered and content-centered. Teachers in programs that tend toward the child-centered end of the continuum believe that the total development of the child should be the focus of education and that children are capable of making their own choices in a planned learning environment. They feel that school experience should be personally meaningful for children, that the process of learning is more important than the product, and that education *is* life and not just preparation for later schooling.

Content-centered approaches place more emphasis on what is taught—the subject matter. This approach is characteristic of most elementary and high school programs. Teachers who choose practices closer to the content-centered end of the continuum tend to be more concerned with what is learned and place emphasis on the acquisition of specific knowledge and skills that they believe to be important for children to learn. What is taught is to a greater extent determined by the teacher.

Every early childhood teacher and program will balance these dimensions in different ways, though the underlying values, philosophy, and view of the learner will influence on which side of the continuum the majority of choices fall. When child development knowledge is not adequately considered, programs may emphasize content without regard to children's needs or they may fail to provide adequate support for children's learning. Such programs are not developmentally appropriate. On the extreme end of the child side of the continuum are *laissez-faire* programs that do not give the structure, stimulation, content, and guidance that children need to grow and learn. On the extreme of the content side of the continuum are *rigid* programs that stress mastery of specific tasks to the exclusion of other goals and that tend to regard children as machines to be programmed rather than as thinking and feeling human beings. Between the two extremes lie a range of alternatives that can contribute positively to children's learning and development (see Figure 10.1).

The decisions you make regarding how to structure choices on the continuum will be influenced by your personal values, the values of your school and community, and the age and abilities of the children you teach. Obviously, most of the choices you make for a group of two-year-olds will be closer to the child-centered side of the continuum than the choices you will make for kindergartners and elementary-school children who have interest in and the

FIGURE 10.1
Child-centered Versus Content-centered Program Continuum

ability to handle more demanding instructional tasks.

Organizing the Curriculum

There are a number of ways to organize curriculum for instruction. Three well-known approaches are (1) subject-centered designs, (2) learner-centered designs, and (3) integrated, or thematic, designs.

Subject-centered Designs

Historically education has focused on the attainment of knowledge, and the curriculum of the school has been presented by subject areas (math, science, social studies, reading, and language arts). Each subject is regarded as having its own distinct content and method. This design is prevalent in most elementary and high schools in which subject matter teaching is generally organized into discrete blocks of time (reading 9:00 to 9:45, math 10:00 to 10:30). Sometimes two or more disciplines, for example math and science, are combined for instruction. Organization by subjects is a useful framework for assuring that all areas of content will be given attention in the program. This traditional teaching approach is not appropriate for teaching young children who want to learn about the world they live in but understand it best as a whole, not as divided into subjects.

Learner-centered Designs

A second major type of design bases learning experiences on the needs and interests of the learners. This design was advocated by the progressive educators described in Chapter 3. Learning is based on children's purposes, on their natural inclinations and ways of learning. Some advocates of this approach believe that all learning experiences should be based on child interest and that the curriculum cannot be preplanned but must emerge from each day's occurrences. The developmental early childhood program in which children have large blocks of activity time to play and explore in a planned environment is an example of a learner-centered curriculum design. Planned activities emerge from teachers' observations and are based on the children's interests and purposes. This approach is appropriate in early childhood classrooms, especially those for two- and three-year-olds, though in itself it may not provide enough intellectual stimulation for older preschoolers, kindergartners, or primary-age children.

Integrated or Thematic Designs

It is also possible and desirable to combine aspects of these two approaches through the use of teaching units based on themes. Theme-based planning combines play and teacher-created experiences into in-depth exploration of topics that are interesting and motivating for children. We have used this approach to structure curriculum and found it effective over the years, especially for children four years old and older.

The term *theme* as it is used in curriculum planning refers to an organizing framework, or a focus for the curriculum. Using a theme as the hub around which appropriate activities are planned allows teachers to integrate several different subject areas into meaningful and worthwhile experiences for children. Themes can involve children in active exploration and problem solving; see *Engaging Children's Minds: The Project Approach* by Lilian Katz and Sylvia Chard (1989). Children's interests or the teachers' ideas about what children would enjoy or benefit from can be sources of the theme. Units based on themes can be tailored to fit the learning styles of a group of children and of individual children in the group. Integrated themes have helped us to think in new and creative ways and have taken us on learning adventures with children.

A theme must be appropriate for the children taught; it should reflect their interests, abilities, and issues of concern to them. A unit on Christopher Columbus would not be appropriate since it could not be meaningfully experienced and is not relevant to a young child's life. A unit on pets (which can be seen and experienced) would be appropriate for young children because they generally have had direct experiences with pets and could easily be motivated to learn more about their own and their friends' pets. Meaningful themes help children make connections. They reflect life and are not separate from it. Children's lives and their environment—their families, cultures, community, or geographic locale—are good sources of themes. Themes based on these topics can contribute to children's awareness and understanding of the world and themselves as well as heightening their sense of uniqueness and pride in their community. While these larger goals are being realized, children engaged in exploring their environment, discussing what they experience, building with blocks, manipulating materials, writing, and cooking are also developing fine-motor and hand and eye coordination, understanding of letters and numbers, discrimination of size, shape, and color, and myriad other skills and understandings.

Communicating the Curriculum to Children

In early childhood programs there are two basic ways that children learn the curriculum content planned by teachers. The first way they learn the content is through child-chosen play activities in a planned environment. The second is through teacher-directed activities. The relative balance of these two processes will vary based on the age and characteristics of the children as well as on the philosophy and characteristics of the teacher and program. Both child-chosen and teacher-directed activities have advantages and disadvantages and are most appropriate with different kinds of content. For example, it is unlikely that a five-year-old would spontaneously learn to read a clock or tie shoelaces without direct teaching, although this might be a learning goal of both teacher and child. Similarly, it is unlikely that any amount of planned activity would teach that same five-year-old to climb a rope, although she might easily learn to do so in focused, self-directed play. Every teacher will seek an optimal balance between child-chosen and teacher-directed activity. As teachers plan they need to ask themselves which activities best meet their educational purposes and how the activities should be balanced in their programs.

Play in a Planned Environment

Through their exploration and self-initiated play activities, children construct knowledge and develop individual skills and interests. Young children need many opportunities to learn and discover through their play each day. Play is the most appropriate learning medium when you want children to explore and discover for themselves. The power of play is that through it children develop skills and knowledge of many kinds simultaneously. At the same time, they enjoy themselves and become motivated to keep exploring and learning.

As we have said in the chapters in this book on play and learning environment, blocks, sand,

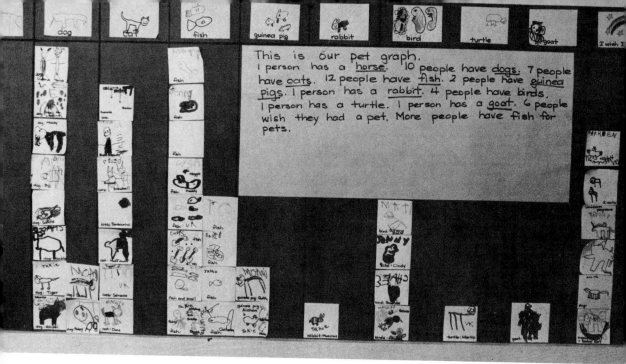

This is our pet graph.
I person has a horse. 10 people have dogs. 7 people have cats. 12 people have fish. 2 people have guinea pigs. 1 person has a rabbit. 4 people have birds. I person has a turtle. I person has a goat. 6 people wish they had a pet. More people have fish for pets.

water, art materials, dramatic play, manipulatives, woodworking, and outdoor play are the cornerstones of the early childhood curriculum. Teachers can provide additional play materials and self-directed activities that support the themes they have chosen.

Teacher-directed Learning

Neither children nor adults live or learn in a vacuum. In every society it is the role of adults to pass on knowledge and skills to children. Much of what young children learn grows out of their day-to-day play experiences, but obviously there is much more to learn. Teachers have knowledge and experiences that are interesting and valuable for young children. These can sometimes be presented best through teacher-directed activities that provide stimulation and ensure that the children focus on a particular topic. Teacher direction is appropriate to introduce children to new ideas and knowledge and to help them make connections that go beyond the basics of interest areas and play materials. A college student of ours noticed that children in

her school were fascinated with bugs on the playground. This observation of children's interest was the springboard for initiating an in-depth study in which children collected and observed insects; read about, wrote about, and drew insects; and visited the entomology department of a nearby university. Teacher-directed learning may take place in one-to-one experiences, small group activities, or large group activities.

One-to-one experiences. When you want a child or group of children to acquire a specific concept or skill it is often useful to plan an activity to present to the children one at a time or to the child who has a specific need or interest. These special teacher-child experiences permit you to concentrate on the child's learning process and participate in a learning dialogue. One-to-one activities allow you to observe and assess a child's knowledge and skill and modify what you do based on the child's response. Large blocks of time for child-chosen activities enable teachers to engage in planned or spontaneous interactions with individual children while the others are engaged in activities. One-to-one instruction is most appropriate in helping children to refine a physical skill, to learn a new skill or technique (a painting technique, forming letters), for conversation, for literacy activities such as key vocabulary and dictating stories (see Chapter 14), and for exploring and discussing observations like why an object floats or sinks.

Small-group activities.   Small-group activities enable you to teach concepts, facilitate an exchange of ideas between children, and have meaningful personal contact with each child. This approach reduces waiting time and works best in activities that involve turn taking, manipulation of materials, and teacher assistance. You are able to attend to the way children respond and can evaluate and modify your teaching right away.

Small groups work best for games like I Spy, for reading stories where you want to generate a lot of discussion, for acting out stories, for creative movement activities, for cooking projects, and for field trips, especially to places like concerts and museums where it will be more meaningful if an adult can discuss the experience with the children.

Children can also be organized into small groups that meet together on a regular basis. These regular experiences can help them to develop some important skills including the ability to listen and talk in a group, to solve problems and make decisions democratically, to take leader and follower roles, and to accept responsibility for the outcomes of their decisions. Small groups develop an identity of their own. When they select a name for their group

they further cement feelings of belonging and responsibility.

Large-group activities.   Large-group activities are valuable when you want children to share a common experience or to hear the same thing. (We use the term *large group* to describe a group of ten to twenty preschool children and fifteen to thirty school-age children—usually a whole class.) Large groups are most appropriate for giving information that is needed by all of the children, for singing, for stories (told or read), and for demonstrations and resource people. They are also effective for group games like dodgeball, and for field trips to a familiar place like a zoo or park (though adults are needed for supervision). Large groups are economical in terms of teacher time, but they are not appropriate when you want to attend to individual needs and responses, when you want children to explore and discover, or for activities like cooking where you want children to be active participants.

We have sometimes observed teachers bringing still larger groups together for activities. Although it is possible to entertain larger groups (several classes or a whole school), it is extremely difficult to do any effective teaching in this kind of setting.

THE PLANNING PROCESS

Planning creates the context for learning to occur. Teachers choose how much they will plan, in what detail, and how far in advance. In every program there is a balance of long-term planning, short-term planning, unit planning, and planning of specific activities.

Long-term Plans

Most teachers make very general plans for a relatively long period, a year or semester, and more specific and complete monthly, weekly, or daily plans. Long-term plans are based upon a combination of broad goals for children and knowledge of their developmental needs. They also take into consideration the predictable characteristics of a group. Every group of young children will begin school with a high degree of reliance on the teacher. At first children will be intensely involved with exploring the environment and testing the challenges and limits of the setting. They are likely to have some difficulty working as a group and staying together. As they become accustomed to routines and school becomes more predictable, children develop confidence in the environment and a sense of membership in the group. As the year progresses they learn to work together and will enjoy more complex challenges. They will also seek new stimulation and, if it is not provided in the context of the teacher's planned curriculum, may supply it in unexpected and undesirable ways. Knowing this will help you to begin with fairly simple and predictable activities and to keep those that are complex and that require a lot of cooperation among children until later in the year.

Long-term plans give a sense of direction for the school year. They are useful for thinking through the kinds of themes that you want to present during the year and making sure that they are balanced in terms of subject matter and developmental goals. It is also useful to be able to share general directions with parents, so that they have advance notice of classroom events that call for their participation. Long-term plans help in making decisions about ordering materials and for providing direction for short-term plans. It will be best if these plans are quite flexible. If you find out that your advance planning was inappropriate or if you discover unanticipated interests or resources, you can change with little regret.

Short-term Plans

You will also write plans that sketch out the major activities of each week and each day. The schedule of daily activities such as story time, circle, and outdoor time, and regular events such as cooking and field trips provide a structure around which you can organize your plan. If you are using a unit-based approach to planning (described in the following section), aspects of your theme will be incorporated in your planning (see Figure 10.2). You will deliberate about the skills and concepts that you want children to develop throughout the weeks and days ahead and you will plan for ways to include areas such as art, science, math, blocks, and dramatic play. Next you plan a sequence of activities that will support the children in acquiring these skills and concepts. You will then write a tentative monthly or weekly plan, review it to see if it is practical and appropriate, and finally write a version that you can use and share with other staff members and parents.

Unit Planning

A unit is a planned series of related teaching activities integrating most curriculum areas and lasting for an extended period of time (two to six weeks). The first step in planning a unit is the choice of the topic—the theme. This involves the teacher or team of teachers thoughtfully considering the values and goals of the program, observations of children's interests and concerns, their own interests and skills, coming celebrations, and a myriad of other factors. A list of possible topics is generated and each item is evaluated.

A team of kindergarten teachers we know chose a unit on marine life for their class when they observed that several of the children were captivated by this topic (one that is relevant and motivating in Hawaii but that would probably not be appropriate in a state with no seashore). When a swarm of bees settled in their treehouse, this same team, after thoughtful deliberation about the potential for generating productive learning, abandoned their plans to begin a unit on gardens and embarked on a study of bees that they felt could accomplish many of the same

educational goals. Children's fear of the bees gave way to fascination as they learned about the social structure of the hive and the production of honey and watched the beekeeper relocate the hive to a site further removed from the classroom. Themes selected by our college students in the last few years that have led to successful integration of subject areas and meaningful learning for children include life cycles, produce from garden to market, flying, family, rain, insects, hospital, trees, and the community.

Some Guidelines for Selecting and Using Themes[1]

Theme possibilities are rich and varied. Used well and thoughtfully, they help children to understand that learning is connected to life. They make planning easier and more fun.

First, be thoughtful in your selection of themes. You and the children will live with the topic that you choose for a period of time, so it should be worthwhile for everyone involved. Several questions will help you to choose wisely:

- Will this topic be interesting and meaningful to the children?
- Are the central concepts *worth knowing*—will study of this topic help children to acquire greater understanding and appreciation of some aspect of the world they live in?
- Are the underlying concepts comprehensible to young children and are the required skills within their grasp?
- Can this topic be taught through direct experience? Children should be able explore it with all their senses.
- Is it flexible enough to meet a range of interests and abilities?
- Can many things can be learned about this topic?

---

[1]Our continuing dialogue with Elizabeth Jones has contributed to our thinking about the appropriate use of themes and to this section.

MAJOR UNDERSTANDINGS

Families are the same: They provide for their members' needs, including their physical needs (for food, shelter, and protection), their emotional needs (for love, connection, and recreation), and their intellectual needs (for education and stimulation).

Families differ: They may have different members, have many or few members, live all together or in different places, and meet their members' needs in differing ways.

Time/Activity	Monday	Tuesday	Wednesday	Thursday	Friday
Circle Time	**Music:** Songs: "You Are the One Your Mommy Loves" Lullabyes to sing to Max's baby. **Discussion:** What do mommies and children do together?	**Music:** Song: "House That's Made of Love" **Discussion:** How are homes the same/different?	**Music and Physical Development:** Finger-play songs: "Here's a Family" "One Little Bird"	**Trip Preparation:** Song: "House That's Made of Love" **Discussion:** What kinds of homes might we see?	**Visitors:** Max's mom and their baby. We will sing lullabyes to the baby and talk to his mom about taking care of the baby.
Activity Time 9:00–10:00 Special activities	**Blocks:** Block families and doll house	**Home Area:** baby care box **Science:** visiting mouse family	**Toys and Games:** Duplo farm family games	**Field Trip:** Neighborhood walk to observe different kinds of homes where families live	**Cooking:** Najecla's favorite spaghetti
	Special activities available in centers, every day all week long.				
Art Activities 9:00–10:00 Easel, drawing materials, and clay always available	My home—box construction	Finger painting	Families magazine collage	Remind parents to send shoes, backpack, school shirt, drink	Sponge printing
Outside Time 10:00–11:00	Obstacle course design	Game: Mother May I?	Hoops and balls		Baby doll and clothes washing
Small Groups 11:00–11:30	Making a group book on how family members take care of each other		Family graph		Illustrating family recipe
Lunch 11:30–12:00 **Books/Stories** 12:00–12:30	*Your Family, My Family*	*Are You My Mother?*	*Big Sister, Little Sister*	*A House Is a House for Me*	*A Baby Sister for Frances*

FIGURE 10.2

Week Plan for Families Unit—Week Two

- Can it generate a variety of activities and learning in a broad range of subject areas?
- Can it be organized to move from more simple to more complex?

Make sure that the theme you chose is complex and interesting enough to be explored in some depth. Weekly themes tend to be an imposition on everyone and promote a once-over-lightly view of content. Plan for several weeks or a month and then stay open to possibilities that emerge from children's or adults' ideas and interests.

Observe the children each step of the way and adapt and change according to their responses to the material. No plan implemented with real children will end up looking as it was originally visualized. Don't get too attached to your plan and don't continue if it isn't working. We once planned and began teaching a unit on feelings for a group of young three-year-olds. While reading a story about a baby who thought her mother didn't love her, we found that the children were extremely concerned with the issue of parental love and care. We realized that the stress of separation was high and that dealing with this dramatic transition in their lives was the real curriculum for these children. We changed the topic to the study of families to help the children connect their experiences at school with their lives at home.

Be sure that the theme is a source of genuine learning and not just way to sugarcoat an inappropriate curriculum. Using dinosaurs, bears, or bees on work sheets to make them more palatable is not even distantly related to the meaningful learning that good thematic planning can generate. Sometimes a theme may give a surface appearance of connecting ideas but may not be meaningful to children and may do nothing to enhance their understanding of the world. We observed a group of three-year-olds "studying" the letter _m_ by making _m_agazine collages and _m_uffins and by coloring a picture of

a _m_onkey. When we asked the children what they had been doing, they responded that they had been cooking, gluing paper, and coloring. Their teacher quickly corrected them saying that they had been studying _m_. This approach failed to integrate children's learning because the central concept was not relevant to this lively group of three-year-olds.

Be careful about using holidays as the basis for thematic planning. Some holidays such as Christmas, New Year's Day, Thanksgiving, and Passover have an impact on children's lives and can be studied in terms of the joys of family celebrations. They are often are made trivial and inappropriate, however, by focusing on a few songs and look-alike craft activities that are devoid of meaning to the children. Other holidays can generate significant learning; for example, Halloween can be used as a springboard for discussing fears and the distinction between fantasy and reality. Holidays like President's Day and St. Patrick's Day have little or no appropriate content for young children. It is also important to remember that holidays have different meanings to different groups of people. For example, many Native Americans regard Thanksgiving as a day of mourning.

Although holidays are times of excitement, they are not necessarily worthwhile curriculum content for children. Your desire to celebrate holidays may stem from the welcome relief they brought to the hard, colorless institutions of your elementary school days. In a beautiful and everchanging classroom designed for young children, such relief is unnecessary.

Writing Unit Plans

The following sections describe procedures for writing plans that we have been evolving over the years for teaching children and for use in our college classes. The process involves a number of interconnected parts that require some work to master. Once learned they give a solid foundation for curriculum planning. The steps for writing a unit plan are as follows:

1. Choose the theme for the unit using the criteria described in the previous section.
2. Think through and then write the rationale for the unit describing why this topic is meaningful to young children and why you are choosing it for this group of children at this time.
3. Brainstorm all of the curricular directions that might grow out of the theme. If the topic is unfamiliar, background reading about the theme will help you to identify and learn important ideas about the subject.
4. Clarify your goals for the unit and decide on the major understandings that you wish children to acquire (Figure 10.3 is an example of a completed curriculum planning chart illustrating major understandings). This is a step that is often omitted in the tendency to generate lots of interesting activities related (though sometimes distantly) to a topic. Since we added this step to our own planning, we have found that we are more focused on helping children gain meaning from the unit.
5. Collect teaching materials and resources from your own, the school, or community library.
6. Develop your initial teaching plan. The curriculum areas plan chart in Figure 10.3 helps to organize activities that support each of the major understandings.
7. Schedule unit activities into your weekly plans, schedule trips and resource people, and begin to write necessary activity plans.
8. Implement your plans, keeping in mind the importance of being open to changes in children's interests and to fortuitous events.
9. Evaluate the unit. There are many ways to evaluate whether children have acquired

the major understandings you have targeted. You can observe their play as it pertains to the unit, have them discuss the topic, dictate stories, or have them write in their journals as a way for you to assess what they have learned. Children who make representational drawings may spontaneously or upon request draw pictures that demonstrate their understanding. For example, following a unit on volcanoes two preschoolers (ages $4\frac{1}{2}$ and 5) were asked to draw a picture (content unspecified) to illustrate the school newsletter. Kerri drew

CURRICULUM AREAS PLAN CHART   UNIT: *Families*

Major Understanding:	1	2	3	4	5
	People come from and/or live in a family	Families provide for their members' needs	Families differ	Family members have roles and responsibilities	Families change
Inquiry Social Studies	Family album	Potluck dinner†	Family sorting workjob	Parent-baby visit Mother-father workjob	Story of the day you were born—parent book
Science	Family tree	Animal family—observation/chart			
Math		Family birthday calendar	Family graph		Brothers/sisters graph
Nutrition		Favorite dinners—cooking activity		Guest chef—mom, dad, grandparent, or other	Baby food sampling
Language	What is a family?—Chart*	Discussion	Puppet families Discussion	Discussion	Talk about pictures
Literacy	My family—group book	Taking care of one another—group book		Family jobs list/book	
Literature	*All Kinds of Families* *The Summer Night*	Houses and homes poems *Big Sister, Little Sister* *Daddy Makes the Best Spaghetti* *If I Were a Mother*	*Your Family, My Family* *Children and Their Mothers* *Children and Their Fathers*	*The Terrible Thing that Happened at Our House* *Bedtime for Frances*	*Arthur's Baby* *Baby Sister for Frances* *My Mother's Getting Married* *My Grandson Lew* *Nanna Upstairs*

CURRICULUM AREAS PLAN CHART UNIT: *Families (continued)*

The Arts Art and Aesthetics	Families art—postcard game	Family activities mural†; Homes—box construction; Illus. families cookbook	Families magazine collage		
Music and Movement	"Here's a Family" "One little Bird"—finger-play songs	Movement activity "You Are the One Your Mommy Loves"	"House That's Made of Love"		"Sweet Little Baby"
Phys. Develop. Fine Motor	Block families	Doll house and family			
Large Motor		Family home Neighborhood walk			
Interest Centers	**Blocks:** Block families, doll house, animals	**Dramatic Play:** Family member prop boxes, family photographs	**Puzzles/Games:** Baby puzzles and lotto, family workjobs	**Science:** Family sorting game, guinea pig mom and baby	**Display:** Prints of families, mural of family photos
	Writing: Family word chart	**Manipulatives** Duplo farm with family and animal family	**Listening** Tape and book sets. *Baby Sister for Frances* and *Bedtime for Frances*	**Library** Selection of library books about families, *My Family* child-made books, family photo albums.	

*Introductory Activity †Culminating activity

FIGURE 10.3
Curriculum Areas Plan Chart for Families Unit

the picture shown as Figure 10.4 which illustrates an erupting volcano, its caldera, and the lava tube that feeds it. Paul drew the form of a piece of lava. Both children were providing their teacher with visible proof of the internalization of concepts relating to a volcano. Similarly, the drawings in Figure 10.5 were kindergarten children's responses to their teacher's request at the end of a unit to draw and label a picture of an insect.

10. Store the materials until they are needed again. We have found it convenient to store unit materials in cardboard banker's boxes. It may be a year or several years before you need them again, but when you do the materials will not have disappeared and,

though changes will need to be made based on new ideas, interests, and materials, you will not have to start over from scratch.

Figure 10.6 summarizes these planning steps in outline form. Figure 10.7 presents several parts of the outline for a unit on families.

Activity Plans

Effective teachers also plan specific activities for each day. Teaching plans for a single instructional event are called lesson plans in elementary schools and special education settings. We prefer to call them activity plans to suggest a somewhat less formal planning approach. Both kinds of plans include a statement of goals or purpose, specify intended learning outcomes,

FIGURE 10.4
Volcano Drawn by a Preschooler

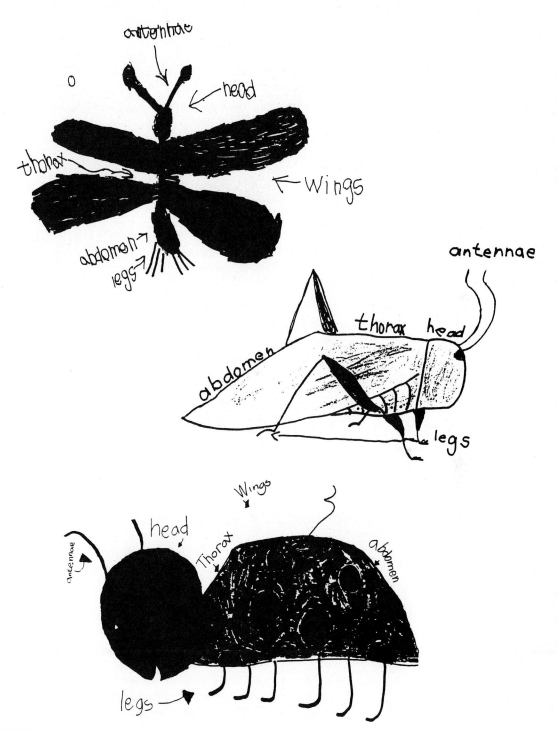

FIGURE 10.5
Drawings by Kindergarteners Showing Their Understanding of the Parts of an Insect

---

UNIT PLAN OUTLINE

Theme: Topic based on appropriate and meaningful content for young children

Children: Age, group size, and characteristics

Rationale: What it is about the topic that makes it worthwhile and relevant to young children and to this specific of group of children at this time

Goals: Broad desired outcomes of the unit—what you want children to understand, experience, try, feel, value, become aware of, learn about, or become more skilled in as a result of this study

Major understandings: Important ideas that you want children to acquire as a result of the experience of this unit—the cornerstone of the unit

Curriculum areas chart: List of activities that will support each of the major understandings in each curriculum area

Integration into learning centers: Ways that the theme can be integrated into the block area, dramatic play area, and other learning centers

Plan for presenting the unit:

Introduction—how you will introduce the unit and capture the children's interest

Activity plans—how you will achieve the unit's goals and help children to acquire the major understandings

Closure—how you will wrap up the unit and help children to review and reflect on what has been learned and experienced

Evaluation: A plan for determining if the unit purpose has been achieved and if the children have grasped the central ideas

Resources: Books for teachers, children's books, records, anthologies, songs, poems, etc.

FIGURE 10.6
Outline for a Unit Plan

list needed materials, describe teaching procedures, and have provisions for evaluation.

Lesson plans include objectives that describe intended learning outcomes in terms of what the children are expected to know or do as a result of experiencing a lesson. Objectives stated in precise terms, called *behavioral objectives,* are often used by elementary school and special education teachers.[2] These objectives describe the desired child behavior in observable terms; for example, the child will cut along a straight line or will identify three shapes. Evaluation of lesson plans considers the degree to which the specific learning objectives were met.

Behavioral objectives enable teachers to assess whether or not their objectives have been met. But under most circumstances their use is not compatible with the philosophy of early childhood education. They predetermine learning so that there is not room for individual choice, they require that all children will be at the same place at the end of a given lesson, and they do not allow for spontaneity or creativity.

---

[2]Discussions with Marjorie Fields have contributed to our thinking about behavioral objectives in early childhood education.

RATIONALE, GOALS, AND MAJOR UNDERSTANDINGS: FAMILIES UNIT

Theme: Families

Children: A preschool class of four- and five-year-olds from diverse ethnic and socioeconomic backgrounds.

Rationale: All children live in some kind of a family. The family is essential to the child's physical and emotional well-being. Children are innately interested in family roles and relationships. Much of the young child's learning begins at home within the family environment. The use of family as curriculum makes a link between home and school.

Family similarities and differences are among the first things that children experience. Children whose families are different from the norm can find this experience difficult and disturbing. A unit on family can help children to realize that family differences are acceptable.

The unit was chosen for this group because the teachers had recently observed a lot of interest in family relationships in the dramatic play area and because two of the children recently experienced changes in their families—a divorce and a new baby.

Goals:

- To help children understand the basic unit of human relationship.
- To make a link between children's homes and school.
- To help children realize that differences between families are acceptable and even desirable.
- To help children learn about the importance of nurturing others and of the critical role that they as family members play now and will play in the future.

Major Understandings:

1. All people come from and/or live in a family.
2. Families try to provide for their members' basic needs for food, shelter, nurture, and a sense of belonging.
3. There are differences between families.
4. Family members have roles and responsibilities.
5. Families change.

FIGURE 10.7

Rationale, Goals, and Major Understanding for a Unit on Families

Moreover, behavioral objectives are not consistent with the belief that children must construct knowledge from their own active involvement with materials and experiences (Lawton 1988, p. 229).

The objectives in activity plans also focus on what the child is expected to gain from the lesson, but they may be broader and include involvement, awareness, and appreciation as well as concepts, understandings, and skills to be acquired. Evaluation is based on the teacher's observation of what children do and say during and following the activity rather than determining if specific outcomes have occurred.

An activity, such as reading a simple, familiar story, will be included in a teacher's weekly plan but generally does not call for a written plan. Locating the book, reviewing it, and spending a few moments thinking about how to structure discussion may be enough preparation. Written plans are necessary when clarity and sequence are crucial or where procedure or content is complex or unfamiliar. If you are a teacher in training, you will want to practice writing activity plans in great detail until you master the process. As you gain experience you will be able to use a much simpler planning process; a few notes may be enough to guide you through the activity. As you present your activities, you will observe children's responses and modify or drop an activity that is not going well. Be ready to change your plans based on shifts in children's interests, a new insight, or a serendipitous event.

Writing Activity Plans

Activity plans are more than an exercise; they are guidelines for thinking and for action and also a way of preserving good ideas that can easily be forgotten if they are not recorded and stored. Carefully thinking through the purpose and sequence of an activity helps to ensure success and is essential for effective teaching. When your planning is good, you will express yourself clearly to children and feel more comfortable. Following is the sequence we use for planning activities:

1. Decide on your purpose and rationale and then choose the activity. We ask our college students, "Why this activity with this group of children at this time?"
2. Think about the concepts, skills, and knowledge you want children to acquire and write your objectives based on these.
3. Check resource books for background information and teaching ideas.
4. Think through and list all of the materials that you will need for your activity.
5. Carefully spell out the procedures. Include a plan for introducing the activity, all the steps

in the presentation, transitions, and closure. Without adequate introduction a good activity may never get off the ground. Without smooth transitions your purpose may get lost in a trample of children and without a well-thought-out closure it may just fizzle out.

The major steps should be simply described without so much detail that you get bogged down trying to follow it, but with enough information that you will be able to use it again at a later date. Be sure not to make assumptions about what children know. Think through what they need to understand in order to do the activity and introduce unfamiliar words and concepts.

6. Gather the materials and present the activity to children. If the activity involves an item that is novel to the children, it may be a good idea to let them get acquainted with it before you begin teaching. (We once planned a sorting activity using different kinds of nuts. Our objective was delayed as we spent several days cracking and eating nuts with the children before we were able to move on to the activity we had originally planned.)

The plan gives you guidelines to follow, but try to remain flexible. If children are interested in different things or if you sense that the plan is not going as you had anticipated, you may find it helpful to redirect or change. As you gain confidence and experience, you will find yourself able to adapt more easily to children's needs and interests.
7. Evaluate the activity to see if your goals and objectives have been achieved. There is no better way of evaluating than sensitively observing children. You can ask questions, observe if and how the material is incorporated in their play, or ask them to draw or write about the topic. Be sure to jot down your thoughts concerning what worked, what didn't work, and your ideas for next time while your memory is fresh.

8. Keep all of your activities and store them in a place where they can be easily located for future use. We like to write a shortened form of our plans on five-by-eight inch cards and store them in small notebooks, file boxes, or on metal rings. You will be glad to have your plans and will be able to use them in the future.

When you first begin to use written plans, you may want to follow them very closely. It is a good idea to know the plan thoroughly so that you can concentrate on the way children are responding. Sometimes what appears to be a disaster in planning may be the result of materials that are too stimulating, mistakes in timing, room arrangement, an activity that is not challenging enough or too challenging for the developmental level of the children, or insufficient opportunities for vigorous physical activity or rest when they were needed. Tried again with an appropriate modification, the other elements of the plan may prove sound. Figure 10.8 gives you our outline for an activity plan. Figure 10.9 is a plan we completed for an activity in the families unit.

ADAPTING FOR DIFFERENT AGES

All children deserve thoughtful teachers who plan for them. Just as children differ, planning for the range of age groups is markedly different. For *infants and toddlers* you develop broad general goals that are applicable to all children based on your knowledge of their stage of development. For example, knowing that toddlers are developing a sense of themselves as capable individuals means that a curriculum plan in any toddler room needs to include lots of opportunities for looking into mirrors, at books with pictures of toddlers, and at photo albums with pictures of themselves; for singing name songs and talking about themselves; and for

pushing buggies, turning on faucets, pouring water, and moving toys from one part of the room to another. It also requires curriculum that meets individualized goals for particular children. If Janelle is afraid of monsters, the curriculum plan needs to include opportunities for her to discuss that fear. If Matthew is having difficulty saying goodbye to his mom, the plan should include lots of talking about how mommies always come back. Most planning will be done on a short-term rather than long-term basis.

The younger the children, the more child centered the program should be. The majority of the program day should consist of play. Children's spontaneous exploration is the core of the curriculum for two- and three-year-olds. For older children planning can be done further in advance and will be more elaborate. Four-through six-year-old children benefit from planned learning experiences based on carefully chosen themes that supplement their play and exploration.

For *primary-age children* learning is more purposeful, project oriented, and structured. They do more elaborate planning for play episodes, are anxious to accurately represent what they have learned, and may seek out resources to make sure that they are doing it "right." Young primary-school children are able to think more abstractly—to represent verbally and through other symbols the reality that they are striving to understand. For example, we recently observed a class of second-grade children studying the harbor. After talking and reading about the harbor and shipping, they took a trip to the harbor where they were able to visit a cargo ship. When they returned to the classroom, they marked the harbor on a city map, wrote stories and painted pictures about their experiences, built ships and harbor buildings out of cardboard, and reenacted the roles of harbor master, chandler, ship's agent, captain, and dock worker.

ACTIVITY PLAN OUTLINE

Activity name: _____ **Theme:** (If applicable) _____
Subject area(s): _____
Brief description: _____
Children: _____
Rationale: (Why have you chosen this activity with these children at this time?)
_____
_____

Purpose: (What are your goals?)
_____
_____

Objectives: (What specific awareness, understanding, and/or skills do you want children to acquire?)
As a result of this activity the children will:
_____
_____
_____

New vocabulary that children may experience in this activity: (If applicable)
_____

What you need: (All materials and supplies)
_____

Space: (Where will you present the activity?)
_____

What you do:

Introduction _____

Procedure _____
_____
_____

Closure _____

Evaluation: (How did it go and what changes might you make next time?)
_____

Follow-up: (What might be possible next steps based on what happened?)
_____
_____

FIGURE 10.8

Outline for an Activity Plan

ACTIVITY PLAN: FAMILIES UNIT

Activity name: Family graph **Theme:** Families

Subject Area(s): Math and social studies

Brief description: A bar graph to compare the number of members in a family

Children: Eight four-year-olds in the Blue Room class

Rationale: As part of the families unit we have been talking about the size of families. Children were confused when I said that I had a little family because they know that I have no "little" children. I think they will understand this concept better if they see it represented graphically.

Purpose: To help children understand two of the major concepts in the families unit: (1) All people come from and/or live in a family and (2) there are differences among families. I hope to have children come to realize that their are many ways to be a family.

Objectives:

As a result of this activity the children will:

1. Gain understanding of some differences between families.
2. Develop awareness of the words *big* and *small* to refer to quantity.
3. Have an experience that contributes to positive self-concept and family pride.
4. Gain understanding of the use of a bar graph to compare quantities.
5. Experience working together in a group and listening to each other.

New vocabulary: *Big* and *small* in reference to quantity, *bar graph*

What you need: One sheet butcher paper approximately 30 inches divided into $2\frac{1}{2}$-inch squares, children's names written beneath columns; squares drawn to portray me and my family members; lots of $2\frac{1}{2}$-inch square pieces of paper (fifty or so); seven to eight paste pots with applicators; two sets of narrow-tip felt markers; yardstick.

Space: Carpeted area near the bulletin board

What you do:

Introduction: Show pictures of my family and talk about what a little family I have. Name the people in my family—paste pictures on graph and show how each picture takes one square. Say "I wonder how many squares your family will make and if you live in a little family or a big family."

Procedure: Pass out squares and have children draw a picture of each family member (discuss with them). As each finishes write the child's name on each square and show him or her how to glue the picture in the column with his or her name on it.

Closure: When all the pictures are glued on, have the children find the columns that are biggest, littlest, the same (use yardstick). Have children tell who is in their family.

Evaluation: From their discussion of the graph I could see that the children understood the concepts. Another time have them discuss family members before they start drawing in order to focus. The children seemed to enjoy it quite a bit—worth repeating.

Follow-up: Make a separate graph or color code the squares for pets next time; Lani had eight dogs!

FIGURE 10.9

Activity Plan for a Unit on Families (see photograph on p. 235)

DISCUSSION QUESTIONS

1. Recall your earliest school experience and share your memories about the kinds of learning experiences that your teachers provided. What was the balance between play and teacher-directed activities? Do you think what was taught was developmentally appropriate and worth knowing? Describe any evidences that you saw of the planning process.
2. How were the learning experiences planned and organized in the early childhood programs you have visited? Were they developmentally appropriate and worth knowing? What might you choose to do differently?
3. Describe the planning processes used in a program you have worked in.
4. To what extent has the planning that you have observed been related to the needs and interests of children? To what extent has it been related to predetermined objectives? What are your thoughts about each?

PROJECTS

1. Observe a teacher-directed learning activity. What do you think the goals and objectives of the activity might be? How does the activity contribute to the accomplishment of the goals? Do you believe the activity was successful in accomplishing its purpose? If not, why not? What implications might this have for your future teahing?
2. Interview a teacher about his or her program goals. Ask about how these are modified or influenced by the community, the interests of children, the concerns of parents, the school administration, and educational trends. How does this affect the experience of children? What implications might this have for your future teaching?
3. Interview two teachers about the kinds of planning that they do regularly, how much time it takes, how important it is to program success, and so forth. Compare their responses. What are your conclusions? What implications might this have for your future teaching?
4. Choose a theme from science or social studies as described in Chapter 14. Use it as an integrating theme for a week's plan for a class of young children. Decide on major understandings and accompanying activities. Using the process described in this chapter, plan for daily large-group and small-group activities, relevant materials for interest centers, and integration of subject areas.

BIBLIOGRAPHY

Armstong, D. G. 1989. *Developing and Documenting the Curriculum.* Boston: Allyn & Bacon.

Biber, B. 1969. *Challenges Ahead for Early Childhood Education.* Washington, D.C.: National Association for the Education of Young Children.

Bredekamp, S. 1987. *Developmentally Appropriate Practice in Early Childhood Programs Serving Children from Birth Through Age 8.* Expanded ed. Washington, D.C.: National Association for the Education of Young Children.

Brown, J. F., ed. 1982. *Curriculum Planning for Young Children.* Washington, D.C.: National Association for the Education of Young Children.

DeVries, R., and L. Kohlberg. 1987. *Constructivist Early Education: Overview and Comparison with Other Programs.* Washington, D.C.: National Association for the Education of Young Children.

Dittmann, L. L., ed. 1977. *Curriculum Is What Happens: Planning Is the Key.* Washington D.C.: National Association for the Education of Young Children.

Joyce, B. R. 1978. *Selecting Learning Experiences: Linking Theory and Practice.* Washington, D.C.: Association for Supervision and Curriculum Development.

Katz, L. G., and S. C. Chard. 1989. *Engaging Children's Minds: The Project Approach.* Norwood, N.J.: Ablex Publishing.

Krogh, S. 1990. *The Integrated Early Childhood Curriculum.* New York: McGraw-Hill.

Lawton, J. T. 1988. *Introduction to Child Care and Early Childhood Education.* Glenview, Ill: Scott, Foresman.

Ornstein, A. C., and F. P. Hunkins. 1988. *Curriculum: Foundations, Principles, and Issues.* Englewood Cliffs, N.J.: Prentice-Hall.

Read, K., and J. Patterson. 1980. *The Nursery School and Kindergarten: Human Relationships and Learning.* 7th ed. New York: Holt, Rinehart & Winston.

Saylor, J. G., W. M. Alexander, and A. J. Lewis. 1981. *Curriculum Planning for Better Teaching.* 4th ed. New York: Holt, Rinehart & Winston.

Schwartz, S. L., and H. F. Robison. 1982. *Designing Curriculum for Early Childhood.* Boston: Allyn & Bacon.

Seefeldt, C., ed. 1986. *The Early Childhood Curriculum: A Review of Current Research.* (Early Childhood Education Ser.). New York: Teachers College Press.

Wiles, J., and J. C. Bondi. 1984. *Curriculum Development: A Guide to Practice.* 2d ed. Columbus, Ohio: Merrill.

CHAPTER ELEVEN

Sensing, Moving, and Growing: Curriculum for Physical Development

And look at your body . . . what a wonder it is! Your legs, your arms, your cunning fingers, the way they move.

—Pablo Casals

In this chapter we discuss the importance of the physical development and the health and safety curricula. The ways in which you can select and create worthwhile experiences to support young children's physical development—sensory and large and small muscle—are presented, as are health and safety education.

W e begin our discussion of curriculum with physical development because the body is the child's connection to the world. Unlike other animals, human beings are completely helpless at birth and spend years gaining full command of their bodies. As young children gain physical skill, they become increasingly able to care for themselves and move beyond the limits that are imposed by their dependency on others. As they gain the ability to control, care for, and use their bodies, they become self-confident and feel more independent. The ability to maintain physical well-being is essential to all other aspects of development. A sensitive, strong, flexible, coordinated, healthy body allows a child to function competently in the world—to grow and learn.

In this chapter we organize the physical development curriculum into four integrated components: sensory, small muscle (sometimes referred to as fine motor), large muscle (sometimes referred to as gross motor), and health and safety.

The physical development curriculum includes learning in other areas as well. A group of children on a hill, with a water source at the top and a few shovels, may be challenged to channel water downward. In the process, they may learn to use tools, solve a physical science problem involving gravity, explore spatial relations concepts such as up and down, and develop communication skills as they cooperate to accomplish the job. A group of five-year-olds playing Red Rover test their strength and stamina, and at the same time they learn some important concepts about social interaction such as taking turns and following rules. To understand many words and concepts children need hands-on experiences with them—imagine trying to explain what *push* means to someone who has never been pushed or given a push. Physical development is a prerequisite to many areas of competence that are highly valued in our society. To learn to read and write children must first develop the ability to make fine visual and auditory discriminations. In addition, writing requires fine-motor skill that emerges from years of practice in the control of the small muscles of the fingers and hands. To appreciate the order and beauty of the world we must first refine our ability to perceive it. To translate ideas and feelings into words or art we must first have many experiences in the physical world.

A DEVELOPMENTAL PERSPECTIVE

The work of Arnold Gesell and his associates, begun in the 1930s, provides much of the information about physical development currently used by early childhood educators (see Chapter 4, Child Development). Gesell contended that inheritance and maturation determined a major portion of an individual's development but that environmental factors could influence it positively or negatively. For normal growth and maturation to proceed children must have nutritious food, affectionate human contact, and adequate opportunities to exercise. Children need protection from disease, injury, and environmental hazards. Day-to-day care needs to be supplemented by periodic medical examinations to make sure that a child's growth patterns are normal and unimpeded by disease.

In addition to having their basic needs met, children need opportunities to move, explore, and manipulate materials, so they can develop their fullest potential for physical sensitivity and competence. They must also learn how to take care of their own bodily needs and how to protect themselves from harm. As a teacher you will use information about physical development, health, and safety to design and plan appropriate curriculum experiences.

Because physical development follows a predictable sequence, you will be able to plan activities that help children move on to the appropriate next steps. The infant develops head control and reaching and grasping skill before sitting and walking. The large muscles closest to the center of the body grow and develop coordinated functions before the small muscles of the hands and fingers. Because mastery of the muscles of legs, arms, and torso must be accomplished first, good early childhood teachers provide many opportunities for active movement. Growing mastery makes large-muscle activity very enjoyable to young children, and it is a feature of much of their play. They gradually go on to develop small-muscle control. The arms, legs, and trunk must learn to work in concert before a child can pump on a swing; scissors cannot be used until coordination and strength of the hand is well developed. Table 11.1 summarizes the development of motor ability from age two through five.

ROLE OF THE TEACHER

Teachers have a vital role to play in the physical development curriculum. Given an appropriate environment and freedom to choose, children create many opportunities for their own physical development. Many of the health and safety concepts and skills that children need are presented and practiced as part of the daily routine of the classroom. It is unnecessary and inappropriate to plan elaborate physical education experiences, like gymnastic classes and many organized games, for young children. Children learn some important skills like hand washing, not from formal teaching, but as a result of your example and guidance throughout

TABLE 11.1

Development of motor ability

	Activity	2	2½	3	3½	4	4½	5
Large Motor	Walking	Heel-toe pattern		On tiptoe	On a line			Backwards
	Running	Just able to run	True running appears	Runs with little stumbling		Runs with good leg-arm coordination		
	Jumping	Jumps down from object with both feet	Jumps off floor with both feet	Jumps in place with two feet together		Jumps skillfully		Broad jumps 2–3 feet; jumps forward 10 times without falling
	Climbing	Walks up and down stairs with some assistance		Climbs stairs with alternating feet holding onto handrail		Climbs jungle gym		
	Balancing	Picks up objects from floor without falling		Climbs up slide and comes down	Hops on one foot	Balances on one foot; walks on balance beam		Turns somersaults
	Skipping					Basic gallop	Skipping	Skillful skipping
	Ball throwing		Responds to thrown ball with delayed arm movements	Catches; throws with some accuracy; kicks ball forward		Throws, catches, and bounces large balls		Catches small ball using hands only; mature ball-kicking patterns; kicks through ball
Small Motor	Drawing	Scribbles		Holds crayon with thumb and fingers; makes dots, lines, circular strokes		Copies circle; imitates cross	Prints a few capital letters	
	Painting	Paints with whole-arm movement		Paints with wrist action				
	Cutting			Cuts with scissors				Cuts on line continuously
	Other skills	Turns knobs	Uses one hand consistently	Rolls, pounds, squeezes, and pulls clay		Holds cup in one hand	Buttons, zips, ties shoes with practice	

the program day. It is important to be attentive to the balance and scope of the physical experiences that children have in your classroom.

Physical development activities are so clearly "play" that planning for them may seem unnecessary, and they may be overlooked in program planning. They may not be adequately planned because teachers may not enjoy this part of the curriculum, because they do not have the pressing need for physical development that children do, or because there is some mess and hazard in the sensory and large-muscle curriculum that may be disturbing.

Small-muscle development opportunities are more frequently planned for as part of the curriculum. Activities that develop coordination and control of the hands and fingers are not messy or noisy and rarely cause adults concern. Indeed, because of the obvious link to adult tasks like writing, computer skills, and assembling materials, small-muscle activities are generally looked on with favor by parents and teachers.

Many of the health and safety activities of the classroom are not recognized as curriculum because they seem so mundane from the adult perspective. It may be true that the time teachers devote to assisting children with toileting, hand washing, and dressing does seem like a nuisance or a distraction from other activities. However, every moment children spend involved in such routines is valuable learning time. They are actively engaged in mastering essential physical skills and concepts. To realize this you need only to observe the delight on the face of a two-year-old who has used the toilet unassisted for the first time; the struggle of a three-year-old attempting to button a shirt; and a four-year-old laboriously cutting the vegetables for a cooking project. You will see immediately that these children are involved in challenging, serious work that will eventually result in gratification and mastery.

Your role is to pay attention to the range of physical skills and attitudes in your group of children so that you can provide them with opportunities and encouragement for development. It is also important to be able to clearly articulate to parents, administrators, and other staff the rationale for total physical development curriculum that includes a proper appreciation for the health and safety curriculum that is embedded in many of the routines of the program day.

SENSORY CURRICULUM

Sensory experience is at the core of the curriculum for very young children. Learning depends on sensory input—hearing, smelling, seeing, touching, moving, and tasting. We are not born with the ability to fully discriminate between different sensations but must become aware of them. Each child must have opportunities to learn to perceive using all of the senses.

By the time children come to you in the preschool setting they may have already been taught to avoid many of the sensory avenues to learning. Touching, smelling, and tasting are often particularly restricted even in children as young as two. They have been given messages like: "Don't taste, it's dirty." "Don't touch, it's dangerous." "It may be poisonous." "Don't touch, you may break it." Looking and listening are generally considered acceptable ways to find out about the world. Although these are valuable for young children, they should not be encouraged to the exclusion of taste, touch, smell, and physical manipulation. If children are to gather and use the information that is available to them in the world, they need opportunities to fully develop each of their senses. The obvious joy a child shows when rolling down a hill, playing with water, smelling a rose, or rubbing fingers along a soft piece of velvet are the observable evidence of how important sensory experience is to young children.

Young preschoolers are in a transition stage between sensorimotor and preoperational modes of learning. In the sensorimotor period (from birth to two years) the senses are the primary mode for gathering information and learning. If the child's ability to receive and use sensory input is severely impeded, normal development will be retarded. For this reason, all preschool and kindergarten curriculums should include a strong sensory component.

Organizing the Content

The senses give you a natural framework for planning and organizing this component of your program.

The *kinesthetic* sense is an internal awareness of movement, touch, and gravity. It is probably the first sensation that human beings experience. Children have kinesthetic experiences in play and when they are touched and held. To remain upright and to make judgments on how we move we need to have the ability to discriminate and control using the kinesthetic sense.

The *auditory* sense, *hearing,* also begins before a child is born. Differentiating between sounds is a major developmental task. Learning to screen the auditory environment—to exclude irrelevant sounds and to attend to what is meaningful—is an important part of language development. In a typical noisy preschool class it is easy to become insensitive to subtleties of sound. We can help children to attend to and differentiate between sounds in music, language, and the world around them.

The sense of *touch,* or *tactile* sense, is a primary mode of learning. The organ of touch is the skin and by its all encompassing nature makes touch a dominant aspect of our lives. Touch gives us information about the world and allows us to make decisions for comfort and safety. Indeed, the survival of an infant has been demonstrated to be dependent on tactile and kinesthetic stimulation (Berger 1980; Papalia and Olds 1982). Early childhood experiences help children learn to identify and discriminate between tactile sensations so they can make judg-

ments about the world based on texture, temperature, and pressure.

We make many decisions based on our sense of *smell*—the *olfactory* sense. We smell bread baking and decide to eat; we smell a rose and bask in the sensation; we smell a dirty diaper and know that it is time to change it. Very young children have limited olfactory experience and may not be able to make clear judgments based on smells. This is one reason why they sometimes drink poisonous liquids like ammonia. Older preschoolers make many choices based on the smell of things and often reject experiences, settings, foods, and people because of an odor which is unfamiliar or which they judge unpleasant.

The sense of *taste* is sometimes called the *gustatory* sense. There are actually only a few taste characteristics—sweet, sour, salty, and bitter. Eating is a multisensory experience. Taste characteristics, together with the aromas of food, create the multitude of flavors that we experience. Texture and temperature (elements of the sense of touch) also influence how we experience food. Infants and very young children explore everything with their mouths, and they do not confine their gustatory exploration to things that we consider edible. In the preschool classroom children can be provided with a range of taste experiences and can develop an understanding of which things are unsafe or unhealthy to put in their mouths.

The sensory mode that we most commonly associate with learning is *sight*. Learning to make visual discriminations begins early in life. From infancy we use visual information to make judgments, but the ability to make fine discriminations takes many years to develop. *Vision,* like other senses, requires opportunities for practice. Because they are so critical in deciphering written language and are relatively easy to provide, visual discrimination tasks are often given a disproportionately large share of teacher attention. This is rarely necessary. Children normally develop visual discrimination as they work puzzles, sort buttons, look at books, and engage with other classroom materials.

Although it is useful to think in terms of planning for the development of each of the senses, it is also important to realize that they need not be learned in isolation. Children involved in a cooking activity touch and compare the flour and salt, smell the banana as it is mashed, experience resistance when the thick batter is stirred, see the bubbles that form as air is beaten in, hear the sizzle as batter is poured in the pan, and taste the finished pancake. To separate these would be difficult and unnecessary—children learn from the combined sensory experience.

The Environment

Teachers who recognize the importance of sensory experiences for young children can create environments that richly support the development of the senses. Most early childhood classrooms have materials that clearly contribute to sensory development: water, sand, mud, dough, and clay. You can add other planned activities using the senses as a framework as we have suggested. Consider each of the senses and evaluate what you could provide to stimulate each sensory modality. Include classroom materials that require matching, sorting, and other purposeful arranging, such as sound cans, sorting boxes, texture boards, pegboards, puzzles, collage materials, and blocks. Many games and materials designed for young children help them to focus on sensory variables, for example, the materials for sensory development designed by Maria Montessori: cylinders that vary in only one dimension—diameter, circumference, or height—and colored chips which children can arrange by gradations in shade and hue. Teachers can also make learning games to develop similar sensory awareness—sound cylinders, color matching games, and feely boxes are teacher-made materials found in many classrooms.

Everyday objects and activities can also encourage sensory exploration. An orange at lunch, an interesting piece of driftwood, the texture of a carpet, and many other ordinary things give children a chance to use all their senses. Collections of objects like rocks, shells, leaves, beans, and seeds give children opportunities to look, touch, and sort.

Materials designed for other curriculum areas are also sensory in nature. The colors in a beautifully illustrated children's book, the different weights and sizes in a set of unit blocks, the sound differences of rhythm instruments, the feel of moving through space on a swing, the cool mush of finger paints or clay, the tastes and smells as children cook applesauce—all are sensory highlights of activities that have other purposes. As you provide experiences to children, you can stay alert to the sensory qualities and encourage their sensory exploration and involvement.

In our own teaching we have used sensory activities that were readily available in our environment. We have enjoyed tasting and smelling days when children brought their favorite items to savor, listening walks when we went to hear what we could hear, and color days when we all wore the same color. When a small group of children and their teachers move beyond the classroom, they encounter many experiences that heighten sensory awareness such as the smells and tastes of the neighborhood bakery and the textures, sights, and sounds of a local park.

Teaching

You support children's exploration by providing space that can be used without fear of mess and materials that can be fully explored without concern about waste. You can help children focus on sensory aspects of materials and experiences by the ways you call attention to them. Materials such as sand, mud, water, clay, and finger paints are sometimes rejected by fastidi-

ous children, particularly when these materials are available only occasionally for short periods. Reluctant children are more likely to learn to use and enjoy materials if they are enjoyed by other children. It also helps when the use of materials moves in a sequence over several weeks or even months, from structured and contained to more open and free form. For example, finger paints might be presented first on a cafeteria tray with small paper, small amounts of paint, and protective smocks. Later activities might involve a group mural finger painting on the tables in the playground, perhaps with sand and gravel added.

Adapting for Different Ages

Sensory experiences are essential for infant-toddler learning, and if you work with children under three, you will be involved in both planned and spontaneous sensory explorations. If you work with children over the age of six, you may find that you are confronted with the challenge of encouraging them to continue with sensory exploration as a valid mode for learning about the world.

Infants and Toddlers

Infants and toddlers transform the most ordinary daily routines into sensory exploration activities. The ripe banana served to an infant is squished and squeezed between fingers and smeared on the face—turned into a tactile, taste, and smell experience. The ensuing mess should not interfere with our ability to see the value of this activity for the child who is learning about the properties of substances.

Learning and development are intimately tied to sensory experience during these years. When we provide for sensory pleasure and exploration, we nurture curiosity and learning. Feelings of security and well-being are gained as an infant strokes the surface of a familiar comfort object such as the satiny border of a blanket or the soft fur of a stuffed animal or experiences a

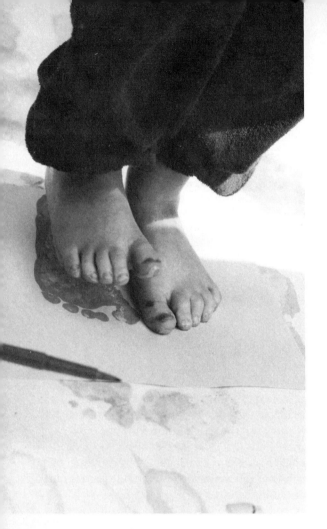

needs people who can appreciate the beauty and variety of nature, art, and music; the sights, sounds, smells, and flavors of a variety of cultures; and all the other sensory joys that contribute to our humanity.

Primary-grade children can continue to have experiences that build sensory awareness and appreciation of the world. They are supported in doing so when they are permitted frequent opportunities to explore and create with art media such as paints, clay, and collage materials. Field trips into natural environments provide a variety of sensory experiences. Visits to view works of art in the community and the display of interesting photographs, art prints, sculpted pieces, pottery, and paintings done by artists heighten appreciation of beautiful and interesting creations. Gardening and cooking are activities to learn from and to give sensual satisfaction. No eating experience is better than that of the peas from your own patch or the tortillas you make with your classmates as a part of a study unit on Mexican culture. Sensory learning is valuable independent of other educational goals, but it can deepen and enrich all learning experiences.

gentle powdering after a bath or diaper change. Children become attuned to sound as caregivers talk, sing, recite nursery rhymes, and join children in responding with surprise, joy, and wonder to unanticipated sounds like the passing fire truck, the boom of thunder, or the creaking of the tree limbs in the wind.

Primary-School Children

As children mature, listening and looking are the senses involved in much of their school learning activities. If you work with primary-school children you can take care to provide experiences that employ other senses and thereby contribute to enriching and balancing their development. We live in a world that needs people who have thinking and doing skills. It is also a world that

SMALL-MUSCLE CURRICULUM

The small-muscle curriculum—learning to co-ordinate the hands and fingers—begins when babies in their cribs reach out to feel, to grasp, and to manipulate. Those initial impulses eventually lead to the competent use of tools. A spoon, a crayon, a hammer, a needle, and a keyboard are all tools that are manipulated by the hands and fingers. The early childhood small-muscle curriculum makes an important contribution to eventual mastery of tools.

Organizing the Content

All small-muscle activities involve control, agility, strength, and coordination. This combination of elements is involved in the multitude of skills that children need to develop. The elements described here provide a useful framework for planning and presenting experiences designed to develop small-muscle skills.

Small-muscle *control* involves knowing what you want your hands and fingers to do and being able to direct them to do it. The direction, size, speed, shape, force, and characteristics of hand movements must be controlled in daily living. To be able to pat a cat and beat a drum requires conscious differing of the force, direction, speed, and size of a similar movement. Time, practice, and many diverse experiences are required to develop this competence.

Agility concerns the ability to move in a precise and intentional way at the speed that is desired. Young children's small-muscle agility is limited. However motivated and intelligent they are, they can rarely master skills such as touch typing, playing the piano, and knitting. Before children can become agile they must gain a great deal of control over the size, direction, shape, force, and speed of other less complicated movements.

Strength concerns the stamina and force that are available to apply to and sustain movement. Children growing up with normal abilities and opportunities to use their hands also develop the strength required to do most small-muscle activities. As children persist at small-muscle activities in preschool, they develop greater strength and stamina.

Coordination means being able to control the interrelationships of hands, fingers, and other body parts. It involves sensory and muscular interplay—hand-eye coordination, moving hands based on visual data, and coordination of the two hands based on visual and kinesthetic awareness (sensing where the hands are in space). Clapping hands, moving spoon to mouth, and stringing beads are examples of activities that require coordinated movement.

Small-Muscle Skills and Activities

The equipment, materials, and activities that you present to young children should provide op-

portunities for all of the small-muscle skills to develop. The following list is intended to help you to ensure that all of the elements are represented in your school curriculum.

Grasping and releasing—whole hand and pincer

Dumping/pouring/spooning

Twisting/turning

Writing/drawing/painting

Tapping/striking

Clapping/slapping/patting

Rubbing/rolling

Folding/tearing

Cutting

Pulling

Stringing/sewing

Tying/buttoning/zipping

Pointing/fingering

As we created this list we were astonished by the complexity of the movements involved and by the sheer quantity of small-muscle tasks that young children need to develop. We thought about which elements and discrete movements were involved in each task. For example, cutting involves all of the elements (strength, control, agility, and coordination) and consists of grasping, directing, releasing tension but not releas-

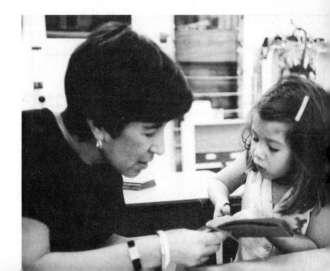

ing grasp, and twisting and turning the opposing hand. No wonder it's hard for young children! Simply feeding oneself requires control and coordination and involves grasping, directing, and releasing an object with enough finesse to avoid spills. The significance of a two-year-old's grasping and dumping can be more readily appreciated as a learning task when viewed as an important step in the mastery of some complicated fine-motor skills.

The Environment

Every classroom for young children needs to have toys and materials that build small-muscle skills. Fortunately, almost all small toys contribute to this development. Most preschools have an area exclusively for construction and manipulative toys such as pegboards, puzzles, and Lego blocks. These need to be sized for the age of the children—younger children need fewer, larger pieces that cannot be swallowed and are easier to manipulate.

Many curriculum materials contribute to small-muscle development. As children cook, use math materials like Cuisenaire rods, build with blocks, probe and investigate science materials, do finger plays, play instruments, and even as they turn pages in a book, they are practicing fine-motor skills. Art activities support small-muscle development. Clay and dough are especially versatile materials with which children develop almost every small-muscle skill. The tools and materials commonly found in writing centers (paper, pencils, pens, crayons, hole punches, staplers, rulers, scissors, stamps, and so on) also develop these skills.

Self-help activities are also major contributors to small-muscle development. As children learn to serve their own food, pour their own beverages, use the water fountain, put on their shoes, and fasten their clothes, they are not only gaining independence but are practicing physical skills. The real challenge of opening your own lunch box and thermos points out the

real-life significance of fine-motor development. Teachers can add pouring activities and lacing frames to help develop these same skills. The materials that are found in the *practical life* area of a Montessori classroom provide this skill development and can be added to any classroom.

Sufficient time, variety, and quantity of materials are needed for children to develop the use of hands and fingers. This time is valuable and children are not "just playing." Children's obvious delight in fine-motor activity is a good indicator of their interest and need for frequent and prolonged practice through play. Daily choice times of at least an hour should include access to manipulative and other materials that support fine-motor development.

Teaching

The most essential thing you need in supporting children's fine-motor growth is knowledge of developmental sequence and sensitivity to individual differences. You will observe children, interpret the meaning of their activity, and provide materials and activities that provide optimal challenge.

When a child is clearly frustrated or bored with a material, you have several choices based on what you know about development and your judgment of the child's skill and personal style. For a child who is struggling to cut a small slip of tissue paper you might offer stiffer paper, note the difficulty, and then make an appropriate comment— "Jenna, I see you tore that paper that was so hard to cut. You solved your problem!" You might decide to stock the shelf with a variety of different weights of paper and more functional scissors, or you could suggest an alternative— "I like to use construction paper when I'm cutting because it doesn't flop."

Sometimes the developmentally appropriate response to a child attempting a difficult task is to design experiences to build prerequisite skills. The child who hasn't yet mastered scissors needs plenty of grasping, tension-release, coordination, and strength-building experiences. Providing dough and clay to build strength and tools like tongs, hole punches, tweezers, and staplers that require similar motor action will contribute to skill in cutting.

Adapting for Different Ages

Throughout every day of our life, from infancy through adulthood, we need to make use of the small muscles of our hands and fingers. As the teacher of an infant or toddler group you take care to provide the materials needed. With primary-age children you may often need to demonstrate and instruct in order to help children learn complex fine-motor skills. For both age groups, adequate amounts of time should be provided for practice of newly emerging skills.

Infants and Toddlers

Newborns will grasp and cling tightly to a finger. Soon they grasp and pull, grasp and release, then pat, slap, bang, and drop every object within reach. In no time at all babies are playing grasp and drop games. They drop toys from their cribs and food from their feeding tables and wail to have the items returned to them so that they can grasp and drop again. Even though the behavior may frustrate adults, it is important infant development and deserves our cooperation and participation for at least a part of each day.

Before they can walk, infants enjoy games and songs that are a part of caregiver and parenting behaviors in every culture. Pat-a-cake and clapping hands to music are among the important educational games of infancy. Push-pull toys fascinate infants and toddlers and they enjoy banging on a drum with a stick or on a food tray with a spoon. Toddlers will fill containers with objects and dump them out and repeat the sequence over and over again. They also begin to master the finer small-muscle control and hand-eye coordination required to stack small blocks, to use a spoon, and to direct a paintbrush or a colored marking pen at a piece of paper. Manipulating playdough can build strength and coordination while giving sensory pleasure. These early years of repetitious small-muscle practice in play are essential for the development of the skill level that enables adults to do things like use a computer.

Primary-School Children

Although they may not have yet mastered typing with speed and accuracy, some primary-school children will have had experiences with a computer keyboard and others may be skilled as pianists and sculptors. Not all will have specialized in these ways, but most do learn how to write readable print and cut accurately with scissors and knives.

A classroom filled with tools, materials, games, and activities that develop fine-motor skill is important for the education of the whole child at this stage of development. Resources may not permit the inclusion of pianos and computers, but children can be interested in and challenged by mastering the use of a donated typewriter, playing a simple tune on a recorder, or learning to weave on a simple loom. Provision of art materials, carpentry tools, and writing and drawing supplies and allowing time and space for these activities help children refine their small-muscle abilities.

LARGE-MUSCLE CURRICULUM

Human beings come into the world unprepared to deal with gravity, to stand upright, and to move through space in a coordinated way. Some mastery over the large muscles of our bodies must precede almost any other learning and skill development. The large-muscle curriculum— that part of the early childhood program that is concerned with the development of children's skill and strength in arms, legs, and torso—is

designed to help children gain and retain physical skills and abilities as they work and play.

The large-muscle curriculum contributes to learning and health in the early years and throughout life. Attention span and concentration are enlarged as children use their bodies in challenging physical activity. Such activity helps to release tension and promotes relaxation. Physical fitness is essential for lifelong health. This area of the curriculum is of critical importance because it can develop the skills and attitudes that will enable children to enjoy physical activity throughout their lives.

Organizing the Content

To become physically competent, children must develop strength, flexibility, agility, coordination, and kinesthetic awareness. These form the basis for the large-muscle curriculum.

The *kinesthetic* sense is stimulated through activities such as climbing, running, jumping, and rolling. Such activities lead to the ability to balance, to identify one's position in space, and to control physical motions. Swinging, turning somersaults, walking on a beam, and jumping on a trampoline are skills that depend on kinesthetic awareness and control.

Strength is the physical energy available for movement or resistance. *Stamina,* or endurance, is the capacity for the sustained use of strength or physical energy. Older children generally are

stronger and have greater and more predictable endurance. Strength and stamina increase as children exert energy and effort for prolonged periods of time in challenging activities like group games, walking, and running.

Flexibility concerns the ease and range of movement. Physical suppleness lessens with age as the muscle system develops and becomes less elastic. An infant easily brings toes to mouth but this flexibility wanes as children get older. One of the goals of the physical development curriculum is to help children retain flexibility while developing muscular strength.

Coordination means being able to move different body parts together in relation to one another. A child pumping a swing pulls arms and legs forward and backward in unison. A baby crawling or a young child climbing on a jungle gym moves arms and legs in opposition. Young children learn to coordinate their bodies first by experimenting, imitating, and exploring movement to gain control. Practice then internalizes the new skill. Opportunities to move freely for large periods of time encourage such experimentation.

Agility involves moving with speed, grace, and precision. A child who can stop abruptly and change directions is agile. Agility requires flexibility, strength, coordination, and a well-developed kinesthetic sense. As children gain agility they feel a sense of mastery. Much of the pleasure children find in large-muscle play stems from the enjoyment of growing agility.

Large-Muscle Skills and Activities

When children engage in a range of large-muscle activities, they develop in each of the areas of physical competence. The following list provides a framework for the physical development opportunities you should offer in your program. Evaluate the environment and schedule in terms of each of the items. There should be space, time, and equipment for children to develop each skill.

Balancing

Walking/running/stopping

Galloping/skipping

Jumping/hopping

Pedalling/propelling

Climbing

Pulling/pushing

Swinging

Swaying/rocking

Twisting/turning

Stretching

Rolling

Crawling

Catching

Punting/striking/kicking

Throwing

Bouncing/dribbling

The Environment

When children have frequent opportunities to engage in active play several times a day, they develop many of the abilities described in the preceding list through their own natural activity. Teachers can provide guidance and encouragement, an environment rich in equipment and materials, and enough time and space for exploration.

Children need equipment for climbing, swinging, throwing, digging, hammering, balancing, and exploring space with their bodies. Large-muscle development opportunities abound in a well-designed play yard for young children. The most desirable outdoor space for a group of young children would include a hill for climbing and rolling, large flat areas for running and galloping, paved areas for wheel toys, dirt and sand for digging, and trees for climbing and shade.

The most important and versatile piece of equipment for large-muscle development is a well-designed and well-constructed climbing

structure. A structure should have different ways to get up and down: ramps, ladders, stairs, slides, firepoles, and cargo nets or webs of tires and platforms of different heights. Smaller pieces of equipment should also be a part of the outdoor environment: rocking boats, balance beams, woodworking tables and tools, hollow blocks, small trampolines, balls, wheelbarrows, wagons, digging tools, trikes, scooters, and balance boards.

Tricycles, blocks, sand and water tables, climbing structures, and rocking boats may require a larger proportion of program budget and space than other equipment, but they are essential for physical development and they will last a long time. Regular trips to nearby parks or gyms can supplement a less than ideal play yard.

Recycled materials can be used to build equipment that can substitute for more costly items. For example, baby bathtubs make adequate water and sand tables. If you can't afford a climbing structure, you can create an alternative with sawhorses, planks, boards, ladders, cable spools, tires, heavy rope, and cargo nets. Logs or telephone poles can serve as a balance beams. If sand is not available, a pile of dirt can serve as a satisfying, if messy, digging substitute. Portable aluminum climbing equipment can be rearranged by you and children either indoors or outdoors. Though less versatile, swings, slides, metal jungle gyms, and other standard pieces of playground equipment also contribute to large-muscle development.

If the climate dictates that you spend long periods of time indoors, you will need to find ways to provide large-muscle development experiences daily. Activities like creative movement, circle games, and physical exercises can give children the chance to use and develop their bodies. Children will, however, need more physical activity than can be provided in a daily activity time. The portable equipment just described—balance beams, trampolines, hollow blocks—can be used indoors when outdoor play is not possible.

Teaching

You support safe, productive, physical activity when you make sure that equipment is free of hazards, appropriately placed, and sufficiently challenging. Your role is to watch carefully so that you are aware of children's growing skill and so that you are available to offer help as needed. Young children can be inadvertently discouraged from climbing, sliding, and swinging by teachers who are overly concerned about possible injury. A useful guideline is that if children are willing to attempt using a piece of equipment, they can usually manage it. If they can get up on a climbing structure they can generally get down from it on their own. Occasionally a challenge will be beyond an individual's capabilities, and you must move to provide assistance. If a child climbs onto something and is not able to reverse the process, you can give instruction and encouragement: "I think you can do it. Put your foot on the bar and move your hand down a little bit—now you can step safely." Even a lift back to the ground, without admonishing the failed attempt, might be appropriate. Children need optimal challenge—equipment, materials, and activities that provide the right degree of difficulty—to develop the skill that is just within their reach.

How you talk can encourage or discourage children's engagement in physical activities. It is best to avoid comments that create comparison and competition between children. Saying "Look how high Sam can climb. Can anyone else climb as high?" may encourage Sam, but the remainder of the children may attempt to reach dangerously beyond their current skill level in order to please you or they may feel inadequate because they cannot achieve the standard you have set. Real encouragement relates only to the individual's accomplishment: "Sam, that's the highest I've ever seen you climb. You're becoming a very strong person." It acknowledges effort and new accomplishments and avoids implying everyone else should be able to do the same thing.

Children benefit from your active involvement in their play. They need someone to toss a ball or to play follow the leader with them, to play guitar and sing as they play ring-around-the-rosy, to explain the rules of What Time Is It Mister Wolf?, to share their triumph as they acquire new skills. By playing *with* children, you encourage and support their activity and you provide a model of an adult who is physically active—a powerful demonstration that being active is natural and pleasurable.

Teacher-led activities that provide practice in developing physical competencies also have a place in the program. These activities can include simple yoga, creative movement, exercises, and group games like tag, dodgeball, and follow the leader. We prefer games that minimize competition and win-lose situations.

Many children develop physical competence from self-directed play in a well-planned and equipped environment whereas others need a good deal of well-planned support. It is important to observe individuals, so that you can encourage reticent children to practice skills they lack and so that you provide adequate challenge for more skilled children. It is also important to provide special opportunities for those children who might never choose to practice a particular skill or those for whom vigorous physical activity is never a choice. Some children curtail their participation because of obesity and may benefit from special encouragement. Children who have definite developmental lags in physical ability may require direct intervention in the form of formal instruction or one-to-one practice. All direct physical training and intervention needs to be carried out in pleasurable play situations, so that the child's attitude will be positive and spontaneous physical activity will become a source of pleasure.

Adapting for Different Ages

Between birth and age eight children make great strides in their ability to use their bodies. The large-muscle development of infants requires quite different support from the teacher than that required by a primary-school child.

Infants and Toddlers

At birth children have little mobility except that afforded them by the adults who carry them. In fact, it is important that they be held and carried for this is how they begin to develop a sense of their position in space and of their bodies as separate from the bodies of their caregivers. The journey from a newborn who is unable to lift his or her head or roll over to a toddler who has the ability to walk, run, jump, climb stairs, and pedal a trike takes thirty-six months.

Within months of birth most babies love to be held upright and push themselves up and down on the laps of willing adults. Such actions help the infant build the strength and coordination that will enable independent standing. Infants should have space in which to practice crawling and stable furniture or stationary cruise bars to hold firmly when they are ready to stand upright and begin their first tentative steps.

Older infants will begin walking with the assistance of wheeled walking frames and even tiny trikes without pedals. Toddlers will still be wobbling when they first attempt stairs. A play structure with two or three broad steps and several safe ways to get back down to ground level will be used well in a toddler room and in the play yard. Pushing or pulling wagons loaded with toys and friends builds strength. By age three many toddlers will have learned to pedal a

trike, throw a ball, and run and stop at will. You support this incredibly rapid rate of development by providing space, time, equipment, and encouragement.

Primary-School Children

Even though primary-school children may take dance lessons, play organized sports, and ride bicycles, the general physical condition of many children today suggests that they do not get regular large-muscle exercise and have not become interested in or skilled at organized games or sports. In many schools large-motor activity is confined to short "recess" periods. In some states no provision at all is made for regular physical development activity periods for primary-school children. Only one state requires daily physical education (Javernick 1988, pp. 18–26). Many teachers strive to make physical activities a more integrated and pleasurable part of school life.

In the classroom, children can enjoy a wide variety of activities that involve large-muscle development but are controlled enough to avoid hurting people and property. Primary-school children can enjoy and benefit from exercises done to music, creative movement or yoga sessions led by the teacher, and temporary obstacle courses and climbing structures.

Organized games have appeal and can be done by quite large groups (even a whole class). Primary-school children benefit from and can enjoy skill practice (throwing, kicking and catching balls, jumping, running relays) if it is conducted in a spirit of play and effort is appreciated as much as success. Field trips can provide exercise in the form of walking and climbing. An occasional teacher-led jog can be a playful diversion from the usual routine. You support physical development when you go beyond the physical education class and recess time mentality and build physical activity into your daily life with children.

PHYSICAL DEVELOPMENT CHECKLIST

Making sure that you are providing for sensory, small-muscle, and large-muscle development opportunities is an important part of your role. You will want to read further to enlarge your repertoire of activities and skills. We have devised the checklist that appears at the end of the chapter to help our college students evaluate their programs, planning, and teaching for a range of physical development opportunities.

HEALTH AND SAFETY CURRICULA

Without safety and health people cannot learn, create, develop skills and share with others. Yet health and safety tend to be given secondary roles in education.

If health education and safety education in your own past consisted of preachy, boring lectures and repetitive drills, you may feel that the topics make dull subject matter for the early childhood years. However, these are the years during which children are most intrigued with learning about caring for themselves. It is the time when the foundations of understanding are formed and the underlying skills and dispositions to care for one's health and safety are established. You have an opportunity to interest children in two subjects that will be important to them throughout their lives.

How do children learn about health and safety? Until very recently education for self-care was the sole responsibility of the family. Children learned through the daily experience of watching their family members care for children and themselves and then by becoming responsible for younger siblings. Today, adults' daily lives are often far removed from their children's lives so children may not observe parents caring for themselves and others.

Typical Western life in the last years of the twentieth century is not as healthful as it once was. Children as well as adults pay a price for a sedentary, urban lifestyle. Fifty percent of American children are judged to be getting insufficient exercise to develop healthy hearts and lungs, and 40 percent of five- to eight-year-olds show at least one risk factor for heart disease (American Academy of Pediatrics 1988). These problems might be remedied in part by introducing children to appropriate health education at an early age.

Accidents are the most common cause of death in young children. Many are outside of children's control, including the most common—fatalities in automobile accidents. But children can learn to avoid some hazards and can learn strategies for coping with others. Safety is an issue in their lives.

As an early childhood educator your responsibility for children's health and safety has three components. The first is to care for and protect children through a safe and healthy environment (see Chapter 7, A Good Place for Children). The second is to empower children through education so they understand and can begin to care for and protect themselves. The third is to educate parents and work with other professionals to promote a safe, healthy home, school, and world for young children.

Health

There are a number of ways that early childhood educators help children to understand and appreciate their bodies and make wise choices about personal care, exercise, and nutrition.

Body Awareness and Personal Care

One of the primary components of the health curriculum is helping children to understand their bodies and how they function. Young children are fascinated with and unashamed of their bodies. They only gradually learn to feel that physical functions like urination are private or shameful.

Teachers of young children need to react to children's interests in their bodily functions in supportive ways. All body parts and physiological processes have names—shin, finger, knuckle, buttocks, knee, forehead, digestion, elimination, saliva, and so on. The words are innocuous and easy to use: "It's hard to breathe when your nose is all plugged up with mucus. If you blow your nose you might be more comfortable." Children who learn accurate terminology in a low-intensity, supportive emotional climate are better equipped to understand and care for themselves. If there are no scary or taboo subjects, children are given an important message: Your body is okay; it is safe to talk with adults about all aspects of how you are feeling.

Body awareness and personal care are also a worthwhile focus for integrating areas of the curriculum. For example, we recently observed a class of four- and five-year-olds who were studying their bodies. They sang songs about body parts and eagerly labeled different parts on life-size outlines of themselves. They compared their heights and weights, made graphs about their eye and hair color, and read books about muscles, bones, and blood. They visited a dentist's office and had a pediatrician come to class.

Providing for children's care and teaching about it are not separate activities. Each time we help children to keep themselves healthy through hand washing after toileting, providing for exercise and rest, toothbrushing, nose blowing, and caring for minor injuries, we have an opportunity to talk about how these contribute to overall health—that children can help themselves to be healthy.

Nutrition

During the early childhood years, we can help children to understand that their health is affected by food and that they can make food

we help them to appreciate the high-fiber, low-fat foods that have been demonstrated by research to contribute to good health. By expanding children's food horizons, we enable them to discover a range of alternatives and help them to develop competence in making wise food choices. Much of what adults experience as children's reluctance to try healthful foods may be the product of their own expectations and biases. Children usually enjoy fruits, vegetables, brown rice, and such exotic dishes as borscht and ratatouille if they participate in preparation and if they know that they will not be forced to eat the food if they don't like it.

Nutrition can be an everyday part of the early childhood program experience. You can best teach nutrition by providing planned experiences that will help children to develop skills and understand concepts, by taking advantage of daily events that involve food like snack and lunch, through cooking in the classroom, and by modeling behavior and attitudes that encourage health-supporting habits.

A few simple concepts form the base of early childhood nutrition education. These do not involve memorizing lists of vitamins and minerals or the four basic food groups. Instead, they involve an awareness of food and the value of good nutrition and the realization that food affects feelings, behavior, and development. Even young preschoolers can come to under-

choices that will help them to grow and be healthy. We have placed nutrition with the physical development curriculum, but clearly it is part of other curricula as well. It connects physical, cognitive, social, and creative development. Because it is used to teach other subjects, nutrition content often gets lost. Nutrition in itself is an important part of the curriculum—something that it is worthwhile for young children to know about.

People's health is linked to their diet. As more and more information is gained, nutritionists are coming to realize that the typical Western diet is not as healthful as was once thought. Children may learn to choose a healthier diet if

---

IN THE CLASSROOM: BODY AWARENESS AND PERSONAL CARE CONCEPTS FOR YOUNG CHILDREN

- People's bodies are all very much alike.
- Body parts have names and functions.
- People differ depending on their age, size, sex, and state of health.
- Children and adults have things they can do to take care of themselves.
- All people need exercise, rest, food, and hygiene.

IN THE CLASSROOM: NUTRITION CONCEPTS FOR YOUNG CHILDREN

- All people need food to grow, live, stay healthy, and have energy for work and play.
- Different foods have different substances that are needed for health and growth. Older preschool children can learn that these nutrients are called protein, vitamins, minerals, carbohydrates, and fat.
- All people need to eat a variety of foods to get all of the nutrients they need.
- All people need the same nutrients, but they need different amounts depending on their age, size, sex, state of health, and the amount of activity they are involved in.
- There are many different kinds of foods that can provide the different nutrients.
- The way that food is grown, processed, stored, and prepared influences its nutritional value.
- Some foods provide many nutrients, some provide very few (for example, sodas provide empty calories, whereas fruit juice provides vitamins, and minerals as well).

stand some basic nutrition concepts, although they may not be able to verbalize them.

Teachers need to model honest appreciation for healthful foods and give children time and several opportunities to try any new or unusual food. A teacher encountering a new food in the school lunch can say, "This looks interesting. It's delicious, but a little different from our usual lunch," rather than looking disgusted and pushing the plate away. If children see adults making food choices that help maintain growth, health, and energy and avoiding non-nutritious foods, they gain nutrition awareness. Poor habits can also be taught by modeling. For this reason you should restrict your consumption of soft drinks and sweets to times when you will not be with children.

Cooking. A range of skills are necessary for children to be competent and independent in choosing and handling food. Children can begin to learn skills surrounding food choice and prepartion including selection, planning, follow-

ing recipes, stirring, pouring, measuring, and serving. Becoming competent at these skills also fosters feelings of self-confidence and positive attitudes toward nutritious foods and cooking. We have been delighted at the competence of experienced cooks aged three and four and surprised at the lack of confidence and skill in first- and second-graders who had not been given cooking opportunities.

Cooking experiences can be integrated into the weekly curriculum. As children cook they become aware of the properties of food and how it contributes to their lives. When they experience the food of other cultures, they are enhancing their appreciation of all people.

In food preparation, it is best to work with small groups. The younger the children are, the smaller the group should be. Choose activities in which children can do most of the work, and remember that everything from setup to cleanup is important. Reduce tasks to child-sized activities to ensure a successful experience. Use tools that work well. Knives that don't cut, eggbeaters

---

IN THE CLASSROOM: CHECKLIST FOR COOKING AND NUTRITION

_____ Unbreakable cooking equipment exclusively for children's use:

_____ Set of nesting bowls	_____ Individual portion bowls (four to six)
_____ Measuring cups and spoons	_____ Stirring spoons
_____ Rubber scrapers	_____ Turners
_____ Bread knives	_____ Sharp paring knives
_____ Small plastic cutting boards	_____ Good can opener

_____ Illustrated cookbooks with simple nutritious recipes

_____ Books for children concerning nutrition

_____ Teacher-made, large, illustrated recipe charts

_____ Hot plate or electric frying pan

_____ Toaster oven

_____ Basic ingredients: flour, salt, baking soda and powder, oil, vinegar, milk

_____ Facilities and equipment for hygenic cleanup and food storage: airtight plastic containers, sink with hot water, refrigerator, dishpan, drain board, sponges, dishwashing soap

_____ Picture collections of foods and food production

---

that stick, and graters that don't grate properly are frustrating and more dangerous than tools that work. It's a good idea to try all recipes before using them with children.

Cooking helps children to feel responsible, independent, and successful. It is a very important vehicle for teaching about nutrition. You can take note of the nutrient contributions of the foods that are being prepared ("The raisins in the snack mix will give us energy on our hike."), help children to notice differences in tastes ("Some of us like the carrots best, other people prefer the celery."), and work with food to preserve the nutrients and enhance the flavor and appearance of the food.

Simple, nutritious snacks make rewarding "cooking" experiences for young children. For example, spreading peanut butter on a slice of celery is not usually thought of as a cooking activity, but it involves food preparation skills that young children need practice to master.

Allowing children to become actively involved instead of remaining the passive recipients of adult services helps them begin to develop the skills and attitudes they will need to take care of themselves.

The times children are actively involved with food and nutrition—during meals, snacks, and cooking and while shopping, gardening, or feeding pets—are times to talk about nutrition. It is interesting to children to talk about where food comes from and how it helps their bodies to grow. Often they echo information they have heard. For example, many children have been told that milk makes them strong or big. You can help to develop the concept by adding a short informative statement like, "Yes, milk has protein in it to help you grow," or "It helps your bones grow and be strong."

The accompanying checklist includes essential materials for cooking with young children. It can be used to evaluate programs and to assist in planning and teaching nutrition and cooking activities.

Substance Abuse Prevention

Today it is common to see substance abuse prevention as a part of the curriculum for children of all ages. It is important to understand what you can do to help young children avoid substance abuse. The roots of substance abuse and its prevention may well lie in the early years, though drugs rarely appear in a classroom for young children.

Feelings of isolation, frustration, and a lack of self-esteem are the heart of substance abuse (Oyemade and Washington 1989). Behind the isolation and negative self-concept of children who abuse drugs, we often find families with problems. Adults in these families often abuse substances and reject their children. They have low expectations of children and are extremely strict or extremely permissive in their parenting. The word *drugs* may never come up as you help children to avoid this hazard. Good preschools have always helped children learn to make connections, handle frustration, and feel good about themselves.

We help to prevent substance abuse by really listening to children, by guiding them so that they learn to solve problems, and by teaching them skills for cooperation. We also help prevent substance abuse by involving parents in the program—by helping parents take pride in their children and by teaching positive parenting skills. Besides building self-concept, you will also provide health and safety curricula in which you discuss food and activities that build health and things that can harm. Such discussions lead naturally to building concepts that decrease the likelihood of substance abuse.

Safety

All of us who care about young children are dismayed when we hear about children being hurt or killed. Traffic and water accidents, fire, and accidental poisoning are the most common causes of death in young children. Young children are also frequently the victims of abuse.

It is not possible for young children to fully protect themselves from the hazards of the natural and human environment. Adults are responsible for providing this protection. Some hazards, however, can be made less potentially threatening with education. To point to only one example, children who are familiar with the way a fully outfitted fire fighter looks will not be as frightened should a Darth Vader look-alike come toward them through a smoke-filled room. Tragically, many children die in fires because they hide from the rescuers whose protective gear looks threatening.

You can help children begin to learn the ways in which they *can* protect themselves. To effectively teach children to be safe requires understanding what hazards are present for young children and the ability to consider the world through children's eyes. The goal of safety is to enable children to be active participants in their own protection rather than passively relying on others. This involves providing information children can understand in a way that they can remember and teaching them skills they can reasonably be expected to master.

It is tempting to teach safety as series of warnings—don't play with matches, don't go near the water, don't run in the street, don't talk to strangers. Unfortunately, don'ts don't work. The temptation of things that are taboo is so great that it is present in mythology and religion in legends like the forbidden fruit, Pandora's box, and Bluebeard's door. Human beings are curious and want to know about what is mysterious, dangerous, and forbidden.

Instead, we can teach about safety as a series of affirmations—things that children *can* do and *why* they should do them. Affirming their ability to take part in their own care and assuring them of our commitment to continue to take care of them to the extent that is needed makes children and adults partners in the effort to ensure safety.

What can young children learn about safety? How can they participate in protecting themselves from hazards? Young children can help keep themselves safe by learning these actions:

- Ingesting only good foods and safe medicines that are given to them by trusted adults and avoiding other substances.
- Cooperating in wearing a seatbelt, avoiding crossing streets unless they are with an adult, using crosswalks, and obeying traffic signals.
- Giving matches to adults, learning to stop-drop-and roll if their clothing catches on fire, recognizing and trusting fire fighters in their fire fighting gear, and practicing safe ways to escape from home and school buildings.
- Playing in pools and other bodies of water only when they are with a supervising adult.
- Saying stop if someone wants to hurt or touch them in ways that feel bad and telling a teacher or parent or other adult if someone has hurt them.

Perhaps even more important, we need to educate parents and ourselves about these dangers. Young children, however competent they may appear, need constant adult supervision and protection.

Teaching about Safety

Teaching young children about safety happens largely in the context of the daily life of the classroom. As you prepare for a field trip, children can help you create the safety rules. The day before the school fire drill you can talk about what a fire drill is for and have children help decide how to have a good one. Safety concepts can be integrated into activities that you are already doing:

- As you sing "Take Me Riding in Your Car," you can modify a verse—"Spree-i-spraddle in the frontseat, spree-i-spraddle in the backseat. Lock the door. Put on your seatbelt. Take you riding in my car!" (Woody Guthrie, "The Car Song").

- Add a painted crosswalk to the trike path for practice.
- Include props and pictures of fire fighters in full regalia in the dramatic play corner.

You can also teach children about safety through a planned curriculum focus. We have seen effective curriculum on fire, home and traffic safety, and on taking care of yourself, all of which made integrating units in preschools, kindergartens, and primary schools

Child Abuse Prevention

All early childhood programs and teachers have the responsibility to protect the children in their care. Much as we would wish it otherwise, it is impossible to "abuse-proof" very young children. There is no single lesson or curriculum approach, no one defensive strategy that will guarantee their safety. In fact, adopting such a curriculum may even lead to a false sense of security, thus endangering children.

The heart of an effective child abuse prevention curriculum is a trained, skilled teacher who shows respect and appreciation for individuals. A teacher who is respectful of others is able to relate to the needs of children and parents for autonomy and privacy and for acceptance of their feelings, ideals, choices, culture, and values. The quality of the relationships that you establish with parents will enable them to feel that they can turn to you with questions and problems concerning their children.

Although there are several popular approaches specifically designed to prevent child abuse by focusing on the concept of private parts, or the ideas of good touches, bad touches, or stranger danger, it is our opinion that these approaches may either mislead, alarm, or arouse the curiosity of children and tend to place responsibility on the relatively powerless child instead of on the adult.

It is essential for children to know that it is okay for them to resist physical intrusion and say, "No, I don't want you to do that to me!" to children and to adults. This means that teachers must respect children's feelings and invite their cooperation rather than insisting on their compliance. Physical force (for example, picking children up and forcing them to be where they do not want to be) can be used only when a child's safety is at stake.

An effective child abuse prevention curriculum is ongoing. It uses the basic principles of early childhood education and development rather than a one-time "innoculation" unit. Such an ongoing program has several characteristics:

- It offers children many opportunities to make choices, including the choice of saying no to an activity, a food, or a suggestion. The right to choose includes the right to accept or reject physical contact, which you will teach by asking, "May I give you a hug?" or saying, "I'm going to pick you up and put you on the changing table now." You should not swoop down and just start doing something to a child.
- It provides many ways for children to learn how wonderful their bodies are through routines, games, songs, movement, stories, and by using proper names for body parts. When children are taught to value their bodies, they may be less likely to passively allow themselves to be hurt.
- It emphasizes understanding feelings and encourages self-expression through words, stories, music, art, movement, and puppetry. Children who can express their ideas, needs, and feelings are better equipped to handle situations in which they are uncomfortable.
- It integrates safety into various topics and activities through discussion, role-playing, and dramatization, so that children learn things they can do to be safe in many familiar contexts—crossing the street, riding in cars, at the beach, at the shopping mall, answering the phone, with a stranger, with a friend.
- It explores differences between secrets and surprises to help children understand that *surprises* are things you are waiting to share

with someone to make them happy (like a birthday present) and *secrets* are things that someone wants you to hide because they are dangerous, wrong, or scary.
- It helps children to feel good about themselves—their characteristics, abilities, and potential. Recognizing and valuing differences and affirming individuality through display, song, celebration, and activities helps children to feel that they are worthy of protection.

Adapting for Different Ages

The health and safety curricula take quite different forms for infants and toddlers and primary-school children than they do for the preschool and kindergarten child.

Infants and Toddlers

Learning about health and safety happens through the routines that the parents and caregivers of infants and toddlers provide. When adults allow infants and toddlers to control what is happening to them as much as possible and explain what they are doing and why, they help even these very young children to be responsible for themselves and ready them to become knowledgeable and competent.

Primary-School Children

Largely self-sufficient, primary-school children can learn about health and safety as interesting subject matter. For these children, health and safety education is empowerment; it helps them feel responsible and is a first step on the road to being a grown-up. They benefit from information that is presented in a straightforward, nonscary manner. They need many opportunities to talk about their ideas. As they learn about safety, they will share their ideas with you and you may find that they have many misconceptions. Their eagerness to learn will enable you to help them to better understand many important ideas.

IN THE CLASSROOM: CHECKLIST FOR PHYSICAL DEVELOPMENT

Program Structure

_____ Stated goals include educating children to care for their own health and safety.

_____ Stated goals include support of physical and sensory development.

_____ Cooking is a planned activity at least weekly.

_____ Children participate in snack preparation.

_____ Access to kitchen equipment is provided.

_____ Daily time for outdoor play and exploration for an hour in the morning and an hour in the afternoon—at least half an hour being continuous.

_____ Daily free choice periods of at least an hour include opportunities to use sensory and manipulative materials.

Environment and Materials

Sensory

_____ Dirt, sand, and water available outdoors

_____ Access to nature

_____ Space where messy materials can be used indoors

_____ Various surfaces for sitting and lying—grass, carpet, textured pillows

_____ Tubs, troughs, or tables for holding water, sand, dirt, mud, and dry material such as sawdust

_____ Scoops, cups, sponges, tubing, house paint brushes, pitchers, sieves, and so on to use with sand and water

_____ Mild soap for bubble blowing and making suds

_____ Shaving cream for finger painting

_____ Materials for mixing—sawdust, pine needles, dry rice, oatmeal, cornmeal, cornstarch mixed with water

_____ Food color and flavor extracts for coloring and scenting water and dough

_____ Rocking boats, balance boards, and swings

_____ Equipment for cooking—measuring utensils, bowls, spoons, hot plate

_____ Art area with finger paint, paste, clay, and dough

_____ Tools for dough and clay—texture mallets, rollers

_____ Unit block area

_____ Materials designed specifically for sensory development such as

_____ sound cannisters, _____ sorting boxes, _____ texture boards, _____ color chips, _____ smelling jars, _____ color wheels, _____ kaleidoscopes

_____ Collections of things to sort by color, shape, size, texture, pattern, smell, taste, weight (seeds, liquids, stones, buttons, food, flowers, leaves, shells, fabric, spices)

_____ Musical instruments and record collections

_____ Puzzles, pegboards

Small Muscle

_____ Tables, chairs, and comfortable floor space for children to work with materials

_____ Art and/or writing area with paper for folding and tearing and a variety of tools: paintbrushes, crayons, marking pens, pencils, hole punch, stapler, typewriter

_____ Dough and clay

_____ Musical instruments

_____ Dramatic play area with dress-up clothes, telephones

_____ Scissors that cut easily and well and that can be used in either right or left hand

_____ Pegs and pegboards appropriate to the developmental level of the children

_____ Puzzles that are complete and appropriate to the skills and interests of the children

_____ Several different kinds of manufactured manipulative toys such as _____ Lego, _____ Bristle Blocks, _____ Crystal Climbers, _____ Linking Loops, _____ stacking rings, _____ Tinkertoys, _____ beads and laces, _____ table blocks

_____ Dressing frames or garments that close in different ways (zipping, buttoning, lacing, tying, snapping)

_____ Games made by teachers such as _____ tongs and things to pick up, _____ pouring activities, _____ spooning activities, _____ jar and lid games

_____ Water and sand toys: pitchers, tubing, funnels, scoops, spoons, measuring implements, sieves

_____ Woodworking area

Large Muscle

_____ Large open outdoor space that is fenced, unobstructed, and relatively level for running, galloping, skipping

_____ Large enough indoor space for large movement activities

_____ Variety of outdoor surfaces—pavement, grass, dirt

_____ Climbing structure that offers several ways to get up and down with adequate space for safe sitting and bars from which to hang

_____ Something to swing from—sling, rope or tire swings, no more than eighteen inches off the ground

_____ Large inflated balls that bounce (ten to twenty-four inches in diameter)

_____ Trikes or push vehicles that are proportioned to the size of the children and are in good working order

_____ Dirt or sand for digging and tools—spades, shovels, hoes, rakes

continued

_____ Woodworking table with wood, hammers, nails, saws, a clamp or vise, hand drill, screwdriver, screws

_____ Balance beam

_____ Wagon and/or wheelbarrow

_____ Large blocks

_____ Planned enjoyable teacher-led large-muscle physical development activities provided regularly—at least once a week

_____ Trips to parks and/or walks at least once a week if the outside environment is inadequate

DISCUSSION QUESTIONS

1. Think of a sensory experience that you especially enjoy (a hot bath, a walk in the woods, putting up a Christmas tree). Compare your thoughts with someone else's. In what ways are they similar or different? What do you feel or think of as you recall this experience? What makes it important to you? How could you bring special sensory experiences into the classroom?

2. Reflect on how physical education, nutrition, health, and safety were taught in the schools of your childhood. What do you remember most vividly? Did these experiences influence what you have done as an adult? Do you use what you learned today?

3. Think about your favorite large-muscle activity—jogging, hiking, dancing. Reflect on what makes the activity especially enjoyable to you. Compare the characteristics of your favorites that make them enjoyable with other people's. Discuss how you could bring different kinds of large-muscle experiences to young children.

4. What talents that involve small-muscle skills have you developed well? (playing the piano, crafts, cooking, sewing, auto mechanics, calligraphy, typing, drawing, crocheting). Think about the kinds of motions that are involved in them. How did you become proficient in your skill? Was it hard or easy to develop? How long did it take? Compare your experience with other people's. What implications might your experiences have for a teacher of young children?

5. Think about what you have observed in curriculum for physical development in programs for young children. Share something that you have seen that particularly impressed you. How might this approach to teaching influence children?

PROJECTS

1. Use the physical development checklist in this chapter to observe an early childhood program. Report on:
   - The extent to which the program seems to support children's sensory and physical development.
   - The classroom's strengths.
   - Some ways that the environment could be improved.
   - What you learned that you might apply to your future teaching.
2. Observe a child for a morning in regard to how she or he is involved in sensory and physical activity. Report on:
   - The ways and circumstances in which the child moves and explores sensory materials.
   - How the environment supports the child's development of strength, coordination, agility, flexibility, and sensitivity.
   - How the teacher supports this child's development.
   - How the program might be modified to enhance the child's development.
3. Observe a teacher for a morning and then interview her or him about how she or he enhances children's physical and sensory development and teaches about health and safety. Report on:
   - Activities and routines you saw that contribute to children's learning in these areas.
   - Any evidence you saw of teacher planning for these areas.
   - The teacher's goals for children.
   - The ways in which what the teacher perceives and what you actually observed match or appear to differ.
4. Write and implement a lesson in physical development, health, or safety using the activity planning form from Chapter 10 (Figure 10.11). Report on how children responded and on how you felt about your teaching. What worked? What might you do differently next time? How might you expand on this experience for children?
5. Compare two early childhood programs in physical and sensory development, health and safety. Report on the ways that the two address these areas—their similarities and differences. Which program seems to best meet children's needs and why? What implications does this have for your future teaching?
6. Compare two classrooms, one preschool and one for infants and toddlers or for primary-school children. Report on how each enhances children's physical development. Talk to the teachers about how they make their curriculum choices in this area.

BIBILIOGRAPHY

American Academy of Pediatrics. 1988. Physical Fitness Facts. *Young Children* 43(2):23.

Barratta-Lorton, M. 1972. *Workjobs.* Menlo Park, Calif.: Addison-Wesley.

Bentley, W. G. 1970. *Learning to Move and Moving to Learn.* New York: Citation Press.

Berger, K. S. 1980. *The Developing Person.* New York: Worth.

Curtis, S. R. 1982. *The Joy of Movement in Early Childhood.* New York: Teachers College Press.

Hill, D. M. 1977. *Mud, Sand, and Water.* Washington, D.C.: National Association for the Education of Young Children.

Javernick, E. 1988. Johnny's Not Jumping. *Young Children* 43(2):18–23.

Oyemade, U. J. and Washington, V. 1989. Drug Abuse Prevention Begins in Early Childhood. *Young Children* 44(5):6–12.

Papalia, D. E., and Olds, S. J. 1982. *A Child's World: Infancy Through Adolescence.* 3rd ed. New York: McGraw-Hill.

Prudden, B. 1964. *How to Keep Your Child Fit from Birth to Six.* New York: Dial Press.

Riggs, M. L. 1980. *Jump to Joy.* Englewood Cliffs, N.J.: Prentice-Hall.

Rowen, B. 1982. *Learning Through Movement.* New York: Teachers College Press.

Seefeldt, C., and Barbour, N. 1986. *Early Childhood Education: An Introduction.* Columbus, Ohio: Merrill.

Skeen, P. G., A. Payne, and S. Cartwright. 1984. *Woodworking for Young Children.* Washington, D.C.: National Association for the Education of Young Children.

Sprung, B. 1975. *Non-Sexist Education for Young Children.* New York: Citation Press.

Sinclair, C. B. 1973. *Movement of the Young Child: Ages Two to Six.* Columbus, Ohio: Merrill.

Torbert, M. 1980. *Follow Me: A Handbook of Movement Activities for Children.* Englewood Cliffs, N.J.: Prentice-Hall.

Whitken, K., with R. Philip. 1978. *To Move To Learn.* New York: Schocken Books.

CHAPTER TWELVE

Creating and Appreciating: Curriculum for the Arts

Every child is an artist. The problem is how to remain an artist . . .

—*Pablo Picasso*

This chapter concerns the arts—music, art, creative movement, and drama—and the development of creativity and the aesthetic sense. In it we discuss children's development in the arts, look at the role of the teacher, provide frameworks for planning creative arts curricula, and suggest strategies for teaching.

In all societies people create and appreciate art, music, and dance. The human need to express ideas and feelings through the arts has existed from the dawn of human history. The arts are vital to the development of children who can feel as well as think and who are sensitive and creative. They nurture an awareness of aesthetics (the appreciation of beauty) that is often destroyed in the pervasive grayness of factories, freeways, and institutional buildings.

The curriculum areas described in this chapter are placed together because they all help children come to recognize and express their feelings and responses, communicate their ideas in new forms, and develop their senses. Although the arts can be a vehicle for many other kinds of learning and creativity is not confined to the arts, we link the two in this chapter because arts are especially appropriate and powerful ways to express creative ideas.

Children are born with an innate awareness and expressiveness in the arts which experiences in early childhood programs help them to retain and develop. Through arts experiences children come to:

- Feel good about themselves as individuals.
- Develop the ability to observe the arts sensitively.
- Develop skill and creativity in art, music, and movement.
- Develop a beginning understanding of the arts disciplines.

- Become appreciative of music, art, and dance from their own and other cultures, times, and places.

Creativity, or originality, is not confined to artists or to people who have great talent or a high IQ. All people are creative when they put together what they know and build something that is new *to them*: an idea, a process, or product. The arts are a primary avenue for developing the ability to think and act creatively. Creativity is easy to see in the arts, but it also occurs in other activities: as children build with blocks, act out roles, use manipulative toys, explore their environment, write stories and play with words, solve problems, and invent games. The creativity of play leaves no lasting product, but it is important to recognize and acknowledge the creativity involved. Children are not always being creative when they are involved in the arts. If they are afraid of not being accepted or feel that their work must meet adult standards, they may make stereotypic "acceptable" products or responses in order to receive approval and praise.

Understanding how young children develop helps teachers to provide a climate that supports creativity and to plan arts activities. Satisfying and successful experiences with the arts occur when you understand what you can reasonably expect of children and when you provide activities that match their needs and abilities. When children's unique expressions are acknowledged, they become aware of their value as individuals, and their self-concept is enhanced. For young children, this is the most important aspect of the arts: the development of awareness and skill and feelings of self-worth.

Neither children nor adults create in a void; creative expression is an outgrowth of other life experiences. Your role is to provide experiences that heighten children's awareness and provide them with inspiration for artistic expression. These may be things as simple as the careful examination of an apple, a visit to a new baby, or a trip to the beach. Creative expression is also stimulated by experiences with the arts. When children have opportunities to view artwork of many kinds, to listen to music, and to attend dance and drama productions, they begin to understand the potential communication power and joy of the arts.

Creativity involves disclosing private thoughts, feelings, and ways of perceiving. Children can only risk this when they feel safe, valued, and encouraged. You support children's creativity by accepting *all* of their feelings, ideas, and creative expression, whether or not they are "nice" or "pretty" by adult standards. Those things that move children and adults are not always the most pleasant aspects of their lives (see Figure 12.1). Nevertheless, if they have the power to evoke strong feelings, they are important, and important parts of life are a part of art.

We often hear teachers despair of their ability to make meaningful creative experiences a part of their classrooms, because they do not feel they are talented or creative. It is not necessary to be an artist, musician, or dancer to help children have good experiences with the arts. Children are not harsh critics and will learn from your participation and enthusiasm. Even if you do not feel that you are talented in the arts, you have a responsibility to children to include them in your curriculum. You can develop a receptive attitude toward the creative expression of children and toward the arts in general. Every community has resources—artists, educators, reference materials—that can guide you to good arts experiences for children.

ART

Art provides opportunities for children to explore and manipulate materials and express their feelings and understanding of the world. Its sensory and physical nature makes it especially appropriate for young children. The primary

FIGURE 12.1
My mommy is mad at me: drawing by a four-year-old

purpose of an early childhood art program is to enhance artistic and creative development. This creative process is most important; the value of a final art product is its relation to the feelings and awareness that it generates in the child.

Creative art activities reap other educational benefits. As children use art media they develop motor control and perceptual discrimination. Language is often inspired and experiences with new vocabulary are provided. Children learn about the characteristics of materials as they work. Confronted with challenges in artwork, children develop problem-solving strategies. As they work with others, their social skills are enhanced. Developing aesthetic awareness and appreciation for the natural world and the world created by people are direct and important benefits of art experiences.

Art and Development

The simple, nonrepresentational character of young children's art and the sequence of children's growth as artists is closely correlated to development. Every child, throughout the world, follows the same sequence of drawing whether using sticks in the dirt or a stylus on a computer digitizer pad (see Figure 12.2). The sophistica-

FIGURE 12.2
Stages of development in children's drawing

tion of the finished product is determined by the child's strength, motor coordination, and cognitive development. Young children view the world simply and attend only to those aspects which currently command their attention. For example, though most four-year-olds are aware of the existence of arms, legs, fingers, and toes, they often create portraits that omit these features and that consist exclusively of a smiling head—the most important feature of a human being and the one they were thinking of as they worked. The sensory pleasure of the art experience and the process of exploration are the primary motivation for very young children's involvement in art. As they mature, children use art to express ideas and to communicate with others, but throughout the early childhood years, they continue to enjoy the satisfaction of "messing about" with materials.

Infants and toddlers experience the world and art as color, texture, form, movement, temperature, and taste. Art is not distinguished from other sensory experiences and is enjoyed in the same ways. A toddler first makes a mark on paper at around eighteen months of age, but the sensory-motor exploration that precedes this is the true beginning of art. This is often referred to as the *scribbling* stage, although adult associations of the word do not do justice to such thoughtful exploration. Children in this stage respond to the world as an extension of themselves. They touch, taste, and smell everything. Creating is very much a kinesthetic experience. Arts experiences must be correspondingly safe, sensory, and flexible. Even though we think of scribbling as referring to drawing, the characteristics of scribbling are also present in children's work with paint, clay, and even collage. By age three children are interested in exploring and manipulating art media. They view the world from their own perspective and have difficulty understanding that the experience of others may be different from their own. Children begin to control and name their "scribbles" but representation is an afterthought. Adults are often eager

to hurry children into representational art, because it is easier to identify and understand what children are communicating in a representational work. A smiling face says more to us than a series of lines of different lengths, widths, and direction, but it is important to allow children to create without representation.

Older preschoolers and kindergartners spontaneously represent their feelings and aspects of the world they know and care about. Development in art at this stage is often called *preschematic,* which means that children represent their world but have not yet developed the regular, recurring symbols that will mark the next stage of art development. Sensory experience and exploration continue to be motivation for involvement in the arts. The easier give-and-take of relationships and eagerness to involve others in their work leads to cooperation with peers. By the primary grades, children have developed a good deal of skill using the basic materials of art and thus enter the *schematic* stage of art. This stage is named for the recurrent symbols (or schema) that children develop in their work. For example, a crowd of people in a drawing would consist of a group of more or less identical figures. Work is more realistic in terms of proportion and color. This is a particularly fascinating stage of artistic development which seems to recapitulate art history in that children's work often is reminiscent of artwork from early historical periods. Work often includes a baseline which defines the bottom of the picture; the rest of the work relates to this line. Perspective may shift within a piece of work. Events in time are often presented across the length of the work and an "X-ray" view allows the artist to represent what is hidden from view. Because of their growing understanding of the world and their increased ability to understand the perspective of others, children at this stage of development can begin to have a more sophisticated appreciation of the work of others and can begin to distinguish art styles and techniques. Children may enjoy trips to art galleries or books about artists at this stage. Table 12.1 summarizes the characteristics of children as artists at various ages.

Framework for Organizing the Content

Curriculum for art consists of two kinds of experiences: studio, where children explore and create using art media; and appreciation or "discipline-based" experiences, where children have opportunities to encounter, discuss, and think about art. Both are valuable and can be part of the regular program for young children. We help children to think about art by being aware of and talking with them about the *elements* that make up works of art. The *processes* are the basic art activities that we provide for children.

TABLE 12.1
Development of Creative Expression in Art

Age	Characteristics as an Artist
Infant/toddler (birth–3 years)	Scribbling stage in art • Experiences art as sensory input • Explores media through all senses • Draws for the first time between fifteen and twenty months following the universal developmental sequence (see Figure 12.2)
Younger preschooler (3–4 years)	Scribbling stage in art continues • Explores and manipulates materials • Experiences art as exploratory play discovering what can be done with color, texture, tools, and techniques • Often repeats an action • Perceives shapes in work • Begins to name and control scribbles • Process not product important; may destroy work during process • Work may not be pleasing to adults
Older preschooler and kindergartner (4–6 years)	Preschematic stage in art • Creates definite forms and shapes • Represents feelings and ideas • Represents what is *known* and *what is important to the child* not what is *seen* or *important to adults* (may not be recognizable to adults) • Work becomes more and more detailed • Preplans and implements • Rarely destroys work during the process • Relationship between aspects of the work
Primary-school child (6–8 years)	Schematic stage in art • Serious effort to master skills • Evaluates own products critically • Uses recurrent symbols in work • Work more realistic in terms of color and proportion • Begins to use different perspectives in work • Use of a baseline to define pictures • Use of "X-ray" view

Art Elements

Every work of art is composed of visual, graphic, and other sensory elements. We experience these elements long before we are consciously aware of them or learn to talk about them. Much of the creative process of art for young children is exploration of the elements of art. Realizing this can help you appreciate children's early artwork and their artistic exploration of art elements.

Line is a part of every painting, drawing, collage, print, or sculpture. Line can be described by kind or quality: straight, curved, wandering, wiggling, jagged, broken, zigzag, heavy, light, wide, thin. Every linear aspect of a piece of art has length, a beginning and end, and direction (up-down, diagonal, side to side). Lines have relationships with one another and other parts of the work. They can be separate, parallel, or crossed. When children fill their paintings and drawings with many different kinds of lines, they are exploring this element.

Colors have qualities and can be referred to by name or hue—red, scarlet, turquoise, magenta. These color names add richness to our experience of color. They can be pure—primary colors (red, blue, yellow), white, and black—or mixed. Different colors are considered to have temperature—coolness at the blue end of the spectrum or warmth at the red end of the spectrum. They have different degrees of intensity or saturation (brightness or dullness) and value (lightness or darkness). Colors change as they mix. They are related to one another (orange is a color that is related to red) and look different when placed next to other colors. Children who combine colors in painting or coloring with chalk or crayons are exploring the nature of this element. Discovering color by mixing takes much experimentation.

Shape, or *form,* in art is far more than geometric shapes like circles, squares, and triangles. Children and artists only rarely fill their work with regular geometric shapes; instead, they combine these shapes with irregular shapes. The forms in artwork can be thought of as filled or empty. In relationship to each other they may be separated by space, connected, or overlapping, or one shape may be enclosed by another. When the boundaries of a shape are completed, the shape is closed; if the boundary is left uncompleted (like a *U* or a *C*) the shape is open. Shapes in three-dimensional art may be solid (like a ball) or may use empty space as part of the form (like a tire).

Space refers to the distance within or between aspects of a piece of artwork. The location of a line, shape, or color is part of the work—center, top, bottom, side, left, right. Space can be crowded and full, sparse, or empty; these conditions give feelings of freedom or cramped enclosure to the work. Space can have balance with other spaces or forms. Boundaries in a work and ideas like inclusion and exclusion are a part of the spatial qualities of artwork.

Design refers to the organization of a piece of work. Children initially work without plan or artistic purpose—art is sensory and exploratory. Nancy Smith (1983, p. 33) refers to children's approach to paper in painting at this stage as a place "to play, a sort of two-dimensional park. . . ." As they gain experience they become aware, and the elements of design enter their work. They are aware of the unity of the work or of a division of elements. A planned, organized piece of work may have a concept (like a circular shape) repeated or varied. The way color, line, and shape are placed may give the work an actual texture or the impression of texture. Elements are used with an awareness of their relationship to one another although effects may be unexpected. Symmetry, balance, and alternation are some of the characteristics found in design.

Art Processes

We use five categories to help organize thinking about the studio art program for young children:

drawing, painting, print making, collage and construction, and modeling/sculpting. In talking to many teachers we have found that these five are the essential processes included in most good early childhood programs; children can enjoy them again and again over time. The basic media are used by child artists and adult artists alike, although there are differences in the complexity of the processes employed.

Children benefit from using the same media over and over and find the same basic activities satisfying over long periods of time. It takes many experiences with the same materials to fully explore their possibilities—clay and paint and crayons, for example, can be available every day.

Drawing involves inscribing a line or figure on a surface with a drafting implement. Unlike paint, drawing materials are nonfluid and need no additional material to mark a surface and so are easy for young children to control. Thick primary crayons provide excellent first drawing experiences. They can be used with greatest facility when they are short and chunky to fit small hands and without encumbering paper wrappers that prevent use of the whole crayon. Felt markers are another good first drawing medium for young children. They require less

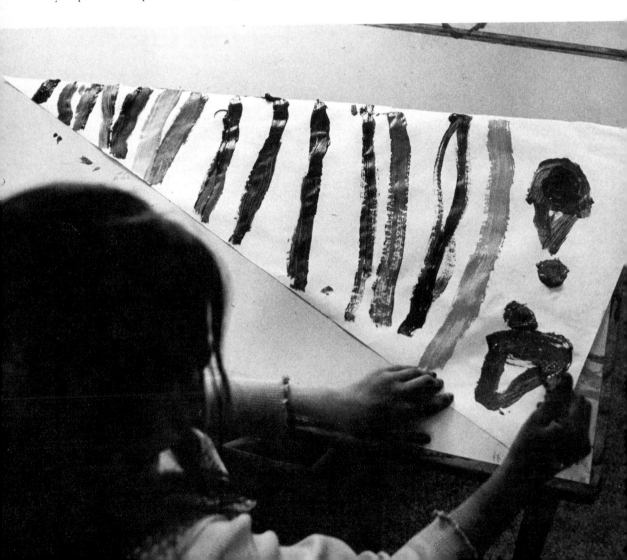

strength than crayons to use successfully and they produce bright, appealing colors. Children will also draw with their fingers and sticks in sand, dirt, snow, fogged windows, fingerpaint, flour dropped on the table during cooking activities, and other media (see Figure 12.2—Stages of development in children's drawing).

Painting is the application of a liquid medium to a surface with a tool like a brush or sponge. When providing paint for young children, it is most important to provide primary colors (red, yellow, and blue) as well as black and white because these colors can be mixed to create all other colors. There are many types of appropriate painting experiences for young children, but one of the most important of these is painting at an easel (or similar surface). Such painting involves the large muscles of the arms and shoulders over which children first develop control as well as the small muscles of the hands and fingers. In addition to easel painting, you will want to provide experiences with finger-painting, watercolor painting, painting with large brushes and water on a fence or wall, string painting, and other variations. We are especially fond of palette painting (using small containers of red, blue, yellow, and white paint to mix on a tray to create a palette of colors). This technique allows children to create their own colors and is similar to the process artists use as they paint. Smith's excellent book *Experience and Art* (1983) gives a detailed explanation of the palette painting technique.

Print making involves using an object to make an image by applying paint or ink to the object and imprinting a surface or by rubbing a flat, textured object that is beneath a surface. Anything that will hold the ink or paint—corks, hands, cookie cutters, spools, feet, paper rolls, fruits, vegetables, and many other things—will make a print. For rubbing, a flat, textured object or surface is placed beneath a piece of paper or similar material and the image is impressed using crayon, chalk, or charcoal. Leaves, surfaces of sidewalks and rocks, fabrics, boards, coins,

inscriptions, and any other interesting surfaces will make attractive rubbings. The creative aspect of print making involves the selections children make as they choose what to print with, the colors to use, and how to arrange prints on paper.

Collage and *construction* entail combining two- or three-dimensional materials. Collage involves attaching relatively flat materials like tissue paper, magazine pictures, cloth scraps, macaroni, ribbons, yarn, leaves, sticks, and sand together with paste or glue. Sturdy construction paper, cardboard, wood scraps, and similar materials make good bases for collage. The skills of cutting, tearing, and folding are often employed in collage. Construction involves three-dimensional materials like paper towel rolls, wood scraps, cardboard boxes, cans, toothpicks, and styrofoam. Sturdy bases are required for glued construction. Woodworking, stitchery, weaving, sculpture, and papier-maché are construction techniques that involve other kinds of materials and skills.

Modeling and *sculpting* involve molding a soft material or carving a hard one to create a three-dimensional work of art. Materials include potter's clay, flour and salt dough (usually called playdough), and oil-based modeling media (sometimes called plasticene). Children form shapes out of these malleable three-dimensional substances. Potter's clay, the most versatile of these, can be used over and over again, can be reconstituted with water, and can be fired (baked in a kiln) for a permanent product. For very young children who do not have adequate strength to manipulate potter's clay, homemade dough provides an introduction to modeling. Children should be given plenty of opportunity to work with modeling materials by sculpting only with their hands. When they are ready for a more complex experience, blunt knives, rounded sticks, and lengths of dowel for rolling make excellent tools. Cookie cutters and similar pattern shapes do not offer a creative experience because they prescribe and limit.

Variations.   In their desire for novelty, we have found that many teachers seek out more and more unusual art activities for their children. Children, however, do not need this kind of novelty. Constantly providing novel art activities may create a situation in which children are kept in a perpetual state of exploration without allowing them to gain the deeper skill and understanding from repeating the same activities many times using familiar media to express ideas and feelings. Variations can be presented when children have thoroughly explored the basic processes and seek variation on their own. Each process can be varied in ways that build on existing skills while heightening interest and providing appropriate challenges. Variation can be provided in several ways:

- Changing the *materials* and *tools* (a new type or shape of paper, the addition of real potter's tools, making homemade paste).
- Changing the *setting* in which the work is done.
- Providing a *motivating experience* (collecting collage materials on a walk, playing music while children work, painting outside, setting a vase of flowers on the table).
- Varying the *technique* or *task* (showing children how to spatter paint instead of paint with a brush, adding a saw to the woodworking materials, instructing children in the use of rolled clay to make coil pots).

Pattern art.   In teachers' efforts to make parents happy they sometimes resort to coloring books and other forms of pattern activities that they call "art." Creative expression, however, is primarily for the artist; it should be a reflection of the artist's ideas and abilities—not the teacher's. Coloring books and teacher-made patterns to be copied by children have nothing to do with the development of creativity or self-expression—in fact, they can be destructive to children's feelings of competence and self-worth. The skills taught this way are almost always developmentally inappropriate and usually lead to children feeling failure and dissatisfaction. The activities take up valuable time that children should be using to develop other skills, awareness, and ideas. They are not a part of good early childhood programs. Viktor Lowenfeld and Lambert Brittain in the eighth edition of their classic work on art education, *Creative and Mental Growth* (1987), have said:

> Art instruction that includes these kinds of activities is worse than no art at all. Such predigested activities force youngsters into imitative behavior and inhibit their own creative expression. These activities make no provision for emotional growth because any variation the child makes can only be a mistake; they do not promote skills, because skills develop from one's own expression. Instead, they condition the child to accept adult concepts as art, art that the child is unable to produce, therefore frustrating normal creative urges. (p. 179)

Similarly, children may sometimes ask you (or other adults in your classroom) to draw a picture for them to color or to take home. Their appreciation for adult efforts may tempt you to draw or paint for them. Such an action has the unintended consequence of discouraging children's creative work and encouraging stereotypes. Since children do not have adult sophistication or skill, they find their own work less and less satisfactory and creativity and learning are sidetracked. Teachers who understand the importance of creativity and art do not draw for children; they do, however, participate in a variety of art activities, for themselves, to model their own enjoyment of working seriously at art.

The Environment

The work of an artist, child or adult, requires a special kind of environment that supports artistic expression by enabling the artist to work with full concentration on the process of creation. It includes materials and equipment that are appropriate to the task, that are functional, and that inspire use. An environment for artistic expression also involves having sufficient time and space for exploration. For young children especially, the environment may be a source of motivation.

When designing an art area for children, you may find it useful to think about an artist's studio: a place designed primarily for art. In a studio, the amount of external stimulation is controlled —people, objects, and sound are brought in when desired as models or for motivation. The work area is well lit, usually with natural light. Materials are organized so that they can be found easily. Work tables and easels are a comfortable size for the artist and the work. Floors, walls, and furnishings are sturdy and washable. Storage is easily reached, smocks are available to protect clothes, and facilities for cleaning up are nearby. Space is set aside for drying work and storing art that is still in process.

It would be difficult to duplicate an artist's studio within an early childhood classroom, but it is possible to include many of its important features. Locate art areas near windows, sinks, and on tile or linoleum. Carefully arrange and maintain storage so that all materials and tools are within children's reach. If storage areas are clearly organized and uncrowded, children will be able to put things away. Make sure that furnishings in the art area are the correct size for the children. Use old or secondhand furniture or cover tables and floors so that the inevitable paint and glue spills are not tragic.

Select art materials that are of good quality and proportioned to the size of the children. Make sure there are enough materials available and that they are stored so that it is easy for children to get them and put them away. If materials are scarce, children may focus on obtaining and hoarding rather than on creative expression. Concentration is encouraged when the space is neither too noisy nor too crowded.

For child artists, like their adult counterparts, the impulse to create may not occur on a schedule. Include basic media (easels, clay, crayons, and so forth) in the daily activity choices and provide other materials several times a week, so that children can express their creative ideas as they occur. In our own teaching we make available a daily smorgasbord of basic art activities including easel painting, palette painting, drawing, collage, and clay as well as a special activity such as stitchery, construction, or print making. We offer the same special activity for several days to enable children to experience it in depth. Great complexity or novelty in art materials is not necessary. Children develop creativity as they find new ways to use the familiar.

Time to use art materials must be long enough for children to thoroughly explore the nature and possibilities of the activity or material and become involved. Little of creative significance occurs if access to art materials is limited to under an hour a day. Children who are repeatedly frustrated at having to leave activities just as they are getting involved may become unwilling to invest energy in art.

Teaching

Your role in art is to provide an environment, materials, experiences, and relationships that support creative development and aesthetic appreciation. A classroom that provides for all of these needs has a *creative climate:* an atmosphere where creative expression is nurtured and where creativity can flourish.

Although it is not necessary for you to be an artist to help young children enjoy art, it *is* necessary to believe that experiences with and participation in art are valuable. Begin by reflecting on the role of art in your own life. If you have had limited experiences with art, treat yourself to an afternoon at a gallery or of quiet perusal of books of art prints at your library. Become aware of the art that you enjoy and share this enjoyment with children.

As you look at and talk with children about art, remember to discuss color, shape, space, line, form, design, and effect—the elements of art. You might say, "You must have used hundreds of dots to fill in that big shape—it makes it stand out on your paper." You may want to write down all the words you can think of to describe an element of art; for example, a line can be jagged, broken, wide, narrow, short, long, curved, flowing, wavy, zigzag, curly, twisted, straight, upright, leaning, turned. These kinds of words give you important things to say about children's work: "You used several kinds of lines in your work—short, narrow ones; wide, jagged lines; and even two wavy lines!"

As children work, it is best, especially at first, to offer only minimal input. Comment on children's effort, innovation, and technique. Avoid asking children *what* they have created. They may have had nothing particular in mind and the question implies that they should have. Instead you can ask them if they wish to tell you about what they have done, and accept it if they do not. Children's creative expression is supported when you demonstrate your genuine appreciation and when your appreciation is broad enough to include the range of children's development. If you reserve appreciation and acknowledgment for work that meets adult standards you communicate to children that you are looking for correct rather than creative responses. Indiscriminate or insincere praise, however, is not an appropriate alternative and renders your comments meaningless. As you gain understanding of the meaning of children's stages of development in art and are charmed by their fresh, nonstereotyped efforts, you will find it easy to be genuine in your appreciation of their work.

Acknowledge children's works by commenting on effort, "You worked hard"; innovation, "You tried it a new way"; or technique, "You covered the whole paper." Refrain from evaluative responses such as good, bad, ugly, beautiful, and messy; instead, help children to become their own evaluators: "What do you like best about it?" "When you do it again what will you do differently?" Children who are encouraged

rather than evaluated develop skills that help them to create their own standards and meet their own goals. When finished artwork is mounted carefully and displayed prominently in the classroom, it also demonstrates to children (and their parents) that you appreciate the work.

Time, teacher acceptance, and encouragement are needed for some children to discover an interest in art. A long period of apparent disinterest or observation may precede participation. Some children may simply be more interested in different kinds of activities and alternative ways of being creative. They may not want to attempt art activities because they already feel they cannot measure up to their teacher's or parents' expectations.

Helping Parents Understand Children's Art

It can be hard for adults, especially parents, to accept the messiness and nonproductive nature of young children's artistic expression. One of your essential roles is to allow this messiness and to help parents understand the importance of their children's art process. As you explain to parents what their children do and what their work means, you are helping them understand your work and the development of their child. Carefully packaging children's work for the journey home also conveys a message. We recently observed a teacher who used ribbon to tie children's paintings in a neat roll. To both the parents and children this said this work is valuable.

Adapting Curriculum for Different Ages

If you work with children who are under the age of three or over the age of six, there will be differences in what you provide as art experiences.

Infants and Toddlers

Art media can offer wonderful, developmentally appropriate experiences for even very young children. Infants do not derive any real benefit from art activities, but toddlers will enjoy the sensory pleasures of art and the sense of empowerment that accompanies acting on art materials. We have sometimes seen adults in infant classrooms holding the hands of their young charges and "helping" them to smear paint across the paper and then proudly presenting the result to the parents with an accompanied, "Andy made this for you today." A year later, twenty-month-old Andy may indeed take paintbrush in hand and delight in the color and texture of the paint and in the power that he has to mark the paper. He still will not have deliberately made anything for anyone, but he will have enjoyed the process and his parents can enjoy the results.

Appropriate activities for toddlers consist of frequent experiences with materials such as large, stubby crayons and watercolor markers with big pieces of paper, easel painting and finger painting, paste and paper, and clay and dough. Food used as an art medium is not appropriate because toddlers are just learning to distinguish between what can be eaten and what cannot be eaten.

Similarly, an infant may enjoy the colors and forms in a Mary Cassatt painting of a mother and child as much as the photo of the baby on the disposable diaper box. The Mary Cassatt print in the classroom will certainly enhance the atmosphere for the adults in the classroom. Toddlers, on the other hand, may examine the work more closely and begin to appreciate it.

Primary-School Children

Primary-school children enjoy and can use fully the open-ended art experiences that have been described in this chapter. With regular access to these materials, they will develop more and more sophisticated artistic skill. But six-, seven-, and eight-year-olds are also ready for additional challenges. If you work with primary-school children, you can begin to teach techniques that

require group participation (for example, mural painting or large construction), that use more difficult or dangerous materials and require greater motor strength and agility (for example, batik or soap carving), that take more planning (for example, building a bird feeder), and activities that have a multistep process that must be carefully followed (for example, pottery).

MUSIC

Music is pervasive. In the heart of a city we experience the "song" of traffic, footsteps, and voices. In the solitude of the country we listen to the harmony of birds, wind, and water. Even before we are born we experience the music of a heartbeat. Music has been called a universal language. It can make us happy or sad, calm or excited; it has been used to evoke feelings of patriotism, sanctity, love, and empathy.

The most important reasons for providing music experiences to children are that they provide a powerful and direct link to emotions; that listening to and making music brings pleasure; and that sharing music with others is an important way to be a part of our culture. Music can also be a path to many other kinds of learning. Because it is an enjoyable experience, it can be an excellent vehicle for developing problem-solving skills ("How could we make motion for a mouse?") and language ("The song says that Aiken Drum 'played upon a ladle,' have you ever seen a ladle?"), and even for pleasantly remembering facts that might not otherwise be easy to recall (many of us have sung the *ABC* song to ourselves to remember whether or not *Q* comes before *R*).

How do we learn to take pleasure in making music—to sing, to play, to create? A hundred years ago there were no radios, no TVs, no record players, and few musical superstars. But every town had musicians, most homes had pianos, guitars, or fiddles, and most people made music. People sang and played with and for each other as entertainment. Singing, like talking, was something that everyone did. Today, many adults have become musically mute and passive because of our technology. Our children will also be mute and passive if we fail to give them music.

Music and Development

Young children's musical responses are strong. From the first moments of life they are soothed by quiet music and respond to a distinct beat with strong rhythmic movement. Music evokes and describes feelings and provides an emotional outlet. As they grow, children may come to express feelings of joy or sadness with a song or aggressive feelings in a dance to rhythmic or dissonant music. They can come to understand, in simple terms, the elements that make up the discipline of music.

Even from infancy, children are active explorers of music (see Table 12.2). They respond to it physically, enthusiastically, and frequently. Crying is a baby's first sound. Pitch, loudness, and rhythm are aspects of a song and a cry. Their

TABLE 12.2
Development of Creative Expression in Music

Age	Characteristics as a Musician
Infant/toddler (birth–3 years)	• Is receptive to music • Responds to music by listening and moving (from birth) and vocalizing (from six months) • Sings for the first time at approximately eighteen months • Uses objects as sound makers
Younger preschooler (3–4 years)	• Is particularly responsive to strongly rhythmic music • Moves and sings to music • Sings spontaneously in play • Has comfortable singing range (D to A above middle C) • Enjoys repeating same song many times • Enjoys using instruments • Responds at own tempo
Older preschooler and kindergartner (4–6 years)	• Can participate in group music activities and games • Can enjoy focused listening activities • Increased singing range from A below middle C to C# an octave above middle C • Increasingly accurate in matching pitch and tempo • Can synchronize movement with music • Can identify and use simple instruments appropriately
Primary-school child (6–8 years)	• Serious effort and ability to master musicianly skills • Able to learn to use adult instruments • Evaluates own music critically • Can sing accurately with sensitivity • Strong sense of rhythm • Enjoys rehearsal and performance • Begins to identify harmony • Can begin to learn notation • Can begin to sing music with "parts"

first vocalizations are akin to song and are called *lalling* and *trilling*. Favorite toys are often objects that make sounds: rattles, chimes, bells, drums, and music boxes. By ten months, infants indicate preferences for music by rocking, swaying, or clapping hands to a favorite tune and by quieting to a favorite lullaby.

By approximately eighteen months, toddlers begin to sing and explore sound. Nursery rhymes and songs are much enjoyed. From age two, they "dance" with swaying bodies, bending knees, and swinging arms. Two-year-olds sing within a limited vocal range and move to music at their own tempo. Through the first two years, music and movement are almost inextricable— to listen, sing, or play an instrument is to dance.

Three- and four-year-olds have a great deal more physical coordination and language skill than toddlers. Their ability to participate in group music activities is much greater. They can reproduce tunes but cannot match their pitch to others. They have a small singing range from about D to A (the range of the "teasing" chant, "Nani nani boo boo, you cannot catch me"). Young preschoolers are among the most active of song creators and they often make up repetitive, atonal songs as they go about their daily activities.

Teachers are very important to young preschoolers so what you do will be important in their musical development. Movement songs are especially enjoyed. You may observe the strong influence of media or pop culture as we did a few years ago when a group of three-year-olds each day built a stage out of hollow blocks, dressed in the flashiest clothes from the home corner, and performed "La Bamba." Rhythm instruments can be played appropriately by young preschoolers who have been given instruction and guidance.

By age four and a half or five, given opportunity, encouragement, and sufficient musical experience, most children sing tunefully in a range that exceeds an octave, understand basic music concepts, remember elaborate songs, move rhythmically to music, and play simple instruments appropriately. If they have had limited music in their lives, children will need additional experience to develop these skills. Four- and five-year-olds can discuss a musical experience in terms of what impact it has on them.

Primary-school children clearly see themselves as learners and enjoy new challenges such as learning to sing a round. Increasing competence can be a matter of great pride and they often choose to practice and perform music and skits with music for others. Primary-school children have the capacity for learning to play chorded instruments like Autoharps and ukuleles. They continue to enjoy singing, particularly when they have a voice in choosing songs. They also like listening to recorded music when there is a related challenge ("Listen for the oboe making the sound of the cuckoo in this piece— how many times does the cuckoo call?"). As children get older, they may become more self-critical and as a result self-conscious regarding their music.

Framework for Organizing the Content

As with art, we use a framework describing the music curriculum that consists of two parts: the *elements* which make up all works of music and the *processes* used by musicians. Understanding both the elements of music and the processes of musicianship gives you the basis for an appropriate music curriculum for young children.

Musical Elements

Elements such as beat, pitch, and phrase are the raw materials out of which every piece of music is made. It is useful for teachers to understand these elements, although they are not meaningful to children isolated from active music involvement. Children can be helped to respond to the elements in their daily experiences with music. As they participate in music activities, they can come to recognize and label some of these concepts ("Let's clap to the beat!" "We sang that song faster than we usually do").

Rhythm involves all of the characteristics that relate to the movement and time of a piece of music. It includes *beat,* the musical pulse that we respond to by tapping our toes, swaying, or clapping. *Melodic rhythm* is the rhythm of the melody or words in a piece of music. When you clap to every syllable of a song as if you were singing it, you are demonstrating the melodic rhythm. Speed in music is called *tempo.* Songs vary in their fastness and slowness, and children can sing songs at different tempos. The points of silence in a piece of music are called *rests.* Children recognize these more easily when they are very distinct, as in the rest that occurs just before the last line of the chorus of "This Land Is Your Land" by Woody Guthrie.

Tone concerns the musical notes. It involves *pitch*, which is the highness or lowness of the notes, and *melody,* or *tune,* which is the arrangement of notes into a singable sequence. Tone also involves the way that musical notes sound. *Tone color,* or *timbre* (pronounced tamber), refers to the characteristic sounds that musical instruments create. Difference in tone color (for example, between a violin and a flute) is one of the elements that children first respond to in infancy and which they strongly respond to throughout early childhood. Children are also very responsive to the loudness or softness of tones, called *dynamics.*

Form involves the structure of musical pieces. Children learn to respond to an *introduction* when you play several chords or the first part of the tune to establish the pitch and tempo of a song before you start to sing. Structurally, all songs are composed of *phrases*, short but complete musical ideas, for example, the first line of "The Eency Weency Spider." *Repetition* occurs when identical musical phrases occur in a song as in the first and last lines of "Twinkle Twinkle Little Star." When similar phrases occur in a song, as in the first two lines

of "Shoo Fly", it is called *variation.* A phrase that is obviously different from the ones that came before provides *contrast,* for example, the third line of "Happy Birthday to You."

Processes of a Musician

As you plan and participate in musical activities with children, you help them to develop the skills and attitudes of a musician. Making music can be both individual self-expression and participation in a social event. It need leave no lasting product—it is valuable for the pleasure that it brings the individuals and the group. The elements of music are used and controlled as children sing and play instruments.

Singing offers many opportunities for children to experience music and to develop musical skills. The songs that you teach will contribute to musical growth and will be more successful if they have aesthetic value (beautiful melodies and/or words). Children will have an easier time learning songs if they are relatively short and simple and have a distinct rhythm. An appropriate vocal range for young children is from approximately the octave from middle C or slightly lower to C an octave higher; the younger the children the more narrow the range. Your repertoire of songs should include pieces with a variety of moods, subjects, and tempos, and should reflect a diversity of styles.

Singing in the preschool needs to be primarily a music experience. Although songs may teach nonmusic concepts, that should not be their primary purpose. Children are being cheated if their music has limited value and is really just a drill on color names, the alphabet, or counting. Excessive use of "limited value" songs dilutes the quality of the music experience.

Many good songs for young children touch on sensitive subjects, the hard edges of life that teachers sometimes try to eliminate from the classroom: death, loneliness, fear, and anger. Children demonstrate by their obvious interest in such songs that they do not need their music sanitized and cute. However, you should be sensitive to children's response to songs that have a strong emotional impact. We once observed a child who became very upset when "John Henry" was sung, perhaps because of the line "he laid down his hammer and he died." It would have been insensitive and disrespectful had the teacher gone on singing this song in the child's presence.

Playing instruments regularly helps children to acquire musical skills. It is neither necessary nor desirable for every child to have an instrument at the same time. This tends to amplify noise and create chaos. Instead, introduce instruments singly in small groups. Let each child have a turn to play and give instruction in the care and handling of the instrument. The musical elements provide a useful framework for learning about instruments. Comparing the sound of a triangle and tone block, for example, and using them to accompany different verses of "Froggie Went a-Courtin'" gives children an experience with timbre.

Composing and *improvising* are the creative outgrowths of the musical skills acquired in singing, movement, and playing instruments. For young children these are very simple variations of musical ideas. You help children to improvise when you ask them for something to do besides clap their hands in "If You're Happy and You Know It." Composing is more complex. It requires creating and preserving a new composition. Notation is too abstract for preschool children (and requires greater musical sophistication on the part of the teacher), but a tape recorder works well to make a record of a child's musical creation. *Musicplay* by Leon Burton and William Hughes (1981) gives a number of suggestions for helping children to develop their own notation.

Listening to music involves appreciating and enjoying music made by others. Recordings can provide children with important experiences with talented musicians, symphonic music, and music from many cultures. Recorded music is so

commonplace that it often is like audible wallpaper—something to ignore. When you use recorded music with children, make your choices carefully and present them as important. To help children to be attentive listeners to recorded music, ask them to listen for a sound, move a part of their body to the beat, or notice what kind of a feeling the music creates in them. Short, evocative pieces of music are best able to

curriculum for young children. Younger children who have lots of opportunities to explore and share music will not feel self-conscious about making music for others. As children get older, they enjoy the challenge of putting together a "show." In early childhood, though, performance should always be secondary to other goals. For preschool children "performances" in which parents and other important visitors are invited to come and participate in a daily music time are preferable to staged presentations where children are on display. Performances for primary-school children are more worthwhile when the children have been given the opportunity to work together to create their performance.

The Environment

Your classroom can be filled with music. Daily experience with music enables children to gradually build and practice a repertoire of skills and songs which will form the base for individual exploration and appreciation. Schedule music sessions at a regular time each day for ten to thirty minutes depending on the age and development of the children.

Every early childhood classroom needs a serviceable sound system and an eclectic collection of recorded classical, folk, jazz, and children's music. Your choices of recorded music help children to be aware of musical alternatives. Your responsibility is to acquaint children with a range of good music, not merely what is easiest or most familiar to you. Children may have plenty of exposure to Top Forty, Sesame Street, and Muzak, but they may never have heard chamber music, folk music, bluegrass, jazz, Gregorian chants, symphonic music, classical guitar, flute, sitar, or opera. Most public libraries have a selection of different kinds of recorded music available for borrowing and you can pick up a new record as you borrow new books.

A collection of simple rhythm instruments that children can play is also essential. Good quality instruments are well made, have good

hold children's attention. Recordings are not a replacement for real people making music. When you play instruments and sing in the classroom, you prove that music comes from people, not mechanical boxes. Have musicians visit your classroom to play short pieces of music for children. They need not be professionals; your next door neighbor's daughter who is studying the clarinet, the high school string quartet, or a parent who plays the banjo will provide a listening experience with live music and real instruments that will impress itself indelibly in the minds of the children you teach. It's best if children are allowed to gently try the instruments themselves.

Performing involves singing, moving to music, or playing instruments for the pleasure of others. It is the least important part of the music tone, and are satisfying to play. They must be sturdy enough to take the enthusiastic handling of many young children. Such instruments are a worthwhile investment that must be stored and handled carefully like any other piece of valuable equipment. Tossed into a box and grabbed again the next time, or left lying on the floor to be stepped on, they will have a short life span. A music center that is carefully arranged with one or two musical instruments and activities to explore makes a good addition to a classroom for children ages four and older.

Teaching

You support children in music through an environment, experiences, and relationships that support musical development and appreciation. A *creative climate* for music, where musical expression is nurtured and creativity flourishes, means that music is frequently present. When music making is a part of classroom, home, and community, children become spontaneous music makers. They hum tunes, make up songs, explore sounds, create rhythms, move to music, and use music to communicate. An environment that supports children's development in music must include live people making and responding to music.

You can help children to be comfortable with music by bringing it informally into the classroom and by formal, planned music experiences. Many teachers bring music into the life of the classroom by playing and singing throughout the day. A teacher we recently observed found or modified a song for each of the children in his group which he then sang to them during outside play time (for example, he sang to one child to the tune of "Michelle, Ma Belle," and to another child to the tune of "La Cucaracha"). If you make up or improvise songs and chants as you work with children, they will follow suit. Another teacher we know always sings a simple tune she created to her class when it's time to go in: "Three-year-old class, it's time for snack. Hurry to the gate so you won't be

late." In like manner, the children in her class often sing about what they are doing.

Although there is much to be gained from spontaneous, informal music, a special time for music each day is essential. The age appropriateness of your plans, your sensitivity to children's responses, and your awareness that music can be very stimulating will contribute to positive, easily managed music sessions. One day the session might be a carefully structured lesson to teach a musical concept using rhythm instruments. The next day it might be a spirited sing-along of everybody's favorite silly songs. Content is not nearly as important as making sure that music happens daily.

Group music times are most successful when you sit with children as you sing, on the carpet or outside under a tree. If you can accompany the singing with a guitar, Autoharp, or ukulele, this will add to the experience. If not, clap your hands, keep time with a drum, or sway as you sing. Piano accompaniment does not offer the intimacy and accessibility of sitting near children and singing with them and it is difficult to manage with groups of young children. Moving to music is a natural response—our toes tap, our heads nod, and our bodies sway almost without our realizing it. Movement helps young children to concentrate on a music session. Hand gestures and finger plays illustrate songs and help children to understand the meaning of the words. Use body movements with songs and encourage children to think of new ways to move.

Adapting for Different Ages

If you work with children who are under the age of three or over the age of six, there will be differences in what you provide as music experiences.

Infants and *toddlers* are active explorers of music but cannot focus on group activities. Provide toys and other objects that make sounds. Sing and play songs and lullabies. Encourage infants' vocalizing and sing with them as they begin to sing. Explore sounds in the environment. Say nursery rhymes and songs. Play recorded music for listening and dancing. Toddlers have a limited vocal range so choose songs that are pitched in the "teasing chant" range (D to A) such as "Twinkle Twinkle Little Star." Appropriate music activities for toddlers consist of frequent experiences with music that use the whole body such as fingerplay and action songs.

Primary-School Children need and enjoy musical challenges. Learning to sing songs that have parts (such as "There's a Hole in the Bucket"), that are complicated (like "Puff the Magic Dragon"), or that are silly (like "The Quartermaster's Store") make good choices for singing activities. Primary-school children enjoy working together to learn to sing a song well. Since they have the capacity for learning to read notation and playing instruments, it is appropriate to teach these skills. Learning about the music or musician is another direction that you can begin to take. Having a goal such as practicing and performing a musical play for others can be a good motivating activity for six- through eight-year-olds.

CREATIVE MOVEMENT

Movement is one of the first ways that adults interact with children—holding, rocking, and bouncing are the earliest movement activities. Young children are nearly always moving. As they move, they learn. Concepts such as rough, smooth, run, creep, and push must be experienced before they can be understood. Children move to play, to express feelings, and to communicate. Creative movement helps young children to express ideas and feelings through body movement.

When is movement creative? When ideas and feelings are expressed through movement in individual ways children are using their bodies as an art medium. This is different from, and not a substitute for, large-muscle activity on the playground or games and exercises such as the "Hokey Pokey." It differs from dance in which the teacher instructs in specific, predetermined ways of moving. In a creative movement activity, children interpret and follow suggestions from the teacher who encourages them to find their own personal, creative, and innovative ways of moving. During these activities, children discover joy and satisfaction in expressing ideas with their bodies and develop a repertoire of movement possibilities. Creative movement offers challenges and new ways to use and practice developing physical skills. As you direct children in movement, you encourage them to make suggestions and express ideas in innovative ways. This supports children's developing imagination and positive self-concept. It is this focus on individual ways of moving that makes it *creative* movement. Social development is enhanced as children learn to move with respect for the group and come to appreciate the creativity of others.

In working with young children, creative movement and drama are closely tied to one another. The motivation for movement activities is often the suggestion to act like a character, animal, or object. Children naturally take on roles in their play and dramatize stories and scenes. With very young children, creative drama and movement are often part of the same activity. As you direct children in creative movement, you may alternate between directions that are exclusively related to body movement ("Bounce.") to directions that are related to a dramatic idea ("Bounce like a ball." "Hop like a rabbit.") to directions that are dramatic ideas as a part of a story or scenario ("The rabbit is hopping slowly now, he hears something. Quickly hop away to your burrow.").

Creative Movement and Development

All children move. In fact, movement characteristics are among the primary ways we define and describe children's development. Most children come to early childhood programs delighted with movement and actively seeking ways to explore, express ideas, and develop physical competence.

Infants respond to the world physically. Learning to control movement is their first challenge. The sequence of physical development from lifting head to walking takes the bulk of the first year of life. Once walking starts, at about one year of age, further movement challenges commence. By approximately two years,

children begin to "dance" with swaying bodies, bending knees, and swinging arms. They learn to manipulate objects in their environment and to catch and kick a ball. They move along to movement songs, balance on a low balance beam, climb on play equipment, and gradually put into place the physical skills that they will need for later development (see Table 12.3).

Three- and four-year-olds can hop, gallop, run, broad jump, and catch large balls. Their ability to participate in group activities is much

TABLE 12.3
Development of Creative Expression in Movement

Age	Characteristics as a Mover
Infant/toddler (birth–3 years)	• Enjoys movement games like This-little-piggy • Gradually develops the ability to creep, crawl, stand, walk, tiptoe, and jump and begins to run • First "dance" at about two—swaying, bending, enjoys moving to music • Begins to try to catch and kick a ball • Can walk on a low balance beam by age three
Younger preschooler (3–4 years)	• Enjoys repetition of movement activities • Enjoys directed movement activities • Learns to hop on one foot • Begins to gallop • Runs efficiently but cannot stop or turn quickly • Jumps for distance • Catches large ball
Older preschooler and kindergartner (4–6 years)	• Can move body parts in isolation with practice • Can participate in group activities and games • Can synchronize movement with music • Runs quickly; controls speed, stopping, and turning • Understands and can move forward, backward, sideways, up, down, fast, slow, lightly, heavily • Gallops skillfully • Skips skillfully by age six • Catches a small ball • Kicks ball in mature style • Balances on one foot
Primary-school child (6–8 years)	• Can do forward roll • Has a strong sense of rhythm • Understands almost all verbal directions • Enjoys new challenges • Can learn dance and movement patterns • Enjoys rehearsal and performance

greater than it was when they were toddlers. They begin to be able to cooperate with their peers and enjoy repetitive, familiar movement activities. Three- and four-year-olds are very active and they often dance and dramatize in play. At this age you may first see children who are too shy to actively participate and who are more comfortable observing. By age four and a half or five, children have gained a great deal of balance and control. They can move their body parts in isolation, can follow most directions, can begin to synchronize movement to music, and can respond quickly and skillfully to a change in directions. Four- and five-year-olds are beginning to have the ability also to understand their role in group activities and can cooperate in group efforts, although they continue to have moments when it is difficult.

Primary-school children have developed many skills and enjoy challenges like gymnastics and team sports. They have a strong sense of rhythm and a great deal of physical control. At this age they may also be more self-conscious and more self-critical and as a result they may hesitate about making mistakes in front of others.

Framework for Organizing the Content

The different *elements* of movement provide a base that enables you to plan and guide creative movement activities that help children to become confident, creative movers.

For the body to be an effective medium for expression, children need to develop *body awareness*—where they are in space (*location*); the *shapes* they can create; the ways they can travel from one place to another, called *locomotor movement;* and the ways they can move while staying in the same place, *non-locomotor movement.* Among the most difficult skills for young children to develop is the ability to move one part of the body while keeping the rest still; this is called *body isolation.*

All movement takes place in *space* which includes *direction* (forward, backward, sideways) and *level* (high, middle, low). *Personal space* is the space right around you, defined by your presence. *General space* is used by the whole group. Activities can help children to use all of their personal space—up high, down low, to the side, in back—and to learn to share the general space. Boundaries (for example, a chalked circle) can define the space for children to move within and around. Space may be filled in different ways while children stay in one place. Images motivate and encourage children to use space in diverse ways. Invite children to think about moving and filling space as if they were balloons, fish, worms, trees, bubbles, or birds.

Time concerns the *tempo,* or speed, of the movement. As you guide creative movement activities, you can include suggestions that encourage children to move at different speeds and levels without touching or bumping anyone else. Young children experience tempo, or time, through a contrast of fast and slow movements. They generally find it easier to move quickly, because slow movements require greater concentration and body control. Slow movement is sustained whereas fast movement can be jerky. Speed can be contrasted by moving body parts at different tempos (raise your arms slowly, shake your hands quickly) or moving the body as a whole at different paces (run, creep, trot, slowly unbend, jump). Imagery of animals, plants, and machines can encourage exploration of speed, and the use of a drum beat or music can help children learn to move to a particular tempo.

Force, the amount of energy used in movement, is another element to be explored. Some movements such as stamping heavily or punching into the air require a lot of force. Others such as tiptoeing or jumping lightly use less. Young children find strong, forceful movements very satisfying, but they also enjoy developing the control needed to move lightly. Activities that involve force may contrast heavy and light movement (stamping and then tiptoeing) and can involve isolated body parts or the whole body while in motion or stationary. Music can evoke heavy or light movements as can images of animals and fantasy creatures (elephants, butterflies, bears, birds, monsters, fairies, giants, ghosts).

Creative movement activities can be quite structured (as when children move parts of their bodies to the beat of a drum) or more open ended (as when children are invited to explore all the ways they can move to music with a scarf).

Children will respond with greater enthusiasm if you weave a story around your creative movement activity. We find the work of Ann Barlin (*Teaching Your Wings to Fly* 1979) and Mimi Brodsky Chenfeld (*Creative Activities for Young Children* 1983) to be useful in designing creative movement activities.

The Environment

An environment for creative movement must be both safe and conducive to creativity. Uncluttered, open spaces with clear boundaries are needed. Wood or low-pile carpeted floors provide the best movement surface. If you use a classroom, push back the furniture to create a safe, open, inviting space. Whatever space you have, it is important to think about how you wish it to be used ahead of time.

The ideal group size for creative movement is from five to twelve children. If you work with larger groups, have the children alternate between moving and being the audience. Regularly scheduled movement activities at least twice a week help children develop skill and build on previous experience. When movement activities occur only infrequently, children do not develop skills and tend to be overstimulated by the rare event.

Teaching

Teachers provide a safe, encouraging, and stimulating atmosphere within which children may experiment in creative movement. A successful movement curriculum takes thoughtful planning. An awareness of the goals of creative movement can guide you. Basic rules for safety need to be established (no pushing, bumping, and so on) and an attitude of respect for individual interpretations and skill levels is essential. We find it important to have a written lesson to use as a map to guide us as we lead children in creative movement activities.

Children's literature can offer motivation for creative movement and drama. A rabbit hopping may become Peter Rabbit fleeing from Mr. MacGregor. Leo Lionni's book *Swimmy* is another example that intertwines the story of a fish with descriptions of the movements of sea creatures and serves as an excellent outline for a

movement-drama session. Creative drama for young children involves their interpretations of story lines and ideas, not memorization of scripts, and should be outgrowths of children's ideas, not production efforts put on by teachers for parents. Some four-, five-, and six-year-olds do become entranced by performance, however. With a skillful teacher, they can begin to extend their developing skills into the performing arts of dance and drama productions.

As children develop confidence and movement skills, they will become able to use movement to express creative ideas with little direction. In the beginning, however, you will need to provide a good deal of guidance. Most children will be delighted to participate in creative movement but a few will hesitate. Children should never be forced to participate in a creative movement activity or ridiculed or criticized for the way they move.

When you first begin creative movement with a group, establish a signal like a hard drumbeat, which will tell the children to freeze. Practice stopping to this signal as a game until they come to understand it as an integral part of every movement activity. This will help you maintain control of the group and will help children focus their movement. Alternate vigorous and quiet activities and begin activities sitting down or standing still before inviting children to move freely around the room. When you have reached a planned or natural ending place, try to finish the activity while it is still going well. End sessions in a way that provides a transition to the next activity: "Tiptoe to the playground when I touch you on the shoulder."

Managing creative movement sessions can be difficult for beginning teachers. Children who have had little experience with structured movement activities can become overexcited and uncontrolled and this can be difficult to handle. If a movement session does not go well, do not blame the children or yourself. Although every group of children is different—some children need very specific limits and others

need lots of opportunity to explore—it is usually best to begin with short (fifteen minutes or less), simple, well-planned, and fairly structured activities and move on to more open activities later. The learning that comes out of these experiences can be valuable for you as a teacher.

Adapting for Different Ages

Movement activities must match the level of physical and language development of the children. If you work with very young children or primary-school children, a successful movement curriculum will have some variations.

Infants and *toddlers* are developing basic movement skills. Their teachers can provide space and activities that encourage them. Take delight in infants' exploration as they learn to move in new ways and participate with them by encouraging them to try new movement challenges. Appropriate movement activities for toddlers consist of frequent experiences with moving and music. The younger the children, the simpler the activities must be. Creative movement activities for toddlers are best provided through simple movement songs and games (like "Jack-in-the-Box" and "The Eency Weency Spider") and by allowing space and freedom to move in response to music. Sustained interest is harder to maintain for very young children because of their more limited language and attention for group activities.

Primary-school children enjoy movement challenges. They can learn simple folk dances and gymnastic routines (make sure they are not risking injury in the ways they are moving). Primary-school children enjoy working together and integrating music, drama, and movement for performance is an enjoyable way to use creative movement in the primary grades. They may also be self-critical. For this reason, it is important to encourage and to avoid adding pressure and to respect children who need time to get involved or who choose not to be involved.

AESTHETICS

Every human being has the potential to develop sensitivity to beauty and the heritage of the arts. Teachers can help young children develop this potential. Aesthetics refers to the love of beauty, to cultural criteria for judging beauty, and to individual taste. Malcolm Ross says:

> Aesthetic perception involves the capacity to respond to the uniqueness, the singular quality of things—to value individual integrity and to reject the cliché and the stereotype. (1981, 158)

Most definitions of aesthetics involve the capacity to perceive, respond, and be sensitive to the natural environment and human creations. For several years we have been exploring the topic of aesthetic development in early childhood because we are concerned that children are not being encouraged to develop their ability to perceive aesthetic qualities. If much of what they are exposed to is without aesthetic merit, they might not learn to appreciate or produce beauty.

Why should you be concerned with aesthetics? One reason is that teachers model and teach about those things that they value. If appreciation of beauty is important in your life, then you will want to share this with children. Another reason is that aesthetic experiences, like play, have intrinsic value. They allow appreciation of a moment for itself. Responding to a lovely sunrise, a painting, or a piece of music requires no coercion. Aesthetic enjoyment provides an avenue through which people can find focus and achieve balance and tranquility in an increasingly fast-moving world. Moreover, children who learn to love beauty in nature and in the arts are likely to want to protect and nourish these valuable resources.

You can support aesthetic development through the experiences that you provide for children. Classroom activities can be designed to help children learn about elements of aesthetics.

For example, postcards and calendars of the work of fine artists (available in museum and gallery shops) can become lotto and card games that children can sort and classify by subject matter, technique, color, or personal preference (Wolf 1984), and beautiful music can be played in the classroom.

Primary-school children can also begin to learn more about art history and criticism and may begin to develop aesthetic preferences. Wolf's art postcard games (as described in *Mommy, It's a Renoir!*) are particularly appropriate for primary-school children. Trips to exhibits and museums and thoughtful presentation of an artist's work can be a valuable part of the curriculum. A seven-year-old friend of ours, for example, became entranced by the work of Van Gogh. He could easily distinguish Van Gogh's work from that of other painters and was particularly fond of the print of *Sunflowers* that his teacher had shared. When introducing primary-school children to art, it is important to guide them in a way that helps the art to be more personal and meaningful. For example, you might ask children to talk about what they see in the different parts of the picture and what the artist might have been thinking and feeling when she or he created the work.

It takes special, additional attention to create an environment that helps children learn to appreciate art. Classroom walls can be adorned with art. The work of fine artists and the work of children both carefully displayed help children to look and focus. In some programs, a particular piece of work is featured and given special prominence. Areas that feature flowers, art prints, sculpture, and beautiful natural objects (called *beauty corners* in British Infant schools) create an island of calm in the classroom and heighten aesthetic awareness.

Books are an especially appropriate way of presenting aesthetic experiences. Books introduce children to different styles and techniques of art (for example, representational, impressionism, cubism, watercolor, wood block, collage). They can also be used as a vehicle for discussing aesthetic impact and children's tastes in art. Consider carefully what you select to put on the library shelves of your classroom. The quality of the illustrations and the design are important criteria in the selection of good books for young children.

Experiences in the natural world also nourish children's aesthetic sense. On a walk in the park or trip to the lake, ocean, or river, stop and help children to reflect on colors, patterns, and textures; focus on tiny flowers or watch a spider spin a web. Special places can be visited over and over again so that children can reflect on the changes in nature over time. These experiences can help them learn to cherish the beauty around them, whether it is found in isolated locations or in rich abundance. They also heighten children's senses and powers of observation and give them the raw material to convert into their own artistic products. A four-year-old friend of ours created a song while sitting in the car and watching a photographer set up his tripod and take a picture of a spectacular rainbow with a misty green valley as a backdrop.

Kona's Rainbow Song

Rainbows are nice, rainbows are pretty
And I see one, a real one, up in the sky.
All of the colors in the world go together to
    make a rainbow.
Rainbows are pretty of all.

Rainbows do light.
Rainbows do everything.

Mothers and fathers do everything for babies.
They change their diapers and take them to the
    park to see rainbows.
You can plant flowers, you can plant leaves.
Everything turns the world.

Planes can fly—babies cannot.

A beautiful rainbow song,
Because we like rainbows.

There is so much walls that we can see.
And rainbows are nice—rainbows are pretty.
And rainbows are part of the life.
And rainbows are sometimes blue,
And sometimes are other colors.

Rainbows can do anything they want to.
They don't have brains like people do.

Rainbows delight!
Rainbows do everything!

Excursions to works of art in your community (for example, to see a sculpture that adorns a public building), to galleries, and to exhibits make worthwhile trips for young children. In almost every town or city there are galleries and museums where works of art can be visited and artists and craftspeople who are willing to share their work with children. For young children, the best experiences with art take place when there is understanding of and arrangement for their developmental needs. It is best if paintings and drawings can be viewed closely and if some objects such as sculpture can be touched. We enjoy taking children to experience beautiful architecture and outdoor art such as large sculptures and murals since these are created to endure hard use and can be explored. Children may want to visit special places many times.

Children need exposure to beautiful environments, to good art, and time to reflect on these things with a caring and thoughtful adult. The way that children are introduced to aesthetic experiences may be as important as the experiences themselves. The early years may be the optimal time to lay the foundation for a lifetime of pleasure and enjoyment.

IN THE CLASSROOM: CHECKLIST FOR CREATIVE CURRICULUM AREAS

Program Structure

_____ Stated goals include the support of the development of creativity and aesthetic awareness through art, music, and movement

_____ Products and performances are considered secondary parts of the arts program

_____ Daily free choice periods of at least an hour include opportunities to use art materials, blocks, dramatic play, and manipulative toys

_____ Daily group music experiences are provided

_____ Creative movement and drama activities are provided regularly—at least weekly

Environment and Material

Environment

_____ Art center _____ Dramatic play area _____ Block area _____ Manipulative toy area

_____ Adequate space for group movement and music activities without protruding furniture or fixtures

_____ Relatively quiet and uncrowded space when music or movement are in progress

_____ Works of art and beautiful objects from nature displayed, some at child's eye level

_____ Children's artwork carefully and aesthetically mounted and displayed

_____ Materials and supplies aesthetically arranged, stored, and organized

_____ Equipment and materials stored so that they are easily found and reached (for example, paper and pens)

_____ Fragile or delicate materials stored to avoid damage (for example, records and instruments)

_____ Equipment and materials available in sufficient quantity so children have plenty of opportunity to use them

_____ Materials that require supervision stored out of children's reach and view (for example, saws and nails)

_____ Storage area for children's completed artwork established at child level and set up so that children can file and retrieve their own work

Equipment, Materials, and Supplies

Art

_____ Trays or cookie sheets to hold materials and delineate space

_____ Airtight containers for storage

continued

_____ Scissors that cut well and can be used in either hand
_____ Paper in a variety of shapes, weights, colors, and sizes including cardboard
_____ White glue and paste
_____ Tempera paint in primary colors (red, yellow, blue), white, and black
_____ Fingerpaint base (bentonite, laundry starch)
_____ Large-format paper for the easel
_____ Paint containers that do not tip when brushes are set in them
_____ Brushes that are one-half- to one-inch wide for easel painting in a variety of lengths
_____ Watercolor brushes, house paintbrushes, feathers, sponges, swabs
_____ Peeled, large crayons
_____ Felt-tip marking pens (nontoxic in both wide and narrow sizes)
_____ Colored chalk _____ Oil pastels _____ Pencils
_____ Hole punch _____ Ruler and protractor _____ Tape _____ Envelopes
_____ Potter's clay _____ Dough _____ Clay boards or mats _____ Dowels or rolling pins
_____ Tongue depressors or blunt knives _____ Clay-working tools
_____ Junk such as paper rolls, fabric pieces, yarn scraps, Popsicle sticks, macaroni, rice, rocks, buttons, wood scraps, seeds, shells
_____ Crewel needles
_____ Small, light hammers _____ Screwdrivers _____ Short saws _____ Vise or a C-clamp_____

Music

_____ Sturdy record player or CD player _____ Tape recorder

Recordings representing a number of eras and styles such as:
_____ Folk music from different cultures
_____ Instrumental music from different time periods and different places
_____ Good-quality recordings designed for children
_____ Meditation music

A variety of good-quality instruments such as:
_____ Tambourine _____ Hand drum _____ Claves and rhythm sticks_____ Triangle _____ Tone blocks _____ Maracas _____ Cymbals _____ Harmony instrument (for example, guitar, Autoharp, ukulele)_____

Movement

_____ Good-quality tunable tambourine or hand drum
_____ Chiffon scarves _____ Streamers _____ Chinese jump ropes_____ Hoops _____ Beanbags_____

Furniture

_____ Small, low tables and chairs or tables low enough for children to sit on the floor

continued

_____ Small table for one child to work alone or with a partner
_____ Low, open storage shelves for art supplies located near the art area
_____ Easel low enough that the smallest child can reach the top of the painting surface comfortably
_____ Drying rack or shelf
_____ Small heavyweight table for woodworking

DISCUSSION QUESTIONS

1. Think of a place that is beautiful to you, that restores your spirit. What kinds of things do you find there? What makes it special to you? Compare your ideas to those of other people—what is similar and what is different about your visions? How could elements of beauty be a part of a classroom? What would need to happen to make this a reality?
2. What kind of experiences did you have in school with art, music, and movement? In what ways did your teachers support or discourage creativity and individuality? How have these experiences affected your feelings about your present-day creativity and ability as an artist, musician, or dancer?
3. Reflect on programs that you have observed. Compare how these have provided creative and aesthetic experiences for children. Was time for art, music, and movement scheduled? Was the environment arranged for children's independent creative expression? Was artwork displayed in the classroom? How did teachers talk to children about their creative efforts? What were the characteristics of the programs you liked best? How did these differ from the programs you liked least?

PROJECTS

1. Use the creative curriculum area checklist to evaluate a classroom on the curriculum for the arts. Report on:
   • The classroom's strengths.
   • Some ways that the environment could be improved.
   • What you learned that you might apply to your future teaching.
2. Observe a child for a morning in regards to how she or he creates. Report on:
   • The ways and circumstances in which the child creates.
   • How the environment supports the child's development in this area.
   • How the teacher supports this child's development.
   • How the program might be modified to enhance this child's learning.
3. Observe a teacher for a half day and then interview her or him about how she or he teaches art, music, and movement and enhances creativity. Report on:
   • Activities and routines you saw that contribute to children's learning.

- Any evidence you saw of teacher planning for creativity and aesthetic awareness.
- The teacher's goals for children in the arts.
- The ways in which what the teacher perceives and what you actually observed match or appear to differ.

4. Write and implement a lesson in art, music, or creative movement using the activity planning form from Chapter 10 (Figure 10.11). Report on how children responded and on how you felt about your teaching. What worked? What might you do differently next time? How might you expand on this experience for children?

5. Compare two early childhood programs in creative curriculum. Report on the ways that the two address the area—their similarities and differences. Which program seems to best meet children's needs and why? What implications does this have for your future teaching?

6. Compare two classrooms, one preschool and one for infants and toddlers or for primary-school children. Report on how each enhances children's creativity and the similarities and differences between them. Talk to the teachers about how they make their curriculum choices in this area.

BIBLIOGRAPHY

Barlin, A. L. 1979. *Teaching Your Wings to Fly*. Santa Monica, Calif.: Goodyear Publishing.

Bayless, K. M., and M. E. Ramsey. 1987. *Music A Way of Life for the Young Child*. Columbus, Ohio: Merrill.

Bland, J. C. 1968. *Art of the Young Child: Understanding and Encouraging Creative Growth in Children Three to Five*. New York: Museum of Modern Art.

Burton, L., and W. Hughes. 1981. *Musicplay*. Menlo Park, Calif.: Addison-Wesley.

Burton, L., and K. Kuroda. 1979. *ArtsPlay: Creative Activities in Dance, Drama, Art, and Music for Young Children*. Menlo Park, Calif.: Addison-Wesley.

Chenfeld, M. B. 1983. *Creative Activities for Young Children*. New York: Harcourt Brace Jovanovich.

——————, 1989. From Catatonic to Hyperactive: Randy Snapped Today. *Young Children* 44 (4):25–27.

Cherry, C. 1971. *Creative Movement for the Developing Child: A Nursery School Handbook for Non-Musicians*. rev. ed. Belmont, Calif.: Fearon Publishers.

Cohen, E. P., and R. S. Gainer. 1976. *Art: Another Language for Learning*. New York: Citation Press.

Cole, E., and C. Schaefer. 1990. Can Young Children be Art Critics? *Young Children* 45 (2):33–38.

Curtis, S. R. 1982. *The Joy of Movement in Early Childhood*. New York: Teachers College Press.

Feeney, S., and E. Moravcik, 1987. A Thing of Beauty: Aesthetic Development in Young Children. *Young Children* 42 (6): 7–15.

Gardner, H. 1980. *Artful Scribbles: The Significance of Children's Drawings*. New York: Basic Books.

Greenberg, M. 1979. *Your Children Need Music*. Englewood Cliffs, N.J.: Prentice-Hall.

Haines, B. J. E., and L. L. Gerber. 1988. *Leading Young Children to Music*. 3d. ed. Columbus, Ohio: Merrill.

Hendrick, J. 1990. *Total Learning*. Columbus, Ohio: Merrill.

Hitz, R. 1987. Creative Problem Solving Through Music Activities. *Young Children* 42 (2): 12–17.

Jenkins, P. D. 1980. *Art for the Fun of It*. Englewood Cliffs, N.J.: Prentice-Hall.

Kellogg, R. 1982. *Analyzing Children's Art*. Palo Alto, Calif.: Mayfield Publishing.

Lasky, L., and R. Mukerji. 1980. *Art: Basic for Young Children*. Washington, D.C.: National Association for the Education of Young Children.

Lowenfeld, V., and W. L. Brittain. 1987. *Creative and Mental Growth*. 8th ed. New York: Macmillan.

MacDonald, D. T. 1979. *Music in Our Lives: The Early Years*. Washington, D.C.: National Association for the Education of Young Children.

Magarick, M. 1975. *Creative Movement: Child Development Associate Module*. Honolulu: Curriculum Research and Development Group.

Montgomery, C. 1976. *What Difference Does Art Make in Young Children's Learning*. New York: Early Childhood Education Council of New York.

Rockefeller, D., Jr. (chairperson) The Arts, Education and Americans Panel. 1977. *Coming to Our Senses: The Significance of the Arts for American Education*. New York: McGraw-Hill.

Ross, M. 1981. *The Aesthetic Imperative: Relevance and Responsibility in Art Education*. Oxford: Pergamon Press.

Rowen, B. 1982. *Learning Through Movement: Activities for the Preschool and Elementary School Grades*. 2d ed. New York: Teachers College Press.

Seeger, R. C. 1945. *American Folksongs for Children*. Garden City, N.Y.: Doubleday.

Smith, N. 1983. *Experience and Art: Teaching Children to Paint*. New York: Teachers College Press.

Sullivan, M. 1982. *Feeling Strong, Feeling Free: Movement Exploration for Young Children*. Washington, D.C.: National Association for the Education of Young Children.

Trubitt, A. 1977. Music. In *Early Childhood Curriculum Modules*. ed. S. Feeney, prepared for early childhood students at the University of Hawaii.

Wolf, A. D. 1984. *Mommy, It's a Renoir!* Altoona, Pa: Parent-Child Press.

——————. 1990. Art Postcards—Another Aspect of Your Aesthetics Program? *Young Children* 45 (2): 39–43.

Zeitlin, P. 1982. *A Song is A Rainbow*. Glenview, Ill.: Scott, Foresman.

CHAPTER THIRTEEN

Communicating: Curriculum for the Development of Language and Literacy

Experience needs language to give it form. Language needs experience to give it content.

—*Walter Loban*

This chapter concerns the language arts—language, reading and writing, and children's literature. In it, we discuss the development of language and literacy and the role of the early childhood teacher and program in the development of language, literacy, and the appreciation of literature.

To understand the world and function in it we need to be able to communicate with others. The strong desire and ability to communicate unites human beings in a common bond. Language is the systematic and symbolic form that represents human thinking. All languages, including nonstandard dialects and unspoken languages such as American Sign Language, share the capacity for breadth and depth of communication. They are infinitely variable and can be used to communicate almost any experience or information. Learning language is one of our unifying characteristics and one of our most important challenges.

Within the curriculum cluster referred to as *language arts,* language is primary. Reading and writing (referred to as *literacy*) are the tools that extend language over distance and time. Literature is the art form that uses language. All depend on a base of oral language.

The goals of the language, literature, and literacy curriculum areas are to help children become enthusiastic, competent communicators who use and enjoy spoken and written language. Programs can foster children's natural desire, ability, and pleasure in communicating with others. Children's school experiences with language and literacy are highly dependent on you, the teacher. Your job is to provide relationships that are supportive, caring, and filled with language in all its forms. As you speak to children honestly and respectfully and listen to them attentively, you are encouraging language use. As you use language to mediate problems, communicate information, and share feelings and ideas, you are demonstrating the usefulness and value of oral language.

In a similar way, the value of written language is demonstrated to children as you use it in your daily activities. When you write a note to a child or parent, a grocery list, or a thank-you letter, or when you read a recipe, story, poem, or book, you model the importance of writing and reading. When children see significant adults in their lives use reading and writing, it provides a powerful incentive to begin learning these skills.

An environment that is rich in language, writing, good books, and other reading experiences is vital. It includes ample opportunities for each child to use language and written words for a variety of purposes, with lots of experiences with talk and print. Good literature will come to be appreciated as children are introduced to many well-written books.

Just as it would be inappropriate to expect every child to master the same physical challenges, so is it inappropriate to expect every child to be able to follow the same verbal directions, enjoy the same books, or have the same interest in written words. A single group of young children may include a range from nonverbal to beginning readers.

LANGUAGE

Language is a shared system of symbols that has structure, rules, and meaning that are accepted and unconsciously known by those who use it. The symbols can be combined, organized, and enlarged to convey an infinite variety and complexity of messages. Except for a few routine phrases like "have a nice day," language is creative. Most utterances have not been spoken or written in exactly the same way before.

It is fascinating to keep in mind that language itself is dynamic and growing. New words come into being every day in response to a changing world. The vocabulary that you use today is slightly different from that which was spoken when you learned to talk; (twenty-five years ago there were no such words as *burnout, networking,* or *yuppie*). Your vocabulary also is different than it will be when today's preschoolers reach adulthood.

Learning to understand and use language is one of the most significant accomplishments of early childhood. Almost all children acquire language without any formal teaching before they enter school; it is a skill that appears to be "caught, not taught." As they forge their language, children develop an inseparable part of themselves as well as a tool for communication, expression, and learning.

Young children learn the customs for language that are familiar in their own homes and communities. They learn to select speech appropriate to the setting: they speak differently in the classroom than on the playground, and differently depending on to whom they are speaking and why. Children learn early to include such nonverbal social features as gestures, facial expressions, body position, and intonation in their style of speaking. They come to understand the expectations and signals for turn taking in conversations.

Both developmental stage and the desire to communicate motivate language learning. Children learn the complex structure, rules, and meanings of language and develop the ability to create their own speech and read and write their own words through processes that are still not completely understood. We know that children need language experiences that are meaningful to them and appropriate to their developmental abilities. For young children, social, physical, and sensory activities are an essential underpinning for talking.

Language and Development

Language development, like physical development, follows a predictable sequence. It is

IN THE CLASSROOM: STAGES OF LANGUAGE DEVELOPMENT

- **Sounds:** From birth infants make and respond to many sounds. Crying, gurgling, and cooing are important first steps in the language-learning process.
- **Babbling:** Babbling encompasses all of the sounds found in all languages. Gradually, babbling becomes more specific with the syllables of the native language being practiced consistently. Before the end of their first year, children engage in *pseudolanguage*—babbling that mimics the native language in its intonation and form.
- **Holophrases:** The first word occurs around the first birthday and evolves to many single words or syllables that stand for a variety of meaningful sentences or phrases in different situations. "Car" said while looking out the window may mean, "Look at the car outside"; "car" said while standing next to the toy shelf may mean, "I want my toy car." A vocabulary of holophrases enables children to communicate with familiar caregivers. Children use successive holophrases to increase their communicative power: "car" pause "go" to indicate "I want to go for a ride."
- **Two-word sentences:** Sentences of two words appear between eighteen and twenty months of age and express ideas concerning relationships: "Mommy sock" (possessor-possession), "cat sleeping" (actor-action), "drink milk" (action-object), and so on. A vocabulary of about 300 words is typical.
- **Telegraphic sentences:** Telegraphic sentences appear next and are short and simple. Similar to a telegram, they omit function words and endings that contribute little to meaning: "Where Daddy go?" "Me push truck."
- **Joined sentences:** As language development proceeds, children join related sentences logically and express ideas concerning time and spatial relationships. They come to understand social expectations for language use and begin to use adult forms of language. Vocabularies expand rapidly, the ability to use words increases, and children intuitively acquire many of the rules of language. By age three children have vocabularies of nearly a thousand words.
- **Overgeneralizations** (sometimes called *creative grammar*): As children become more sophisticated in their language, they overgeneralize rules in ways that are inconsistent with common usage, for example, *"I comed home"* for *"I came home."* Correct forms are temporarily replaced as rules are internalized.

related, but not tied to, chronological age. Regardless of the language being learned or the culture in which it is learned, language develops at generally the same stage of life and through the same processes. Within any group of young children of a similar age, there are differences in language facility and individual style.

Although individuals vary in the speed of language acquisition and in how much they speak, the language learning process is universal. Psychologists and linguists have long theorized how children learn language. The behaviorist view, popular until the late 1950s, that language is gradually built up through imitation and reinforcement is now regarded as inadequate to explain the creative nature of speech. The predominance of children's invented words and phrases unlike any spoken by adults are among the many clues that children play a creative role in constructing their own language and do not simply learn by rote.

Linguist Noam Chomsky, as described by Bruner (1983), proposed that humans must have an innate ability to process language, which he referred to as a *language acquisition device* (LAD), in order to explain why children are able to produce word forms and sentences they have never heard. Chomsky's work sparked interest in finding out what young children naturally understand about the structure of language when they start to talk—for example, identifying similarities in the ways all young children combine words or use grammatical forms. Even though this research helped scientists and educators understand the formal features of language (*what* children do), it did little to explain *how* young children learn to speak.

Language and thought go hand in hand; however, the exact nature of the relationship is not clear. Jean Piaget and Lev Vygotsky, two developmental theorists, both studied children's language development and have helped early childhood educators to understand the relationship of children's cognitive growth and the development of language.

Piaget was concerned with how language influenced the development of thinking. He observed that preschool children's speech was more often *egocentric* (talking aloud to oneself) than *socialized* speech (dialogue with others). He suggested that egocentric speech is merely an accompaniment to activity—that it reflects thinking rather than expanding it. Children become capable of acquiring and using language *only* as they develop concepts. In this view experience is most important; language is acquired in social contexts *after* concepts are in place.

Vygotsky (1962, 1978) argued that children learn language as an interaction between innate maturation and the stimulation of social experiences. The development of language allows children to organize and integrate experience, in other words, to develop concepts. Vygotsky observed the egocentric speech of childhood (which he called *external* speech), but he interpreted it as the *means* by which children develop concepts and plan actions. In this view language is essential for understanding and organizing experiences. Communication with others is vital because children develop language in relationships with more competent speakers (adults and older children).

Although there are clear differences between these two views, both agree that a strong relationship exists between thinking and language, between concepts and the words used to express them. There is also agreement that children's development of language is part of an active mental process. It involves constructing intuitive rules that guide behavior. Experiences with the world *and* language-filled relationships are vital.

Before speaking, children make and respond to many sounds. Crying, gurgling, babbling, and cooing are important parts of the language-learning process. Caregivers respond to the sounds infants make, and important language abilities are established. Current theories of language development proposed by Jerome Bruner, Gordon Wells, and others follow Vygotsky's view that early social experiences form the basis for language development. Bruner (1983) proposes that these experiences form a *language acquisition support system* (LASS) to assist Chomsky's LAD.

The communication between infant and caregiver helps us understand how children learn to talk. Adults act as informal guides to support and foster language learning through these interactions. Routines are the major context for language learning: "dialogues" between adult and infant during feeding and changing, games like peekaboo, naming objects and events as they occur, picture book reading, and nonverbal play. By their first birthday children generally speak their first word and more words soon follow. Bruner suggests that caregivers provide a temporary framework or *scaffold* for language by assuming young children intend to communicate, by listening carefully, and by assisting only as much as needed. In early conversations, caregivers provide some of the child's responses. As the ability to participate is demonstrated, the adult adjusts and gradually permits the child to take over on his or her own.

As children learn language, they master a complex task that involves a system of speech sounds *(phonology)*, grammatical forms and relationships *(syntax)*, meaning *(semantics)*, and socially based customs for language use *(pragmatics)*. Exposure to everyday speech and a desire to interact socially contribute to children's construction of their own understanding of language principles. Many experiences with language used in context help children to understand and use new words. Vocabulary grows quickly.

Experimentation with all of the language elements is essential. *Overextensions* of a particular word are common. For example, a toddler of our acquaintance called the family cat "key-cat" and overextended the word to label the neighbor's dog, a furry toy, and the lady across the street who had three cats. Similarly, older children *overgeneralize* grammatical rules, "I holded the baby bunny." These are natural parts of children's active language development; they help us realize that children analyze and construct language rather than merely imitate or learn by rote. This process of exploration is not affected by instruction or correction but by speaking and listening. By the age of five or six, most children have mastered the basics in all of these areas in their native tongue; they have "learned language."

Framework for Organizing the Content

Oral language is used for a variety of purposes—to direct others, to express needs and direct one's own behavior, to establish and maintain relationships, to call attention to oneself. Language can also be used to ask for and give information, to interpret our experiences, to play, and to create imaginary scenes or think about events that are not happening in the present. Most young children have ample experience using language for directing behavior and other interpersonal purposes. When they first come to school, some children may have had little opportunity to use language to describe and explain their experiences or to talk about things beyond the here and now of immediate events. Differences will reflect the wide range of possible ways language was used by individual caregivers and social groups. If you become familiar with the different uses of language, you will be able to see where children's opportunities for talking might be extended and to ensure that a range of language opportunities are encouraged in your classroom.

Informative Language

Informative language is used to share facts and opinions with others. In classrooms, children as

well as teachers need opportunities to practice using language to exchange information. You may need to provide a model of this kind of talk and a great deal of encouragement. You must be a careful and respectful listener. Children who learn that you will listen to them and take them seriously will come to feel pride and delight in their own abilities. These children may be the ones that often say, "Did you know that . . .", "My Mommy says . . .", "I saw . . ."

Descriptive Language

As you work and talk with young children, there are many chances to describe experiences in words. Many parents and teachers naturally model the use of descriptive language, particularly with very young children. They talk about what is happening, giving a running commentary as they go through an activity: "Dylan sure seems to be enjoying himself on the trampoline. Look how his hair flops up and down as he jumps." Skillful teachers make sure ample time is left for children to contribute. Children may need your help to become specific in their talk. For example if a child says, "I got the stuff," you can expand by saying, "Oh good, you brought the sawdust and scraper. Now we can clean the mouse cage."

Reasoning Language

One of the things children may experience for the first time in the early childhood program is the language of cause and effect. Reasoning language helps children to understand the relationships between actions, "If we go out while it's raining we'll get wet," and relationships between people, "If you invite him over he may play with you." Young children need help as they learn to use language for reasoning and solving problems. Teachers often instruct children to substitute specific words or phrases. They suggest alternative ways to express problems, "Tell him you want him to stop taking your blocks," and model problem-solving language,

"Please don't put that bucket on my lap, it's getting me wet." Children then try out the new language in their play situations.

Language of Imagination and Recall

Children first talk about the here and now. Eventually they begin to talk about things they remember, things that happened outside of school or in the past. Some children learn to use language to build imaginary scenarios for their play; others have little experience with this kind of talk. If children are not familiar with this use of language, they will need adult modeling and support to learn to talk to create or recall things not present.

Language Play

Young children often use language in playful ways. They invent silly words, use "naughty" language, state things they know to be incorrect as a joke (teacher: pointing to a new hat the child is wearing, "What's that?"; child: giggling, "A watermelon!"), experiment with sounds, and make up rhymes ("Swinging, ringing, pringing, flinging, minging.") Such language play may help children begin to develop a conscious awareness of language itself, the kind of thinking about language they will need as they learn to read. Thinking and talking about language require greater sophistication than using language to communicate. Playing with language may help children to develop this important awareness. Nonsense words, rhymes, jokes, tongue twisters, and "silly talk" in literature and conversation foster language play.

The Environment

Most children learn language well at home in their interactions with family members. We can draw on this natural environment as a model for a classroom that supports language development. In a natural language environment, people communicate about meaningful events; real people use real talk about the real things they are doing. The classroom language environment is very different from a home environment because of the high child-adult ratio (a low classroom ratio of five to one would be a very high ratio for a home), so there may be fewer opportunities for children to talk with adults. To support language development in school, teachers need to make time and create an environment in which conversations between adults and children and among children are encouraged.

The overall organization of your program will influence children's talk. You set the stage for language development by preparing a language-rich environment filled with interesting things to do, see, and talk about. Plan classroom activities that will enable children to see connections with similar experiences outside of school (for example, cooking, gardening, caring for pets) and they will have much to talk about. Provide enough time and space for children to come together and converse as they work and play. Value the buzz of conversation and do not demand silence as an indication of order. Let the children know that talking to each other is worthwhile and something that you want them to do. Engage in conversations with children that are dialogues, not teacher monologues. Use classroom volunteers such as parents or students to increase the opportunities for extended conversations between children and adults.

Routines and daily activities also provide opportunities for language development. Lunch, snack, and transitions are also conversation times. Daily music, movement, meetings, art, and story times involve language.

Teaching

You will not actually instruct children in a subject called language (a discipline studied by linguists and other scholars). Instead, you will help children develop language by using it. As children act out roles in block and dramatic play areas, they develop variety and complexity in their language. As they work together on group projects, they use language to plan, compare, and describe. Comfortable areas to talk in and materials like picture books, puppet theaters, dramatic play props, language games, flannel boards, and art projects motivate language. When children take trips, they share experiences that they will enjoy talking about. You can plan activities that help to develop language, for example, creating a web of words as in Figure 13.1 to describe the frog that is visiting the classroom.

The kinds of language described in the curriculum framework can be used as a guide to ensure that you are using language for a number of different purposes. Use variety and specificity in the words you choose to direct or describe ("It's on the top shelf next to the striped basket."). Ask open-ended questions (those that do not require a particular answer, see Chapter 14 for examples) and expand children's language naturally without being distracting or making corrections.

Explore words and play with language. As children show interest in words talk about them. In our own teaching we use a vocabulary that is slightly more complex than the children's (and only slightly less complex than the language we use in talking to one another) to help them learn new words in context and to help them become curious about language. Recently, in talking to a group of four-year-olds, the word *distressed* was used ("Katherine is too distressed to come to circle right now.") Ben who is four and a half years old asked, "Why do you use words we don't understand?" The response was, "So that you can learn them too—what do you think distressed means?" Ben answered, "Sad and mad."

Trust that all children have language facility you can nurture. Hesitant or shy children may require a longer time to speak or answer questions, and it is important to be patient and give them enough time. In addition to planning for language experiences, take advantage of the unplanned moments when language can occur.

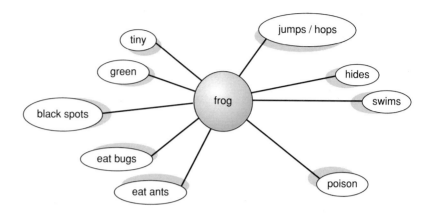

FIGURE 13.1
Web of Words

How you talk with children is important. Children need a chance to express their ideas, to tell about the things they know and that are important to them, to be able to make sense of their experiences. In conversations you can help children by allowing them to take the lead and then following their topics, showing interest, and encouraging them to continue the discussion. It is not necessary to plan specific questions to use when you have conversations with children. Questioning by adults may seem like a test, and some children will focus on finding the answer expected by the adult rather than on doing their own thinking.

Adapting for Different Ages

Infants and *toddlers* need teachers who spend time in conversation with them. A natural model of teaching is even more important in programs for children under the age of three than it is in programs for older preschoolers. They need adults who engage in a dialogue of words, sound, and action. If you work with infants and toddlers, you will spend focused time talking and listening. Like their parents, you will be among a small group of adults who knows the special language of a particular child.

If you work with *primary-school children,* the language teaching task remains a natural part of daily interactions with children. Because of children's growing ability to think about language, you can begin to talk to children about words. Language games, language challenges, and humor like puns and riddles can add great richness and excitement to the curriculum. School-age children take special delight in learning the particular vocabulary of their intense interests. Knowing the long and complex scientific names of the dinosaurs, the words of complicated jump rope rhymes, and the complicated descriptions of the paraphernalia of a fantasy character are all examples of the power of language and the new abilities of a school-age child.

LANGUAGE AND CULTURE

Culture, as well as developmental difference, affects language use. School customs can be quite different from those of home and may require a greater adjustment for children from some social and cultural groups than for others. As a teacher of young children, you will need to be aware of and sensitive to the social customs for talking children have learned. Children from some cultures learn to show respect for adults by remaining silent and looking away, whereas those from other cultural backgrounds learn to maintain eye contact and speak up. Anthropologists of education (Bryce-Heath 1983) have found that children from different cultural backgrounds learn different ways of talking about and expressing the meaning of events. Ways of telling stories, looking at picture books, and asking or answering questions may also be affected by cultural differences.

There are variations in the way individuals speak. Some variations are personal; they relate to word and phrase preferences and individual characteristics such as voice quality. Other variations relate to the language that is used, valued, and taught in a particular locale. In the United States, Canada, Australia, and Great Britain, for example, English is spoken as the primary language but there are regional differences. When the differences are distinct, they are called *dialects*. Dialects vary from the dominant language in vocabulary, pronunciation, and grammatical rules. Often they vary in the rules for forming plurals, negatives, and past tenses, for example, "ain't" for "isn't."

In the United States, there are variations of English that have roots in other languages. They use English words but are sufficiently different from standard English to be considered separate languages. These variations are called the *Creole* languages, *Gullah* in South Carolina and Georgia, and *Pidgin* in Hawaii. They use some non-English words and substantially different grammar, and they are quite difficult for most speakers of standard English to understand.

Black English, spoken among the black population of urban ghettos in the northern United States and throughout the South, uses elements of southern dialects and words and structure that reflect a Creole language. Although it has greater differences from standard English than most dialects, it is not considered a separate language.

Language differences have deeper implications, however, than simple grammatical or pronunciation variations. Because language is intimately connected to the way we live, a language expresses a particular culture's unique perception of the world. Certain languages, for example, have fewer names for colors than English; hence, the colors themselves are probably perceived differently. The Inuit culture of the Arctic, to point to another example, has many different words to describe snow. Language, then, is more than written and spoken communication. It is an intrinsic part of our culture and reflects a distinctive vision of the world.

For children to become confident, effective communicators, they must first feel comfortable speaking. Whatever language they speak, it is vital that you accept and respect their language. Although dialects have sometimes been characterized as inferior, they are in fact, simply different. Like standard English, they are flexible, capable of expansion, governed by rules, and expressive. Speakers of a dialect communicate effectively in day-to-day interactions in their own communities. Standard English (sometimes called the school dialect) has no inherent superiority for communicating or for thinking. It is, however, widely used and understood as the language of education, literature, business, and technology. Consequently, teachers are generally expected to provide a model of standard English. Programs aimed at changing oral language through drill and practice separate talk from meaning. They are likely to be ineffective and may have a negative effect on children's self-concepts by demeaning their natural expression.

In our diverse society you may have children in your class whose first language is not English. At one time these children were considered disadvantaged, and the job of the teacher was to develop the child's skill in English while decreasing the use of the native tongue. Knowledge of two languages is now generally viewed as advantageous and continued development in

both languages is an important goal in the education of these children.

To support bilingualism teachers need to actively value the child's first language and culture. Janet Gonzales-Mena (1981) suggests that the basis for teaching young children whose first language is not English must be relationships within a program for total development; ideally, teachers who speak both languages should be involved. This view of learning a second language is consistent with knowledge of language development, but it is not always possible. Indeed, we have experienced classrooms in which children came from eight different language backgrounds. A United Nations translator would have been the only solution. Creative monolingual teachers can work successfully with the non-English-speaking children in their classes by using the resources available to them. They learn key words and phrases in the child's language; they have children use their first language to teach the group words, songs, and games; and they encourage bilingual family and community members to participate in the classroom. Most importantly, they build strong relationships with the children and their families and help them feel comfortable sharing their language and culture in the school. Reading, home visits, and discussions with the parents will help you develop under-

standing of children whose backgrounds are different from your own.

LITERACY

Reading and writing are facets of communication, tools to unlock ideas, and adventures. *Literacy* describes the interconnected processes of reading and writing. *Emergent literacy* is the evolving process by which children become literate without formal instruction. William Teale and Elizabeth Sulzby (1986, p. 1) define the period of emergent literacy as the span "between birth and the time when children read and write in conventional ways."

Until recently, an intense debate over whether or not young children should be taught to read was common. Proponents of more academic programs for young children argued for drill in phonics and other skill-oriented procedures. Another view presented reading and writing as requiring instruction in a set of skills that could not be taught until children had demonstrated certain "readiness" behaviors, for example, large- and small-muscle skills, visual and auditory discrimination, sequencing ability, and the ability to follow a left-to-right orientation. Readiness skills, and not reading and writing, were viewed as appropriate preschool activities, and teachers were warned away from encouraging children's interests in written language.

In the past several years, this great debate has altered as some radically different ideas have been accepted. Educators now acknowledge that preschoolers in our society come to school with many ideas about reading and writing. Good teachers have always provided some experiences for young children that contribute to their emerging concepts about reading and writing. However, it is not drill, rote learning, or workbooks that provide meaningful literacy education for young children. Much more than isolated skills to be mastered, reading and writing are in programs for young children because they are part of children's lives and the lives of their families who live in a literate world.

Literacy and Development

Children who live in our print-filled world have early awareness of written language and develop concepts about it from a very early age. Learning about reading and writing does not wait for children to be declared officially "ready."

Young children learn to speak at an early age, a complex and difficult task. They learn through everyday experiences with language with thoughtful adults who pay attention to their growing skills. It is becoming clear that the foundations for making sense of written language start long before reading; they start with early social uses of print. Everyday experiences and supportive adults who interpret and call attention to print give children opportunities to actively explore and think about written language.

Much current research has its basis in Vygotsky's suggestion that we look for what happens before writing and reading and how literacy is supported in children's social interactions. Children do not wait for formal lessons to begin to formulate ideas about written language. Some children even begin to read and write without instruction, although careful investigation shows that they usually live in homes where many experiences with written language are available and they have much adult support.

Stages of Literacy Development

Current research makes evident parallels between the development of literacy and language. Like language development, literacy appears to follow a sequence in which social interaction about print plays an important role. Like oral language development, expression (writing) is as important as reception (reading), and like language learning, literacy is an active process whereby children construct rules or models that help them make sense of experiences with print.

Exploring and refining. Children who are cared for by literate adults have many experiences with books and writing before they have the ability to hold a book or pencil. In homes where books and writing tools are available, they are both children's toys and the everyday objects used by adults. Like other toys and everyday objects, they are *explored* by children from the time they are allowed to hold them. They are looked at, felt, mouthed, shaken, and thrown. Parents and other important caregivers in a child's life model and teach the behavior that is appropriate with these raw materials of literacy. Observing this modeling, children at an early age come to *refine* their understanding of how books and writing work. From about the time they begin talking, around their first birthday, they start to demonstrate that "book behavior" involves looking at pictures and not playing with or manipulating the books as toys. They learn that writing occurs on paper and has special characteristics.

Cultural relevance and conventions. Marie Clay (1975) and others have found that children begin to grasp principles of how print works as they explore and attempt to create graphic forms that resemble letters. In their early concepts of writing children rarely look for connections between spoken words and their written forms. They explore the graphic features of print, finding that it follows certain rules: linearity, repetition of individual elements, directionality, variation of symbols, arrangement and spacing of letters on a page. Children who grow up with print may distinguish their "writing" scribbles from their drawing scribbles. Writing often consists of more regular and more individual marks than drawing. Like the sequence of drawing, children follow a sequence in learning to write and many three-year-olds start to distinguish letters and letterlike forms from scribbles.

The two-year-old son of a graduate student we know was amply supplied with crayons, markers, and paper. At times he would use these and scribbled in typical toddler fashion. He often chose, however, to use the pens with which his father wrote drafts of his papers. The toddler used these pens quite differently. He held them tensely and made tiny lines that squiggled and ran from one side of the page to the other. This child demonstrated that he had refined his knowledge of writing and had developed concepts about it.

Children make guesses or assumptions about how print works as they explore; for example, many young children believe that a certain number of characters (at least three or four) must be written before a message or "word" can be read. These early concepts must be revised as the child's thinking progresses to accommodate new information. In this way meaning is "constructed" by each child.

Jerome Harste, Virginia Woodward, and Catherine Burke (1984) found that many young children from all socioeconomic backgrounds in the United States "read" print as it appears in their environment; for example, they read the golden arches of the McDonald's sign and understand the purpose of the red, white, and blue U.S. mail symbol. This is called reading *contextualized* or *environmental* print and it is one of the first signs that children are beginning to attend to print and understand some of the communication purposes of reading and writing.

Books, too, have a specific mode of use. Children learn to start at the front cover and go through page by page. After having many enjoyable everyday experiences, they develop a positive regard for books (and a predisposition to read and write). As children develop understanding of books, they demonstrate awareness of basic story structure by retelling familiar stories and pretending to read books to themselves or others using language forms that sound like "book language." Understanding the purposes and characteristics of books and the ability to comprehend and find personal meaning in story reading are essential underpinnings for later reading success. Gordon Wells (1981) found that the best way to predict later success in reading was to observe how well young children understood the conventions of print used in books.

Over generalization. As children begin to recognize a connection between speech and print, they construct rules to explain the relationship. For example, a four- or five-year-old child who is familiar with a few alphabet letters may begin to write "words" by matching letter names with sounds in speech (for example, *M* to stand for mommy). As children gain greater sophistication they might write one letter per syllable (*ME* to stand for mommy) and later one letter to stand for each sound (*MME* might now stand for mommy). Many children independently produce readable written messages using this *invented spelling* before they receive formal instruction in writing. A child we know wrote *hp vlnti* on a valentine. Children's invented spelling often uses the sounds of the letter name. For example, engine might be spelled *NJN* and dress might be *GS*. The first conventionally spelled word a child writes is likely to be his or her own name. Invented spelling continues to be an important process in children's learning in primary school. Unlike the "social" knowledge of rote memorization which is known only because others say it is true, the successive approximations of children's writing demonstrates that they are constructing knowledge of reading and writing that is internal. Children gradually develop rules and generalizations about written language for themselves; often they proceed through stages in which they hold inaccurate or partially accurate concepts as they attempt to sort out how written language works.

Formal reading and writing. There is no one moment when children make the transition to formal reading and writing. The stages just described are part of an ongoing process. For one child the progress from thinking about written words to adult-like reading and writing may be astonishingly rapid, whereas for another it may be an agonizingly slow process. We have known children who seemed to be almost fully self-taught readers who needed such limited assistance, for such a brief amount of time, that their learning could hardly be followed. We have also known children who took a very long time. However long the journey to literacy, it is a trip that brings a lifetime of benefits and one in which you, the teacher, can share the joy and wonder.

Framework for Organizing the Content

Literacy is acquired because it is meaningful. Motivation and thinking about literacy arise from within the child. Each child learns to read and write as an individual; each child puts together ideas in ways that make sense that is personal and pleasurable. The curriculum for literacy must be similarly individualized. Before you plan a curriculum, it is important to understand how each child is putting together ideas about the relationship between print and meaning.

Adult-conceived reading tasks, such as matching uppercase to lowercase letters or tracing letter forms, frequently do not match children's concepts about written language. Reading and writing require conceptual development that resists direct teaching. Instead, knowledge construction depends on experiences that are within a child's understanding.

The elements of the literacy curriculum are straightforward and consist of four major parts

which are discussed in the sections that follow on environment and teaching:

- Providing experiences with the written word.
- Reading with children.
- Writing with children.
- Talking with children about print.

The Environment

An important way you support emergent literacy is by including reading and writing throughout the classroom. For example, have a name label on the rabbit's cage and label shelves and containers with pictures of the contents. Similarly, decorations can heighten print awareness. Alphabet charts and posters that include writing, signs, and book covers put reading and writing into the environment.

With older preschoolers, kindergarten and primary-school children, use print throughout the classroom for purposes that will make sense to them. Have name cards to read, copy, and use in activities; label games, materials, shelves, belongings, and children's work. Use charts and lists that include children's names. Put up signs and labels for various areas of the classroom; refer to the signs when talking to children. Use charts that include both print and pictures: recipe charts, stories, directions, words to songs, poems. Read them to children.

As children begin to notice the graphic elements of print, they will incorporate them into artwork. Children's own writing can also decorate and label the classroom. We observed a preschool classroom where a child made a poster showing step by step how to make a new art project that he had invented. His teacher wrote the steps as he dictated them and the other children came and followed his words and drawings. On the door to the bathroom in this same classroom one of the children had written a request *"Pls REBR To FH tiLT,"* (Please remember to flush the toilet).

A Writing Center

Every classroom for young children needs many different kinds of writing materials that are readily available, so children can try writing on their own. You will need a variety of unstructured materials including different types and sizes of paper (envelopes, note cards, paper to be made into little "books," notepads) and different writing tools (pencils, erasers, markers of various widths, crayons). Other materials might include sets of small plastic letters (both uppercase and lowercase) for constructing words and sentences, three- or four-inch wooden letters for tracing, a letter stamp set for printing, and a typewriter or a computer with a simple word-processing program designed for children.

Children can use these materials for exploring, producing messages, artwork, or self-selected writing practice. Older preschoolers may begin to write the words they know (their names and words like *love*) and use invented spelling. Classrooms where writing supplies are available to children and where there are words to copy encourage children to write to communicate.

Books Throughout the Classroom

Literature stimulates children's interest in words and in reading. Reading materials like newspapers and books and writing experiences like making out a receipt can be incorporated into the dramatic play area. Reference books can be part of the science area. Writing materials can be available in the block and science areas so that children can label their work, draw or write about their experiences, or ask a teacher to take their dictation. Books of all kinds, magazines, and newspapers can be kept as reference material throughout the classroom as well as in the library area. Be sure children understand that they have permission to explore the books—they are not just for adult use. Include books that adults use (encyclopedias, dictionaries, some books with few or no pictures) as well as those specifically written for children, so children will have a broader exposure to what reading means. Include child-made "books" in the classroom library or book area.

Puzzles, Games, and Workjobs

Children who are beginning to be interested in reading will enjoy using games, puzzles, or workjobs that use letters and print. Some of these materials can be open ended, for example, a set of alphabet letters that can be spread out on the floor or a basket of wooden letters for tracing and coloring. Other more defined tasks might include workjobs in which small items are sorted by beginning sounds. These activites have the kind of personal "fit" needed by young children in various stages of literacy development. Avoid group lessons that present isolated literacy tasks out of the context of children's real-life experiences.

Teaching

Children show you their developing awareness of written language in many different ways. Some begin to take an interest in favorite storybooks as they read along, point to the print, or retell the story. Others recognize or discuss the meanings of signs or labels frequently encountered. Most children are exposed to symbols, signs, and printed messages all around them in the form of traffic signs, logos for products on packages, and in television advertising. Adults make use of and refer to these forms

of messages and discuss them with children: "Look, there's the big *S;* we're at Safeway." Children's first interest is often in their own names which they recognize and wish to write; they may print their initial, saying, "That's my *J.*" Some children will pretend to write and read messages in their play. Familiar books may be "read" to a group by a child who pretends to be the "teacher."

All of these activites are evidence that print has been noticed and is being explored. In most programs for four- and five-year-olds, some children will be actively interested in learning about written language, while others will display little interest. Interest in print is sometimes demonstrated even by very young children; we recently observed a two-and-a-half-year-old laboriously writing "names" (strings of scriptlike symbols) on the paintings of all of the children in her group.

Supporting children in becoming literate requires a special kind of effort. It requires a watchful eye and sensitive ear so that you notice children's efforts and know the children you teach. It requires really being with children so that you remember events that are important and that become a part of initial writing and reading. The parallel with language can be made: caregivers who really know the beginning talker will understand that "Nini" means a special blue ribbon and similarly, teachers who really know a beginning writer will be able to read the "writing" in Figure 13.2 and know that it spells Theresa.

FIGURE 13.2
Sample of Beginning Writing

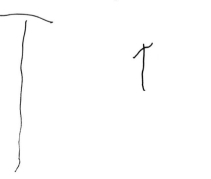

Providing Experiences with the Written Word.
As young children experience print in their
day-to-day lives, they gain literacy concepts. They
learn that print communicates and that a collection of increasingly recognizable letters tend to
be connected with the same experience time
after time; they also learn to view themselves as
a part of a community that uses print.

Reading with children.   Children who are read
to frequently and spend time with books during
their early years often become successful readers. They begin to see that what is read must
make sense and are able to make connections
between their own experiences and books.
Hearing stories read gives children familiarity
with the elements of a story and with "book
language" which is different and more formal
than day-to-day speech. Today, researchers are
looking more specifically at what concepts children gain as they are read to and at the kinds of
supportive adult interactions that take place as
children learn to read.

Children develop an appreciation of books
when they experience them in the company of
an adult who makes reading a time of warm

sharing. As they hear books read children
become familiar with the print, match spoken to
written word, and relate the illustrations to the
content. When you read to individual children,
you will have an opportunity to talk about the
books and print at the level of the child's interest
and understanding and will be able to assess
that understanding. The section that follows
on children's literature describes how you can
select a wide variety of good books for children.

When you read to the group, you are
ensuring that all the children have an experience
with books and you are demonstrating that
reading is a worthwhile part of the school day to
which you are willing to devote your time and
attention. Some of the newest materials for
emerging literacy, Big Books, are designed so
that children in groups get some of the benefits
of being read to one-on-one. The accompanying
box suggests some things to do as you read with
one or two children at a time to help them build
concepts about print.

Try to find other adults to read one-on-one
with children (parents, volunteers, nonteaching
staff, students, siblings). Let children "read"
familiar picture books to you and to classmates.

IN THE CLASSROOM: READING WITH A CHILD
TO DEVELOP CONCEPTS ABOUT PRINT

- Keep favorite books in the classroom over time and re-read favorite stories.
- Talk about the author; show the child the author's name in the book.
- Read so that the child can see the print.
- Let the child turn the page as you read.
- Sometimes point out words or punctuation like ! or ?.
- Talk about the story, its meaning, and the child's own experience.
- Refer to books after you have read them at other times and make connections
  to life.
- Point out the front of the book and the back of the book.
- Turn the book upside down and talk about how silly it looks and why you
  can't read it like that.

Some children enjoy trying to match print to known messages; for example, they may like to read along with the words of familiar songs, rhymes, poems, or tapes and records. Storytelling, puppets, flannel board stories, and dramatizations of books are other ways to help children begin to understand books and experiment with creating stories.

Writing with children. One way children come to see that print is a way to communicate is through dictating to adults. As a group or as individuals, children can create stories and books based on trips or familiar experiences that are illustrated and hung on charts or bound in books for the classroom library. This technique is called *language experience.* It helps children understand the connection between written and spoken language and builds a sense of what it feels like to be a reader and a writer. We have seen it used successfully in many preschool and kindergarten classes.

Creating a book or story using children's words can be successful even with very young children. We recently observed a classroom for two-year-olds where the teacher created small books of photos of each child's family and home. As she looked at the book with the child, she wrote down what the child said. The next time they brought out the books the child's words were the text of the story. When you are taking dictation for a story with older children, write so they can see what you are doing. Talk informally about the words as you write, pointing out words or letters as you take dictation. Write what the child says, using his or her natural form of expression, when you are recording the child's language.

Another technique that uses the words of the child to develop reading skills is called *key vocabulary.* It is described by Sylvia Ashton-Warner in her book *Teacher* (1963). Key vocabulary involves having children dictate and keep a file of words that have special meaning to them, such as *mommy, daddy, kiss,* and *rocket.* As children become familiar with the words and want to use them in their writing, they can create personal dictionaries.

Storyplaying is a technique evolved by Vivian Paley and described in her book *Wally's Stories* (1981). A child dictates a story which he or she later directs as the teacher reads it aloud and other children act out the parts. Storyplaying contributes to children's language ability, to their creative imagination, and to their emerging literacy, as well as being a powerful outlet for feelings.

An excellent and highly motivating way to involve children in literacy activities is to build them into the dramatic play center. Suggest that the children write labels, lists, signs, or whatever fits the situation as they act out scenes from life. A lot of writing can be found in a home, hospital, barber shop, or even on a photographic safari in the jungle.

You encourage and value children's attempts to produce writing and explore reading when you provide time and acceptance of their "free" writing, including scribble writing and pretend writing. Help them write their own name when they show interest in doing this. Encourage them to, "Try to write all by yourself" or "Pretend you can write it." Children may wish to copy (or even trace) print that is of interest to them. We came into a classroom one day to discover four-year-old Anna copying the names of all the children and teachers in her class onto a diagram of a circle—to show them all where they should sit.

As children begin to understand more about written language, you can support their efforts to communicate through writing. You can focus on the process, on what children are doing and how they are doing it, and on the *ideas* they are trying to express. Encourage them to write with invented spelling. Assist children who are beginning to write on their own by answering questions and providing specific information or help. Accept efforts and focus your comments on their approximations of print. Your most essen-

tial contribution is to encourage children to try to write. You can do this by inviting them to write for themselves and to their families and friends or to you.

To help children understand reading, encourage them to read back messages they write and to "read" dictation you have written for them. Often children will be able to convey the sense of what has been said if not the exact words. Feedback that has personal meaning seems to be the most effective way to help children begin to develop literacy concepts. For a child who expects adults to be able to read anything that looks like print, specific feedback such as "This doesn't look like any word I know" provides new information that conflicts with the child's expectations. Such conflicts require the child to adjust his or her thinking to make sense of this new information.

Base any help you provide on a child's requests and immediate needs within self-selected writing or reading tasks. Respond to children's thinking and questions as they are pursuing their own ideas about written language. For example, a child who is trying to find a friend's name on a list may read "Sam" as "Steven" because he is looking only at the first letter. You could point out what the child knows, "You're right—there's an S in both names!" and also call attention to the differences, "But Steven's name is a lot longer than Sam's."

Modeling

It is important that you visibly enjoy reading and writing yourself. Adults who enjoy and use reading and writing for themselves provide a powerful model for children. Teachers often write and read in the classroom and comment on their use of books as resources: "I wonder what ingredients we'll need for the lasagna; I'm going to look it up here in my cookbook." Your appreciation of children's literature and your visible enjoyment of reading demonstrate that it is a worthwhile and pleasurable experience. Some teachers have a short quiet time set aside when everyone, teachers included, take out a book and read.

Take advantage of every opportunity to use print in the natural ongoing activities of your classroom; encourage the children's interest, allow them to explore print and writing on their own, and provide follow-up activities. You might also create simple stories for the children and talk about your thinking as you write.

Show your writing to children when they express interest, tell them what you are doing, and answer their questions so they will begin to understand adult purposes for writing. Recently, while one of us was writing an observation of a teacher, a child questioned, "What are you doing?" This led to a discussion, "I'm writing about the things that children and teachers are doing in your school. Then I can remember it and talk with your teacher later about the things that she can do to help you learn." The child asked about specific words and later in the day brought her own written "message" to share.

Adapting the Literacy Curriculum for Different Ages

Literacy is sometimes said to begin at birth. Literacy education continues throughout the years of schooling. The approach to literacy varies with children's developmental needs and interests.

Even though *infants* and *toddlers* do not need reading instruction, they gain powerful messages from their teachers and the environment. They can be fascinated by the magic of the printed word when it applies to them. We observed two two-year-olds looking at a "pocket chart" of school enrollment. They asked the director about the cards, were anxious to find themselves, and stopped to touch their names whenever they went past the office. A room for infants and toddlers, like one for older children, should have books and words throughout. Like the teacher of older children, the infant-toddler teacher should be a model of a person who loves and uses reading.

Programs for *primary-age children* generally have a well-defined curriculum for literacy. If the curriculum includes the emergent literacy teaching philosophy and techniques presented here, the teachers need only make sure that they include reading and writing opportunities across the curriculum and that they recognize the importance of and encourage children's creative spelling and grammar. The suggestions presented here are even more important in programs that are currently using traditional basal readers or workbook-based reading and writing curriculums. We have known creative primary teachers who have offered the less appropriate workbooks and other curriculum materials as a choice for children in addition to a rich, appropriate emergent literacy model. They have won over amazed principals and parents—the children learned to read and write, and more importantly, they wanted to!

LITERATURE

Children who love books come to love reading. Children who have many positive experiences with literature come to love books. Literature is not merely the carrot with which we motivate children to read; in a very real way, it is the most important reason for learning to read. Through good literature, children experience both language and art and learn about the world and relationships. Literature can provide information and motivate exploration, creativity, a concern for others, and a love of reading.

Not all books are literature, and not all children's books contribute to development. Literature can be defined as "work of excellence that has permanent value: the poetry, stories, and other writing that we will continue to use over the passage of time" (*Webster's II New Riverside Dictionary* 1984). Children's literature is relatively new. Time has not yet defined which books will endure.

Until the twentieth century children's literature was not recognized, either academically or by publishers, as a separate or important part of literature. Most "classic" picture books have been written in the past fifty years. The past twenty years has seen an explosion of children's literature. Some of the new books are works of artistry that delight children now and will for generations to come.

Good literature for young children has the qualities that we look for in all literature. It shows respect for the reader, it is not condescending; it does not stereotype, preach, or moralize; it has integrity (that is, honesty and truthfulness within the context of the story); it uses aesthetic language; and in some way, it helps the reader to understand and feel more deeply. Good literature teaches by example. In *The Story of Ferdinand* the message about peace and nonviolence is positive and not overstated. Illustrations are essential in children's books and should enhance and enlarge the experience of the words. They should be executed beautifully, with care and craftsmanship, in a medium that is appropriate to the content of the book.

Children generally are not able to purchase books or make unlimited use of libraries, so it is up to adults to present a range of quality literature from which children can make choices. Since many parents are not acquainted with the qualities that characterize good literature for children, the task of providing guidance often falls to teachers. As children's literature has become an accepted product, it has also become a vehicle for marketing. Most grocery stores, variety stores, and even bookstores have a shelf of children's books that accompany television shows, movies, and related paraphernalia. These are advertisements not literature and they do not belong in early childhood programs.

Literature and Development

The best, most honest, and most beautiful children's book may not be best for every child. It is important to select a variety of books that are appropriate for the developmental level of the children. Very young preschoolers have not yet developed the fine-motor skills necessary for turning pages carefully, have an attention span that is relatively short for seated activities, are limited in experience and vocabulary, and are primarily interested in their own experience of the world. For these children, books should be durable with heavy pages and hard covers (board and cloth books for toddlers), relatively short, and concerned with experiences that the child knows or can relate to. For example, *The Runaway Bunny* by Margaret Wise Brown deals with feelings of anger, love, and security that all children have experienced. It is best if books for young preschoolers are written in a straightforward manner with easy-to-interpret words and illustrations.

If you work with older preschoolers or kindergartners, you can include stories that deal with events and characters that are beyond their realm of experience and longer stories with more complex words and plots and more intricate and subtle illustrations. Older children will also have more distinctive personal likes and interests. While a book like *Where the Wild Things Are* by Maurice Sendak seems to have almost universal appeal because of its illustrations of monsters and its underlying subject matter of power, anger, fear, and belonging,

other books appeal to some individuals more than others. Some children are moved and entranced by the moody poetry of *Dawn* by Uri Shulevitz, others enjoy the rhythmic silliness of Beatrice Shenck de Regnier's *May I Bring a Friend?*, and still others enjoy a well-told tale like William Steig's *Sylvester and the Magic Pebble*. Knowing children, their interests, their developmental level, their attention span, and the day-to-day events in their lives will help you to pick books that are appropriate and meaningful.

Framework for Organizing the Content

Presenting literature to young children involves choosing books thoughtfully, designing space for group reading and independent exploration of books, reading with skill and responsiveness, and designing experiences to expand on literature.

We find it useful to think of the following categories of books to help ensure that we provide a variety for children. Each kind of book serves a different purpose and appeals to different children at different times, supporting their existing interests and helping to build new ones.

Fiction

Fiction for young children can illustrate life, enchant, instill a love of literature, entertain, and bring happiness. To be effective, the author must respect childhood and children's lives. The author's ability to communicate in ways that create memorable, believable characters and the illusion of reality in time and place (even in a fantasy) develops an understanding of life's experience. A story's plot is more than a mere recounting of events; it encourages children to understand the reasons behind events. The point of a good story need not be heavy handed—stories that preach or devalue their experience will not appeal to children. Both fanciful fiction or fantasy (real people doing fantastic things and fantastic characters doing real things) and realistic fiction are important and belong in early childhood programs.

Fantasy can be a book specially written for children or a retelling of a traditional story. Fantasy is among the most important of childhood activities, so it should come as no surprise that fantasy comprises much of the literature of childhood and the traditional literature of nations. Characters in fantasy have fantastic adventures but personalities very like the children we teach and the adults in their lives. It is this similarity coupled with the delight in pretend that makes fantasy so appealing to children. Although, by definition, fantasy cannot be real, it delights because it has its own logic and rules that remain true for the story. Sylvester, the unfortunate donkey in *Sylvester and the Magic Pebble,* finds a pebble that grants wishes when held. He can turn himself into a boulder but cannot transform himself back without touching the magic pebble. The realism within the fantasy allows children to put themselves into the story.

Folklore is a part of our heritage that children can begin to enjoy in early childhood. Folktales touch on themes and questions that have universal appeal and universal similarity— magic, good and evil, joy and sorrow, the origins of the world and the creatures in it. Folktales are satisfying in their construction; they have a clear beginning and ending and are concise. They appeal to children's sense of justice and humor. Retellings of familiar fairytales like Susan Jeffer's lushly illustrated *Snow White* and of less familiar folktales like Verna Aardema's *Why Mosquitoes Buzz in People's Ears* are an important part of the classroom library.

Realistic fiction is a more recent addition to the literature of childhood. Authors of good realistic fiction write of childhood with an affectionate, unsentimental voice. Lucy Sprague Mitchell, who influenced so much of today's early childhood education, was one of the first to call for realistic stories for preschool children (Sutherland and Arbuthnot 1986). Books like Margaret Wise Brown's *The Noisy Book* and

Marjorie Flack's *Angus and the Cat* are two of the now classic stories that were written in the 1930s (sometimes called the golden age of children's literature) in response to this new awareness.

In the past, realistic fiction failed to pay adequate attention to minorities, disabled, and other groups of children, and in so doing, gave children in these groups no one to identify with in the books that they read. Today's stories often include characters that are disabled, poor, ethnically diverse, and who live in families as varied as those of real children. An important characteristic of these books is that the plot is relevant to children and central to the story and not just a vehicle for a well-meaning message. Ezra Jack Keats's *Peter's Chair* is about a little boy who does not want to give up being the baby of the family—he happens to be black and lives in a large urban setting.

Informational Books

All children are curious. They explore the world and want to know how things work and why. Informational books written in understandable, direct language; aesthetically worded and illustrated; and related to the experience of children can broaden their understanding. To teach and entertain they *must* be factually accurate, current, not overgeneralized, and not filled with half-truths. To enhance interest and not bore, they must be well paced and skillful in their presentation of concepts. Illustrations help to convey more than the words alone can. To be appealing and accurate without being demeaning or insincere is the great challenge of informational books for young children. Milicent Selsam has written a number of fine informational books for young children including, *Animals of the Sea* and *A First Look at Spiders.*

Informational books can be a vehicle to promote a host of goals. Some address scientific, social, and environmental concerns once thought inappropriate or too controversial for the young—concepts like birth, death, sex, racism, aging, war, and pollution. When well written and well illustrated, these books help children to understand aspects of their lives about which they have vital concern. Others that are written to meet a societal demand for curriculum material on a current issue or fad may be inappropriate for young children. They are often promoted as a cure for social ills. If the book was produced hurriedly to address a short-lived concern, the language used and style of illustration may be sentimental, stereotyped, or carelessly executed. If the subject matter is inappropriate, the books generally treat the subject in a superficial, simplistic, or inaccurate manner. Books for preschool children that purport to teach them how to avoid sexual abuse or drugs usually do more to alleviate the worry of the purchaser than ensure the welfare of children and should not be confused with literature or protection.

Mood and Concept Books

Mood and concept books sensitize children to ideas, feelings, and awareness. They help to expand the realm of an individual's experience. Into this category we place books that use organizing frameworks like the alphabet, aesthetic experiences, elements of design, colors, shapes, and numbers. Wordless books are generally a part of this category. They encourage children to think and use language. Concept books are most valuable when they provide a sense of joy and wonder in the world and are not used to drill children on concepts. There are a wealth of choices in this area: Jan Ormerod's beautiful wordless book about a child's morning *Sunlight,* Anita Lobel's *On Market Street,* Mitsumasa Anno's *Topsie Turvies,* and a host of beautiful photography books by Tana Hoban such as *A, B, See!* are a few of our favorites.

Poetry

Poems appeal to young children. They have a natural response to rhythm and rhyme and will often speak in the singsong cadences of Mother Goose. Rhymes and finger games are nearly universal forms of literature passed down from parent to child around the world. *Nursery rhymes* of all cultures include common themes—animals, unusual or grotesque people, street cries, games, fantasy creatures, clapping and finger play, riddles, tongue twisters, nonsense, counting rhymes, proverbs, and simple verse stories. Collections of rhymes and poems belong in every classroom.

Many books for young children are written in poetry. Poetry that is sometimes, but not always, rhythmic and rhymed presents mood and melody in language in a natural and unforced manner. Poetry helps to enhance children's understanding of the world and develops their sensitivity to language. It can inspire and move children or calm them. Poetry is more than rhyming words. Poetry consists of words carefully chosen that remain in memory long after they are gone, words that have music and power. Children are surprisingly interested in hearing poems and an illustrated anthology of poems for children in the classroom library may become a favored book. Individual poems illustrated as books like Clement Moore's *The Night Before Christmas* (a particularly appealing version has been illustrated by Tomie de Paola) make a good introduction to those uncertain of poetry. Robert Louis Stevenson's *A Child's Garden of Verses,* Edward Lear's *Book of Nonsense,* and A. A. Milne's collections *When We Were Very Young* and *Now We Are Six* are other good choices to share with young children.

The Environment

A comfortable, well-stocked library area in the quietest corner of the classroom enhances children's experience with books. A low shelf designed to display the front covers of books enables children to select and replace books themselves. Soft pillows, artwork, a rocking chair, and an adult lap to sit on attract children to a library corner. For reading to groups, a quiet area of the classroom with adequate lighting and comfortable seating enables children to hear the words and see the pictures, thereby setting the stage for positive literature experiences.

Group book times should occur daily and can last from ten to twenty minutes, depending on the interest and developmental level of the children. Although books can be read to quite large groups, smaller groups will have more positive and longer book times. In order for children to fully benefit from being read to, they must first be interested. Bored, uncomfortable, hungry, or overtired children will not be able to lend their full attention to books.

Teaching

You have three important roles in the literature curriculum:

- Making wise literature selections and creating an environment filled with books.
- Presenting literature to children through book reading, story telling, and acting out of stories.
- Helping parents to make literature a part of their children's lives at home.

Every classroom needs a variety of different kinds of books that change regularly. Part of what creates active, eager readers is the sense of adventure that accompanies making a choice and opening a new book. Make sure that the books represent diverse ethnicities, lifestyles, cultures, appearances, races, ages, and activities among people. Mothers should not be cast solely in the role of nurturers. Families should include single parents and only children. Minorities should appear in many professions and activities. Girls as well as boys should be adventurous and outgoing, feeling and creative. Grandparents should sometimes be attractive and active as well as aged and infirm.

There are different ways of reading to children depending on your purpose and the type of book you are reading. When you are reading books to children, it is important to read the words the author has written. This gives children the experience of rich language, one of the most important parts of literature. Children who are beginning to attend to reading also will develop understanding of the constancy of print. It is usually best to read the text continuously without interruption. This helps children to develop the sense of the story and the flow of the book's language and it helps groups of children to remain attentive.

More personal connection and dialogue is possible when you read to one or two children at a time. When reading a book with one or two children, comments and questions can help develop understanding of the story experience by enlarging on events in the books: "I wonder what the Gunniwolf wants. The little girl seems to be going deeper into the jungle. Why do you think the Gunniwolf talks like that?" Such interaction can help you to become better attuned to children's needs, feelings, and interests. Questions and comments can also serve as a bridge between the child's life and the book: "Little Sal is filling her bucket with blueberries just the way we filled our buckets with crab apples when we went to the farm." One of your most important goals in presenting literature to children is to help them develop understanding and love of books. They should never feel pressured by questions about books; if they feel that storytime is quiz time they may avoid reading altogether.

Reading a story to a group requires skill and practice. You prepare by being well acquainted with the story and with the children. When reading to a group sit on a stool or low chair to help children see. Make frequent eye contact while reading so you keep in touch with children's responses. Children will be more attentive if you speak in a clear, audible voice and if your expression relates to the content of the story. Your natural conversational tone contains distinct differences and nuances that you can use as you read.

Literature is enhanced when it is not isolated from other classroom experiences. It can be a launching point for many other kinds of activities. For example, a memorable phrase such as "Cats here, cats there, cats and kittens everywhere, hundreds of cats, thousands of cats, millions and billions and trillions of cats" (*Millions of Cats,* Wanda Gag 1929) may be the perfect response to a squirming litter of kittens if children know and love the book.

Books and poems have tremendous potential for motivating children in creative drama and movement. It is a rare group of young children, for example, that do not spontaneously begin to take on the role of the monkeys in Slobodkinas's *The Peddler and His Caps* after hearing it one or two times. With the addition of a few props and some teacher direction, you can introduce a new dimension to children's innate dramatic sense. Flannelboards and puppets are effective ways to present literature to very young children. They also contribute to the experience of older children who appreciate props that can be manipulated and who enjoy using the materials for their own storytelling.

Poems that are "stuck" in books may never make their way into your mouth or children's hearts. We have used *poetry posters,* developed by our friend Kay Goines, as a way to bring poetry into the classroom. A poetry poster is a poem written on a piece of poster-sized paper, illustrated by a teacher or parent, and hung in the classroom to bring the poem to the children and you.

Some recorded stories and poems for children add an extra dimension to a familiar book. We especially enjoy recordings of authors reading their own work and accomplished actors reading stories. It is vital to remember that no recording, however good, is a substitute for daily reading time with a teacher. Many recordings are made without aesthetic awareness or respect for children and are not appropriate classroom materials. These often have been designed to be sold in grocery stores and seem to be the literary equivalent of the candy and junk food displayed at checkout stands.

Similarly, there are many fine films and videotapes of good children's literature and others that do not contribute to children's development. After a child has had exposure to a book, a film or videotape can add new dimensions and enlarge on children's experience. Videotaped books are certainly preferable to typical children's television programming. We do not believe that either, however, deserves a prominent role in the classroom.

Helping Parents Make Literature Choices

One of the important things a teacher can do is to help parents use and choose good books for their children. Few parents have spent time learning about good literature for young children. Their own early experiences and the books that are marketed by department stores may be their primary sources. A simple and effective way to help parents is to make good classroom books available for overnight borrowing. Your careful explanation of how important reading is to children and how special the books are to you will help ensure that they are returned undamaged. Special book borrowing envelopes or bags can be used to record the titles of the books borrowed and to protect them

as they travel to children's homes and back to school again in the morning. Establishment of this routine will help children later when they begin to use public libraries. You can also prepare children by taking field trips to the local library and by encouraging parents to take regular trips to the library with their children to borrow books and to attend library-sponsored story hours.

Adapting for Different Ages

Infants and *toddlers* need teachers who use books and oral literature in the day-to-day context of play and routine. They enjoy repeating rhymes, playing rhyme-accompanied games, and simple board, cloth, or picture books.

Primary-school children enjoy picture books they can read themselves like Arnold Lobel's *Frog and Toad* and Else Minarik's *Little Bear* series and predictable books like Bill Martin, Jr.'s *Brown Bear, Brown Bear.* Because of their greater attention span they can appreciate listening to longer picture books such as Chris Van Allsberg's *The Polar Express* and books with few pictures like Mary Norton's *The Borrowers,* Laura Ingalls Wilder's *Little House on the Prairie,* and E. B. White's *Charlotte's Web.*

If you work with primary-school children, the task of teaching literature is much broader. School-age children take special delight in gaining new skills, in sharing special books, in writing books, and in reading all the books by a favorite author. As you work with primary-school children, discussion can expand to include many aspects of literature. Continue to read to children for pleasure and to let them enjoy a book that is just beyond their reading skill.

IN THE CLASSROOM: CHECKLIST FOR THE LANGUAGE AND LITERACY CURRICULUM

Program Structure

_____ Stated goals include support of language and literacy development, and appreciation of literature.

_____ Daily free choice periods of at least an hour include opportunities for children to talk to one another and adults, explore printed material, use writing equipment and art materials, and look at books.

_____ Daily schedule includes planned story times.

_____ Trips are a regular feature of the program.

Environment and Materials

_____ Well-equipped centers designed so that small groups of children can work and talk together

_____ Block center	_____ Library area
_____ Writing center	_____ Listening center
_____ Manipulative toy area	_____ Art area
_____ Dramatic play area	_____ Science area

_____ Comfortable outside space for playing, sitting, and talking; for example, benches in the shade, a water table, a climbing structure with space for sitting, and a sandbox

_____ Interesting activities in the yard such as gardening, digging, animal homes, bird feeders

_____ Printed materials, charts, and signs displayed in the classroom

_____ Shelves and cubbies labeled with words and pictures

_____ A parent bulletin board and parent message pockets

_____ Samples of children's graphic productions and beginning writing displayed in the room and reproduced in the newsletter*

_____ Children's books kept in parent area to encourage parents to read to children

_____ Interesting objects, pictures, and photographs that children can talk about displayed in the classroom at child's eye level

_____ Books and reading materials found in relevant interest centers; for example, newspapers or magazines in the dramatic play area and illustrated science books in the science center

_____ Language-related workjobs and learning games*

_____ At least two puppets

_____ At least two toy or disconnected telephones for children's use in dramatic play

Writing Center

_____ Tables and chairs proportioned to the children
_____ Marking pens in narrow and broad widths, pencils, and crayons
_____ Standard-size paper and note cards
_____ Recycled envelopes to hold messages
_____ Stapler, hole punch, tape, yarn to tie books together*
_____ Name cards and/or key vocabulary collections*
_____ Wooden letters for tracing—lowercase and uppercase*
_____ Folders to hold each child's writing*
_____ Illustrated children's dictionary*
_____ Letter stamp set*
_____ Alphabet poster*
_____ Typewriter*
_____ Word Cards

Library Center

_____ Selection of books appropriate to the developmental level of the children which shows characters of diverse race, culture, age, and social class without moralizing or stereotyping by gender or other characteristics

_____ Realistic fiction	_____ Mood and concept books
_____ Poetry	_____ Wordless books
_____ Child-authored books	_____ Informational books
_____ Fanciful fiction	

_____ Photograph albums with photos of children from the class and their families on trips, at work, at play, at school, and at home
_____ Beautifully illustrated books that include different styles of artwork—photographs, prints, drawing, painting, collage
_____ Bookshelf that displays book covers
_____ Book jackets and posters for decoration
_____ Comfortable, clean carpeting and pillows to rest on
_____ Good lighting—neither too harsh nor too soft
_____ Flannelboard with pieces that can be used by children

*Items most appropriate for older preschoolers and not generally appropriate in a classroom for two- and three-year-olds

DISCUSSION QUESTIONS

1. What are the things you read and write as an adult? Do you do a lot of reading and writing? How much is for work, how much for pleasure? How do you feel about literature and about the other reading and writing you do? How do you think your feelings are affected by your experiences as a child in school? Compare your thoughts with someone else's. In what ways are they similar or different?
2. What are all the ways that you can think of that you use language? Do you think of yourself as a competent, skillful talker? In what circumstances are you most comfortable? Do any situations make you uncomfortable? Why? Compare your feelings with those of another person. Do your feelings about language have any implications for your work with young children?
3. Discuss the books you loved as a child. What did you love about them? Why were they important to you? How did you discover those books? What books would you like to share with children? Do your childhood experiences have any implications for your work with young children?

PROJECTS

1. Use the language and literacy curriculum checklist to evaluate a classroom on the communication curriculum. Report on:
   • The classroom's strengths.
   • Some ways that the environment could be improved.
   • What you learned that you might apply to your future teaching.
2. Observe a child for a morning in regard to how she or he communicates. Report on:
   • The ways and circumstances in which the child communicates.
   • How the environment supports the child's development in this area.
   • How the teacher supports this child's development.
   • How the program might be modified to enhance the child's learning.
3. Observe a teacher for a morning and then interview her or him about how she or he teaches language, literacy, and literature. Report on:
   • Activities and routines you saw that contribute to children's learning.
   • Any evidence you saw of teacher planning for communication.
   • The teacher's goals for children in communication.
   • The ways in which what the teacher perceives and what you actually observed match or appear to differ.
4. Write and implement a lesson in language, literature, or literacy using the activity planning form from Chapter 10 (Figure 10.8). Report on how children responded and on how you felt about your teaching. What worked? What might

you do differently next time? How might you expand on this experience for children?

5. Compare two early childhood programs in the communication curriculum. Report on the ways that the two address the area—their similarities and differences. Which program seems to best meet children's needs and why? What implications does this have for your future teaching?

6. Compare two classrooms, one preschool and one for infants and toddlers or for primary-school children. Report on how each enhances children's ability to communicate. Talk to the teachers about how they make their curriculum choices in this area.

BIBLIOGRAPHY

Ashton-Warner, S. 1963. *Teacher*. New York: Simon & Schuster.

Barratta-Lorton, M. 1972. *Workjobs*. Menlo Park, Calif.: Addison-Wesley.

Bissex, G. 1980. *Gnys at Wrk: A Child Learns to Write and Read*. Cambridge, Mass.: Harvard University Press.

Bruner, J. 1983. *Child's Talk: Learning to Use Language*. New York: W. W. Norton.

Bryce-Heath, S. 1983. *Ways with Words: Language, Life and Work in Communities and Classrooms*. New York: Cambridge University Press.

Bryen, D. N. 1971. *Inquiries into Child Language*. Boston: Allyn & Bacon.

Butler, D., and M. Clay. 1983. *Reading Begins at Home*. Portsmouth, N.H.: Heinemann Educational Books.

Cazden, C. B. 1975. Play with Language and Metalinguistic Awareness. In *Dimensions of Language Experience,* ed. C. B. Winsor. New York: Agathon Press.

_____ , ed. 1981. *Language in Early Childhood Education*. rev. ed. Washington, D.C.: National Association for the Education of Young Children.

Chomsky, C. 1971. Write First, Read Later. *Childhood Education* 47(6), 296–299.

Clay, M. M. 1975. *What Did I Write? Beginning Writing Behavior*. Portsmouth, N.H.: Heinemann Educational Books.

Cochran-Smith, M. 1984. *The Making of a Reader*. Norwood, N.J.: Ablex Publishing.

Dumtschin, J. U. 1988. Recognize Language Development and Delay in Early Childhood. *Young Children* 43(3):16–24.

Durkin, D. 1980. Is Kindergarten Reading Instruction Really Desirable? In *Ferguson Lectures in Education, 1980: Lecture Symposium of the 1979–1980 Series*. Evanston, Ill.: National College of Education.

Dyson, A. H. 1988. Appreciate the Drawing and Dictation of Young Children *Young Children* 43(3):25–32.

Ferreiro, E., and A. Tebrosky. 1979. *Literacy Before Schooling,* trans. K. G. Castro. Portsmouth, N.H.: Heinemann Educational Books (translated 1982).

Fields, M. V. 1989. *Literacy Begins at Birth*. Tucson, Arizona: Fisher Books.

Fields, M. V., and D. Lee. 1991. *Let's Begin Reading Right: A Developmental Approach to Beginning Literacy.* 2d ed. Columbus, Ohio: Merrill.

Genishi, C., 1988. Children's Language: Learning Words From Experience. *Young Children* 44(1):16–22.

Genishi, C., and A. H. Dyson. 1984. *Language Assessment in the Early Years.* Norwood, N.J.: Ablex Publishing.

Gonzales-Mena, J. 1981. English as Second Language for Preschool Children. In *Language in Early Childhood.* rev. ed., ed. C. B. Cazden. Washington, D.C.: National Association for the Education of Young Children.

Graves, D. H. 1984. *Writing: Teachers and Children at Work.* Portsmouth, N.H: Heinemann Educational Books.

Hall, M. A. 1981. *Teaching Reading as a Language Experience.* 3d ed. Columbus, Ohio: Merrill.

Harste, J., V. Woodward, and C. Burke. 1984. *Language Stories and Literacy Lessons.* Portsmouth, N.H.: Heinemann Educational Books.

Hubbard, R. 1988. Allow Children's Individuality to Emerge in the Writing: Let Their Voices Through. *Young Children* 43(3):33–38.

Hymes, J. L., Jr. 1958. *Before the Child Reads.* Evanston, Ill.: Row, Peterson.

Jacobs, L. B., ed. 1965. *Using Literature with Young Children.* New York: Teachers College Press.

Jalongo, M. R. 1988. *Young Children and Picture Books: Literature from Infancy to Six.* Washington, D.C.: National Association for the Education of Young Children.

Jones, E., ed. 1988. *Reading, Writing and Talking with Four, Five and Six Year Olds.* Pasadena, Calif.: Pacific Oaks.

Kawamoto, E. 1989. Emergent Literacy. Unpublished manuscript, College of Education. University of Hawaii, Honolulu.

Meek, M. 1982. *Learning to Read.* Portsmouth, N. H.: Heinemann Educational Books.

Moskowitz, A. 1978. The Acquisition of Language. *Scientific American* 239(5):82-96.

Palewicz-Rousseau, P., and L. Madaras. 1979. *The Alphabet Connection.* New York: Schocken Books.

Paley, V. G. 1981. *Wally's Stories.* Cambridge, Mass.: Harvard University Press.

Parker, R. P., and F. A. Davis, eds. 1983. *Developing Literacy: Young Children's Use of Language.* Newark, Del.: International Reading Association.

Pflaum-Conner, S. 1986. *The Development of Language and Reading in Young Children.* 3d ed. Columbus, Ohio: Merrill.

Read, C. 1971. Preschool Children's Knowledge of English Phonology. *Harvard Educational Review* 41(1).

Schikedanz, J. A. 1978. Please Read that Story Again! Exploring Relationships Between Story Reading and Learning to Read. *Young Children* 33(5)48–55.

Sholtys, K. C. 1989. A New Language a New Life. *Young Children* 44(3):76–77.

Sutherland, Z., and M. H. Arbuthnot. 1986. *Children and Books.* 7th ed. Glenview, Ill.: Scott, Foresman.

Teale, W., and E. Sulzby. 1986. *Emergent Literacy: Writing and Reading.* Norwood, N.J.: Ablex Publishing.

Tough, J. 1977a. *The Development of Meaning.* Boston: Allen & Unwin.

_____ . 1977b. *Talking and Learning: A Guide to Fostering Communication Skills in Nursery and Infant Schools.* Portsmouth, N.H.: Heinemann Educational Books.

Vygotsky, L. S. 1962. *Thought and Learning.* Cambridge, Mass.: MIT Press, 1962.

_____ . 1978. *Mind in Society: The Development of Higher Psychological Process.* Cambridge, Mass.: Harvard University Press.

Wells, G. 1981. *Learning Through Interaction: The Study of Language Development.* New York: Cambridge University Press.

Wilkinson, A. 1971. *The Foundations of Language.* London: Oxford University Press.

CHAPTER FOURTEEN

Discovering and Thinking: Curriculum for Cognitive Development

It is little short of a miracle that modern methods of instruction have not already completely strangled the holy curiosity of inquiry, because what this delicate little plant needs most, apart from initial stimulation, is freedom; without that it is surely destroyed.

—*Albert Einstein*

The universe is the child's curriculum.

—*Maria Montessori*

In this chapter we will focus on how the early childhood curriculum can be designed to support children's growing understanding of the world they live in. We discuss inquiry processes that are the building blocks of children's construction of knowledge and how these contribute to concept development. We look at the curriculum areas that are most directly involved with cognitive development: math, science, and social studies. Although the primary focus is on cognitive development, the social studies component has to do, in large part, with social and emotional development as well.

Young children have a compelling curiosity to figure out why and how the world works. They learn by doing—by observing and manipulating concrete materials and interacting with their environment. Through play they acquire and order knowledge. From their earliest months, they observe and identify phenomena, discover relationships, search for answers, and communicate their discoveries. They construct knowledge as they explore, experiment, and act upon their environment. Children are individual in their ability and differ in the way they learn.

Math, science, and social studies extend into every aspect of curriculum and of life. Children inquire and develop concepts as they play and participate in all curriculum activities. Experiences in mathematics, science, and social studies are uniquely suited to the development of thinking and problem solving and are the areas of the curriculum in which cognitive development is a primary emphasis.

A DEVELOPMENTAL PERSPECTIVE

The development of thinking is a fascinating area of child development. The work of Jean Piaget is most enlightening to those interested in this topic because of his careful observations of the characteristic ways that children's thinking and concept development occur. Piaget discovered that children's thinking is very different from the logical thinking of adults and is reliant on direct, repeated sensory experiences. His work has helped educators to understand that children's cognitive development proceeds through stages just like physical development—it is as foolish to attempt to rush a child past a stage of cognitive development as it would be to attempt to teach a crawling infant to jump.

Piaget described three kinds of knowledge. *Physical knowledge,* the knowledge of external reality, is the understanding that is gained from simple interaction with the physical world. For example, by holding and playing with a ball a child learns about its properties—its texture, its shape, its weight, its squishyness, and its tendency to roll away and bounce.

Logico-mathematical knowledge is constructed from direct experience. It is based on comparison and relationship. For example, a child sees similarities between a tennis ball and a playground ball in shape and roll and bounce characteristics, and the child contrasts their differences in size, color, texture, and weight. Through the experience of many balls, the child begins to develop an idea of ball as a single category based on shared characteristics. Logico-mathematical knowledge depends on one's own experience; it is not arbitrary or dependent on others.

The third kind of knowledge is *social knowledge.* As implied in the name, social knowledge depends on what we have learned from others and not on direct experience of objects or events. It is based on what people decide. Balls are used for play, and different kinds of balls are used for different games.

In traditional educational settings teachers have often taught math, science, and social studies as social knowledge. This 8 is called *eight.* The earth goes around the sun. Boise is the capital of Idaho. Piaget's description of cognitive development as constructed knowledge suggests that in order for children to really understand math, science, and social studies, they must have opportunities to explore and act on the real world to establish relationships and construct their own knowledge.

Concept Development

Children's minds and bodies are actively involved in giving meaning to their experiences. Through their activities they develop concepts to help them make sense of their experience. A concept is a mental image or word picture that is communicated in a single word or combination of words—it has a general not a specific meaning. As a child repeatedly experiences the characteristics of an object, animal, person, or event and mentally combines and organizes these, a concept is formed. For example, an infant may have constructed the concept door based on many repeated experiences including a slam, mother returning through this spot, the way to get where you want to go, pinched fingers, a light source at night, and the barrier to what is desired. Concepts are generalized as children recognize the common attributes of objects, people, ideas, and experiences. In the door example the initial concept of door may only refer to the door of the bedroom. As many doors are experienced, the concept is generalized and different doors are recognized: the door of the family car, the door of grandma's house, the automatic door at the supermarket, and finally doors in general. Although the doors differ greatly, the common characteristics are recognized and the concept is established.

A child's ability to understand and develop a concept depends on cognitive maturation and the availability of relevant experiences. Concepts differ in how difficult they are for children to understand. Whether or not a concept is developmentally appropriate for a young child and likely to be understood is related to its degree of abstraction and complexity.

Concepts can be thought of as existing on a continuum from concrete to abstract. The *concreteness* of a concept refers to whether it can be directly experienced or observed. Concrete concepts are accessible to children. They can be experienced through the senses—seen, heard, held, felt, touched, tasted. Concepts that depend on information outside of direct experience are abstract and cannot be completely understood by a young child, regardless of how hard an adult may try to provide the experience through language. This makes events, times, and places that cannot be directly experienced in some way (Africa, World War II) and abstract concepts (justice, liberty) mostly meaningless to young children.

The *complexity* of a concept, the amount of information needed to define it, is the second quality that affects a young child's ability to understand it. Children acquire concepts of low complexity more quickly than those of high complexity. Some concepts are available to children through direct experience but involve many interrelated ideas. These cannot be understood because young children's capacity for creating and retaining connections between such ideas has not yet developed. The concept of wind is both relatively simple and concrete; it is defined primarily by one's experience of it against the skin and its ability to move objects about. The concept of weather, however, is complex and requires the grasp of numerous other supporting concepts including evaporation, wind patterns, cloud formation, low- and high-pressure areas, and precipitation. Young children will not understand the phenomenon of weather because the overall effect requires attending to a variety of attributes simultaneously.

Inquiry Processes

The processes that children use to learn about the world and to construct concepts are referred to as inquiry processes. To inquire means to ask, to discover, to think, to take risks, to make mistakes, and to learn from mistakes. It is not learning correct answers. If we teach science, math, and social studies as predetermined knowledge that children must acquire by rote, then we do not help them to develop higher-level thinking skills or to learn to inquire. Inquiry for young children involves the organization of experiences through exploration. Inquiring children use sight, sound, taste, smell, touch, and the kinesthetic sense to gain general and specific information that will contribute to the development of concepts. Curriculum specialists identify between ten and fifteen distinct inquiry processes, but the few processes listed in the accompanying box apply best to young children who learn from concete experience.

IN THE CLASSROOM: INQUIRY PROCESSES USED BY CHILDREN

- **Exploring:** Using the senses to observe, investigate, and manipulate.
- **Identifying:** Naming and describing what is experienced.
- **Classifying:** Grouping objects or experiences by their common characteristics.
- **Comparing and Contrasting:** Observing similarities and differences between objects or experiences.
- **Hypothesizing:** Using the data from experiences to make guesses (hypotheses) about what might happen.
- **Generalizing:** Applying previous experience to new events.

Role of the Teacher in Cognitive Development

Children approach the world with a sense of wonder and an almost infinite curiosity. The role of the early childhood teacher is to create the climate in which each child can discover the power of ideas and generate concepts about the world. It is important to be responsive to children and open to the many aspects of life about which they are curious.

Although all children are curious and actively try to understand the world, it is possible to destroy the delicate flower of inquiry. Children continue to learn and inquire when they are encouraged to be autonomous and to ask questions. If, instead, they are convinced that they should memorize without thinking and digest facts because they have been fed to them by an authority, then they lose their curiosity. This is the great danger of teaching what we know instead of encouraging children to find out on their own. To help children to question, to inquire, you must accept and encourage autonomy. In exchange you will gain active, eager learners who think and reason instead of learning by rote.

For thinking and problem solving to take place you must provide a learning environment that is both stimulating and reasonably ordered. There must be space, interesting equipment and materials, and lots of time to explore how things work and to develop and test ideas. Activities that stimulate inquiry and lead to concept development need to be carefully planned. When you design curriculum experiences, you will want to think about the developmental appropriateness of the concepts to be learned.

Many kinds of learning cannot take place within the confines of the classroom. The world beyond the school walls provides more than a pleasant vacation from school routine. It is vital for children to see and experience the real world. This is particularly true if you work in a setting where children's experiences have been limited. A teacher friend of ours in another state recently took her class to see the ocean—a two-hour bus trip that had never been made before by the majority of the poor, inner-city first-graders. At the shore one of the children came to her barely able to speak he was so excited, saying, "Robin! . . . Water! . . . Sand! . . . Moving!" He had not known that the ocean moved. His understanding of ocean and shore would have been mere social knowledge without this direct experience. It takes effort to take children beyond the school. Learning trips can take extra personnel, money, and special planning. They are worth the effort.

Communication That Supports Inquiry

Talking with children as they explore and discover is one of the most important things you will do in the cognitive areas of your program. Skilled teachers target their comments, questions, and activities to make optimal use of the natural curiosity of children. You can make statements about your own wonder and curiosity. Supportive comments on the discoveries and explorations of children encourage further inquiry. Questions help children to notice detail, make comparisons, and come to conclusions. For example, if several children are exploring what happens when one of them narrows a faucet with a finger, making the water spray out, you might comment: "I wonder what makes that happen? You found a way to change the water flow. Can you make it come out slower (faster)? What do you have to do to change it? Why do you think that happens?"

Teachers express a sense of curiosity about and appreciation of the world in statements like, "I wonder why the clouds are moving so quickly?" "Look at how different each shell is." "The baskets all nest together, the little ones inside the big ones." "I wonder why cats purr—I wish I could." "The mother bear is looking after her cubs—every mother seems to do that." "I can feel the rabbit's heart beating quickly and hard—I wonder how she's feeling?" Statements like these model an inquiring mind. They help children to form concepts but do not hand them pre-formed ideas.

Children learn to inquire and become active problem solvers when they are encouraged and supported in doing so. They need to understand that it is acceptable not to have an answer or to have the "wrong" answers. Giving information is not your most important role. Facts about the world pronounced by teachers often deprive children of the opportunity to learn through inquiry. For example, we once observed a child who found a praying mantis and eagerly asked his teacher what it ate so that it could be kept alive. The teacher admitted that she did not know but asked, "How can we find out?" This resourceful four-year-old questioned other adults and finally looked through a book about insects in the science area and found a photo-graph of a praying mantis. He took it to his teacher and she read to the group about the dining habits of this insect. They proceeded to feed the praying mantis on ants and beetles. Had the teacher simply said, "It eats bugs," the learning would have been much less meaningful to the child.

Open-ended questions encourage children to think. They say to the child, "Tell me more." Questions are open when they can be answered in a number of different ways and have more than one correct answer. You can develop skill in asking open questions by practicing until you can ask them with comfort. The following are the beginning phrases of some open-ended questions:

• What do you see? (hear, feel, smell)
• How are these the same? (different)
• What do you think about . . .?

- How do you know . . .?
- What do you think would happen if . . .?
- How do you think we could find out . . .?

A closed question has only one correct or acceptable answer, for example, "What color is this bead?" "Is this a circle?" Closed questions are often useful for learning whether children have acquired a concept or piece of information, but they do not stimulate inquiry. In most classrooms, teachers use a mixture of open and closed questions. The kind of mix is influenced by values, objectives, and the nature of the particular situation. Awareness of the purpose of each type of question can help you to make conscious choices about which to use. If you wish to stimulate children to inquire, you will ask many open-ended questions.

The silence that a teacher allows between statements or questions is also an important factor in how children respond. Researchers have found that three to five seconds is the average amount of silence that occurs between teacher questions and the child's response or a follow-up comment from the teacher. They found that if the teacher waits only one or two seconds, one-word responses are most frequent. If the wait lasts for several seconds longer, children respond with whole sentences and complex thoughts that represent more creativity and increased speculativeness. (Costa 1974, p. 60)

MATHEMATICS CURRICULUM

Mathematics is a way to structure experience to form ideas and concepts about the quantitative, logical, and spatial relationships between things, people, and events. During the early childhood years, young children come to think of themselves as part of a community of people who use number to order and communicate about their world. In the same way that young children will pretend to write and read, they will label

distance and ages with numbers ("My doll is twenteen." "It's thirty-fifty miles.").

The development of mathematical thinking is a long process that consists of far more than simply knowing how to count and manipulate numbers in computations. Math concepts cannot be taught. They must be constructed. How is not fully understood. Like the development of language, these concepts appear to evolve as children mature and have many experiences with the real world. Adults make assumptions about what children know and about what they need to know based on adult understanding of practical skills such as using money, balancing a checkbook, and reading a clock. Children's thinking, needs, and development, however, are different.

The conceptual underpinnings of practical skills are based on many years of concrete experiences that may not seem to relate to mathematics. Concepts such as more and fewer, far and near, similar and different, short and tall, now and later, first and last, over and under, precede later mastery of complex mathematical concepts. Teachers participate by providing an environment, materials, and activities that support children's inquiry into math.

Appropriate Math Concepts for Young Children

The work of Piaget and others has led to an investigation of the kinds of math concepts children are capable of grasping and the ways they can best acquire them. Young children develop concepts of classification, space, number, measurement, ordering (seriation), patterning, and time. The discovery of what young children can learn has led to a rethinking of the traditional content of the math curriculum. The curriculum should lead toward the ability to think logically and to creatively solve problems found in daily life. Counting and shape and numeral recognition are no longer considered sufficient content for a preschool or kindergarten math program.

Many misconceptions exist about what number is in the early childhood years. Most adults assume that the ability to count and understanding of number are the same thing. This is not true. Being able to count reflects the ability to memorize and mimic certain behaviors (touching and saying a number). It is a rote activity unless the child has a concept of number (oneness, twoness, threeness, and so on). Only then does the child understand that the name represents a specific quantity. A parent of our acquaintance proudly told us that her four-year-old child "knew" numbers up to twenty. Indeed, the child could recite the words *one, two, three,* and so forth in proper order. When asked to point to a stack of six blocks from among several piles of six or less, she could not choose the stack of six. Despite her rote counting skill, she clearly demonstrated that sixness was not a concept she understood.

Children only gradually come to really understand number despite rather easily learning to count using number names in the correct order. They use counting as a reliable tool when

underlying number concepts are in place—usually around the age of seven. Children do not understand number until they understand:

- There is a one-to-one correspondence between each number name and an object in the set being counted.
- The number name applies not only to the last object named but also to the entire set of objects.
- Other number names mean more or less than the number.
- Number is the same regardless of what objects are counted.
- The physical arrangement of the objects does not influence how many there are.

Numeral recognition is a visual-perceptual task that is unrelated to the concept represented by the numeral. Until children develop the number concept and understand that the word represents the concept, they are not able to understand the meaning of the symbol. Numerals and their names are social knowledge—useful for communicating once the underlying concept is in place. Although young children may appear to be reading numerals, a closer look at their understanding will usually demonstrate that they are naming the shape of the numeral rather than understanding the number concept. Children who are beginning to identify numerals and letters, for example, often add these to their paintings and drawings because they enjoy their new-found ability to identify and make these shapes—they are design elements rather than symbols for quantity or sound.

The practice of memorizing shape names (triangle, circle, square, and so on) is a sensory-perceptual and labeling task that is a minor part of helping children develop an understanding about the relationships between physical objects in the world. Children are learning about shape and space as they experience position, distance, boundaries, and shapes in relation to their world.

Each of these experiences represents a particular kind of learning. Because they are so limited and are generally taught without connection to the larger world of mathematics, they do not help children gain the concepts that are needed for later mathematical and logical thought.

Children are discovering math concepts in the course of the ordinary activities and routines of classroom living. You can help them develop these concepts by providing a math-rich environment in which each child has the raw materials needed for understanding important mathematical concepts and relationships. You also can plan specific activities to give children a broad range of math experiences.

Framework for Organizing the Content

The math content of our childhoods—addition and subtraction facts—is no longer regarded as a good foundation for children's learning about mathematics. What then is the content that young children need to help them make sense of the physical and social world and to help them understand abstract mathematical concepts later in their school careers?

Classification is one of the ways that we organize and understand daily life. It is an important skill for children to learn. To classify means to sort or group people, objects, ideas, or events by shared characteristics. When children understand that they can group things together based on the ways they are alike and exclude them based on the ways that they are different (negation, or "not like"), they have developed the basic concept of classification. Objects that are grouped together are considered to be part of a set. As they become more sophisticated and flexible in the categories they use, children are developing a more profound understanding of classification. Children are learning to group things according to their common attributes when they hang dresses up, place all the dishes in the cupboard, put all the large beads in a basket and all the small beads in a can, and sort buttons by size, shape, color, number of holes, or type of shank.

Space involves the way one object or set of objects relates to others based on position, direction, and distance. Children develop concepts about space as they notice the relationship of their bodies to other people and objects and when they observe spatial relationships between people and objects. The concept of position may be developed in day-to-day activities such as putting away the blocks—the long ones on the bottom shelf and the short ones on the top shelf. The concept of direction may be discovered as a child first drives a tricycle forward and then backward. When a child kicks a ball to a nearby child and then to a faraway child, the concept of distance is being explored.

Number refers to ideas that concern quantity and order. Number is actually several complex, related concepts. *Quantity,* or the amount, is what we usually think of when we refer to number. A *set* of objects has a certain quantity that is unchanging and unrelated to the physical act of touching and naming ("1,2,3") the objects. Children can learn to compare quantity and to determine more, less, fewer, or the same amounts. Learning to comprehend position (first, second, third, and so forth) is another number concept. *One-to-one correspondence* is a precursor of counting and understanding of number. Children must first learn that objects matched one for one (for example, a napkin for each person) share the same quantity before they can understand number.

Young children learn about number by exploring and describing arrangements and combinations of objects. Repeated opportunities to use many kinds of objects in play and in practical life situations are important, so that children can manipulate and talk about number and so that they begin to understand that number is unrelated to specific objects and instead is a tool to describe and understand the world.

Measurement is the process of comparing size, volume, weight, or quantity to a standard. Adults use numerically expressed standards such as meters, ounces, or dollars. Measurement is a practical part of math that we use with children informally all the time. ("We need three cups of flour in this dough recipe." "I bet you grew two inches last month." "We need another foot of ribbon.") Measurement for children is making comparisons of things in their immediate environment. Children discover the concept of measurement when they experiment to find out how many unit blocks equal the width of the carpet, count how many cups of water fill a large container at the water table, or compare their height to the heights of their friends and teachers. Children need experience comparing *length, mass* (heavy or light), *capacity,* and *temperature.* Older children will also begin to use *money*—another, more abstract, standard.

Seriation takes place when objects are ordered in a sequence based on a difference in the degree of some quality such as size, weight, texture, or shading. Children gain experience in seriating when they arrange things in their environment, for example, themselves from shortest to tallest, balls from smallest to largest, or color chips from palest to darkest.

Patterning is another form of ordering based on repetition. When children create bead necklaces with alternating colors, arrange parquetry blocks, or sing the chorus after every verse of a song, they are experiencing patterns.

Time concepts develop as children notice the *sequence* of events in their daily lives; for example, lunch is always followed by rest time, and a story about zoo animals is read before a visit to the zoo. *Duration* is another time-related concept. Children begin to understand as they notice such things as outdoor play lasting a long time in comparison to book time which lasts for a short period.

Geometry refers to the properties of two- and three-dimensional objects and their properties. Children know a great deal about geometry by interacting with the world. Geometry in early childhood education is a real-world experience. Children can identify how objects are similar and different in shapes and properties. As they manipulate blocks, puzzles, games, and toys, they are learning about geometry.

The Environment

A math area equipped with carefully chosen equipment and materials can encourage children to experiment and thus discover many math concepts. Purchased equipment like attribute blocks (regular shapes which vary in size, thickness, and color), Cuisenaire rods (small colored blocks that are numerically related), colored cubes, pegboards, measuring tools, and seriation materials like stacking cups are designed to enhance math learning. Unit blocks provide excellent experiences for the development of number, spatial, seriation, and classification concepts. Computer programs are starting to be developed that provide math experiences for young children that are more than rote drill.

Some allow children to program and some provide experience with patterning, seriation, and number. Computers can be very motivating, and if the software is thoughtfully and appropriately designed, computers can supplement an experience-based math program for young children.

Teacher-made activities like button sorting, lotto games, and matching activities foster mathematical learning. Good sources for ideas for teacher made math games are Mary Barratta-Lorton's books *Workjobs* (1972), *Workjobs II* (1979), and *Math Their Way* (1976) and Lalie Harcourt's *Explorations* (1990). Math learning opportunities occur throughout the classroom and the program day. Manipulative games, water play with measuring cups and containers, dramatic play areas, outdoor exploration where spatial concepts like top-bottom, in-out, and up-down are experienced all teach mathematical concepts.

Teaching

Even though you cannot directly teach math concepts, you *can* support children as they discover them for themselves. It is important for you to notice when and how mathematics is meaningful to the children you teach. A child who is comparing and arranging things in sets and using ideas of quantity is providing you with important information. When children do these things, you can add additional activities and ask stimulating questions that will provide opportunities to help them learn.

You support children in their development of math concepts by encouraging them to be aware of the ways that many kinds of things (objects, actions, and events) relate to one another—snack comes before circle time; fish, birds, and mice are all alive; grown-ups are bigger than children; running is faster than walking.

Children may begin to be aware of math when you use math ideas in your conversations, "Would you like your cracker whole or in two

pieces?" Set math tasks and ask children questions: "Which beads do you think belong together? Why?" "Can you find a doll that is smaller than this one but larger than this one?" "Can you cover the mat with blocks? What kind will you use? Why?" "How many cubes do you think will fit along the side of the box?" Help children by encouraging them to question, to think, and to share ideas with one another. Ask questions about math (Do you have as many as I do?) and be prepared to forego questioning when children do not appear interested.

Providing children with many opportunities to manipulate objects, including those made as "math" teaching equipment (like Unifix cubes or Cuisenaire rods) and other equipment that lends itself to mathematical relationships (like blocks and button collections) supports the development of math concepts. Children also learn about math in their relationships with their peers. With other children they will be challenged ("You got more than me!" "I don't want to be second!") and they will need to work out mathematical problems in meaningful and concrete ways.

The world and our daily lives are filled with math. Children can become math conscious. Talking about time, dates, ages, amounts, size, money, and other math ideas is both natural and a necessary preparation for later understanding. Children who have a background with the concrete experiences upon which math is based come to see themselves as individuals who use number and measurement as important tools in daily life.

Children learn about math as they handle the routines of the day. When each child has one cracker and rests on one mat, one-to-one correspondence is experienced. As children learn the sequence of the daily schedule, learn to pour half a glass of milk, or learn to cut their apples in two parts, they are using math. These are only a sample of the potential of the total school environment for exploring math concepts. Look closely at exactly how your classroom supports math learning, so you can better evaluate what you might do to expand and enrich the existing possibilities.

Adapting for Different Ages

The development of math concepts is clearly a developmental process. While a "doing" approach to math is appropriate throughout the early childhood years, what children are doing will vary.

Infants and *toddlers* are learning about math throughout their waking moments. An infant reaches and touches a mobile and learns about space and distance. A toddler gives one floppy toy dog to each parent and learns about quantity. Fitting a block into a sorting box is a lesson in geometry. Using the category "moo" to describe all the large four-footed animals seen in a field and "bowwow" to describe all the small furry animals around the house is a sorting experience. Trying to wear daddy's or the doll's shoe is an experience in measurement. We provide lots of math experiences for infants and toddlers. They learn math by being free to explore in their natural, instinctive way. You can support them in this self-initiated exploration and observe with amazement and appreciation the way that human beings learn math.

Primary-school children are eager to learn to use math in the practical ways that grown-ups do. They, too, want to be competent in making number, measurement, and time work for them. They also continue to need the base in real experience with sand, water, blocks, and manipulative toys. Primary-school children can start to use math in real life. For example, in cooking they can use standard measurement and note its usefulness. Just as young children needed repeated experience of three things to comprehend threeness, older children need many opportunities to manipulate sets of twelve things to comprehend that twelve really breaks down into sets of three and four. Otherwise, like one of the authors of this text, they may believe until adulthood that multiplication tables are magic formulas to be memorized and not simple aspects of reality to be understood.

SCIENCE CURRICULUM

In early childhood programs, science is the process of exploring the earth and the creatures that live upon it in ways that young children can understand. Science, like play, is an active and involving process. When children play they think fluently. Rebecca Severeide and Edward Pizzini in their article The Role of Play in Science (1984) compare play and science:

> Play is fanciful, divergent, and subjective. Scientific inquiry is logical, linear, systematic, and objective. Yet scientists often solve problems most effectively and innovatively when they pursue solutions in the spirit of play. (p. 58)

For many adults science is a scary, mysterious field involving a collection of facts and complex concepts that are only learned from a manual in a lab. For others it is specific information that adults know and that must be told to children. Teachers who have maintained their own playfulness and enthusiasm for science view it as a process of exploration and experimentation through which they and children together find out about the world. These teachers work with children to figure out how to learn the answers to questions through observation, research, or experimentation.

One of the ways science educators help us to remember that science is indeed an active process is by renaming it "sciencing." Sciencing is active; it implies trying things—things that work and things that do not work. It means a joyful risk-taking approach to learning.

Framework for Organizing the Content

Although it is not necessary to be a scientist or to know a great deal of scientific information to offer science experiences in your classroom, you do need to appreciate the value of science and be aware of subject matter suitable for young children. Science for young children can, and should, be much more than a fish tank and a rock collection in a corner of the classroom.

The science curriculum can be divided into two broad categories: *biological,* or *life science,* and *physical science.* Like other curricula for young children, science is not isolated or clearly divided into separate subjects.

Biological or Life Science

Children are naturally curious about living things: what they are, how they live, their life cycles. The way things move and change makes them intriguing and renews children's interest. Many concepts basic to the fields of biology, physiology, and ecology are explored, discovered, and validated by young children in their daily lives.

We call the study of plants and animals— their structure, origin, growth and reproduction—*biology.* The young child is filled with wonder about where the butterfly came from, how a bean grew into a plant, how the bulging mother mouse got the babies inside her, and why the dog has four legs and the spider has eight. The raw materials for the study of biology abound in and around the classroom. Biology is an integral part of every young child's life. As you work with children, you will help them to observe, compare, and contrast living things and to ask questions about what they see. As children observe the transformation of a caterpillar into a butterfly, the seed into a plant, and the pregnant mouse into a family, they are having concrete experiences with reproduction, growth, and change.

Physiology is the science dealing with the functions of living organisms or their parts. Physiological concepts are directly accessible to young children. Starting with their own bodies, they notice functions such as breath, movement, sensation, and digestion. Interest in their own

growth can lead children to explore and learn about physiological structures such as bone and muscle systems. Children's fascination with their own bodies and with animals at home, in the classroom, and in nature can be used as the springboard to further discovery.

Ecology is the science of the relationships between living things, their environments and each other. We are dependent on the resources of the earth for survival and, consequently, we have responsibility for them. We are teaching ecology when we help children understand that animals and people need clean air and water and a safe, healthy environment and that they can participate in taking care of the environment. Ecology can be taught to young children as you read, observe, and talk about the animals and plants in your environment; as you observe how people affect the environment (for example, noticing where people have trodden the grass away or where they have planted a garden); as you observe how garbage is collected and disposed of; and as you notice the effects of litter. A visit to the zoo to see animals that are in danger of extinction, and for older children to learn about the kinds of habitats the endangered animals need and how they are threatened, also teaches a lesson in ecology.

Physical Science

The study of matter, form, and change is called physical science. Children explore and observe the properties of the earth, the sky, and matter, for example, reactions to temperature and force and interactions. Concepts basic to physics, geology, and chemistry are experienced and explored by young children in the course of daily activity. Children's curiosity is aroused by these subjects when they have personal impact.

Physics is the study of matter, energy, motion, and force. When children explore speed, leverage, balance, gravity, and mechanical systems, they are experiencing physics. Children first become aware of the physical properties of the world through exploratory play. A toy is dropped and falls to the floor. An unbalanced pile of blocks collapses. A rock dropped into a puddle makes rings of ripples. It takes many repeated experiences such as these for children to grasp that they are predictable phenomena which can be generalized. These are children's first physics experiments.

Chemistry deals with the composition, properties, and transformations of substances. Children are experiencing chemistry when they watch their dough disintegrate in the water table, see the oil separate from the rest of the salad dressing, and observe the interaction of vinegar and baking soda. Cooking provides opportunities to observe chemical transformation through the use of heat, moisture, and the combination of substances. Chemistry for young children does not mean combining magical powders that are unrelated to daily living, instead it is the exploration of the commonplace.

Geology is the scientific study of the origin, history, and structure of the earth. Children experience geology as they observe and discuss the common features of the earth such as mountains, rocks, and fossils. They are experiencing geology when they ask questions such as "Where does the sand come from?" "What made the mountains?" "Why did all the dirt wash away in the rainstorm?" As children walk over hills and look at the layers of rock formations, they are experiencing geology. Young children's concepts of geology are limited to what they have experienced repeatedly.

Astronomy is the science that has to do with the universe beyond the earth's atmosphere— the sun, moon, planets, and stars. Although young children do not have a hands-on experience of astronomy, they do note the cycle of day and night, the heat of the sun, the waxing and waning of the moon, and the stars in the sky. They are exposed to media concerning space through television, movies, and books. Fantasy and fact are intertwined and are difficult for children to separate in this age of space explo-

ration and satellites. Children will be curious about these phenomena, and school can give them a place to talk and read about astronomy and the exploration of space. The most accessible astronomical phenomena—the cycles of the sun and the moon—can sometimes be observed during the program day.

The Environment

The environment of the school affects the scope and variety of the science curriculum. An outdoor play area with trees, grass, sand, dirt, water,

bugs, and other creatures provides a laboratory for science experiences. Earthworms dug from the ground, insects discovered beneath the overturned rock, and seedlings growing after a rain are ideal starting places for exploring living things. Children on a seesaw may discover concepts about balance and leverage. The frozen water puddle in the early morning that melts by noon and is miraculously gone as children leave for home provides a chemistry lesson. If you look and listen to children as they interact in the outdoor environment, they will provide you with many ideas for science experiences that you can explore together.

A science area in the classroom can be a laboratory for teacher-initiated activities and child discoveries. If an earthworm is brought into the area, a science problem is posed: what does this creature need to survive? Together, children and teachers may solve the problem based on their observations or by referring to books or resource people. Tools and materials for exploration can be stored in a science area: magnifying glasses, magnets, dissection equipment, trays, bug boxes, animal cages, tools for manipulating and taking apart a clock or radio, and measuring equipment like scales and rulers. The area can include ongoing projects such as aquariums, terrariums, animal families, and plants. Learning materials, such as a sink and float game, and picture collections for sorting and describing may be stored and used in the science area. The area can also contain science reference books.

Some appropriate and worthwhile science experiences require moving beyond the school setting. Science learning trips can be as simple as a nature walk in the neighborhood or can be more elaborate trips to locations like the zoo, aquarium, preserve, farm, museum of natural science, forest, seashore, or mountains. Whether your trips are nearby and spontaneous or more distant and carefully planned, they will promote more science learning if there is enough time for children to learn by discovery. This is facilitated by allowing small, unrushed groups of children to visit sites where they can explore and discuss experiences as they occur.

Teaching

Your main teaching role in science must be the preservation and encouragement of the natural curiosity of children. To maintain children's attitude of playfulness toward science, you need to view children's difficult questions as an opportunity to model the attitudes of the scientist: curiosity, questioning, willingness to explore and solve problems.

Children's natural curiosity is the beginning place for your science curriculum, but it is not the end. The framework described provides you with a tool for thinking about the kinds of experiences you will provide. Children should have experience with both biological and physical science areas.

When there is a subject about which children are interested, you can plan specific activities. We have observed teachers and children conducting experiments on the needs of seedlings (what happens if one is kept in the dark?), the effect of time on a carrot, keeping track of the progress of monarch caterpillars, and composting garbage to make soil for a garden.

When science inquiry opportunities occur in planned or spontaneous activities, you can guide children's curiosity and help turn a pleasant experience into one that has deeper learning potential. For example, a small group of children looking at a squirmy family of baby mice will be delighted by their tiny pinkness and their mother's felicitous care. They may not spontaneously realize that the babies are seeking milk, that their eyes are closed, or that these babies are like many other babies, including themselves in some ways. To encourage thinking and concept development ask children questions such as "Why do you suppose the baby mice were squirming?" "What do you think will happen if their mother goes and runs on the wheel?" "What do the babies remind you of?" Part of your role is to find just the right resource (a person or a book) to expand the children's knowledge. As you model an inquiring and respectful attitude toward the world, you help children to become scientists. Science, rather than being scary or mysterious, is everyday, accessible, infinitely interesting, and definitely worth knowing.

Your own spirit of scientific inquiry will affect what is learned and the attitudes that children develop about science. We once observed a group of children and a teacher who were fascinated and curious about an animal skeleton they had found along the side of the road. They took the bones back to the classroom for further exploration. Another teacher responded to their find with repulsion. Fortunately, the group's teacher was not deterred and they spent several days examining, reassembling the skeleton, counting the bones and teeth, and figuring out that it had been a dog—a wonderful lesson in scientific inquiry!

Adapting for Different Ages

All young children are natural scientists. Their play is full of exploration. This is true for an infant who is learning about physiology as she first discovers her toe. It also is true for a second-grader who is catching tadpoles after school. The task for teachers of younger and older children is to recognize what is most appropriate sciencing for the stage of development and interests of the children.

Infants and *toddlers* seek many repeated experiences with the world to develop a foundation of understanding. The infant who drops his bottle from his high chair is exploring physics as is the toddler who plays endlessly with the water faucet. The great majority of science learning occurs as a matter of course when infants and toddlers interact with the environment. When you pay extra attention to what very young children are experiencing, you can enhance this learning. Infants and toddlers explore physiology as you play games with fingers, touch and name body parts, and talk about eating, drinking, digestion, elimination, breathing, and sleeping ("You drank a lot of water and now your tummy is really full." "The cold water feels good going down." "Sheila has toes and Max has toes. Everybody has toes!"). In programs for infants and toddlers special care needs to be taken to making the living plants and animals accessible to view and safe for and from children. Sensory activities like playing with sand and water provide opportunities for beginning experiences with physics, chemistry, and geology.

Primary-school children can continue to experience sciencing as play. This is quite different from a traditional model in which children may do hands-on experiments only to duplicate the results in the textbook rather than to explore and find out. Selma Wasserman and George Ivany in their lovely book on science curriculum, *Teaching Elementary Science: Who's Afraid of Spiders?* (1988), describe what they refer to as the *play-debrief-replay* model for teaching sciencing. In this method the teacher sets up a science play center with materials to explore. Children "play," explore the materials freely; "debrief," discuss what they have done with a teacher who assists them in reflecting on what they have observed; and then "replay," try it again with the same materials. If you are fearful of such an open approach to science remember you can begin with materials that are very safe and that make very little mess as children are learning to be self-sufficient. As you and the children become more experienced, you can take greater risks and have greater learning adventures.

SOCIAL STUDIES CURRICULUM

The social studies curriculum for young children concerns relationships among people and between people and their environment. In early childhood classrooms the social studies can and do include a myriad of topics related to the social (and sometimes behavioral) sciences.

Although there is general agreement today among early childhood educators that social studies can be taught in meaningful ways to young children, there is little consensus regarding content and organization.

Many adults remember social studies as dull subjects unrelated to the real world and requiring the memorization of dates, names, and places. Learning was fragmented and the usefulness of the content in people's lives was not made clear. Others have memories of interesting and exciting social studies experiences, which suggests that the subject matter can be taught in pleasant and memorable ways. Adults' recollections may vary so much because a number of different fields are included in what we call social studies and there is a wide range of methods by which subjects are taught.

We have found that when properly communicated, the social studies can help children to see some of the significant patterns in their lives and to explore topics that are of interest to them. Social studies can include their own feelings, family, community, locale, and personal history. The subject matter is not to be studied in isolation but as a part of their lives—an exploration of who they are. It can be a source of vital and exciting school experiences.

Through social studies young children can have important learning experiences:

- They begin to learn about and accept themselves.
- They begin to learn about and accept others.
- They gain understanding of the people and relationships around them.
- They become acquainted through direct experience with concepts from a number of different social science fields.

Like math and science, social studies concepts are learned best when they are lived. It may take more thought and planning to provide direct experiences with social studies than it does to put out math manipulatives or magnets and animals in the science corner. Social studies involve taking children out into the world of people and relationships or bringing the world to them.

Frameworks for Organizing the Content

Social studies content can be organized in many ways. In fact, it seems that it is rarely approached exactly the same way. Three approaches that are often used are the expanding horizons model, organization by disciplines, and organization by social and political concepts.

The Expanding Horizons Approach

Traditionally, social studies content for elementary-school children was organized around a pattern called the expanding horizons approach (see Figure 14.1). It assumed that children's experiences with social studies should begin with things close to home that can be directly experienced and gradually move to include topics less close to home—the child's state, nation, and the world.

This model has merit because it starts with the child and what appears to be directly experienced. Children in the 1990s, however, often have much more information and direct contact with the world beyond the home and school, and they may be constrained by this

approach. Nevertheless, the approach is still reflected in most social studies textbook series for elementary programs.

Social Science Disciplines Approach

The social studies encompass many fields. As subject matter in an early childhood program, social studies can contain aspects of a number of social and behavioral sciences. The goal is to provide beginning experiences with key concepts of these disciplines.

Anthropology is the study of the way people live in different cultures. Every person lives in and comes from a culture. Young children can easily see that cultural heritage is defined in differences: foods, dwellings, clothes, languages, beliefs, music, and dances. With guidance they can learn about the similarities—our common humanity. Members of all cultures have language, rituals, and celebrations and provide their members with food, shelter, protection, and clothing. Children can become aware of and develop pride in their own cultural heritage while learning that differences contribute to a society that is rich and interesting. By comparing and contrasting what is familiar with what is less well known, we can help children to understand that people want and need similar things and have different ways of meeting those needs. By looking at differences as valuable and interesting, we help children to accept diversity.

Families of culturally diverse groups of children we have worked with have taught us about their cultures by sharing items of clothing and other special artifacts, as well as by teaching us songs, dances, language, and recipes. As the culmination of one study, the children illustrated a book of recipes from the many different cultures and gave it as a holiday gift to the families. Children experienced that although there were differences among cultures, these differences were ways of caring for similar needs: a futon and a bed were both comfortable places to sleep; chopsticks, forks, and fingers

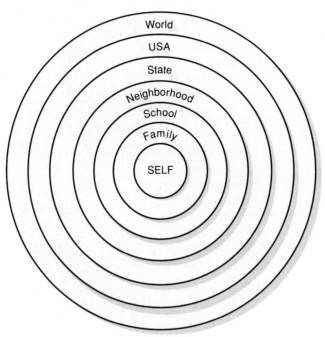

FIGURE 14.1
Expanding Horizons Approach

were all good tools for getting food to the mouth; a kilt, a kimono, and a lavalava all covered bodies and were fun to dress up in. As the parents participated, children began to understand that this special part of them added to who they were and that culture enriched us all.

Economics is the study of how groups of people consume, produce, and deliver goods and services. For young children economics means: all people need and want things (food, clean water, clean air, safe homes, clothing, medical care, work, education, transportation, entertainment); people work to get the things they want and need; there is not always enough for people to have everything they want and need. When we divide the leftover snack among all of the children who want some, when we limit the number of children who can use a highly attractive toy; and when we pay bus fare to go on the bus or purchase ingredients for cooking at the local supermarket, we are teach-

ing young children about economics. In preschool and primary classrooms sociodramatic play of stores, restaurants, and so on provide opportunities to develop concepts about economics.

Geography is the study of earth and its features and the effects of human activity. Geographers today organize their field into several major areas.[1] Those that can be taught in meaningful ways to young children include the following: (1) *location* which addresses the questions where is it and why is it there; (2) *place* which looks at the question what is it like—those physical and human characteristics that make the place special; (3) *human-environment interactions* which look at how people adapt to a place and how they change it as well;

---

[1]This material is taken from Diana Ginsburg's M.Ed. project called Geography in Early Childhood Education.

and (4) *movement/spatial interactions* which address the questions of how we depend upon people in other places and how the transportation of goods and people affect our lives. Young children can also begin to develop the most important tool of geographers, the ability to make and use maps.

Many familiar preschool activities can provide a foundation for developing geographic concepts and skills. As we take trips into the world beyond the school walls and represent what we have seen through maps, photographs, and drawings, we are studying geography. Children are also learning about geography as they learn to closely observe the geographic features of their environment. We have seen young children study geography by mapping their school in their world with blocks or on paper (see Figure 14.2), taking a trip to the harbor, creating imaginary islands out of papier-maché, examining relief maps, and looking at a globe to see where a child was going on a vacation.

History is the study of the events that make up the past of humankind. Teachers of young children often attempt to teach history through songs and crafts. Although making a Pilgrim hat and singing a song about Abraham Lincoln may be directly experienced, they have little to do with teaching history and cannot be understood by young children in any meaningful way. The story of Lincoln may not be teachable to most four-year-olds, but they can learn about history—the history of their own classroom or family or the story of their own birth.

Teaching history to young children involves making them aware of the passage of time and how time affects plants, animals, and people. Children experience the duration of time as they discuss the sequence of events for the day or wait for bread to come out of the oven. A weekly trip past a garden or a construction site gives clear evidence of the changes that take place over time. Looking at their own baby pictures lends dramatic credence to the idea that time affects them. Children also learn that everything

and everyone has a history—a story of what happened before. We can help children to learn their own history: "What happened on the day you were born?" "What did your Mommy do when she was your age?" "Remember when we went to the aquarium?" Making group books, taking classroom photos, and encouraging children's families to share their stories about the child's past are good ways to teach history to young children.

Psychology is the study of mind, emotion, and behavior. Young children can come to understand that all people have feelings both pleasant and unpleasant, that there are many different feelings, that feelings are natural and acceptable (both their own and those of other people), and that everyone has much the same feelings but sometimes for different reasons. They can learn that when we experience negative feelings, it is important to talk about them rather than to hurt other people on the outside or ourselves on the inside. In a related area, teachers help children learn to distinguish fantasy from reality—an important task of the early childhood years. Unlike adults, young children are open about their feelings and fantasies. In play, in stories, in songs, and in discussions you can develop ideas about feelings and fantasies in age-appropriate ways. Dictating and acting out stories are some of the activities you can use to help children to express feelings and understand fantasy.

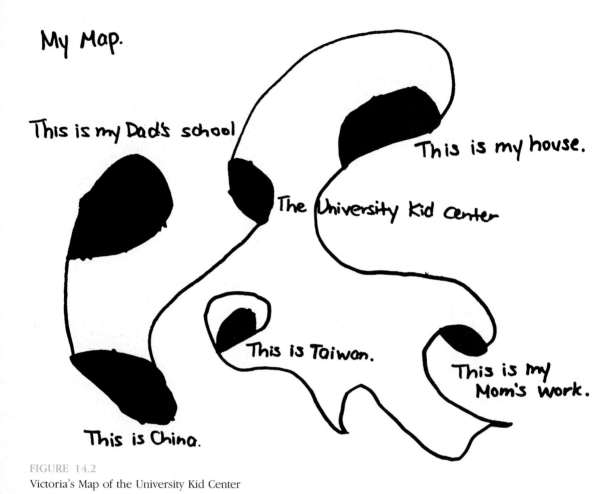

My Map.

This is my Dad's school

This is my house.

The University Kid Center

This is Taiwan.

This is my Mom's work.

This is China.

FIGURE 14.2
Victoria's Map of the University Kid Center

Sociology is the study of human society, its development and organization. For young children it includes the study of the ways that people live together in communities like schools and neighborhoods and the ways that they make decisions and rules and the reasons for those rules. Sociology is being taught when groups of five-year-olds talk about and vote on what the classroom rules will be; when groups of four-year-olds divide up classroom chores on the basis of what is fair; when groups of three-year-olds take turns in suggesting songs for the group to sing; and when groups of two-year-olds learn to keep helping with cleanup until it's all done.

Social and Political Concepts Approach

There is a good deal of interest today in teaching young children the social and political concepts that have an impact on our lives. This social studies content goes well beyond the traditional disciplines and includes topics such as understanding feelings; awareness of aging, the elderly, and death; caretaking and compassion; developing a positive self-concept; learning about disabilities; racial differences; cultural differences; resisting stereotyping; and cooperation and conflict resolution. Many books can help you to address this important part of your curriculum. Some that we have found helpful are *Anti-Bias Curriculum* (Derman-Sparks 1989), *Social and Moral Development in Young Children* (Edwards 1986), *Learning to Be Peaceful Together* (Hopkins, Winters, and Winters, n.d.), and *Diversity in the Classroom* (Kendall 1983).

The Environment

Social studies content can contribute to wonderful and interesting classroom environments. You will not have a special area for social studies, though the block and dramatic play areas are important places for children to act upon themes from the social studies. Writing and art areas in which children can record and report their experiences are important to social studies as is a well-stocked library with many carefully selected books that will enhance and extend social studies themes. The current social studies topic can be exhibited on the walls and bulletin boards of the classroom.

Social studies are part of your classroom environment when they reflect cultural diversity. The dramatic play area can include multiracial dolls, culturally diverse clothing, and props for a variety of ages and careers. The classroom can be decorated with fine art posters and photographs that reflect many kinds of people from many cultures. You may have to seek out props for blocks and puzzles that show diversity of age, sex role, and race. Similarly, materials that extend children's awareness of history, place, and community (such as old photos, fire-fighter props, and photographs of different environments) support social studies learning.

The world beyond the school is the classroom for social studies. It would be difficult, and a little silly, to teach about the community without ever venturing into it or to study geographic features without ever going to look at them. As you teach children about social studies, you will want to make use of the environment surrounding your school; indeed, it will profoundly influence what social studies areas you will pursue. If you teach in New York City you will have a different social studies curriculum than if you teach in rural North Carolina or the Pacific Northwest. Whether you teach about community via a trip to the five shops located on your street or by walking to the taro patch down the block, you can use the environment beyond the school to teach economics, anthropology, geography, sociology, and history.

Teaching

We do not set out to teach young children the abstract concepts associated with the social science disciplines as we might do with older children. It takes thoughtful planning based on knowledge of child development to weave these topics into meaningful learning experiences for young children. In the real world of early childhood classrooms, we use the social studies to help develop important attitudes and values and to communicate ideas that help children understand and appreciate their world.

Basic teaching strategies include direct experiences in the classroom, direct experiences in the world, follow-up on experiences, and good questions. One of the most important ways to teach social studies to young children is to bring them into contact with the people and activities about which they are learning. This requires a teacher who is awake to the social studies learning possibilities inherent in the children, families, community, and program.

Because social studies encompass such a broad area and can be approached in so many different ways, they are an excellent tool for organizing and integrating curriculum. Food preparation, visits from resource people, songs, dances, artifacts (from a family, culture, or place), books, and trips all contribute to concept development in the social sciences. Follow-up activities can occur in every area of the curriculum. Children gain deeper understanding when they re-create and re-experience concepts in dramatic play, artwork, writing books, block play, songs, and games.

As a teacher, you can teach sensitive social and political concepts by providing a model of a strong, competent, compassionate, active person regardless of your gender, age, race, or culture. Your own feelings about age, race, class, handicapping conditions, and sex role will communicate to children, and you will want to make sure that you give positive, affirming, antibiased messages. You can make sure that books, puzzles, pictures, and other educational materials present a similarly nonbiased view.

It is important to learn to talk thoughtfully and openly to children when social and political subjects come up. Think ahead about some of the things that you might do and say to help extend their understanding of things that worry and perplex them. A four-year-old in a group that one of us taught brought a newspaper photograph to school that showed a starving child in Cambodia. His concern led to a study of a geographic area and a political situation that we would never have chosen, but the subject interested the group and led to worthwhile, if sobering, learning.

For a number of years we have developed social studies content in our classrooms using a curriculum framework that focuses on six questions. These questions connect social studies directly to the lives of children and incorporate the social science disciplines and social and political themes just discussed (Feeney 1976). Activities based on the questions help children gain self-awareness and acquire beginning social studies concepts. Through the questions adults can also see the relevance of classroom social studies activities to children's lives and can help make the subjects meaningful to them.

A curriculum that addresses the question "Who Am I as a Person with Feelings?" helps children to understand concepts about feelings and to accept and deal with feelings in constructive ways. The question "Who Am I as a Member of a Family?" helps children to understand concepts of anthropology and sociology that deal with similarities and differences in families. "Who Am I as a Member of a Community?" helps children learn about the people in communities—what they do, how they get the goods and services they need, and how and why rules are made to protect them. "Who Am I as a Person from a Culture?" helps children to understand their culture. "Who Am I as a Person in a Place?" teaches about how the features of the earth influence how we live. The question "Who Am I as a Person in Time?" addresses duration and sequence of events in daily life. (See Chapter 9 for an example of a unit on families.)

Adapting the Curriculum for Different Ages

We have talked about the social studies curriculum for preschool and kindergarten classrooms, but it is rich subject matter for even the youngest children and can be a source of joy in learning for older ones.

Infants and *toddlers* learn about social studies as we carefully select what we bring into their environment. What do the books and photographs show? Do they show many kinds of people and places? Do they refute age and gender stereotypes? Infants and toddlers also learn about social studies from the things that we do, say, and reveal in our expectations. They learn about power and rules by the way we treat them. They learn about acceptance and bias from us.

Primary-school children can use the tools of the social scientist. They can read and record information in a systematic and thoughtful way. You can involve primary-school children in planning and teamwork and you can create more elaborate, product-oriented activities. In some of the photographs in this chapter you can see a group of second-graders in Hawaii who were busy studying the harbor. Some children investigated and set up a supply store (the ship's chandler); others built models of the buildings that they had visited. Some investigated the loading procedures. Some mapped, wrote, and illustrated books about the harbor. These children used both the tools of the social scientist and the play of children to learn more about a subject that was interesting and meaningful to them.

IN THE CLASSROOM: INQUIRY CURRICULUM CHECKLIST

Program Structure

_____ Stated goals include support of play, discovery learning, questioning, and problem-solving skills.

_____ Time for independent play and exploration comprise the majority of the program day in at least one-hour time blocks.

_____ Planned small-group activities are provided daily.

_____ Cooking is a planned activity at least weekly.

_____ Children participate in snack preparation.

_____ Trips related to science, math, and social studies, taken at least biweekly.

_____ People who can share skills or demonstrate concepts visit the classroom.

_____ Planned science, math, and social studies activities are drawn from the interests and experiences of children.

Environment and Materials

_____ Low tables and chairs so children can work alone or in small groups

_____ Science center and math center (or a combination of the two)

_____ Unit block center

_____ Art center

_____ Outdoor environment: dirt, plants, insects, birds, playground equipment

_____ Space and equipment for gardening

_____ Water for classroom use by children

_____ Access to kitchen equipment

_____ Useful throwaway materials such as jar lids, corks, cotton

_____ Plants and animals that are cared for by children

_____ Chart stand and paper

_____ Dramatic play center

_____ Space for using mud, sand, dough, and water

_____ Tubs and trays for various purposes

_____ Collections of objects, both natural and made by people, for children to sort and classify in different ways

continued

Math

_____ Attribute blocks or beads
_____ Partitioned trays for sorting (for example, ice cube trays or egg cartons)
_____ Seriation games and toys (for example, nesting cups, sound cannisters, texture games, color chips)
_____ Puzzles
_____ Cuisenaire rods
_____ Colored cubs
_____ Shape-sorting boxes
_____ Measuring implements: rulers, cups, spoons, tapes, yardsticks
_____ Coins and play money for the dramatic play area
_____ Balance
_____ Purchased games such as lotto games, number games, and card games
_____ Teacher-made games
_____ Parquetry pieces
_____ Pegboards
_____ Working clock at child's eye level
_____ Beads for stringing

Science

_____ Aquarium to use for fish, plants, mice, and so forth
_____ Magnifying glasses
_____ Jars for specimens (for example, baby food jars)
_____ Machines to examine and disassemble and reassemble
_____ Screwdrivers (flat and Phillips), pliers, wrenches, and hammers
_____ Thermometer for observing temperature variation in water and air
_____ Screen cages for temporarily housing insects, lizards, and other life forms
_____ Factual books about science topics: books written for children, well-illustrated reference books for adults, child-made books, teacher-made books on subjects of interest
_____ Picture collections of animals, plants, geographic and astronomic features, machines
_____ Probes, tweezers, tongs, and scissors
_____ Sponges, eye droppers, tubing

continued

Social Studies

_____ Children's books and child-authored books about feelings, families, community, culture, place, and time kept for reading in the library

_____ Picture and poster collections of people from your area and from other places, times, and cultures working, playing, interacting, caring for home and family, displaying emotion, celebrating, shopping

_____ Artifacts of feelings, family, and so forth (for example, all children bring a favorite stuffed animal, family photographs, eating utensils from different cultures)

_____ Record collections that include music from various ethnic and cultural backgrounds and representing different moods and feelings

_____ Dramatic play clothes and props representing different roles, ages, work, play, cultural groups

_____ Materials for creating books: paper, pens

_____ Teacher-made games that illustrate social studies concepts (for example, sorting photograph cards into happy and not happy or arranging pictures in the sequence of a family's day)

_____ People and animal figures for block play

DISCUSSION QUESTIONS

1. Reflect on how math, science, and social studies were taught in the schools of your childhood. What do you remember most vividly? Did these experiences influence what you have done as an adult? How do you use what you learned in your life today? Compare your feelings with someone else's. In what ways are they similar or different? What are the implications for you as a teacher?

2. Think about what you have observed in math, science, or social studies in programs for young children. Share something that you have seen that particularly impressed you. How did the environments support inquiry in these areas? What kinds of teacher talk and questioning did you observe? How might these approaches to teaching influence children?

3. What inquiry subject area do you most look forward to presenting to young children? About which do you feel most apprehensive? Why?

4. Think of a time when you were really curious and excited about learning something. What made it interesting? What did you do to find out more about it? Do you still remember what you learned? How do you use it?

PROJECTS

1. Use the inquiry curriculum checklist to evaluate a classroom in math, science, and social studies. Report on:
   - The classroom's strengths.
   - Areas needing more attention.
   - Some ways that the environment could be improved.
   - What you learned that you might apply to your future teaching.
2. Observe a child for a morning in regards to how she or he is involved in math, science, and social studies. Report on:
   - The ways and circumstances in which the child discovers, inquires, and solves problems.
   - How the environment supports the child's development of inquiry.
   - How the teacher supports this child's development of inquiry.
   - How the program might be modified to enhance this child's learning.
3. Observe a teacher for a morning and then interview her or him about how she or he teaches math, science, and social studies. Report on:
   - Activities and routines you saw that contribute to children's learning in these areas.
   - Any evidence you saw of teacher planning for math, science, and social studies.
   - The teacher's goal for children in the development of inquiry.
   - The ways in which what the teacher perceives and what you actually observed match or appear to differ.
4. Write and implement a lesson in math, science, or social studies using the activity planning form from Chapter 10 (Figure 10.11). Report on how children responded and on how you felt about your teaching. What worked? What might you do differently next time? How might you expand on this experience for children?
5. Compare two early childhood programs in math, science, and social studies. Report on the ways that the two address these areas—their similarities and differences. Which program seems to best meet children's needs and why? What implications does this have for your future teaching?
6. Observe two classrooms, one preschool and one for infants and toddlers or for primary-school children. Report on how they are similar and different and how each enhances children's development of inquiry. Talk to the teachers about how they make their curriculum choices in this area.

BIBLIOGRAPHY

Barratta-Lorton, M. 1972. *Workjobs.* Menlo Park, Calif.: Addison-Wesley.

————. 1976. *Math Their Way.* Menlo Park, Calif.: Addison-Wesley.

_____. 1979. *Workjobs II.* Menlo Park, Calif.: Addison-Wesley.

Carlsson-Paige, N., and D. Levin. 1985. *Helping Young Children Understand Peace, War, and the Nuclear Threat.* Washington, D.C.: National Association for the Education of Young Children.

Costa, A. 1974. *Basic Teaching Behaviors.* San Anselmo, Calif.: Search Models Unlimited.

Derman-Sparks, L., and the A.B.C. Task Force. 1989. *Anti-Bias Curriculum: Tools for Empowering Young Children.* Washington, D.C.: National Association for the Education of Young Children.

Edwards, C. P. 1986. *Social and Moral Development in Young Children.* New York: Teachers College Press.

Elkind, D. 1974. *Children and Adolescents: Interpretive Essays on Jean Piaget.* 2d ed. New York: Oxford University Press.

Feeney, S. 1976. *Child Development Associate Module: Social Studies.* Honolulu: Curriculum Research and Development Group.

Flavell, J. H. 1977. *Cognitive Development.* Englewood Cliffs, N. J.: Prentice-Hall.

Forman, G., and D. S. Kushchner. 1977. *The Child's Construction of Knowledge.* Monterey, Calif.: Brooks/Cole.

Ginsburg, D. 1989. Geography in Early Childhood Education. Unpublished M.Ed. project, Department of Curriculum and Instruction, University of Hawaii.

Harcourt, L. 1990. *Explorations.* Menlo Park, Calif.: Addison-Wesley.

Harlan, J. 1988. *Science Experiences for the Early Childhood Years.* 4th ed. Columbus, Ohio: Merrill.

Herrera, S., and H. D. Their. 1974. *Beginnings.* Teacher's Guide (SCIS). Chicago: Rand McNally.

Hill, D. M. 1977. *Mud, Sand, and Water.* Washington, D.C.: National Association for the Education of Young Children.

Hirsch, E. 1984. *The Block Book.* Washington, D.C.: National Association for the Education of Young Children.

Holt, B. 1977. *Science with Young Children.* Washington, D.C.: National Association for the Education of Young Children.

Hopkins, S., J. Winters, and L. Winters. n.d. *Learning to Be Peaceful Together.* Fullerton, Calif.: Concerned Educators Allied for a Safe Environment.

Judson, S., ed. 1984. *A Manual on Nonviolence and Children.* Philadelphia: New Society Publishers.

Kamii, C. 1982. *Number in Preschool and Kindergarten: Educational Implications of Piaget's Theory.* Washington, D.C.: National Association for the Education of Young Children.

Kendall, F. E. 1983. *Diversity in the Classroom: A Multi-cultural Approach to the Education of Young Children.* New York: Teachers College Press.

Mitchell. L. S. 1934. *Young Geographers.* New York: John Day.

Neugebauer, B., ed. 1987. *Alike and Different: Exploring Our Humanity with Young Children.* Redmond, Wash.: Exchange Press.

Saracho, O. N., and B. Spodek. 1983. *Understanding the Multicultural Experience in Early Childhood Education.* Washington, D.C.: National Association for the Education of Young Children.

Seefeldt, C., ed. 1987. *The Early Childhood Curriculum: A Review of Current Research.* New York: Teachers College Press.

—————. 1989. *Social Studies for the Preschool-Primary Child.* 3d ed. Columbus, Ohio: Merrill.

Severeide, R., and E. Pizzini. 1984. The Role of Play in Science. *Science and Children* 21(8): 58–61.

Shultz, K. A., R. P. Colorusso, and V. W. Strawderman. 1989. *Mathematics for Every Young Child.* Columbus, Ohio: Merrill.

Smith, R. F. 1981. Early Childhood Science Education—A Piagetian Perspective. *Young Children* 36(2): 3–10.

Sunal, C. S. 1990. *Early Childhood Social Studies.* Columbus, Ohio: Merrill.

Wasserman, S., and G. W. G. Ivany. 1988. *Teaching Elementary Science: Who's Afraid of Spiders.* New York: Harper & Row.

Wichert, S. 1989. *Keeping the Peace: Practicing Cooperation and Conflict Resolution with Preschoolers.* Philadelphia: New Society Publishers.

Wolf, D. P. 1986. *Connecting: Friendship in the Lives of Young Children and Their Teachers.* Redmond, Wash.: Exchange Press.

PART V

SPECIAL RELATIONSHIPS

This final section acquaints you with additional skills, beyond regular classroom practice, needed by teachers of young children. Chapter 15, Working with Children with Special Needs, will help you identify and work with children who require special knowledge and attention, and Chapter 16, Working with Families, provides an overview of the teacher's responsibilities to families.

CHAPTER FIFTEEN

Working with Children with Special Needs

Do what you can with what you have.
        —*Theodore Roosevelt*

In this chapter, we help you think about and prepare to work with children who differ from others in ways that require special knowledge and attention. We describe some characteristics of children with special needs and discuss the preparation, planning, and teaching strategies required to provide an optimal learning environment for them. We also explore the personal dimension of examining your thoughts and feelings about working with exceptional children and their parents, and the ways in which you can help other children to accept their classmates with special needs.

A s a teacher, you will encounter some children whose needs require additional knowledge and expertise in order for you to work effectively with them. As we thought about the children we have known and taught, we realized that there are many ways to have special needs. An individualized approach to

teaching is required for all children—from the unusually active to the very quiet or exceptionally sensitive. A child from a different culture, a child who speaks another dialect or language, a child who learns like a three-year-old but has the feelings of a six-year-old, a child who wears glasses, a child from a single-parent family, a child with a lisp—all have special needs. In every early childhood classroom, there are at least as many special needs as there are children. All children require thoughtful planning and teaching.

Some children face greater challenges in their lives than others. Their needs may be harder for the teacher to meet and their differences are such that you will want to learn some new ways to teach and communicate with them. Some children may have a significant disability or delay in one or more aspects of growth and learning; others may be coping with a serious illness such as cancer or AIDS. Then there are others who may learn more at a more rapid rate than other young children; they, too, require individual attention in order to be stimulated and challenged.

Many terms have been used to describe these children—*handicapped, disabled, special-needs, exceptional*, and others. According to Norris Haring and Linda McCormick (1990, p. 82)

> An *exceptional child* is one who is different enough from the "standard" or "average" child to require special instructional methods, materials, services and possibly equipment in order to attain desired learning objectives. Children may differ in the rate at which they learn when compared to age-peers *or* they may learn differently due to loss of physical and/or sensory functions. Generally speaking, parents and professionals . . . favor using the term *special-needs* for all of these youngsters including those at risk for later difficulties.

Two valuable guidelines to adopt in speaking of children with special needs are to speak of the child first and the disability second (for example, a child with cerebral palsy, not a spastic child) and to emphasize the child's *abilities* not the disabilities.

Early identification and intervention can get needed help for a child at a time when it will be most effective. As a teacher, you get to know each child within the natural context of classroom activities. Your knowledge of child development and your observational skills have prepared you to identify a child who seems different in one or more significant ways from other children in your group. For example, in the class of a teacher friend, there was a child who seemed to drift off in daydreams. Annie was not making progress comparable to that of the other children. The teacher's well-intentioned response was to be patient and understanding and to calm parental fears. Regrettably, it was later determined that Annie suffered from a form of epilepsy. The daydreaming episodes were actually petit mal seizures. Her developmental lags were caused by this undiagnosed condition. If a teacher does not know the signs of certain physical, emotional, or mental conditions, or if a teacher chooses to overlook indications of possible difficulties, there may be a delay in getting help for the child. Early intervention can help avoid certain developmental repercussions that may be more difficult to remedy as the child gets older.

In your career, you will have many opportunities to work with children who have special needs. There will be those whom you are the first to identify as having special needs; there will be already identified children who are placed, full time or part time, in your classroom either because "mainstreaming" in a regular early childhood program is the best placement or because no appropriate program is available.

The presence of a child with special needs will affect many aspects of your classroom. Your training in early childhood education will have prepared you to view each child as unique—with different skills, interests, and needs—but you will want to acquire additional knowledge of appropriate techniques that can enhance your capability to be an effective teacher for each individual child. Remember that your best source for basic information about the child will be the child's parents. Pediatricians, therapists, and special education teachers are other resources for information to help you understand and work with the child. And your foundation of knowledge about meeting the basic needs of *all* young children will be one of your most valuable assets.

POLICY AND PROGRAMS FOR CHILDREN WITH DISABILITIES

The care and education of children with special needs is a field with its own history and traditions. Today's emphasis on bringing these children into the mainstream of society through placement in regular education classrooms has resulted in a merging of two distinct and different approaches to education: special education and early childhood education.

The challenge of providing education for all children, including those with disabilities, was first confronted in the early 1900s when compulsory school attendance laws were enacted. Public and private residential schools were established for the severely handicapped. Special classes evolved in regular public schools when behavior problems arose as a result of educating children with special needs in regular classrooms.

From the 1920s to the 1960s, most of these children were segregated into classrooms in separate school buildings, far from main activity areas. Usually only those children with mild disabilities, who were considered "ready" for education, were included in public school classes. Children with more severe and multiple handicaps were confined to institutions or residential schools. The Civil Rights legislation of the early 1950s is often credited with providing the impetus for work to secure the rights of the handicapped in this country. When the Supreme Court ruled that separate education for racial minorities could not be considered "equal" (*Brown* v. *Board of Education* 1954), the ground was laid that segregated schooling for any purpose was questionable.

In the mid-1960s, special classes in the public schools became an issue of controversy. Some saw them as dumping grounds for problem children, including those who were culturally different, with no real attempts to meet their educational needs. At this time, too, some educators began to question whether special education classes were the best approach; they suggested that these children could learn better in regular classes. Adding to this ferment, parents, who had banded together to lobby for special education legislation, took their concerns to court. Several important court cases in the early 1970s affirmed the right of all children with disabilities, regardless of severity, to a public education.

Preschool-aged children with disabilities were first served in demonstration programs in 1968 when Congress passed P.L. 90-538, the Handicapped Children's Early Education Assistance Act. Then in 1972, Head Start was mandated by P.L. 92-424 to reserve 10 percent of its enrollment for children with disabilities as a prerequisite for continued federal funding.

P.L. 94-142, the Education for All Handicapped Children Act (1975), required that all children with disabilities be provided with free appropriate public education. In most states this legislation did not lead to the provision of free public programs for preschool-aged children with disabilities, even though small incentive grants were available to those states that developed such programs. Subsequent amendments to P.L. 94-142 have redefined the population to be served, specifically referring to children from birth through age eight. P.L. 98-199 (1983) and P.L. 99-457 (1986) offer financial assistance and technical assistance to school systems for programs for infants and toddlers with disabilities. These laws also emphasize the role of parents and families in making early intervention efforts work.

IDENTIFYING CHILDREN WITH SPECIAL NEEDS

Fifteen eager four-year-olds are eating morning snack. It is now the middle of the school year, and they have all learned the ropes of making snack a pleasant time. Except Jeremy. Jeremy cruises the edges of the room, stopping briefly to dump a puzzle from a shelf and run his hands through the pieces, only to be distracted by the morning's paintings drying nearby. As he passes a table of children, his attention is again deflected. He tries to squeeze his body onto a chair occupied by another child. The result is a struggle in which Jeremy quickly loses interest. This has disrupted snack for the other children and Jeremy himself has been unable to participate appropriately in an important classroom activity.

Jeremy's behavior is usually like this. His actions consistently precipitate conflicts with other children and adults. He seems unable to engage for any length of time in meaningful activity. As his teacher you might feel irritated and frustrated. You know from your training and experience that many young children are easily distractible at age four. Jeremy's case seems extreme. You suspect that Jeremy may need extra help to cope with the demands of the preschool classroom.

For many early childhood teachers, a situation similar to this one becomes their first experience in working with a child with special needs—a child whose condition has not been formally identified and who is not yet receiving any appropriate intervention. For other teachers, it is not unusual to have children with mild disabling conditions (such as hearing impairments, speech impairments, visual impairments, asthma, epilepsy, or diabetes) placed in their preschool classrooms. And it is becoming increasingly common for children with more serious handicaps to be formally or informally mainstreamed.

The behavior of a child like Jeremy may perplex or upset you. Your feelings can cue you to a possible problem and the need for some extra help to best serve the child's needs. Many conditions that are only mildly disabling are first detected when a child enters an early childhood program. You have an opportunity to identify and help these children who will benefit from a careful evaluation and special services. What steps do you take when you believe a child in your classroom has a condition that may require special help? Start by observing the child in some systematic way. Begin to note all the ways the child is functioning appropriately and similarly to other children in the class. Then pinpoint those ways in which his or her behavior and skills are significantly different. Make written anecdotal records, being careful to make objec-

tive statements about what you observe the child doing: When is this behavior manifested? In what contexts do you see it occurring? Is it age-appropriate behavior? Once you have a more objective view of the child's behavior, you can decide whether step two—getting help—is necessary.

Share your observations and concerns with a coworker, head teacher, or director. The support they provide will help you sort out and organize your thoughts and feelings. Colleagues can also offer useful insights from a more objective point of view. Ask them to make an independent observation of the child in the classroom. Consider possible modifications of classroom environment and schedule that might have a positive effect. Sometimes adult expectations for children's behavior are "developmentally inappropriate." The resulting problems are ones that we have created for the children and ourselves.

When you are ready, schedule a conference with the child's family. The best time to do this is after you have collected observational data and researched the available community resources. Avoid approaching parents by saying, "I want to talk with you about Jeremy." Such a statement invariably arouses their anxiety to such a degree that open communication becomes difficult, if not impossible. Instead, Ellen Galinsky (1988) suggests making a simple statement about the problem: "Jeremy has some difficulty in getting involved in play activities either alone or with other children. I'd like to talk with you about what we're trying at school and see what works for you at home. Can we get together some afternoon this week to discuss this?"

Start the meeting on a positive note. Parents appreciate hearing what you especially enjoy about their child, so begin with positive comments; tell them what you see as their child's strengths and capabilities. Then share those observations that caused your concern; show parents the written observations you have recorded. Build an alliance with parents by asking them if and when they have ever observed similar behavior and how they have handled it. Together you can explore various possibilities and ideas on how to find some answers to the questions you have raised.

Often parents have had concerns but have not known whether or where to turn for help. They may be relieved to learn that you are committed to supporting them in the process of getting answers to these questions. The information and insight you offer may prompt them to arrange for their child's referral for evaluation, or they may ask the school to arrange for the referral. However, some parents may react fear-

fully. They will reject the possibility that something could be "wrong" with their child and prefer to believe it is something the child will outgrow. In such cases, you can explore other avenues for getting help and classroom support, while you continue working with the parents toward an eventual referral. All parents need reassurance that getting extra help for their child does not mean they or their child will be rejected by you or the early childhood program.

Be persistent. As an early childhood educator, you will naturally feel responsible for doing your best to get help for a child who may have special needs. But it is not necessary to assume

total responsibility. Enlist the support of your director or head teacher. Ask for a list of community resources. Both public and private agencies provide screening, evaluation, and consultation for children with special needs. Your own school may be able to provide such services. A good place to begin looking for help is your state, county, or local department of health or department of education. If they do not provide the services you require, they can probably direct you to the appropriate agency. Private agencies such as the Association for Children with Learning Disabilities or children's hospitals are another resource for help.

CHARACTERISTICS OF CHILDREN WITH SPECIAL NEEDS

Eligibility for government-sponsored programs is determined by identifying children who have certain characteristics. Children with these characteristics frequently have difficulty learning. They may develop more slowly in some domains because of a physical, sensory, intellectual, or behavioral problem. These are long-term conditions, not the result of a temporary incapacity due to illness, injury, or short-term stress. These children will require special kinds of learning experiences and/or professional treatment to adapt to or overcome their condition and to achieve their fullest potential. An unfortunate and harmful consequence of establishing eligibility for special programs is the labeling of children by the nature of their disability. As an early childhood educator, refrain from falling into the trap of referring to any child by a label. Use the child's name.

The severity of a disability can vary widely. The severity will determine to what degree special techniques, equipment, or materials will be needed to help the child learn. In general, children with mild and sometimes moderate disabilities are included in regular programs. Four general areas of functioning may be limited

by disabling conditions: mobility, communication, information acquisition, and information processing. Children may have more than one area of dysfunction. In addition to your knowledge about children with disabling conditions, you will need special knowledge and skills to deal with children who are gifted, children who come from families experiencing unusual stresses, and children who have been physically, sexually, or psychologically abused or neglected.

How to Identify and Work with Children with Special Needs

Teachers of young children may be the first to recognize the possible existence of abuse, giftedness, a physical disability, sensory impairment, emotional problems, speech difficulty, or developmental delay. Major impairments are almost always detected by physicians or parents prior to the time children enter early childhood programs. Although you should be alert to physical and behavioral characteristics that suggest the need for evaluation, it is not your role to diagnose a disability. This chapter does not attempt to acquaint you with all the information you need to recognize the signs and symptoms of various exceptionalities. An excellent reference book that does this well is *Children with Special Needs in Early Childhood Settings* by Paasche, Gorrill, and Strom (1990). As the authors point out, a single symptom such as poor coordination can have many causes.

In the case of a child who has an identified disability, there may be a temptation to become an expert on the causes, symptoms, and nature of that particular disability. Even though all that knowledge may help you deal with your anxiety, it will not help you to know the needs of individual children. To know the children, you must observe and find out what they like, what makes them happy, what do they do well, what is hard for them to do, and what they need help with. The disability is not the child. No two children with the same disability are alike. There are, however, some sound strategies that will help you work with a child with special needs in the classroom.

Children with Physical Disabilities

Children with a physical disability may be unable to control or easily move their bodies. They may have difficulty coordinating body movements, or may have been born without a limb or have had a limb removed in an accident or for medical reasons. Neurological impairments are caused by damage to the brain, spinal cord, or nerves. Orthopedic impairments are caused by direct damage to the bones, joints, or muscles. Problems associated with pregnancy and birth, hereditary and genetic factors, injury, or disease may cause a physical disability. Many children who are physically disabled may have additional problems such as hearing loss or mental retardation. Others may have just the single handicap.

You want to encourage a child with a physical disability to participate as fully as possible in your program. Some adaptations of your classroom environment may make this easier. Adjustments of table height or easel height, the relocation of certain supplies and toys to make them more accessible, and the rearrangement of furniture are some things to consider. As the extent of a child's mobility and coordination is particular to the individual child (not to the disability), be sure to consult with the parents and the physical therapist before you make changes. Ask also about what adaptations can be made to standard preschool equipment like tricycles to enable the child to engage in as many regular activities as possible. Let the child discover abilities and limitations by trying out activities, and encourage independence through teaching self-help skills such as dressing or eating.

In consulting with the parents and therapist, find out about appropriate activities enjoyed by the child that can be used or adapted for use with the whole class. For example, body awareness activities will be helpful in improving all the children's appreciation for and understanding of their bodies. Emphasize activities that give a child with a physical disability the opportunity to play with other children. Preschool children are often fascinated by any special equipment—for example, walkers or wheelchairs—used by a

---

IN THE CLASSROOM: SOME CHARACTERISTICS OF CHILDREN WITH PHYSICAL IMPAIRMENTS

Children who are mildly or moderately physically impaired may:

- Be clumsy and walk or bump into things often.
- Have difficulty with motor activities involving large muscles, such as crawling, climbing stairs, or riding a tricycle.
- Have difficulty with activities involving eye-hand coordination, such as stringing beads, building a tower of blocks, or cutting or drawing (also a sign of possible visual impairment).
- Have poor speech because of inability to control their breathing and the muscles needed in articulation.
- Have difficulty chewing or swallowing.
- Show a lack of stamina and display overall weakness.

classmate. Check with the parents—they may be willing for the other children to satisfy their curiosity by trying out the equipment.

Children with Visual Impairments

During the early childhood years, all children are learning to coordinate, control, and focus their eye muscles. Visual impairments are often not diagnosed until a child enters a school program. A child whose inability to see well interferes with easy participation in daily activities is considered visually impaired. A child with partial sight may have a *visual acuity* problem that is correctable with glasses. The field of vision may be limited or eye movements may be uncoordinated, making it difficult to focus. Few children have no seeing ability at all. Many can see light and dark areas or broad shapes but not details. Some have peripheral rather than frontal vision.

The development of children whose blindness occurred after birth more closely resembles that of other children, but the development of children who are blind at birth tends to be much slower. Lacking visual stimulation which encourages exploration of the environment, children with visual impairments usually lag in physical development. Many large- and small-muscle activities are learned by imitation: children watch and then copy the movement. But movement will be perceived as dangerous when the consequence of movement is getting hurt by bumping into things. Fear of movement may in turn affect social development as young children's social play is generally physically active and centered on toys. Not surprisingly, children with visual impairments may be advanced in speech and language and may excel at listening and memory activities.

There are many things you can do to help a child with a visual impairment enjoy and benefit from your program. Provide good overall lighting and try to avoid having areas of glare or deep contrasts between light and shade. Keep the room arrangement and traffic patterns simple and uncluttered and when a change is needed, have children participate in making it. When introducing an activity or game, use detailed description to accompany your actions. Place the child with low vision close to you for circle activities such as action songs, finger plays, and stories. Give the child larger toys and materials to which you have added either different textures for tactile appeal or sounds for auditory appeal. Encourage the child to sit where the activity can be best seen and to tell you what is wanted or needed. Teach the child to look in the direction of the person speaking rather than looking away. Remember that social cues such as facial expressions that express feelings may not be seen and you will need to assist with verbal descriptions.

Children with Hearing Impairments

Children are considered hearing impaired when they have difficulty understanding and responding to speech or sounds. The problem may be in perceiving the volume or clarity of sound. When children cannot hear, even with the use of a hearing aid, they are said to be deaf. Children who are hard of hearing have a permanent but less severe hearing loss in which the use of a hearing aid is helpful. Damage to the outer or middle ear (*conductive loss*) and damage to the inner ear or the nerves that carry sound to the brain (*sensorineural loss*) can occur before or

IN THE CLASSROOM: SOME CHARACTERISTICS OF CHILDREN WITH VISUAL IMPAIRMENTS

Children with vision problems may:

- Rub their eyes excessively, squint, or frown.
- Shut or cover their eyes; tilt or thrust their head forward.
- Hold objects close to their eyes and show difficulty with tasks requiring close use of eyes.
- Stumble over objects.
- Be unable to see distant things clearly.
- Be irritable or blink frequently when doing close work.
- Have inflammation or other eye problems such as swelling or styes.

after birth. Sometimes the loss is temporary, caused by a middle ear infection, but frequently, untreated infections of this nature can cause permanent hearing loss.

When children cannot hear a language model, they have difficulty learning to speak. Spoken words may be unclear and difficult to understand. The rhythm and voice quality of speech may sound odd. Social interactions are hindered when it is difficult for children to express feelings or needs or to have others understand them. Cognitive skills may be slower to develop if hearing loss has resulted in a language delay.

Whether a child's hearing loss is temporary or permanent, there are many familiar techniques that you can use to help. By placing yourself facing the light source and at the child's eye level, you will be able to establish eye contact and thus attract and hold attention. In a

IN THE CLASSROOM: SOME CHARACTERISTICS OF CHILDREN WITH HEARING IMPAIRMENTS

Children with hearing impairments may:

- Have trouble paying attention, especially in group activities.
- Not answer when called.
- Get confused about directions or not understand them at all.
- Frequently give the wrong answer to questions.
- Often say "what?" or look confused by questions, statements, or directions.
- Have poor speech, substitute sounds, omit sounds, or have poor voice quality.
- Avoid people; prefer to play alone.
- Get tired early in the day.
- Turn one side of the head toward sounds, indicating a hearing loss in one ear.

group activity, have the children sit in a circle, so all faces will be visible. Address the child by name, speak clearly in a normal voice, and use simpler phrasings, but whole sentences. When a child seems not to understand, rephrase your sentence instead of repeating it. Also, the use of visual clues and gestures will aid understanding, but remember the child needs time to direct attention to the object or gesture and then look back at you. Encourage participation in activities like dramatic play and puppetry. If the child is receiving speech therapy, ask the therapist for ideas of games you can adapt for the whole class. And if the child uses a hearing aid, ask the parents to teach you how it should be worn and cared for — you can't tell just by looking whether the hearing aid is actually functioning!

Children with Speech or Language Impairments

Problems with speech and language occur quite often in young children. Some disfluency is part of normal speech development; so are errors in articulation. However, speech and language problems may be associated with one or more of a variety of factors: speaking another language, a hearing impairment, cleft palate, autism, cerebral palsy, attention deficit disorder, an emotional problem, or a learning disability. Some of these are permanent, some are temporary.

Children with *receptive language* problems have difficulty understanding the meaning of words or the way words are put together. Children with an *auditory processing* problem may be unable to tell the difference between speech sounds (auditory discrimination), may be unable to isolate the important sounds from a noisy background, may have trouble remembering what they hear, may confuse the correct order of a series of sounds, and may consequently have problems forming concepts. Children who lack the ability to use language effectively (a problem with *expressive language*) have difficulty verbalizing ideas, selecting the appropriate word from a more limited vocabulary, or employing correct grammatical structures.

IN THE CLASSROOM: SOME CHARACTERISTICS OF CHILDREN WITH SPEECH OR LANGUAGE IMPAIRMENT

Children with speech or language difficulties may:

- Not be talking by age two.
- Not speak in two- or three-word sentences by age three.
- Be very difficult to understand after age three (still relying mostly on vowel sounds and omitting the beginnings and endings of words).
- Use poor sentence structure after age five, such as, "Me school go."
- Stutter after age five.
- Have poor voice quality.
- Have difficulty hearing speech sounds.
- Have difficulty understanding what is said.
- Appear shy and embarrassed when speaking.
- Have trouble following directions, describing things, using correct parts of speech, or putting words into sentences, compared with other children.

Children with *speech* problems have trouble being understood. There are many normal articulation errors in preschool children as, for example, in substituting an "f" sound for "th." When these articulation difficulties persist beyond the age of five, or if a child's speech is typified by unusual pitch, volume, or voice quality, an evaluation by a speech therapist is in order.

When a child in your classroom has a speech or language problem, you want to be careful not to interrupt, rush, or pressure him or her. Model correct language, using simple constructions and vocabulary, and expand the child's own comments. Provide many opportunities to enjoy language use by building upon experiential learning activities (such as field trips) and incorporate songs, rhymes, and chants into daily routines.

Children with Intellectual Impairments

Although all children learn at different rates, some children have a significantly slower overall rate of learning and development. They appear much younger than their chronological age and during the preschool years are already having difficulty learning skills and developing concepts. They may be unable to remember what was learned or to use the information to solve problems in new or unfamiliar situations. Children who are intellectually impaired have trouble developing and using language, playing cooperatively, initiating activities or interactions, and learning to function independently. Intellectual impairments, often called retardation, can occur before, during, or after birth.

Children with mild intellectual impairment may seem little different than the youngest children in an age group. Children with moderate intellectual impairment will have greater difficulties in self-help skills, motor development, social skills, and language development. In general, they tend to behave like children about half their age. Children with severe intellectual impairment will usually have so many areas of dysfunction that integration into a

---

IN THE CLASSROOM: SOME CHARACTERISTICS OF CHILDREN WITH INTELLECTUAL IMPAIRMENTS

Children who are mildly to moderately retarded may:

- Be unable to follow directions that contain more than one or two steps.
- Not be able to independently choose an activity.
- Have a tendency to imitate rather than create.
- Have poor eye-hand coordination.
- Be slow to learn simple games or classroom routines.
- Be very slow in learning language.

regular program is rare. Since there is no certain way to discover exactly how retarded a preschool child may be, do not prejudge what a child can do and can't do. The best approach is positive: encourage the child to try.

When you have a child with some degree of intellectual impairment in your classroom, relate as you would to a slightly younger child. Give your directions one step at a time; simplify and guide daily routines; allow more time to make a transition. Try using shorter sentences and a simplified vocabulary. Spend time showing a new activity and use a multisensory approach to teaching. Repetition of the demonstration may be needed until the activity is mastered. After that, give many opportunities to successfully practice the new skill. Encourage growing independence by emphasizing self-help skills.

Children with Learning Disabilities

The term *learning disabilities* is used to refer to assorted problems exhibited by children with normal intelligence but below age-level functioning. Children with learning disabilities are usually extremely uneven in development. For example, they may have good motor skills but have a considerable delay in language. In school-age children, these inconsistencies often lead to their being accused of not trying hard enough or of being lazy, uncontrollable, or stubborn. During the early childhood years, learning disabilities are difficult to identify. Your knowledge of the normal developmental range of behaviors and skills may help you assess whether a child should be evaluated for a possible learning disability.

Many children with learning disabilities exhibit an inability to attend. They may show impulsive behavior beyond what seems developmentally appropriate. Sometimes these children have been called hyperkinetic or hyperactive or have been said to have minimal brain dysfunction. These symptoms are now referred to as *attention deficit disorder*. The problem occurs more frequently in boys and tends to appear by age three. Children with an attention deficit disorder are easily excitable, have trouble waiting for explanations or taking turns, and can seldom pause long enough to relax, watch, or listen. Many cannot tolerate physical restriction. Jeremy, the child in the example at the beginning of this chapter, may be suffering from this disorder. Do not assume that every active young

---

IN THE CLASSROOM: SOME CHARACTERISTICS OF CHILDREN WITH ATTENTION DEFICIT DISORDERS

Children with attention deficit disorders may:

- Be impulsive, acting quickly without thinking about the consequences.
- Have a short attention span, being unable to concentrate on one task or activity long enough to complete it or switching from activity to activity without seeming to gain satisfaction.
- Have difficulty organizing and completing work and lack goal direction.
- Be distractible, having trouble paying attention to the task at hand and being unable to redirect attention to the original task once distracted.
- Be hyperactive: being constantly in motion even when surroundings are quiet, being restless and fidgeting all the time.

child has an attention deficit disorder. Children with this problem are identifiable because of the extremes of their behavior.

You may find it important to provide a lot of structure for a child with a learning disability. Simplify the physical environment and reduce visual stimulation. Define the child's work or play area and position yourself nearby so you can offer assistance or encouragement. Make picture charts showing the sequence of actions in a daily routine such as getting ready for nap. Warn the child of changes in schedule and state your expectations for behavior clearly.

Children with Behavioral, Social, or Emotional Problems

Frequent and severe emotional difficulties can result from a number of different causes including inadequate nurturing, abuse and neglect, physical injury, or biochemical imbalance. Some stressful life events such as death, divorce, separations, and moving can provoke temporary signs of emotional distress. Emotional problems interfere with the development and mainte-nance of meaningful relationships and with the development of a positive and accurate sense of self.

In mild and moderate cases, children with emotional problems tend to be more aggressive, unhappy, anxious, or withdrawn than their peers. Children with severe problems are much more extreme in their reactions and usually require care in specialized settings. Severe qualitative abnormalities in functioning and be-havior may be characterized by withdrawal, anxiety, or aggression. Unusual behaviors such as self-mutilation, rocking, running with arms flapping, extreme fearfulness, withdrawal, or total loss of self-control may be displayed.

If you have a child in your group who seems to require an unusual amount of adult supervi-sion and assistance, or one who is overlooked because he or she so rarely interacts with others, carefully document your observations and share

your concerns with the family. A child may exhibit symptoms of emotional disturbance in response to highly stressful situations such as divorce or death in the family, because of abuse, or as a learned behavior pattern. In any case, the child may benefit from some sort of short-term treatment.

A child with emotional problems may be difficult for you to handle not only because the child is so intense, but also because there is so much disagreement among experts about the causes, classification, and treatment of these conditions. You will need someone to help you understand and work with such a child. It is helpful to have several mental health profession-als available for consultation who are in tune with the school's philosophy and who have worked successfully with its children and fami-lies in the past.

Children Who Have Been Abused or Neglected

A child who is abused or neglected has another kind of special need that you need to learn to identify and respond to. Child abuse may be defined as intentional physical and/or emotional maltreatment of a child by an adult, usually a person responsible for the child's welfare. Mal-treatment of children is a destructive response of adults with poor coping and caregiving skills when confronted with too much stress in their lives. Stress factors such as low income, inade-quate housing, unemployment, isolation or the absence of family support systems, having a child with a disability, and unwanted pregnancy are often exacerbated by family conflict, substance abuse, and mental health problems. Frequently, the abusing adult was abused as a child and thus learned to use physical, sexual, or verbal vio-lence as a means of controlling or disciplining a child and releasing tensions and frustrations.

When you see symptoms of emotional dis-turbance in children and observe physical inju-ries such as burns or unusual bruises or marks at

IN THE CLASSROOM: SOME CHARACTERISTICS OF ABUSED OR NEGLECTED CHILDREN

Children who have been abused and neglected may be:

- Overly compliant and passive or show extreme avoidance of confrontation with children and adults.
- Extremely demanding, aggressive, and filled with rage.
- Prematurely competent; for example, they may prepare meals, take the bus alone, or care for younger siblings when it is neither developmentally nor culturally appropriate to do so.
- Extremely dependent in behavior.
- Developmentally delayed or regressed with infantile behavior.

different stages of healing on a variety of body planes, be alerted to look more closely at these children. Careful observation of children's imaginative play may provide additional clues. Children often reveal intense feelings and concerns in their play themes. An example would be acting out the violent adult, with another child or a doll as a passive or powerless victim.

In cases of neglect, a child's attendance may be inconsistent, or arrival and pickup may be late. The child may appear hungry, underweight, unwell,, unclean or inappropriately dressed. Some neglected children demonstrate unusual competence in self-help skills and assume adult responsibilities, yet have difficulty playing cooperatively with other children or handling changes in the daily routine. This type of behavior often indicates that a child has had to learn certain survival skills such as dressing and feeding without assistance, because a nurturing adult has not been available. It is important to remember that as much as we value independence in children, it is not developmentally appropriate for a three-year-old to prepare breakfast every morning or for a four-year-old to walk to school alone each day.

Certainly a major signal for concern is when children show precocious sexual awareness in play or talk. This may be the outward evidence of sexual abuse such as being made to observe adult sexual behavior or of being the unintended witness of sexual acts. You will want to be aware of the tone and pattern of parent-child interactions. Does the child seem consistently frightened or intimidated when with the parent?

When parents withhold emotional support and positive attention or make strong verbal attacks, characterized by threats of physical harm, name calling, or profanity directed at the child, you must consider the likelihood that the child is being subjected to emotional abuse.

Parental discipline and child abuse are part of a continuum. This makes it difficult sometimes to discern whether there is simply a difference in values and cultural norms or there is real abuse to the child. The director of a center in a community with a large Samoan population had to reexamine her criteria for what behaviors she would consider physically abusive to children in light of the fact that a physical response to children's misbehavior was almost universally accepted by that community as proper parenting. Middle-class teachers may incorrectly identify children as neglected when in reality what they are seeing is not strictly neglect, but the result of family poverty or lack of education.

Remember that it is important to use our child protection laws not just as a deterrent to child abuse and neglect, and not as a judgmental and punitive response to instances of abuse and neglect, but as an occasion for educating all parents about what fosters the healthy growth and development of young children.

Teachers have a professional responsibility and are mandated by law to report suspected cases of child abuse or neglect. It is your responsibility as a teacher and an advocate for children to be aware of the indicators of abuse and neglect and to report suspected cases to the appropriate agency, so that the child and family can receive the help they need as soon as possible. The program where you teach should have a policy of informing parents of the school's reporting obligation as part of their orientation to the program. Staff should receive written procedures for how to report suspected cases. If your program does not have these policies and procedures, urge the administration to develop some immediately. Offer to help and get other staff members involved. Refer to the NAEYC Code of Ethical Conduct (see Appendix 1) for ethical guidelines and seek the support of trained specialists. With so much public attention focused on reported cases of child neglect and abuse, especially sexual abuse, many communities have created special task forces or expanded services to deal with the problem. Be sure you know what is available in your community.

The child who has been abused has special needs, many of which the preschool setting can meet if there is thoughtful planning. In order to rebuild a healthy self-concept and the ability to trust adults, extra time and attention must be devoted to the child. One person in a teaching team should be designated as the child's primary teacher, responsible for being physically and emotionally available to meet the child's needs for positive attention, care, comfort, and positive discipline. The consistency of that adult's loving firmness can help the child realize that adults can be trustworthy, predictable in their reactions, and in control of themselves and the environment. To the greatest extent possible, what the child experiences in the way of daily routines, activities, and expectations should be carefully structured to promote feelings of mastery, security, and control. Sensory activities, such as dough and water play, can be used by the teacher first as a way to foster the nurturing relationship and then as a bridge between that bond and the encouragement of a normal interest in play activities and socialization with other children and adults.

Children with Special Gifts and Talents

Children who have unusual strengths, abilities, or talents are often called gifted. They are highly individual in their development and abilities. In fact, there seems to be more variety among them than there is among other children. There is no single measure that can identify giftedness in children. They may have a single unusual strength or ability, such as a child who has a phenomenal ability to remember, read, or perform music at a very young age. They may also have both a gift and a disability, as did the son of a friend of ours who had unusual verbal and artistic ability *and* dyslexia.

If you have a child in your program who has many of these characteristics, you should make observations and then talk to the parents about what this may imply for the child's future education. You will want to encourage the child by providing many opportunities to develop and extend interests. The best learning materials offer some challenge because they are open ended, require active involvement and self-direction, and stimulate thinking. Find out what this child really wants to know or do, and then find the materials that will support the desire to learn. You may have to consult experts and find materials designed for older children. The child who is gifted has less need for structure and often can work quite independently. Large

IN THE CLASSROOM: SOME CHARACTERISTICS ASSOCIATED WITH CHILDREN CONSIDERED GIFTED

Children who are gifted may:

- Exhibit intense curiosity, ask many questions and conduct investigations into how things work.
- Develop passionate interest in one particular topic or in a series of topics.
- Have advanced reasoning ability, demonstrate the capacity for abstract thinking and the use of symbol systems at an early age.
- Be highly independent in thought and behavior.
- Be unusually perceptive and aware of people and things in their environment.
- Have extraordinary memories.
- Show great persistence in self-chosen tasks; are motivated to pursue the interest and accomplish a goal at a self-determined high standard.
- Have advanced language ability with an unusually large and sophisticated vocabulary, and the ability to use and appreciate humor.

blocks of time for exploration enable concentration. You support learning by giving the materials and the time and by being available as a resource. Variety and the introduction of new materials on a regular basis are important.

MAINSTREAMING CHILDREN WITH SPECIAL NEEDS

Mainstreaming is a term coined to emphasize the importance of educating children with special needs in the mainstream of society rather than at home, in institutions, or in special segregated classes. In mainstreaming it is assumed that since all children differ in abilities, interests, and needs, classrooms can be designed to provide learning experiences for all children.

More and more children with special needs are being mainstreamed into public schools as a result of a federal law (P.L. 94-142) that requires that all children with disabilities have access to a "free, appropriate public education, in the least restrictive environment." The law requires an individualized education plan (IEP) for each child identified as handicapped. Because that law includes children as young as three years, some children with special needs are being mainstreamed into preschool settings as well as elementary schools. You may have a child with a disability placed in your classroom. If a child already in your classroom is identified as having special needs, he or she may remain there. If you know you will have a child with special needs in your classroom, the suggestions in the accompanying box may be helpful.

Preparing Yourself and Children for Mainstreaming

We have already talked about your feelings as a teacher in the process of identifying and getting help for a child with special needs in your classroom. As you work with the child on a day-to-day basis, you may request extra guidance from your supervisor or a consultant as you adapt to this new teaching experience. For example, how do you help other children

IN THE CLASSROOM: RECOMMENDATIONS FOR PREPARING YOURSELF FOR MAINSTREAMING

- Learn about a child's special needs by talking with the child's parents. They will be your best source of information for how the child functions at home.
- Consult with the child's doctor, therapists, or other teachers who have worked with the child for additional information. Ask whether the child is taking any medication and whether there are side effects. Ask what special classes or forms of therapy the child participates in, and find out if there are precautions, limitations, or requirements you should know about.
- Determine what services will be available to support your work.
- Ask specific questions such as, "How can I make group time relevant to this child and also meet the needs of other children?"
- Brainstorm with the experts and consultants available to you.
- Be flexible and easy on yourself; you can learn from your experience.

understand and accept a child with special needs? How can you best work with the child's parents who may need a different type of working relationship with you? How can you get special training that would help you be a more effective teacher for this child? Who can help you learn to use sign language, to respond to a seizure, or to use special equipment? In addition, you may want to request volunteer assistance or a reduced class size so that you can continue to provide every child with a quality program.

For your personal orientation, remember that an effective way to prepare yourself to work with any child is to ask yourself, "Who is this child as a whole person: likes, dislikes, learning style, friends, personal qualities?" This approach reminds you that a disability or special need is only one characteristic of a person—children are more alike than different. Do this exercise frequently and eventually it will become automatic to respond to the child as an individual first and as a person with a disability only when it is appropriate to do so. For example, Amanda wears a brace on one leg. When she sits on the floor to work a puzzle or stands at an easel to paint, your first response will be to her competence at working the puzzle or the beauty of her painting, *not* to the brace on her leg. When she is on the playground and cannot run or climb like the other children, you will help her find alternatives. Your focus will be on what she can do, not on what she cannot do.

You many find yourself encountering feelings about a child with special needs that you are not "supposed" to have. For example, if you were Jeremy's teacher, you might find yourself overwhelmed and exhausted. It might be difficult to keep from reacting negatively to such an unfocused, perpetually moving child. Yet it will be important to do your best to remain positive and supportive, for we know that children with attention deficits and other disabilities can develop low self-esteem, become negative, do very badly in school, and may develop symptoms of emotional disturbance when they are in nonsupportive environments.

It is especially important to remember that you must balance the special needs of an individual child with those of the entire group.

Occasionally a child with special needs may demand so much of your time that you find yourself in an ethical dilemma: it is impossible to meet the needs of this one child and still provide a good experience for the other children. If the situation is actually harmful to the safety and welfare of the other children, it will be necessary to drop the child from the program unless you can find an acceptable alternative. One preschool we know has made arrangements with the special education department of the state university to provide student volunteers to assist gifted and disabled children in their setting. Even if your school is not located near a college or university, you may be able to find volunteers through a public service agency or club.

In another case, a friend of ours told us about Kevin, a child with a neurological impairment, who drooled continuously. Our friend, an excellent preschool teacher, was surprised to find herself feeling repulsed by Kevin's drooling. It brought up childhood memories of another youngster who had been teased and tormented by other children, including herself, as the neighborhood "dummy." Our friend took care to spend extra time with Kevin, made an effort to see him as a whole child, and eventually found that not only did she forget about her response to his drooling, but she also deeply treasured this child's sense of humor and his affection toward her. She also worked hard to help the other children in her class accept Kevin— something you want to do for every child in your group.

Preparing the other children in your group requires sensitivity on your part. A simple explanation of the disability with some examples that they can relate to a personal experience is probably the best method. You might say about a child with an expressive language problem, for example, "Mark has trouble saying what he wants to say sometimes. Do you ever want to tell someone something and the words come out all mixed up?"

Making a special child appear to be too different is not wise, because other children may then become excessively helpful and overprotective or they may exclude the child believing he or she is not capable of participating. You can help young children understand that no one can do everything, that everyone of us has strengths and weaknesses. By teaching children that all of us need the opportunity to try, you enable them to see that when we try things on our own, we have a better chance of acquiring skills and competencies. Show the children in your class specific ways they can include a child with a disability in their play. For example, you might encourage them to help a child with little vision feel the shape of an elaborate block structure and then to give verbal guidance so that the child can place blocks in the structure.

Answer children's questions about disabilities as honestly and directly as you can. Help them understand any differences they may observe. You could say, "Rose wears a hearing aid so that she can hear us when we talk to her." With the child's permission, other children may want to try the hearing aid. Or you may be able to ask a speech therapist to bring some hearing aids for children to try and to explain how they work.

Be ready to assure other children that a disabling condition isn't "catching." Older children may initially laugh at or ridicule any child who is different. Remember that this response is fueled by their own embarrassment. It provides you with an opportunity to talk about the wide range of differences among people and the value of helpful and respectful relationships. Teachers report time and again that the caring relationships developed among the children are an overwhelming positive outcome of mainstreaming. Your warm, accepting attitude will provide a powerful model for the development of these relationships.

Modifying the Program

Play is the primary vehicle for learning for all young children. Sometimes teachers become so concerned with remedial tasks that they forget that children, with or without disabilities, need the same opportunities for play. Play is particularly important for children who have disabilities because it is through play that they experience those feelings of mastery, resourcefulness, and competence that are so crucial for development of a positive self-concept.

To facilitate play, provide children who have disabilities with support and guidance in coping with fear about unfamiliar experiences. Allow them additional time to develop comfort and competence in play situations and assist them in learning specific play skills they may need. You may include more time for directed teaching and take a more active role in helping them strengthen newly developing skills.

Children with special needs, like other children, need opportunities to engage with a variety of both open-ended and specific-purpose materials. Clay, paint, and blocks stimulate exploration and creative play. More defined activities such as lotto, puzzles, and pegboards provide experiences in developing and strengthening specific skills and problem-solving strategies. Some materials can be adapted for use by children with disabilities. For example, yarn or masking tape wrapped around pencils and marking pens makes them easier to hold and use.

A daily routine that includes a variety of learning experiences is just as important to a child with special needs as it is to other children. Free play and teacher-directed times, child- and teacher-chosen activities, and large as well as small groups, all provide opportunities for learning.

Plan individual sessions with a child with special needs several times a week or on a daily basis. The focused attention of an adult helps the child and allows you to concentrate on the child's particular interests and needs. You may need to enlist help from volunteers or support from your coworkers to allow you to schedule this individual time.

Planning

Your knowledge of what is developmentally appropriate for young children in general will guide your planning as you decide what materials and activities to use, how to introduce them, and what responses you will expect. For some children, especially those who are intellectually impaired, a *task analysis* approach in planning is a useful tool. This involves breaking down tasks or skills into their component parts and teaching them separately as a series of subskills, not unlike the way you slowly help a toddler learn to pull up his or her pants. You may find it helps to break down such tasks as putting on clothes and going to the bathroom for certain children who require practice with each subskill for a period of time before they can succeed with the overall activity. You may want to attend a special education class or workshop to learn about task analysis.

Classroom observation supplemented by data from assessment instruments can help your planning. They enable you to identify a child's strengths and weaknesses and help you discover the best conditions and teaching strategies for learning. You can then understand where the child experiences difficulty and will be able to set objectives and design activities that will help you meet those needs. Coworkers or volunteers may be needed to free you to take the time necessary to do systematic observation.

Teaching Strategies

Children with certain disabilities may have difficulty paying attention. To help children focus on the task at hand, use attention-getting words such as *look*, *listen*, or *watch me* and allow children to touch and manipulate materials.

When children are highly distractible, you can control the amount of stimulation by simplifying the task or by presenting only one part at a time. Keep transitions short within and between activities. Be sure that all procedures are planned and materials organized so that long lapses can be avoided. Include many opportunities for individual and small-group activities. Large-group activities may be overstimulating and require more waiting than some children can tolerate.

Be especially careful to pay attention to children's efforts at communication whenever and wherever they occur. If the child has difficulty with expressive language, listen closely in order to decipher communication. Ask to make sure you have understood what was meant, "You have a bunny like that at your house?" If a child has difficulty understanding language, simplify your speech somewhat. Encourage children to talk about their feelings during times of stress, frustration, or excitement. And encourage talking among children. When a child shares with you or calls your attention to something, acknowledge this and sometimes redirect the communication to another child, "Tell Willie what you told me."

When helping children to develop concepts, focus on contrast by giving lots of positive and negative instances. For example, if you are helping children to develop the concept of a circle, present contrasting shapes so children can see "circle" versus "not circle," and present many real-life examples such as a bracelet, saucer, hoop, and so on. Present examples of the concept throughout the day: join hands to make a circle at group time, eat round crackers for snack, make circular vegetable prints during art. In general, teach much the same way you would with other children, but keep in mind that you may need to spend a longer period of time with some children with special needs.

Working with Parents

We know that parents who learn that their child has a disability often go through a grieving process much as if the child had died. Indeed, they have suffered a loss—the loss of their image of their ideal child and the loss of some of their dreams, hopes, and expectations for that child. They will experience denial, anger, despair, and finally, acceptance. You may encounter parents at any point in this process and it is important for you to understand and accept their feelings. It may be hard for you to feel as if you've reached parents if they are somewhere in the first three stages. Keep in mind that if properly supported, the process resolves itself in acceptance; that is, although the parents would not have wished their child to be disabled, they are able to view the disability as a fact of their lives. Your role is to be patient and understanding in the early stages of the process and to demonstrate the ways in which you can help their child learn to cope with and compensate for the disability.

Even though you cannot be on call to parents twenty-four hours a day, you will want to be sure that the parents of a child with special needs have regular access to you. Conferences should feel "safe" to parents, so that they can hear information about their child without feeling it is prejudiced or judgmental. The anecdotal records you keep on the child can serve as the basis for a dialogue between you and the parents. Make a special effort to collect data on children with disabilities; the more data you have, the easier it will be to see progress that you can share with the parents. Having a sharing notebook for each child may make it easier for some parents who are more comfortable with sharing a concern in writing than in speaking to you directly.

Parents must be involved in decisions about and give their consent to any services their child receives other than the usual classroom routine. You may be the bridge for parents to therapists

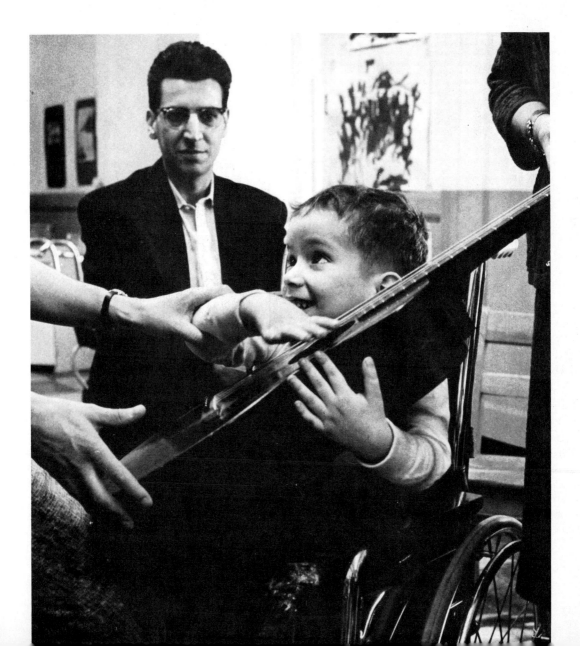

or other professionals who will work with their child. Your role will be to ensure that communication is clear among home, school, and professional helpers.

Just as it is important to avoid making a child with special needs appear too different, so it is necessary to help the parents feel a welcome part of the ongoing life of the school. If the family is new to your school, be sure they meet other families at school functions or when they drop off or pick up their child. You might say, "Mrs. Brown, I'd like you to meet Mrs. Nishimoto. Her daughter Lisa was Nicole's partner on our field trip today." Don't hesitate to ask the parents of a child with a disability to help at a work day or provide field trip transportation just as you would any other parent. But realize that some parents will benefit from a short respite from the ongoing responsibility and involvement with their child, whereas others will derive benefit from building relationships with other parents.

If the family has been in your program for a while before their child is identified as having a disability, you may need to increase the frequency of parent communication in order to get help for the child. Also make a special effort to keep those parents involved in ordinary events. Even if they can't participate much while they are adjusting to this new dimension of their lives, later they will appreciate being kept informed.

Confidentiality is one of the issues you will face whether the family is new or an ongoing one. How much is appropriate to reveal to other parents about a child's disability? Other parents will have questions you must be prepared to answer. Parents, like their children, may need to be reassured that the disability itself or the child's behaviors are not "catching." They need to know that children rarely adopt any developmentally inappropriate behavior displayed by a child with a disability. It is important to keep private specific details about the disability or the family. To a pointed question you might reply, "Amy needs extra help in some ways. If you'd like to know more about it, you might want to ask her parents." You can offer general reassurance, emphasizing the benefits of learning to accept differences and to be caring and respectful in relationships with all people. You should also encourage other families to help the parents of a child with a disability feel welcome. Your own attitude will provide a positive model.

A FINAL NOTE

Almost every chapter in this book contains information that will help you work with all kinds of children—children who differ in the color of their skin, hair, and eyes, in physical size, in language spoken in the home, and in their skills and abilities to understand and function in the world. That same information is valid for working with children with special needs. You may find it useful to adapt some of your usual teaching practices and to find an extra measure of patience and acceptance within yourself. You will benefit from the help and support of parents, coworkers, your director, health specialists, and perhaps volunteers. You have the potential for an unprecedented learning experience in your own development as a teacher. You will learn specific information about different disabilities. You will develop interpersonal skills as you help coordinate the collaboration of individuals who will provide help for the child. And you will learn the meaning of the paradox of our shared humanity within the wide spectrum of individual differences.

DISCUSSION QUESTIONS

1. Think about your own abilities and disabilities. How have they affected your life? How did they influence your childhood experiences? What do you wish your teachers had known or felt?
2. Think about the ways that disabled children were a part of your early school experiences. How do you think your teachers felt about these children? How did you feel? What implications does this have for your teaching?
3. Recall a relationship or an interaction that you have had as an adult with a handicapped individual. How did you feel? Did the experience change your ideas about disabled people? How?
4. Explore your thoughts and feelings about working with children with special needs. Are you comfortable? Why or why not? What implications do your answers have for you as a teacher?

PROJECTS

1. Observe an early childhood classroom that mainstreams a child with special needs. Report on how the teacher attempts to meet the child's needs. Describe your impressions of the teacher's attitudes and values regarding this work. Reflect and then comment on the effect this has on all the children in the class.
2. Interview a teacher of a mainstreamed child to find out what procedures were followed in identifying and planning for the child's educational experience. Describe this process and your feelings about it.
3. For at least an hour observe and imagine yourself in the place of a child who you suspect has a disability. Try to experience the program as the child might. Describe what you think the child's experience may be. Based on this experience, suggest how the program might be adapted to meet this child's needs.
4. Observe a disabled child in a regular preschool setting. Report on what you would do if you were going to have a conference with the child's parents. What would you tell them? What questions would you ask? How would you create a climate of safety and trust within the conference?
5. Find out what services your local departments of education and health and/or social services (and other agencies) offer to handicapped children under the age of five. Write a pamphlet about this information for teachers; include phone numbers and names of contact persons.

BIBLIOGRAPHY

Allen, K. E. 1980. *Mainstreaming in Early Childhood Education*. Albany, New York: Delmar.

Braun, S. J., and M. G. Lasher. 1978. *Are You Really Ready to Mainstream? Helping Preschoolers with Learning and Behavior Problems*. Columbus, Ohio: Merrill.

Cartwright, G. P., C. A. Cartwright, and M. E. Ward. 1981. *Educating Special Learners*. Belmont, Calif.: Wadsworth.

Featherstone, H. 1980. *A Difference in the Family: Life with a Disabled Child*. New York: Basic Books.

Galinsky, E. 1988. Parents and Teacher-Caregivers: Sources of Tension, Sources of Support. *Young Children* 43(3):4.

Goldman, N. T., and S. Rosenfield. 1985. Meeting the Needs of Preschool Gifted Children. In R. H. Swassing, *Teaching Gifted Children and Adolescents*. Columbus, Ohio: Merrill.

Haring, N. G., and L. McCormick. 1990. *Exceptional Children and Youth: An Introduction to Special Education*. 5th ed. Columbus, Ohio: Merrill.

Jordon, J., et al. 1977. *Early Childhood Education for Exceptional Children*. Reston, Va.: Council for Exceptional Children.

Kaplan-Sanoff, M., and E. F. Kletter. 1985. The Developmental Needs of Abused Children: Classroom Strategies. *Beginnings* 2(4):15–19.

Koplow, L. 1985. Premature Competence in Young Children: A False Declaration of Independence. *Beginnings* 2(4):8–11.

Meisels, S. J. 1978. *Developmental Screening in Early Childhood Education*. Washington, D.C.: National Association for the Education of Young Children.

Murray, K. 1985. Reporting Child Abuse: What Are Teachers' Responsibilities? *Beginnings* 2(4):35–37.

Paasche, C., L. Gorrill, and B. Strom. 1990. *Children with Special Needs in Early Childhood Settings*. Menlo Park, Calif.: Addison-Wesley.

Piazza, R., and R. Rothman. 1979. *Readings in Preschool Education for the Handicapped*. Guilford, Conn.: Special Learning Corporation.

Protecting Children, Centers, Teachers, and Parents from Child Abuse: A Center Checklist. 1985. *Beginnings* 2(4): 42–43.

Research for Better Schools. 1978. *Clarification of P.L. 94-142 for the Classroom Teacher*. Philadelphia: Research for Better Schools.

Smith, S. L. 1979. *No Easy Answers*. Cambridge, Mass.: Winthrop.

Souweine, J., S. Crimmins, and C. Mazel. 1981. *Mainstreaming: Ideas for Teaching Young Children*. Washington, D.C.: National Association for the Education of Young Children.

CHAPTER SIXTEEN

Working with Families

Just keep in mind though it seems hard I know,
Most parents were children long ago—incredible.
                              —*H. Rome*

This chapter focuses on the importance of children's families and of building relationships with them in early childhood programs. We discuss the awareness, knowledge, and skills you need to work productively with families. These include appreciation of parenting, skill in building relationships, ability to communicate information about child development and early childhood education, and knowledge of resources for families. We explore a variety of ways that programs can involve family members—information sharing, participation in the program, and education.

Children come to school wrapped in the values, attitudes, and behaviors of their families. Although your first challenge and primary role is working directly with children, you need to see and support each child as a part of a unique family whose members are also important teachers. Families today take a variety of forms which sometimes include adults other than parents (stepparents, siblings, grandparents, and other relatives or friends) who may assume parental roles. To simplify the wording of this chapter, we speak of both parents and families and in so doing are speaking of the entire cast of adults who play an intimate and significant role in a child's life. When we speak of parenting, we are discussing that nurturing done by these important adults.

You probably chose to become a teacher because of your interest in and allegiance to children. You may not have recognized working with parents as a part of your job. The needs of children cannot be adequately met, however, if you do not also take families into consideration. The relationships that you build with parents will bring about collaboration between home and school to enhance children's development. Contemporary research suggests that the most effective programs for young children are those that involve their families.

Interacting with families can also be gratifying. Parents who recognize the importance of their children's early years appreciate your

405

efforts and skills as few others can. Since parents know their children best, they will be the first to notice when your work has had a positive impact. As you enrich their children's lives and help them with the task of parenting, you can develop warm relationships that may even blossom into friendships. Learning that you have made a difference to a family is among the most rewarding experiences that a teacher can have.

Relating to parents has its own unique challenges and demands. The awareness and sensitivity that you have developed in your work with children are also important as you work with adults. Adults need relationships in which they feel safe and respected just as children do. Parents may differ in their needs, interests, awareness, knowledge, and skill, but there are similarities among them. Parents are concerned with the welfare of their children. They want the best for them and want to be kept informed of the important events of their children's lives away from home. The basis for your relationships with parents is your commitment to a joint venture of providing good experiences for children.

You do not need to become intimate friends with parents, nor do you need to be the ultimate authority on child rearing to be effective in working with them. You have yourself to offer, a knowledgeable professional who cares about their children and who is able to relate to family members to support their child's growth.

Working with families may seem difficult at times, because you have fewer skills in working with adults and because the results of this work are not always easy to observe. Unlike their young children, parents cannot always live in the moment; the attention they have to give their child's teacher is limited by their concerns for other, possibly more critical, aspects of their lives. If you are a young teacher with no children of your own, you may feel that you are viewed as inexperienced or incapable. Working with adults may seem more problematic than working with children because adults may seem more likely to make negative judgments.

Just as you examined your attitudes about working with children, you will want to look at your values and attitudes regarding your relationships with parents. You will also want to think about whether you can accept a variety of approaches to child rearing that reflect differences in values, cultures, and lifestyles. You will encounter differences in values about education and about child rearing with some of the parents with whom you work, and you will want to be prepared to deal with these differences in constructive ways without assuming the role of expert or assigning blame. It may be difficult to feel accepting of parents whose goals for children are very different from yours. Because of your commitment to children, it may be hard to accept parents who appear uncaring or who seem to treat a young child in a harsh or inappropriate way. Sometimes it may be difficult to distinguish between behaviors that simply reflect a difference in values or skills and those that are abuse—where you have a legal and ethical obligation to intervene. Keep in mind that parenting *is* difficult, that there are few resources available, and that the great majority of families *are* doing the best they can given their circumstances.

WHAT YOU NEED TO KNOW TO WORK WITH FAMILIES

The knowledge and skills that you developed to work with children will serve you well as you work with families. The following additional knowledge and skills relate specifically to the part of your work with families:

- Understanding of what parenting is like.
- Understanding how relationships are built.
- Knowing how to communicate information to adults.
- Knowing how to support families in stress.

Today's world is extremely complex. Television pervades almost all of our lives and instant replay of historical events makes the world seem much smaller than it once did. Violence is widespread, as are reports of abuse against children. The context of growing up now is quite different from what we remember in our childhoods—one that implies new responsibilities for those who care for young children.

Your work with families will be enhanced by your awareness of the many aspects of parenting—the joys as well as the difficulties. Being sympathetic and supportive is easier when you realize that parenting is not an easy task. The stresses can sometimes overshadow the pleasures. Parenting involves a day-in and day-out responsibility that is unrelenting and that cannot be ignored or avoided. You can help parents renew their pleasure in their child's special stage and enjoy the process of parenting.

It is also helpful to understand that people enter into child rearing with many kinds of expectations. The reality of parenting is almost certain to be different from the expectation. As parents develop, they seem to follow a relatively predictable sequence. Ellen Galinsky (1981) describes the early childhood years as the time when parents are learning to be nurturers and learning to define themselves as authority figures in the family.

The purpose of the family has enlarged from the performance of specific survival functions such as providing food, shelter, clothing, and supervision to ensure children's physical well-being (Pickarts and Fargo, 1971). It now includes the more abstract tasks of providing psychological security and skills in dealing with an increasingly complex and dangerous world. Society's view of family roles has changed over the past several decades. Today we are more aware of the importance of the early years, and parents are told that they need specialized skills to aid in their child's development. Some families feel pressured to hurry their children into the activities that are supposed to ensure success—music, dance and athletic lessons, early academics, and entrance into the best preschool in order to achieve access to the best primary school, high school, and even college.

Methods of child rearing have changed since today's parents were children. Strict discipline versus total permissiveness has given way to a number of different and sometimes contradictory approaches. The process of learning about

these approaches and choosing those that are consistent with personal values and style and the temperament of the child is complex.

The very structure of the family has also been changing. The extended family is disappearing; families move frequently so there is a loss of community. Single parents and stepparents are commonplace, and you can expect that many of the children in your care will come from such families. Newly "blended" families that include a stepparent's children, the children of a parent's new marriage, grandparents, and other related and unrelated adults are also common. When a family changes, the experience is usually stressful, even if the change is positive and wanted. There are many things that teachers can do to let families know that their structural diversity is accepted. One of the

simplest but most important things teachers can do is to learn the names of all the important players in the child's life and include these in their information sharing.

Financial uncertainty is another factor that may be very much a part of a family's life. It hardly needs to be said that both parents are often part of today's work force. More than half of all preschool-age children have working mothers. Families in which two parents are working must deal with multiple roles and the resulting time and energy constraints. Moreover, there is a dramatic increase in one-parent families (most frequently mothers) who are operating under severe financial constraints. Today, one in five American children has a single parent and one in five is poor. It is estimated that by the year 2000 this will increase to one in four (Children's Defense Fund 1989.) We are concerned today about the large numbers of homeless children and how to provide educational programs for them.

Changes in the nature of child rearing require new skills and responses that many adults are not prepared for. They may find it difficult to develop the skills they need and to find resources for acquiring them, especially if they are struggling to survive financially. They may be forced to rely on social agencies, including schools, to perform many of the roles that were once the responsibility of the extended family. The early childhood program can be a good place for providing support to parents. Your good relationships with parents will help them feel easier about turning to you for assistance and about sharing some of the responsibility for their child with you.

Building Relationships with Families

In order to work effectively with families you need to focus on building good relationships with them. Although this need not be difficult or time-consuming, it does require thoughtfulness and attention. Good relationships with families do not develop simply because you have good intentions.

Relationships begin with the attitudes that you hold and express. All people are more trusting and open in an atmosphere of concern, respect, acceptance, and individual attention. The things that you do to build such an atmosphere for families in your program are usually small, easy to overlook, and as simple as the courtesies you extend to your colleagues and friends.

In good relationships individuals feel welcomed. You can accomplish this if you know names, greet individuals daily, and have provisions for regular sharing of information with parents. Since all relationships are based on sharing and trust, begin by learning about each other. Take time to find out what family members are interested in, what they do, and what they care about. Share information that will help parents know something about you—remember, though, it is not appropriate to share *your* personal problems. Acknowledge events and transitions in the child's life at school and in the family's life at home. Recognize and share a family's joys and sorrows. Be scrupulous about maintaining confidentiality: nothing destroys trust faster than idle gossip and broken confidences.

You will want to convey to parents that you are committed to hearing their concerns (at an appropriate time) and that you will face problems with them, rather than avoiding issues or insisting on your own methods. Skills in active listening, giving I-messages, and avoiding roadblocks will help. Sometimes you may feel that listening to families' concerns is extra work. Remember that the time you spend with parents may ultimately contribute to the relationship and to the child's well-being at home and in school.

Communicating Information to Adults

Your knowledge of child development influences your relationships with children and serves as a basis for the kind of program you plan for them. You need to be able to clearly communicate your understanding of this theory to parents so they can understand why the program is a good one for their children.

Communicating specialized information may involve translating the professional terms that you use with your colleagues into words that have meaning to the uninitiated. Simply saying that you provide opportunities for motor development is not as valuable as letting parents know that creative movement, swinging, sliding, trike riding, and climbing help their child to develop skill, strength, and coordination in the arms, legs, and torso and that using pegboards, the easel, puzzles, and beads help develop skills in manipulating with hands and fingers that will be essential in learning to write. Additionally, all of this may not be nearly as meaningful as letting parents know that physical competence and the related confidence that it brings also contribute to social and academic success.

Both parents and teachers have information that contributes to the child's well-being and that allows them to meet each other on equal ground. Parents bring knowledge and experience of their child as a unique human being, and you bring your theoretical knowledge of children in general. Both types of information are vital if you are to create the best possible educational experience for each child.

You will be comfortable with what you are doing and better able to explain your program choices and rationale when your decisions are based on knowledge of children and curriculum and on clear value choices. As you explain what you do and why, it is important to separate and communicate your *preferences* in teaching and child management from your *knowledge* about what constitutes appropriate, desirable practice in teaching and relating to children. As parents observe your approach to curriculum and classroom management and learn more about the rational for what you do, they will learn more about development and will have a broader understanding of their choices. For example, you can tell parents that you have chosen not to provide workbook experiences for young children because you know that they learn concepts through real experiences. You might then show parents a sorting activity in which children make discriminations similar to a workbook task; and share some ways that similar activities (such as sorting and putting away the silverware) might be provided at home.

Learning how to provide families with information that is meaningful to them is a skill that you will develop with time and experience. Share what you know and be willing to admit what you don't know but are willing to learn more about. Remember that you and the parents both have worthwhile ideas and that neither of you is infallible. You *are* the professional in these situations, however, and although you want to be respectful of parents, you also need to act on your best professional judgment. If the requests of parents violate what you know to be best for children, you have an ethical responsibility to do what is right for children, but you will want to explain the reasons for your choice to the parents.

As an accessible professional with knowledge of a range of choices, you may find yourself being asked for advice or may feel a strong desire to offer it when you are not asked. We have found that it works better to offer such advice in a tentative fashion. To a parent who has difficulty coping with a whiny child at a late pickup you might say, "All of the children seem to get cranky when they're hungry and it's close to supper. I have found that it helps when parents bring a small, nutritious snack to give to them on the ride home."

How to Support Families in Stress

Even though you are not a counselor, you will need to have information and strategies for supporting families during times of stress. Some kinds of stress are relatively minor, perhaps the result of juggling the responsibilities of a busy life; others are more serious.

As a teacher of young children you may be the first professional who identifies a problem that has an impact on a child. Problems may be as simple as a change in schedule that is causing a child to have difficulty staying awake in school or as serious as a case of child abuse or neglect.

Family Changes

Families often need assistance when there is a change in family structure such as a new baby, death, divorce, or remarriage. One of the simplest ways that you can help is by keeping a child's school life as stable as possible during the period of the change. You will want to have knowledge of programs such as children's guidance and divorce clinics, mental health services, family mediation organizations, and neighborhood resources in order to help parents find needed assistance for dealing with these transitions.

As a person who works closely with a family in today's society, it is almost inevitable that you will find yourself being asked to play a supportive role for one or both parents in divorce or child custody conflicts. Since these conflicts can be traumatic, policies and procedures need to be established before a problem occurs. A clear policy statement can help parents understand that your primary commitment is to the child's welfare and that such problems are by no means unique or a sign of parental failure. When a divorce or custody battle does take place, it can be tempting to express a preference for one or another parent. Keep in mind that you serve a child better by maintaining neutrality unless the child appears endangered. In cases where family members are in conflict, the NAEYC Code of Ethical Conduct states in section P-2.10: "We shall work openly, sharing our observations of the child, to help all parties involved make informed decisions. We shall refrain from becoming an advocate for one party" (Feeney and Kipnis 1990).

Abuse and Neglect

One of the most difficult situations faced by a teacher of young childen is addressing a case of suspected child abuse or neglect. Every program should have written policies that notify parents of the program's obligation to report child abuse and neglect and of policies designed to protect children.

You have an ethical, and in most states a legal, obligation to report suspected cases of abuse or neglect of children (discussed in Chapter 15, Working with Children with Special Needs), but you also need to continue to work with the family with sensitivity and respect. When you suspect that child abuse or neglect might be occurring you need to confer with the family and attempt to develop mutually acceptable strategies; provide consultation and parent education as appropriate and make referrals to agencies that might help the family deal with potentially abusive behavior. If you are convinced that the child is being abused and you make a report to a child protective agency, you should inform the parents that the referral has been made unless you believe that this might result in harm to the child.

Make every effort to maintain positive relationships with the parents at this time: focus on positive aspects of the child in discussion and make an effort to notice and comment on attempts to handle the child's behavior in a constructive way. Parents who are under the stress of an investigation of child abuse will need extra support from staff, not less. Let the parent know that your goal is to support the family and help them cope better. Avoid adversarial comments that make the parent feel inadequate or incompetent. Neither child nor parent should be labeled as "abused" or "abuser" and confidentiality should be scrupulously kept.

INVOLVING FAMILIES IN EARLY CHILDHOOD PROGRAMS

Family involvement in early childhood programs can run the gamut from programs that act as an extended family and involve parents at all levels to those in which teachers talk to parents rarely and only when there is a problem. In ideal situations parents and teachers work closely in a variety of ways. Parents can participate in classroom activities, plan or attend parent education programs, serve on policy-making groups, and contribute to the program through work on facilities, fund-raising, and lobbying in the community on its behalf.

Family involvement begins when you provide parents with information about the kinds of involvement available to them in your program. It is important to find out some things about the family members: what they want and need, their level of interest in the program, their time constraints, and the kinds of activities in which they might enjoy participating.

Sharing Information

You help parents understand and support your program by sharing information with them. It helps them to contribute and to be better equipped to work with their children at home when they know what you are doing and why.

The first opportunity to share information with a family will occur when they visit your program to learn about it and to decide if it is right for them. Staff members aid parents in their decision making by exchanging information with them. You will need to provide an understandable explanation of what is done in the program and why. You also will want to encourage parents to tell you what their child is like and what kind of program they are seeking. During your discussion you can share, in an unbiased way, what you know about other program alternatives in your community. This is especially important if you suspect that what is desired by the family is different from what your program offers. Such an open sharing of information sets the stage for a truly collaborative effort between school and home. It also increases the likelihood that the family will become committed to the school and find meaningful, fulfilling ways to become involved in the school community.

Once a family has chosen your program there are other avenues for continuing and expanding this new relationship. At the beginning of a school year or when there are a number of new families, you may wish to have an orientation meeting. These meetings tend to work best when they combine information sharing with an opportunity for socializing. We have found it effective to begin a meeting at the end of a day when the families arrive to pick up their children; we provide for a shared meal and informal conversation, followed by introductions and information about the program. Participation will be facilitated if you can offer child care for older and younger children as well as those enrolled in the program.

The initial visit and a good orientation meeting are useful in setting the climate for teacher-parent interactions and family involvement; however, they are only the beginning of an ongoing process of communication. The basis for your relationship with parents is your knowledge of and your commitment to their child. Because of previous experiences with schools and teachers, parents may not feel comfortable in their initial contacts with you. In the beginning, you will need to take the lead and assume the bulk of the responsibility for building the relationship. You can accomplish this by frequent and positive sharing of information about the school's activities and your experiences with and observations of their child. Sharing the small joys and sorrows of the child's life creates a bond between you and the family.

Good daily communication with families requires flexibility and creative planning, and it is important to use all the avenues that are available to you. Keeping in contact with busy working parents involves a special effort. Responsibility for greeting these parents at early arrival or late departure may need to be assigned to one staff member, because you may not get to talk to these parents during your normal work hours. A message center where each family has a mailbox or message pocket helps to make communication easier. A summary of the day's experiences can be posted here. In some programs this is also where journals are kept. Teachers and parents share information about the child through the journals in which they both read and write frequently.

As you observe children, you can keep both mental and written notes to share at the end of the day in the journal or by phone call: "Christopher worked really hard in the block area today. He was very persistent and figured out how to make his tower as tall as the shelf. His face shone with delight when he finally was able to make his tower strong enough not to topple."

Families can be informed of the activities of the program by reading a week's plans posted near the sign-in area or sent home each week. Bulletin boards, notes, and newsletters offer opportunities to explain aspects of the program in greater detail, to solicit assistance from families, and to provide information about child development and other topics of interest. These techniques are most successful if they are very visible, attractive, short and to the point, and easy to read. If reading them is built into some other routine, such as sign-in, they are more likely to get the parents' attention.

Another way to communicate to families that they are valued parts of the program is to create a parent corner near the entrance to the school or classroom. This area might have a comfortable adult chair or couch, reading material, coffee or tea, pictures of the children at play, or even a slide and tape presentation about the program. Parents may enjoy talking to one another in this area or a child and parent might spend a quiet moment there together.

If some of the parents in your program have special communication needs, if they are non-English speaking, or if literacy is a problem, then you will need to make a special effort to ensure that you communicate with them. Bilingual parents might be designated translators and other parents might be readers for those who have difficulty reading. Information can be presented graphically as well as in written form to enhance communication. The guiding principle in reaching everyone is to present the same information in many different modes and forms.

Addressing Parents' Concerns

Because parents are so deeply concerned about their children, it is inevitable that issues and questions will arise regarding the care and education that their children are receiving. In good relationships moments of concern and questioning lead to open exchange of information and ideas and often to greater insight into values and goals.

Very predictably, parents have concerns about their child's health and safety in the program, about the care of their child's possessions and clothing, and about the purpose of play and the child's academic progress. Despite a good relationship, addressing these concerns can be worrisome to either parent or teacher. It is essential that parents feel heard, that their issues are addressed, and that their efforts and judgment are respected. If you consistently display sensitivity in dealing with their concerns, it is more likely to be reciprocated. To be prepared as a teacher you need to be able to respond to questions and concerns in ways that keep the lines of communication open and without being defensive or devastated by being questioned or challenged.

Parents' questions may arise from the nature and philosophy of the program. Young children's programs often are quite different from other kinds of educational settings. The materials and experiences provided seem to bear little

relationship to conventional learning. Parents may wonder why their children play so much, why they are not learning "academic" skills, why they come home so dirty, and why you let them do things that appear dangerous.

The concerns that parents have about play often reflect a lack of understanding of how young children learn. Parents may relax as you help them understand that children learn in significantly different ways from adults and that the development of motor and perceptual skills forms the base of later, more abstract learning. Since the most recent formal educational experiences of most adults have usually been in lecture situations, they may have lost touch with the learning that goes on in active, hands-on experiences. Remind them of the things they have learned by doing—cooking, driving a car, bathing a baby, using a computer—and that *doing* is an important way of learning too. Explain the sequence of development in very concrete terms: "Children first have to learn to tell the difference between obvious things like blue round beads and square purple ones before they can tell the difference between more subtle things like numbers and letters." This will help adults to see the purpose of the activities that you do with children.

When parents do not agree with you about the curriculum, it is essential that you take their concerns seriously and not dismiss them. It is equally important that you speak from your own knowledge and experience of developmentally appropriate practice. We are teachers because of our specialized expertise and it is our responsibility to address parents' concerns with sensitivity from the knowledge base of the field. For example, dialogue with a parent who has expressed a concern about a four-and-half-year-old learning to read might sound something like this:

PARENT: You know, I think it is time that you start teaching Rebecca to read. She is always looking at books and she can read the names of all the stores at the shopping center.

TEACHER: You're right. Rebecca is expressing a strong interest in reading lately. I've noticed that she is spending time at the writing center and is incorporating letters into her paintings and drawings. She doesn't want me to write her name on her work anymore—she wants to do it by herself. I've been fascinated to watch this because it's just what I've been reading about how children develop literacy (that's the new term for beginning reading and writing). What the specialists are saying is that children learn to read and write through their experiences with reading and writing in their day-to-day life.

PARENT: What about teaching her letters and words? I bought a workbook at the drugstore last week and Rebecca has been coloring all the pictures. I can't keep her away from it. Why aren't you teaching her anything like that at school?

TEACHER: What I've been doing here at school is introducing a word bank for each of the children. Here's Rebecca's file of "special words." She has all the names of her friends and family. I've also been introducing more print into the room. You know back at the beginning of the year I put up some labels on different things in the classroom—look here, where I put *chair* on this chair. Because Rebecca and a few of the other

children have been so interested, we've been labeling others things together. Rebecca asked to put *squeakers* on the mouse cage. She and Joni made this word book together right after that.

The messes inherent in the sensory development, art, and science curricula are also the topic of frequent parental concern. Knowing the purpose of these activities may make them easier for families to appreciate. Discomfort may be eased if the activities are announced in advance, if children are sent to school in play clothes, and if you provide smocks to protect clothing from damage.

Some parents may be astonished and alarmed by the physical challenges that children undertake in the school setting. They may never have allowed their children to climb to the top of the jungle gym or to use functional saws, scissors, or cooking equipment. They may not understand why you do. Families often cannot provide independent or adventurous physical activities. They may not be aware of what young children can safely do with close supervision. People vary greatly in their judgment of what is or is not dangerous. Parents may judge an activity or piece of equipment based on their own experience. We find it helpful to let parents know that we share their concerns and then go on to talk about the value of the activity and the safeguards that we take. You can let parents and children know that you won't allow or encourage children to attempt activities that are clearly beyond their capacities, but that your situation safely provides opportunities for exploration that contribute to development.

Conducting Parent Conferences

A conference provides you and parents with time to share information and perceptions. It provides for in-depth and personal exchange of information that is not possible in other ways. A central purpose of your conference is to form an alliance with parents to help the child grow and learn. During conferences, you may explore issues relating to the child at home and at school. This is a time when personal or family problems may become known to you. You can then help parents express and clarify their feelings and values, provide information, and help them develop their skills and resources. Regular conferences support your work and build parent-teacher relationships. If conferences are held rarely or only in the event of a problem, they will be more stressful and less productive.

Planning will help you to spend conference time effectively. First you will need to plan for quiet, undisturbed space and sufficient time. Providing these ensures that the conference will be unpressured and productive. Scheduling ten parent conferences for twenty minutes each on one day is neither an effective nor pleasant way to plan for this important part of your role as a teacher.

You can prepare for the conference by looking over your anecdotal records, assessments, samples of work, and other records on the child. You might write a summary or fill out a checklist to use as a conference guideline. We have used the developmental checklist in Chapter 6 for this purpose.

Parents may be apprehensive if they do not understand the purpose of the conference. You will want to begin by explaining that you and they are there to share information and get to know one another better. Assure them that you welcome their ideas and questions, that the conference is a joint process. As you share your perceptions of their child in school, try to describe what the child *does* rather than saying what he or she *is:* "Matthew usually watches the others use a new piece of equipment before he tries it. He seems to like to have a quiet space and a long period of time." Do not say, "Matthew is very shy." In positive conferences the child's areas of strength are discussed and other areas are looked at in terms of growth and direction for parents and teacher.

When it is necessary to discuss a problem, assume that solutions can be found. You can use conference time to clarify the issues, agree on goals, develop a plan of action for home and school, and decide when you will meet again to evaluate what you have done.

It is natural and necessary for parents to be intense, emotional, and partial to their child. Teachers play a different role—they must be less intense and more objective. In approaching conferences assume that parents have good intentions and that they will share honestly as you do. You may disagree with one another because of your different experiences in life and with the child, but you are ultimately on the same side—the child's.

Parent Involvement in the Program

You play an important role in encouraging and supporting parent participation in your program. Involved parents can work with the children, orient other parents to classroom participation, provide input into program policy, and strengthen the relationship of the entire program to the community. When parents participate as volunteers they can enrich your program and enable you to do more. They support children's experience when they work with individuals and small groups in the classroom and accompany you as you take children on trips outside the school environment.

When parents volunteer in the classroom, everyone can benefit: the parents, the teachers, and the children:

When *parents* participate in the program they:
- Have an opportunity to learn about the teacher's way of guiding growth and development.
- Gain firsthand insight into the meaning of the curriculum that they may be able to apply at home.
- Gain a sense of competence and a feeling of being needed as they contribute to the program.

When parents participate in the program *children:*

- Have a chance to see their parents in a different role.
- Become acquainted with adults who have skills, feelings, and ways of relating that are different from those of their own parents and teachers.
- Have more individualized attention available to them.
- Experience a richer curriculum.

When parents participate in the program *teachers:*

- Have a chance to expand their program because of the improved ratio.
- Can learn from the knowledge and expertise parents bring and share.
- Have an opportunity to observe the relationship between parent and child.
- Have a chance to develop a more meaningful relationship with individual parents.
- Have more opportunity to interact with individual children.

It takes a while for teachers and parents to get comfortable, so begin in easy stages. It is easy to invite parents to visit and observe their child in the classroom. With just a little additional planning and work, parents can be invited to come for special occasions such as a birthday party or a special child-prepared luncheon. More thought and preparation are required when parents work with you and the children in the educational program. To ensure a successful first experience for the parent, have them begin with a simple task such as reading a story to two or three children or assisting you as you set up activities. It is important to allow parents to participate in ways that feel comfortable and natural to them and to offer them support in developing skills. As they gain skill, parents can take a more active part in the classroom by planning with you and possibly sharing unique abilities or special knowledge.

You may need to make an effort to ensure that fathers as well as mothers participate. Fathers may feel that the early childhood program is not their natural province, and they may not be certain that they have anything to contribute. In fact, most fathers will be perfectly comfortable doing the activities just suggested. They may require a special invitation from you to feel assured that they are welcome.

An orientation to learn routines and procedures is imperative both to help parents feel prepared and to ensure that they understand program philosophy and policies so that quality can be maintained. A satisfying classroom experience is enhanced when parents and teachers can find time to cooperatively plan activities and meet at the end of the school day to discuss, share experiences, and give each other feedback. Remember that when parents participate, you have the additional responsibility of supervising them.

A card file containing information about activities and jobs that need to be done is useful for letting parents know what kind of participation is needed and will be welcomed. Posting written statements in each area of the classroom describing the purpose of the activities and how adults can interact with children is another good technique for supporting participation.

Family members who lack the time or who are uncomfortable participating in the classroom may be involved in a variety of other ways. It is important to be especially aware of including options for single-parent families who may have greater stress and less time (but no less interest) than two-parent or extended families.

Some family members may volunteer to use their skills to create items for classroom. Others may enjoy making educational materials at home. If people express an interest, help them get started by organizing a workshop on how to create learning games. Involve them in identifying what specific learning games would help round out the curriculum in their child's classroom. This workshop should include ideas for useful junk to save and materials to be purchased.

As families become involved and committed to the program, they may recognize its budgetary limitations and offer to help in finding additional resources. They may be willing to spearhead or participate in fund-raising events or grant-writing projects. Others may be willing to join together with the staff to do renovation, repair, or cleanup projects. Many programs hold special days periodically at which families and staff work together cleaning or doing repairs on the facility. These workdays are better attended if parents have had some say in what most needs doing and can choose their jobs based on skill and interest. To ensure a successful workday, someone or a committee must identify the work to be accomplished, gather the required equipment and materials, arrange for child care and food, and make sure that the jobs can be done in the designated time. If participants can end the workday with a feeling of accomplishment, they are more likely to volunteer for another one.

Parents can also be involved in groups such as advisory and policy boards. This form of involvement can help your program more accurately reflect the interests and needs of the families you serve. Parents who participate in policy-making feel that the program truly belongs to the families and their children. They are willing to expend more of their energy and resources because of their greater commitment. The program thus gains valuable parental advocacy and skill.

As the classroom teacher, you are the person most likely to know the special interests, concerns, and talent of the parents of the children with whom you work directly. Parents, children, and the program benefit when you invite families to participate in your classroom and attend special events or when you help them to find additional avenues for involvement.

Parent Education

Traditionally, many programs for young children and their families have included parent education activities. Parent education can help parents understand the importance of their role in their child's development and education. As they come to know and trust you, some parents will seek advice about problematic areas in their relationship with their child. When you find commonly shared areas of concern among parents, you can structure opportunities to provide them with appropriate information about child development, early childhood education, and parenting skills.

Parent education can take many forms. You may act as a direct provider of education or you may help parents find other resources. Informally, you may talk with parents and model effective strategies for interacting with children in the course of your daily contacts. Such informal parent education can be very powerful. More formal educational methods such as newsletters, workshops, parent discussion groups, and parenting courses can also be provided. Schools we have worked in have offered many educational services to parents including a weekly newsletter with a feature called "Help Your Child Learn at Home"; workshops on making and choosing toys, preparing children for kindergarten, language and reading, and nutrition; courses on parenting skills; and parent-coordinated support groups.

Parent education can encompass many topics. The only limits are the imaginations of the families and staff. Obviously, many of the topics will be beyond the skills and expertise you gain in your preparation to become a teacher of young children. However, you need only be aware of the special skills and interests of the families and community members who are and have been involved in your program and you will likely have a vast store of resources for a family education program. Family members who understand the values and goals of the program will often be willing to share their special skills and knowledge and even invite their friends to contribute.

Just as other aspects of the early childhood program, a family education program requires some careful planning. Probably the single most important step in planning is to survey the parents to learn what they most wish to learn about. It is disconcerting to invite an expert on child development to speak to a group of parents and present your speaker with a nearly empty house. If you explore the reason for a low turnout for such an event, you may discover that the topic was a staff idea and that the parents

would have come to a meeting on another subject. It is also important to realize that the success of a parent meeting is not measured by the number of bodies in the room but by the impact on the individuals who did attend.

Assessing the interests and needs of parents can be accomplished in a variety of ways. Small groups of parents can get together and brainstorm everything they would like to learn about children and family life. Even if the representation is small, the initial list of topics can be distributed to the rest of the families for additions, comment, and prioritization. After an initial list of topics has been generated, you can distribute the list in subsequent years with space

for parents to indicate topics they would like to know more about and those in which they have special knowledge and skill that they would be willing to share with others. Do leave space for adding new topics.

When you have a list of topics relevant to the families currently enrolled in your program and a good idea of some likely presenters or knowledge of other sources of the desired information (films, videos, printed materials), you can begin to plan your program. Printed materials can be made available to families in the special area or room you provide for them in your facility. Films and videos can also be screened in a family lounge or area of the school if you have the appropriate equipment.

Workshops, courses, or lectures, like all other parent meetings, need to be scheduled at a time that is convenient for family members. If provisions for child care, a meal, and a comfortable location are offered, participation will be enhanced. Finally, to ensure a well-received session, it is essential that someone from the program communicate with the presenters about the skill and knowledge level of the families and check to be sure that the presentation will be lively and appropriate. We have found that the best learning experiences for adults almost always include an opportunity for active participation as well as the presentation of information.

DISCUSSION QUESTIONS

1. Recall the ways your family participated in your educational experiences. How did the school encourage family participation? What impact did family involvement have on your attitude toward school?
2. Think about a program that you have observed or worked in. What kinds of family participation did you observe? What appeared to be the attitudes of the school staff toward family involvement?
3. What do you see as your potential strengths and weaknesses in working with families? What kinds of family involvement would you feel most comfortable with? What might be difficult?

PROJECTS

1. Choose two early childhood programs. Interview the director or parent involvement coordinator in each to discover the kinds of family involvement available, the program's philosophy regarding family involvement, and the ways the program communicates with families. Observe the school environments and note any efforts to communicate with families (for example, parent bulletin boards). Compare and contrast the programs and discuss what you learned from your exploration.
2. Choose two early childhood programs. Collect a sample of the materials that each program gives to families: brochure, application, handbook, newsletter,

policy statements, and so forth. Compare and evaluate the materials based on the ideas presented in this chapter. Discuss how the programs appear to differ in their philosophies and attitudes toward families. What did you learn from this experience that may be helpful to you as a teacher?

3. Interview one or two parents of children in early childhood programs. Ask them to talk about the day-to-day experience of parenting a young child. What do they expect from their child's program in terms of information and support? How well do they think the program is doing in providing these things? Report on what you learned and its implication for you as a teacher.

BIBLIOGRAPHY

Berger, E. H. 1987. *Parents as Partners in Education.* 2d ed. Columbus, Ohio: Merrill.

Bredekamp, S. 1987. *Developmentally Appropriate Practice in Early Childhood Programs Serving Children from Birth through Age 8.* Expanded ed. Washington, D.C.: National Association for the Education of Young Children.

Children's Defense Fund. 1989. *A Vision for America's Future: An Agenda for the 1990's.* Washington, D.C.: Children's Defense Fund.

Elkind, D. 1981. *The Hurried Child: Growing Up Too Fast, Too Soon.* Menlo Park, Calif.: Addison-Wesley.

Feeney, S., and K. Kipnis. 1990. *Code of Ethical Conduct and Statement of Commitment.* Washington, D.C.: National Association for the Education of Young Children.

Galinsky, E. 1981. *Between Generations: The Six Stages of Parenthood.* New York, Times Books.

Gordon, T. 1974. *Parent Effectiveness Training.* New York: David McKay.

Hetznecker, W., L. E. Arnold, and A. Phillipps. 1980. Teachers, Principals, and Parents: Guidance by Educators. In *Helping Parents Help Their Children,* ed. L. E. Arnold. New York: Bruner/Mazel.

Honig, A. 1975. *Parent Involvement in Early Childhood Education.* Washington, D.C.: National Association for the Education of Young Children.

Katz, L. 1980. Mothering and Teaching—Some Significant Distinctions. In *Current Topics in Early Childhood Education.* Vol. 3, ed. L. Katz. Norwood, N.J.: Ablex Publishing.

Lawrence, G., and M. Hunter. 1978. *Parent-Teacher Conferencing.* El Segundo, Calif.: Theory into Practice Publications.

Lightfoot, S. L. 1978. *Worlds Apart: Relationships Between Families and Schools.* New York: Basic Books.

Powell, D. R. 1989. *Families and Early Childhood Programs.* Washington, D.C.: Research Monographs of the National Association for the Education of Young Children, No. 3.

Pickarts, E., and J. Fargo. 1971. *Parent Education: Toward Parental Competence.* New York: Appleton-Century-Crofts.

Rappoport, R., R. Strelitz, and Z. Strelitz. 1980. *Fathers, Mothers and Society: Perspectives on Parenting.* New York: Vintage Books.

Ricci, I. 1980. *Mom's House/Dad's House.* New York: Collier Books.

Stevens, J. H., and M. Matthews, eds. 1979. *Mother/Child, Father/Child Relationships.* Washington, D.C.: National Association for the Education of Young Children.

Stone, J. G. 1987. *Teacher-Parent Relationships.* Washington, D.C.: National Association for the Education of Young Children.

Taylor, K. 1981. *Parents and Children Learn Together.* 3d ed. New York: Teachers College Press.

POSTSCRIPT

We hope this book has helped you to reflect on yourself as a teacher or as a prospective teacher of young children. If you have been enrolled in a college program, you have probably had opportunities to interact with children from a variety of backgrounds in a number of different kinds of settings. Through these experiences you may have made a commitment to teaching and learned about your strengths in working with children and adults and about the areas in which you need to work harder. You may have also thought about the kind of teaching situation that might best reflect your interests, abilities, and style.

If you are looking forward to your first teaching position, there are some things you should be aware of. We have found that no training program, no matter how good, can prepare you completely for the real world of teaching. The first year can be hard and stressful, partly because everything is new, but also because beginning teachers tend to have unre-

alistically high expectations of themselves. Indeed, if you have read this whole book, you may be overwhelmed by what is expected of you. Remember that we focused on the ideal of early childhood programs based on what we believe is best for children. We have no expectation that a first- (or even fifth-) year teacher can do all of it well all of the time.

"Who am I?" and "Who am I in the lives of children?" are questions that need to be asked over and over again in the career of a teacher. Going back to these questions will help you to reflect on the very basis of what you do and why you do it. The answers will become clearer, deeper, and more meaningful as you gain new awareness and understanding through your experiences with children.

As a teacher of young children, you will be caring for the future by doing the most important and vital job in the world. This is easy to say, obviously true, and easy to forget in the day-to-day press of working in an early childhood program.

You Are Caring for the Future by Caring for the Children

Tomorrow's adults, in their most vulnerable stage of life, are in our hands today. Today's children need to be protected so that tomorrow's adults will be safe and healthy. No human being survives without nurturing. Today's children need nurture so that tomorrow's adults will be strong and sensitive people who like themselves and take care of themselves. Today's children need encouragement so that tomorrow's adults will be creative thinkers, discoverers, and problem solvers. They will have some big problems to solve. Today's children need guidance so that tomorrow's adults will be appreciative of this fragile world we live in and so that they care about skill, artistry, and beauty. Today's children need to learn to cooperate and solve problems so that tomorrow's adults will be peacemakers at home and in the world; so that they think for themselves; and so that they care for others—those who are like themselves, those who are different, and those who are in need.

You Are Caring for the Future by Caring for Yourself

You are the only tool you have. There is no book, toy, video, or computer program, no matter how impressive or expensive, that can substitute for a human being who knows about, cares for, and is sensitive to young children. *You*

are it, the vital ingredient in caring for children and thus caring for the future.

All you have to give is yourself—your caring, your energy, and your commitment. But many of us feel self-indulgent when we focus on taking care of ourselves. Our families, our work, our other obligations often seem to have a more valid claim on our time and energy. To accomplish the demanding task of teaching young children, you need to be in good physical and emotional health. You need to take care of your body by paying attention to nutrition, exercise, and relaxation, so that you can be your best.

You need to nurture your mind so that you stay excited and motivated as a learner. Observing children is like an ever-changing kaleidoscope; understanding them is the first, and usually most lasting, intellectual challenge for teachers. Adults are ready for different kinds of learning at different times just as children are. There are a number of sources and kinds of information that are helpful in providing intellectual challenge for teachers. As a beginning teacher you invest most of your energy in the task of teaching. You will need the advice of colleagues and articles with lots of practical suggestions. As you gain experience and confidence, you will seek more challenge and inspiration and will pursue more in-depth study of the field.

You need to feel that you are appreciated, meaningfully connected to others, and that your job is worth doing. And you need to nurture your spirit. Take time for reflection, for sitting in a beautiful garden, for spending time with a friend, for literature, art, and performance. These things are valuable and as necessary to the spirit as food to the body.

In your first year of teaching work to set realistic goals for yourself, to find your strengths and build from them, and to acknowledge your mistakes and learn from them. It is important to remember that you, like the children you teach, are a person in the process of development. If you apply the same developmental perspective

to yourself that you do to them, you may be able to acknowledge your growth instead of lamenting your shortcomings.

You Are Caring for the Future by Caring for Our Profession

It is difficult to care for children in a field that does not receive the recognition and compensation it deserves. By becoming advocates for our profession and for our children, we can make a difference. Early childhood educators have started to make a difference and the nineties are an exciting time in early childhood education. We are on the threshold of a new era that is visible in accomplishments such as standards for teacher preparation and accreditation for quality programs; the growing number of states providing programs for four-year-olds; concern with early childhood certification in public schools; growing recognition of early childhood education by professional groups; and support for national child care legislation.

When you join a professional group like the NAEYC, when you speak to a friend or a legislator on behalf of quality, when you stand up for developmentally appropriate practice in your school, when you write a letter or make a phone call to your senator or representative, you are caring for your profession. By caring for your profession you are caring for the children and you are caring for the future of us all.

You Are Caring for the Future by Making a Commitment to the Field of Early Childhood Education

The NAEYC's Code of Ethical Conduct (see Appendix 1) is accompanied by a Statement of Commitment that sets forth the personal obligations that need to be made by an early childhood educator in order to further the values and live up to the responsibilities of the field. Reflect on the statement and let it guide you as you embark on your new profession of early childhood education. As your colleagues in this important venture, we welcome you.

APPENDIX ONE

The NAEYC Code of Ethical Conduct

PREAMBLE

NAEYC recognizes that many daily decisions required of those who work with young children are of a moral and ethical nature. The NAEYC Code of Ethical Conduct offers guidelines for responsible behavior and sets forth a common basis for resolving the principal ethical dilemmas encountered in early childhood education. The primary focus is on daily practice with children and their families in programs for children from birth to eight years of age: preschools, child care centers, family day care homes, kindergartens, and primary classrooms. Many of the provisions also apply to specialists who do not work directly with children, including program administrators, parent educators, college professors, and child care licensing specialists.

Standards of ethical behavior in early childhood education are based on commitment to core values that are deeply rooted in the history of our field. We have committed ourselves to:

- Appreciating childhood as a unique and valuable stage of the human life cycle;
- Basing our work with children on knowledge of child development;
- Appreciating and supporting the close ties between the child and family;
- Recognizing that children are best understood in the context of family, culture and society;
- Respecting the dignity, worth and uniqueness of each individual (child, family member and colleague);
- Helping children and adults achieve their full potential in the context of relationships that are based on trust, respect and positive regard.

The Code sets forth a conception of our professional responsibilities in four sections, each addressing an arena of professional relationships: 1) children, 2) families, 3) colleagues, and 4) community and society. Each section includes an introduction to the the primary responsibilities of the early childhood practitioner in that arena, a set of ideals pointing in the direction of exemplary professional practice,

Stephanie Feeney and Kenneth Kipnis. 1989. Code of Ethical Conduct and Statement of Commitment. *Young Children* 45(1):24-29.

and a set of principles defining practices that are required, prohibited and permitted.

The ideals reflect the aspirations of practitioners. The principles are intended to guide conduct and assist practitioners in resolving ethical dilemmas encountered in the field. There is not necessarily a corresponding principle for each ideal. Both ideals and principles are intended to direct practitioners to those questions which, when responsibly answered, will provide the basis for conscientious decision-making. While the Code provides specific direction for addressing some ethical dilemmas, many others will require the practitioner to combine the guidance of the Code with sound professional judgment.

The ideals and principles in this Code present a shared conception of professional responsibility that affirms our commitment to the core values of our field. They publicly acknowledge the responsibilities that we in the field have assumed and in so doing they support ethical behavior in our work. Practitioners who face ethical dilemmas are urged to seek guidance in the applicable parts of this Code and in the spirit that informs the whole.

SECTION I: ETHICAL RESPONSIBILITIES TO CHILDREN

Childhood is a unique and valuable stage in the life cycle. Our paramount responsibility is to provide safe, healthy, nurturing and responsive settings for children. We are committed to supporting children's development by cherishing individual differences, by helping them learn to live and work cooperatively, and by promoting their self-esteem.

Ideals:

I-1.1   To be familiar with the knowledge-base of early childhood education and to keep current through continuing education and in-service training.

I-1.2   To base program practices upon current knowledge in the field of child development and related disciplines and upon particular knowledge of each child.

I-1.3   To recognize and respect the uniqueness and the potential of each child.

I-1.4   To appreciate the special vulnerability of children.

I-1.5   To create and maintain safe and healthy settings that foster children's social, emotional, intellectual, and physical development and that respect their dignity and their contributions.

I-1.6   To support the right of children with special needs to participate, consistent with their ability, in regular early childhood programs.

Principles:

P-1.1   Above all, we shall not harm children. We shall not participate in practices that are disrespectful, degrading, dangerous, exploitative, intimidating, psychologically damaging or physically harmful to children. **This principle has precedence over all others in this Code.**

P-1.2   We shall not participate in practices that discriminate against children by denying benefits, giving special advantages or excluding them from programs or activities on the basis of their race, religion, sex, national origin, or the status, behavior or beliefs of their parents. (This principle does not apply to programs that have a lawful mandate to provide services to a particular population of children.)

P-1.3   We shall involve all of those with relevant knowledge (including staff and parents) in decisions concerning a child.

P-1.4   When, after appropriate efforts have been made with a child and the family, a child still does not appear to be benefitting from a program, we shall communicate our concern to the family in a positive way and offer them assistance in finding a more suitable setting.

P-1.5   We shall be familiar with the symptoms of child abuse and neglect and know community procedures for addressing them.

P-1.6   When we have evidence of child abuse or neglect we shall report the evidence to the appropriate community agency and follow up to insure that appropriate action has been taken. When possible, parents will be informed that the referral has been made.

P-1.7   When another person tells us of their suspicion that a child is being abused or neglected but we lack evidence, we shall assist that person in taking appropriate action to protect the child.

P-1.8   When a child protective agency fails to provide adequate protection for abused or neglected children, we acknowledge a collective ethical responsibility to work toward improvement of these services.

SECTION II: ETHICAL RESPONSIBILITIES TO FAMILIES

Families are of primary importance in children's development. (The term "family" may include others, besides parents, who are responsibly involved with the child.) Because the family and the early childhood educator have an interest in the child's welfare, we acknowledge a primary responsibility to bring about collaboration be-

tween the home and school in ways that enhance the child's development.

Ideals:

I-2.1   To develop relationships of mutual trust with the families we serve.

I-2.2   To acknowledge and build upon strengths and competencies as we support families in their task of nurturing children.

I-2.3   To respect the dignity of each family and its culture, customs and beliefs.

I-2.4   To respect families' child-rearing values and their right to make decisions for their children.

I-2.5   To interpret each child's progress to parents within the framework of a developmental perspective and to help families understand and appreciate the value of developmentally appropriate early childhood programs.

I-2.6   To help family members improve their understanding of their children and to enhance their skills as parents.

I-2.7   To participate in building support networks for families by providing them with opportunities to interact with program staff and families.

Principles:

P-2.1   We shall not deny family members access to their child's classroom or program setting.

P-2.2   We shall inform families of program philosophy, policies, personnel qualifications, and explain why we teach as we do.

P-2.3   We shall inform and, when appropriate, involve families in policy decisions.

P-2.4 We shall inform and, when appropriate, involve families in significant decisions affecting their child.

P-2.5 We shall inform the family of accidents involving their child, of risks such as exposures to contagious disease that may result in infection and of events that might result in psychological damage.

P-2.6 We shall not permit or participate in research which could in any way hinder the education or development of the children in our programs. Families shall be fully informed of any proposed research projects involving their children and shall have the opportunity to give or withhold consent.

P-2.7 We shall not engage in or support exploitation of families. We shall not use our relationship with a family for private advantage or personal gain, or enter into relationships with family members that might impair our effectiveness in working with children.

P-2.8 We shall develop written policies for the protection of confidentiality and the disclosure of children's records. The policy documents shall be made available to all program personnel and families. Disclosure of children's records beyond family members, program personnel and consultants having an obligation of confidentiality shall require familial consent (except in cases of abuse or neglect).

P-2.9 We shall maintain confidentiality and shall respect the family's right to privacy, refraining from disclosure of confidential information and intrusion into family life. However, when we are concerned about a child's welfare, it is permissible to reveal confidential information to agencies and individuals who may be able to act in the child's interest.

P-2.10 In cases where family members are in conflict we shall work openly, sharing our observations of the child, to help all parties involved make informed decisions. We shall refrain from becoming an advocate for one party.

P-2.11 We shall be familiar with and appropriately use community resources and professional services that support families. After a referral has been made, we shall follow up to ensure that services have been adequately provided.

SECTION III: ETHICAL RESPONSIBILITIES TO COLLEAGUES

In a caring, cooperative workplace human dignity is respected, professional satisfaction is promoted and positive relationships are modeled. Our primary responsibility in this arena is to establish and maintain settings and relationships which support productive work and meet professional needs.

A. RESPONSIBILITIES TO CO-WORKERS

Ideals:

I-3A.1. To establish and maintain relationships of trust and cooperation with co-workers.

I-3A.2 To share resources and information with co-workers.

I-3A.3 To support co-workers in meeting their professional needs and in their professional development.

I-3A.4 To accord co-workers due recognition for professional achievement.

Principles:

P-3A.1 When we have concern about the professional behavior of a co-worker, we shall first let that person know of our concern and attempt to resolve the matter collegially.

P-3A.2 We shall exercise care in expressing views regarding the personal attributes or professional conduct of co-workers. Statements should be based on firsthand knowledge and relevant to the interests of children and programs.

B. RESPONSIBILITIES TO EMPLOYERS

Ideals:

I-3B.1 To assist the program in providing the highest quality of service.

I-3B.2 To maintain loyalty to the program and uphold its reputation.

Principles:

P-3B.1 When we do not agree with program policies, we shall first attempt to effect change through constructive action within the organization.

P-3B.2 We shall speak or act on behalf of an organization only when authorized. We shall take care to note when we are speaking for the organization and when we are expressing a personal judgment.

C. RESPONSIBILITIES TO EMPLOYEES

Ideals:

I-3C.1 To promote policies and working conditions that foster competence, well-being and self-esteem in staff members.

I-3C.2 To create a climate of trust and candor that will enable staff to speak and act in the best interests of children, families, and the field of early childhood education.

I-3C.3 To strive to secure an adequate livelihood for those who work with or on behalf of young children.

Principles:

P-3C.1 In decisions concerning children and programs, we shall appropriately utilize the training, experience and expertise of staff members.

P-3C.2 We shall provide staff members with working conditions that permit them to carry out their responsibilities, timely and non-threatening evaluation procedures, written grievance procedures, constructive feedback, and opportunities for continuing professional development.

P-3C.3 We shall develop and maintain comprehensive written personnel policies that define program standards and, when applicable, that specify the extent to which employees are accountable for their conduct outside of the workplace. These policies shall be given to new staff members and shall be available for review by all staff members.

P-3C.4 Employees who do not meet program standards shall be informed of areas of concern and, when possible, assisted in improving their performance.

P-3C.5 Employees who are dismissed shall be informed of the reasons for their termination. When a dismissal is for cause, justification must be based on evidence of inadequate or inappropriate behavior which is accurately documented, current, and available for the employee to review.

P-3C.6   In making evaluations and recommendations, judgments shall be based on fact and relevant to the interests of children and programs.

P-3C.7   Hiring and promotion shall be based solely on a person's record of accomplishment and ability to carry out the responsibilities of the position.

P-3C.8   In hiring, promotion and provision of training, we shall not participate in any form of discrimination based on race, religion, sex, national origin, handicap, age, or sexual preference. We shall be familiar with laws and regulations that pertain to employment discrimination.

SECTION IV: ETHICAL RESPONSIBILITIES TO COMMUNITY AND SOCIETY

Early childhood programs operate within a context of an immediate community made up of families and other institutions concerned with children's welfare. Our responsibilities to the community are to provide programs that meet its needs and to cooperate with agencies and professions that share responsibility for children. Because the larger society has a measure of responsibility for the welfare and protection of children, and because of our specialized expertise in child development, we acknowledge an obligation to serve as a voice for children everywhere.

Ideals:

I-4.1   To provide the community with high quality, culturally sensitive programs and services.

I-4.2   To promote cooperation among agencies and professions concerned with the welfare of young children, their families and their teachers.

I-4.3   To work, through education, research and advocacy toward an environmentally safe world in which all children are adequately fed, sheltered, and nurtured.

I-4.4   To work, through education, research and advocacy toward a society in which all young children have access to quality programs.

I-4.5   To promote knowledge and understanding of young children and their needs. To work toward greater social acknowledgment of children's rights and greater social acceptance of responsibility for their well-being.

I-4.6   To support policies and laws that promote the well-being of children and families. To oppose those that impair their well-being. To cooperate with other individuals and groups in these efforts.

I-4.7   To further the professional development of the field of early childhood education and to strengthen its commitment to realizing its core values as reflected in this Code.

Principles:

P-4.1   We shall communicate openly and truthfully about the nature and extent of services that we provide.

P-4.2   We shall not accept or continue to work in positions for which we are personally unsuited or professionally unqualified. We shall not offer services that we do not have the competence, qualifications, or resources to provide.

P-4.3   We shall be objective and accurate in reporting the knowledge upon which we base our program practices.

P-4.4   We shall cooperate with other professionals who work with children and their families.

P-4.5 We shall not hire or recommend for employment any person who is unsuited for a position with respect to competence, qualifications or character.

P-4.6 We shall report the unethical or incompetent behavior of a colleague to a supervisor when informal resolution is not effective.

P-4.7 We shall be familiar with laws and regulations that serve to protect the children in our programs.

P-4.8 We shall not participate in practices which are in violation of laws and regulations that protect the children in our programs.

P-4.9 When we have evidence that an early childhood program is violating laws or regulations protecting children, we shall report it to persons responsible for the program. If compliance is not accomplished within a reasonable time we will report the violation to appropriate authorities who can be expected to remedy the situation.

P-4.10 When we have evidence that an agency or a professional charged with providing services to children, families or teachers is failing to meet its obligations, we acknowledge a collective ethical responsibility to report the problem to appropriate authorities or to the public.

P-4.11 When a program violates or requires its employees to violate this Code, it is permissible, after fair assessment of the evidence, to disclose the identity of that program.

The NAEYC Statement of Commitment*

As an individual who works with young children, I commit myself to furthering the values of early childhood education as they are reflected in the NAEYC Code of Ethical Conduct.

To the best of my ability I will:

- Ensure that programs for young children are based on current knowledge of child development and early childhood education.
- Respect and support families in their task of nurturing children.
- Respect colleagues in early childhood education and support them in maintaining the NAEYC Code of Ethical Conduct.
- Serve as an advocate for children, their families and their teachers in community and society.
- Maintain high standards of professional conduct.
- Recognize how personal values, opinions and biases can affect professional judgment.
- Be open to new ideas and be willing to learn from the suggestions of others.
- Continue to learn, grow and contribute as a professional.
- Honor the ideals and principles of the NAEYC Code of Ethical Conduct.

*The Statement of Commitment expresses those basic personal commitments that individuals must make in order to align themselves with the profession's responsibilities as set forth in the NAEYC Code of Ethical Conduct.

Ethical Cases*

You can use the following ethical cases as a starting place for thinking about ethics. Reread the section on core values in Chapter 1 and the Code of Ethical Conduct in Appendix 1 and use them to think about what the good early childhood educator should do in the following situations.

ETHICAL CASE 1: THE ABUSED CHILD

Mary Lou, a five-year-old in your school, is showing the classic signs of abuse: multiple bruises, frequent black eyes, and psychological withdrawal. Her mother, a high-strung woman, says Mary Lou falls a lot, but nobody at the center has noticed this. There were two times when Mary Lou's father seemed to be drunk when he

picked her up. The law says you must report suspicions of abuse to the Children's Protective Office. But, in your experience, when the authorities get involved they are usually unable to remove the child from the home or improve the family's behavior. Sometimes the families simply disappear, or things become worse for the children.

ETHICAL CASE 2: THE WORKING MOTHER

Timothy's mother has asked you not to allow her four-year-old son to nap in the afternoon. She says, "Whenever he naps he stays up until 10:00 at night. I have to get up at 5:00 in the morning to go to work. I am not getting enough sleep." Along with the rest of the children, Timothy takes a one-hour nap almost every day. He seems to need it in order to stay in good spirits in the afternoon.

*Stephanie Feeney, Ethical Case Studies for NAEYC Reader Response, *Young Children,* vol. 42, no. 4, pp. 24–25, 1987.

ETHICAL CASE 3: THE DIVORCED PARENTS

Martin is the recently divorced father and custodial parent of four-year-old Tracy. Carla, the girl's mother (and the noncustodial parent), visits her often at the school during the day. Tracy's father has changed since the divorce. He always has a stressed expression on his face and avoids contact with the staff. He neglects to sign Tracy out—a violation of school policy—and has twice caused minor damage with his car in the parking lot. Tracy is now absent two or three days a week and is usually late for school when she comes. Tracy's father became very angry at the staff and his daughter when Tracy's lunch box was misplaced. Some of the teachers are a bit afraid of him, calling him "the ticking bomb." Efforts to talk with him have been unsuccessful. Despite the absences, Tracy has seemed healthy and well-adjusted though in recent weeks she has difficulty completing school tasks.

Carla has heard rumors that her former husband is behaving strangely. She tells you she is unable to reach her daughter by telephone or pick her up at the times specified in the court agreement. She asks what is happening and if you have concerns about Martin.

ETHICAL CASE 4: THE AGGRESSIVE CHILD

Eric is a large and extremely active four-year-old who often frightens and hurts other children. You have discussed the situation repeatedly with the director, who is sympathetic but unable to help. The parents listen but feel that the behavior is typical for boys his age. They won't get counseling. A preschool specialist from the Department of Mental Health has observed the child, but her recommendations have not helped either. Meanwhile, Eric terrorizes other children and parents are starting to complain.

You are becoming stressed and tired and your patience is wearing thin. You and your coteacher are spending so much time dealing with Eric that you are worried the other children are not getting the attention they need.

ETHICAL CASE 5: THE "ACADEMIC" PRESCHOOL

Heather has been a teacher at a preschool for several years, seems happy there, and receives a good salary. She has just gone back to school to get her CDA credential; she has been assigned as your trainee. You have gone to observe her class and have seen three- and four-year-olds using workbooks for long periods of time each day. The daily program also includes repetitious drill on letters and numbers. Children are regularly being "taught" the alphabet and rote counting from one to a hundred. You also notice that most interactions are initiated by adults and that children have few opportunities to interact with materials.

You have mentioned to Heather that you do not think that the school's curriculum is appropriate for preschool children. She replies that she had a similar reaction when she began working there, but that the director and other teachers assured her that there was no problem with the curriculum. They told her that this is the way they have always taught and that parents are satisfied with it.

ETHICAL CASE 6: THE STAFF-CHILD RATIO

When you began your job as teacher in a class of three-year-olds, you were not well informed about state regulations. You found your work extremely tiring and after some time you learned that regulations in your state require a staff-child ratio of no more than one to twelve for three-year-olds. You are teaching alone in a group that sometimes has as many as seventeen children in it. When the licensing worker comes to inspect, the director explains that the cook is part of the staff and works regularly in your classroom.

DISCUSSING ETHICAL CASES

A good way to begin to understand ethics and learn how to resolve ethical dilemmas is to practice discussing ethics with your colleagues using cases like these. Although there is no one way to discuss an ethical issue, the following strategies will help you:

- Discuss the case and identify that core values that seem to be in conflict.
- Restate the problem in terms of what the good early childhood educator owes to children, parents, colleagues, directors, and themselves.
- Brainstorm all possible solutions without evaluting them.
- Critically evaluate each solution and try to reach consensus about what the good early childhood educator would do. If you cannot reach consensus, acknowledge both majority and minority viewpoints.
- Use the NAEYC Code of Ethical Conduct to identify what sections of the code guide the early childhood professional.

Personal Favorites Book List

This is a list of books that have influenced us personally and professionally. We recommend them to beginning teachers as an introduction to the field or to experienced teachers who may have missed some of them.

We selected these books because they were readable, inspirational, or at the forefront of some school of educational thought or new instructional approach.

• • • • •

Author	Title
Ashton-Warner, Sylvia	*Teacher*
Axline, Virginia	*Dibs in Search of Self*
Ayers, William	*The Good Preschool Teacher*
Bettelheim, Bruno	*Love Is Not Enough*
Chilton-Pearce, Joseph	*The Magical Child*
Dennison, George	*The Lives of Children*
Dewey, John	*Experience and Education*
Elkind, David	*The Hurried Child*
Erikson, Erik	*Childhood and Society*
Fraiberg, Selma	*The Magic Years*
Ginott, Haim	*Teacher and Child*
Goodlad, John	*A Place Called School*
Gordon, Thomas	*Teacher Effectiveness Training*
Greenspan, Stanley, and Nancy T. Greenspan	*First Feelings*

Holt, John	*How Children Fail*
	How Children Learn
Hunt, J. McVicker	*Intelligence and Experience*
Hymes, James L.	*Teaching the Child Under Six*
	Early Childhood Education: An Introduction to the Profession
Jersild, Arthur	*When Teachers Face Themselves*
Jones, Elizabeth	*Dimensions of Teaching-Learning Environments*
	Joys and Risks of Teaching Young Children
Kohl, Herbert	*36 Children*
Kuroyanagi, T.	*Totto-Chan*
MacCracken, Mary	*Circle of Children*
Maslow, Abraham	*Toward a Psychology of Being*
Mitchell, Lucy Sprague	*Young Geographers*
Moustakas, Clark	*The Authentic Teacher*
Neill, A. S.	*Summerhill*
Paley, Vivian	*Wally's Stories* (and all others)
Read-Baker, Katherine and coauthors	*The Nursery School* (all editions)
Riley, Sue Spayth	*How to Generate Values in Young Children*
Rogers, Carl	*Freedom to Learn*
Silberman, Charles	*Crisis in the Classroom*
Skinner, B. F.	*Beyond Freedom and Dignity*
Smilansky, Sara, and Sheftaya, Leah	*Facilitating Play*
Sommer, Robert	*Personal Space*
Steinfels, Margaret O.	*Who's Minding the Children?*
Williams, Roger	*You Are Extraordinary*
Yonemura, M. V.	*A Teacher At Work*

• • • • • •

Organizations, Journals and Newsletters

Organizations

ACEI
Association for Childhood Education International
11141 Georgia Ave., Suite 200
Wheaton, MD 20902

ACT
Action for Children's Television
46 Austin St.
Newtonville, MA 02160

Children's Defense Fund
122 C St. N.W.
Washington, DC 20001

DDCDCA
Day Care and Child Development Council of America
1401 K St., N.W.
Washington, DC 20005

ERIC/ECE
Educational Resource Information Center on Early Childhood Education
805 W. Pennsylvania Ave.
Urbana, IL 61801

NAEYC
National Association for the Education of Young Children
1834 Connecticut Ave., N.W.
Washington, DC 20009

OMEP
Organization Mondiale pour L'Education Prescholaire and the U.S. National Committee for Early Childhood Education
81 Irving Place
New York, NY 10003

SACUS
Souther Association for Children Under Six
P.O. Box 5403
Brady Station
Little Rock, AR 72215

Journals

Child Care Information Exchange
P.O. Box 2890
Redmond, WA 98073

Childhood Education
Association for Childhood Education International
11141 Georgia Ave., Suite 200
Wheaton, MD 20902

Day Care and Early Education
Human Sciences Press
72 Fifth Ave.
New York, NY 10011

Dimensions
Southern Association for Children Under Six
P.O. Box 5403, Brady Station
Little Rock, AR 72215

Early Childhood Research Quarterly
National Association for the Education of Young Children
Ablex Publishing Company
355 Chestnut Street
Norwood, NJ 07648

Interracial Books for Children Bulletin
1841 Broadway
New York, NY 10023

Journal of Research in Childhood Education
Association for Childhood Education International
11141 Georgia Ave., Suite 200
Wheaton, MD 20902

Young Children
National Association for the Education of Young Children
1834 Connecticut Ave., N.W.
Washington, DC 20009

Newsletters

Child Health Alert
P.O. Box 338
Newton Highlands, MA 02161

ERIC/ECE Newsletter
805 W. Pennsylvania Ave.
Urbana, IL 61801

Nurturing News: A Forum for Male Early Childhood Educators
187 Caselli Ave.
San Francisco, CA 94114

How Who Am I in the Lives of Children? *Addresses the* CDA Units

CDA Units	*Chapters in* *Who Am I In the Lives of Children?*
Unit 1: Introduction to the Early Childhood Profession	Chapter 1: The Teacher and Values Chapter 2: History Chapter 3: The Field of Early Childhood Education
Unit 2: Ways to Study How Children Grow and Learn	Chapter 4: Child Development Chapter 5: Play Chapter 6: Observation and Evaluation
Unit 3: Ways to Set Up A Safe, Healthy Learning Environment	Chapter 7: A Good Place for Children Chapter 8: The Learning Environment
Unit 4: Positive Ways to Support Children's Social and Emotional Development	Chapter 9: Relationships and Guidance

NAME INDEX

SUBJECT INDEX